Worlds of Hurt presents a coherent rendering of the relationships between individual trauma and cultural interpretation, using as its focus the Holocaust, the Viet Nam war, and the phenomenon of sexualized violence against women. Survivors of these traumas constitute themselves as unique communities and bear witness to their traumatic experiences both privately and publicly. Each community has a vested interest in its own story and the stories told about its members by outsiders. The survivors themselves write a "literature of trauma" born of the need to tell and retell the story of the traumatic experience, to make it "real" to the victim, the community, and the larger public. In so doing, they draw on their understanding of previous traumas and other survivor communities, using them both as validation and cathartic vehicle. When traumatic stories are told and retold, they enter the vocabulary of the larger culture and become tools for the construction of national and cultural myths. The desires of the survivors and of the state are often in conflict, since the goal of a survivor is change, while the state is frequently interested in preserving the status quo.

Worlds of Hurt

CAMBRIDGE STUDIES IN AMERICAN LITERATURE AND CULTURE

Books in the series

Continued on pages following the Index

Worlds of Hurt

Reading the Literatures of Trauma

KALÍ TAL

CAMBRIDGE UNIVERSITY PRESS

Published by the Press Syndicate of the University of Cambridge
The Pitt Building, Trumpington Street, Cambridge CB2 1RP
40 West 20th Street, New York, NY 10011-4211, USA
10 Stamford Road, Oakleigh, Melbourne 3166, Australia

First published 1996

Printed in the United States of America

Library of Congress cataloging in publication data applied for

A catalog record for this book is available from the British Library

ISBN 0-521-44504-3 Hardback

For Robert Berkey

I can't think of him without smiling.

Contents

Acknowledgments

In the eight years since I began work on this book, I have received a great deal of intellectual and emotional support from my colleagues, my mentors, and my friends. I'd like to take this opportunity to name them, and to thank them.

Robert Stepto's assistance was essential to my project—in the cold environment of Yale University's graduate school and American Studies Program, he offered me warm shelter. My teachers John Blassingame, Deborah Thomas, and David DeRose provided me with advice and support during the difficult years I spent in the Ph.D. program at Yale and made it possible for me to complete my degree and retain both my sense of proportion and my self-respect—to laugh instead of cry when a Director of Graduate Studies remonstrated me for my "willfulness. I would also like to thank Herman Beavers, Jennifer Memhard, Wendy Kuppermann, Barbara Ballard, David Luebke, Ramona Douté, and Linda Watts for their friendship, given generously (sometimes at great personal cost) in the wake of the divisive and bitter politics of the Yale clerical and technical worker's strike of 1984.

My intellectual debts date back to my undergraduate days at the University of California at Santa Cruz, and I'd like to acknowledge the influence of Marge Frantz, J. Herman Blake, Larry Veysey, Harry Eastmond, John Dizikes, Phyllis Rogers, and Michael Cowan.

My colleagues at the U.S. Holocaust Memorial Museum deserve thanks for sharing their expertise and insights with a curious newcomer to the field. Linda Kuzmack, Radu Ionid, and Emily Dyer were extremely helpful. David Luebke, a good friend in graduate school, became a valued colleague at the Museum, suggesting new and interesting material for me to examine, reading my drafts, and offering constructive criticism of my work. Joan Ringelheim also gave me a great deal of help, advice and support.

Through my work with the journal *Viet Nam Generation*, which I founded in graduate school and continue to publish and edit, I met many people who have helped me out along the way. My thanks go to Phil Jason, Susan Jeffords,

Bill King, Harry Haines, Marc Jason Gilbert, Tony Williams, Renny Christopher, and Dan Scripture, as well as others too numerous to name.

The Vietnam veteran writers and poets with whom I have had the pleasure and privilege of working are a remarkable group of people. Bill, Anne, and Leela Ehrhart have opened their home and their hearts to me. Peter Brush read my manuscripts and gave me a new perspective on the Marine Corps. John Baky has supplied me with countless useful references and a steady stream of acerbic and invaluable commentary on the field of Vietnam War literature. He also created the index for this volume. David A. Willson is a fine bibliographer and an unequaled collector of popular culture artifacts that he has generously shared with his colleagues; he is also the funniest and most perceptive man I know. Alan Farrell allowed me to escape to his cabin when I needed peace and quiet, and Alan's carefully considered response to an early draft of the manuscript was a most helpful critique. Thanks also to Marc Adin, Horace Coleman, David Connolly, Helmuts Feifs, Jim Lynch, Gerald McCarthy, Leroy Quintana, and Dale Ritterbusch.

A special thanks to Joe Amato, David Erben, Charlotte Pierce Baker and Elizabeth Wilson for asking good questions.

Finally, I'd like to thank those closest to me. My brother, Tal Herman, has been an unflagging source of moral and material support. Cynthia Fuchs is my theoretical and analytical "better half"—without our conversations and correspondence I would not have been able to conceive of, much less complete, this project. My partner Steven Gomes, keeper of knives and keys, has given me the space and the incentive to finish this work—marking an ending and a new beginning.

Worlds of Hurt

1

Worlds of Hurt

Reading the Literatures of Trauma

The fact that a situation is ubiquitous does not absolve us from examining it. On the contrary, we must examine it for the very reason that it is or can be the fate of each and every one of us.

– Alice Miller[1]

Daughter: What does "objective" mean?
Father: Well. It means that you look very hard at those things which you choose to look at.

– Gregory Bateson[2]

On December 1, 1991, Elie Wiesel presented former Secretary of State Henry Kissinger with the Elie Wiesel Remembrance Award. The Award honors individuals who survived the Holocaust, "and then somehow contributed – through their work, writing, art, or philanthropy – to the welfare of the Jewish people and humanity."[3] The announcement of the awards ceremony, which took place at a State of Israel Bonds dinner, appeared in the "Chronicle" column of the *New York Times*. It merited only a short paragraph in the back pages of the paper, and seemed, on the surface, entirely unremarkable – a simple case of Nobel Prize winners patting each other on the back, famous men gathering together to praise one another.

Elie Wiesel is a professional Holocaust survivor. Beginning with the publication of his autobiographical novel, *Night* (1960), and continuing through his long career as an author and activist, Wiesel has promoted the memory of the genocidal campaign waged by the Nazis against the Jews. Terrence Des Pres, who has written in strong support of Wiesel's work, noted, "As a survivor and a witness [Wiesel] is accorded a respect bordering on reverence."[4] Throughout his career Wiesel has confirmed his belief that the survivor–witness bears a terrible burden – a duty to both the living and the dead to testify, to tell the world of the horrors he has seen. At the same time, Wiesel believes, testimony is never adequate, that it can never bridge the gap between language and experience: "Could the wall be scaled? Could the reader be brought to the other side? I knew the answer to be No, and yet I also knew that No had to become Yes."[5] Wiesel has long insisted that "those who have not lived through the experience will never know,"[6] and he laments the days when discussion of the Holocaust was "still in the domain of sacred memory, was considered taboo, reserved for the initiates. . . ."[7]

Henry Kissinger emigrated from Germany to the United States in 1938 with his parents and his brother. Kissinger was 15 years old when he departed Europe for America, and he never experienced the hardships of the ghettos or concentration camps of the Third Reich. His claim to the title of "Holocaust survivor" derives from the fact that 26 members of his family were killed at Auschwitz. Such broad inclusiveness calls into question the value of the categorical distinction, since so many American Jews might also qualify as "survivors."

The irony of Elie Wiesel designating Henry Kissinger – who wasn't "there" – a fellow survivor is heightened by Kissinger's involvement in another genocidal campaign, one which Wiesel publicly deplored. Wiesel visited Cambodia in 1980 and wrote of his sympathy for the victims of the Pol Pot regime: "How could a Jew like myself, with experiences and memories like mine, stay at home and not go to the aid of an entire people? . . . As a Jew I felt the need to tell these despairing men and women that we understood them; that we shared their pain; that we understood their distress because we remembered a time when we as Jews confronted total indifference. . . ."[8] By 1980 it was generally accepted in reputable academic and intellectual circles that the campaign waged by Nixon and Kissinger to bomb Cambodia back into the Stone Age had destabilized the Cambodian government and caused the political and economic upheaval that enabled the Khmer Rouge to seize power.[9]

Though Wiesel's decision to grant Kissinger honorary survivor status does not mark the first occasion Wiesel has chosen to engage in morally questionable public behavior (at the height of the Gulf War he honored George Bush with a humanitarian award on behalf of the B'nai B'rith) it is certainly the first time that he has bestowed the title of survivor on someone who spent the years of the Nazi regime in such comfortable circumstances. It seems to me that Wiesel has, finally, completely ungrounded himself. For if Henry Kissinger is a survivor, what then is Elie Wiesel? The difference between the two men is now, apparently, only a matter of degree – a question of which one survived "worse" horrors.

I begin with the story of Wiesel and Kissinger because it illustrates the problem which lies at the heart of this book. In order to understand the implications of Wiesel's action, we must look backwards to the time before his connection to the Holocaust went unsaid. We must remember that Elie Wiesel was not always already Elie Wiesel. We must do this even though the best and the brightest of the critics of Holocaust literature warn us against it:

> To read a book by Elie Wiesel is one thing; to read it with knowledge of the man as a survivor and a witness, and further to read it with at least some knowledge of the ghettos, the cattle cars, and the killing centers, is another, very different experience.... Much of the time the full impact of his prose depends on knowing *who* is speaking and *what* he is speaking of, while neither is actually clarified.[10]

How does one learn "who" Wiesel is, and gain "some" knowledge of the Holocaust? And which "who" and which "some" are the right ones? During and immediately after the Holocaust, information and testimony came from thousands of survivors and witnesses (like Wiesel himself, who was not yet already "Elie Wiesel"). There were many voices and none of them were famous yet. By what process was Wiesel selected from ten thousand others? How did Wiesel become the "who" he is, the voice of "the" survivor?

These questions about Elie Wiesel raise deeper questions: What is the connection between individual psychic trauma and cultural representations of the traumatic event? What does the act of testimony, of "bearing witness" mean to an individual survivor, to a community of survivors? How are testimonies interpreted by different audiences? What does the designation "survivor" mean, and who has the right to confer that title? What happens when a survivor's story is retold (and revised) by a writer who is not a survivor? How are survivor's stories adapted to fit and then contained within the dominant structure of social, cultural and political discourse?

It is difficult to articulate such questions, and impossible to answer them within the framework of traditional academic disciplines. I draw from a wide variety of methodological approaches and use the analytic techniques devised by scholars in "area" studies – women's studies, African-American studies, Holocaust studies, and cultural studies. In such interdisciplinary work, boundaries are fluid and context becomes all-important. This is not, therefore, a study of *all* survivors in *all* circumstances. I do not believe in universally applicable, "normative" models. I am an Americanist, with a specialty in post-World War II culture in the United States, and I draw my examples from that place and that time.

This study focuses on three distinct traumatic events, and their representation in contemporary U.S. culture: the Holocaust, the Vietnam War, and sexual abuse of women and children. On the face of it, this may appear an outrageous comparison – as if, perhaps, I chose my subject matter on the basis of its sensational nature. This is not the case. My awareness of the connections between these events has evolved gradually, and sometimes painfully over a period of years. My decision to complete this book was made with full knowledge of its controversial nature. My aim is to force readers to question the "sacred" nature of the Holocaust as subject matter, to encourage them to be critical of the recent tendency to elevate the American veteran of the Vietnam War to the status of "hero," and to acknowledge the existence of an ongoing campaign of sexual violence and oppression waged by many men against the women and children of the United States.

In addition to insisting on the importance of contextualizing my subjects, I believe that it is only fair to the reader to provide enough information for her to place *me* in context. In the words of Holocaust scholar Philip Hallie:

> My way of understanding good and evil . . . involves proper names and particular circumstances, and a felt obligation to look closely at these. One of those proper names is my own. Narratives need narrators, and storytellers have much to do with the nature and style of their stories. For me, ethics is partly a matter of autobiography, partly a matter of history and philosophy. Personal candor is part of narrative ethics for me.[11]

In addition to the public information on my curriculum vitae, I feel the following facts are important for my reader to know.[12]

I was born in 1960. I am a white woman. I am a Jew, born of Jewish parents, and brought up in their completely secular household. I was raised in a multiethnic, multiracial extended family – my mother's father divorced his Jewish wife and married my Episcopalian Puerto Rican step-grandmother, who was already the mother of several children from her previous marriage. Through my many uncles and aunts, who were often present in our home, I was exposed to elements of Puerto Rican and black culture, as well as to the ways in which racism is manifested in a close-knit multiracial family. I was sexually abused as a twelve-year-old by adult friends of my maternal grandfather. My sexual identification is primarily heterosexual. I was raised in an upper-class environment, with all of the privileges that entails.

I have offered the reader this information not in the spirit of confession or testimony, but in the attempt to live up to the standards set by other feminist critics, such as African-American theorist Valerie Smith, who suggests that "if those of us working on the connections between race, class, and gender in cultural productions acknowledge the relation of our theoretical work to our personal circumstances, then we will be able to expand the radical possibilities of our scholarship."[13] I consider it necessary not only to admit, but to *define* my subjectivity – such a definition seems to me to make the sort of Gramscian "good sense" that political scientist Joan Cocks describes:

> Good sense is thought that is self-knowing . . . It is self-critical. . . . It is finally . . . self-active, fashioning its own independent world-view, and working to make that view systematic, unified, and rigorous. . . .

The cultivation of such self-knowing, self-critical, self-active thought is
. . . a preliminary condition for people giving a conscious direction to
their own activities and taking "an active part in the creation of world
history."[14]

Like Cocks, I believe that "cultural–political theory inquires primarily into
consciously lived life"[15] and that such an inquiry "makes its major moves back
and forth between some individual train of thought or action or sensibility
and the larger, collective political and cultural world."[16] Any act of cultural
criticism, in this estimation, ought to be a self-conscious act – one in which
the critic acknowledges that her choice of subject has meaning, and that a
choice of subject is itself open to interpretation. As Des Pres observed, "There
are always, for any subject under the sun, worldly conditions to be met –
social, political, cultural – when asking: Why this event? At some point, also,
one must ask: Why me?"[17] I have attempted to make this question – Why me?
– integral to my approach.

I believe that the responsibility of the cultural critic is to present a continuous challenge to the assumptions upon which any communal consensus
is based – to insist that nothing go without saying. When cultural critics seek
to expose and then question the rationales for specific community practices,
we situate ourselves in opposition to dominant discourse. We question our
own beliefs, and the beliefs of others. We appeal to people's "good sense," and
we measure our success by the amount of argument we generate. We actively
work towards the breakdown of consensus, at which point, "assumptions that
could previously be taken for granted become one set of theories among
others, ideas that you have to *argue for* rather than presuppose as given."[18] Such
a process is not infinitely reductive, nor does it promote the notion that all
theories are equally valid.

Unlike the most playful of the deconstructionists, we do not seek to prove
that there is, finally, no solid place to stand. We have moved beyond the
discovery of the reductive power of the question "why?" Every human being
possesses a core set of beliefs rooted in faith. Cultural critics seek to establish
a mode of discourse in which each person can first uncover and acknowledge
his or her beliefs, and then test them, compare them to the beliefs of others,
understand their implications, and modify them to reflect a changing understanding of the world. Our end goal is a community based on the full and
informed participation of all its members – a community where difference is
not only accepted but cherished because it provides us with new frames of
reference and new ways of understanding ourselves.

The subject of this work is psychic trauma; its cultural–political inquiry
moves back and forth between the effects of trauma upon individual survivors
and the manner in which that trauma is reflected and revised in the larger,
collective political and cultural world. In the cases of the Holocaust, the

Vietnam War, and the campaign of sexual violence waged against women and children, I examine three strategies of cultural coping – mythologization, medicalization, and disappearance. Mythologization works by reducing a traumatic event to a set of standardized narratives (twice- and thrice-told tales that come to represent "the story" of the trauma) turning it from a frightening and uncontrollable event into a contained and predictable narrative. Medicalization focuses our gaze upon the victims of trauma, positing that they suffer from an "illness" that can be "cured" within existing or slightly modified structures of institutionalized medicine and psychiatry. Disappearance – a refusal to admit to the existence of a particular kind of trauma – is usually accomplished by undermining the credibility of the victim. In the traumas I examine, these strategies work in combination to effect the cultural codification of the trauma.

Traumatic events are written and rewritten until they become codified and narrative form gradually replaces content as the focus of attention. For example, the Holocaust has become a metonym, *not* for the actual series of events that occurred in Germany and the occupied territories before and during World War II, but for the set of symbols that reflect the formal codification of that experience. There is a recognizable set of literary and filmic conventions that comprise the "Holocaust" text. These conventions are so well defined that they may be reproduced in endless recombination to provide us with a steady stream of additions to the genre:

> [I]n the minds of some, the "Holocaust Novel" may now be seen as an available subgenre of contemporary fiction, to be written by anyone who is on to and can master the "formula." ... [Readers of this literature] will be taken rather swiftly and effortlessly through the whole "pattern": the prewar normalcy and the coming of trouble; the beginning of a propaganda campaign against the Jews and racial and religious incitement against them; the incipient threats at first against a few, and then openly against the many; the bureaucratization of terror and the growing "banality of evil"; the exploitation of slave labor and the emergence of the child smugglers; the omnipresent disease and hunger; the imposed quotas; the strikes and other temporary shows of resistance; the roundups and transports; the camps; the corpses; and a few survivors. None of this is "easy," but neither is it beyond the reach of a competent writer.[19]

Once codified, the traumatic experience becomes a weapon in another battle, the struggle for political power. "The role of political power," as Foucault explains, "... is perpetually to re-inscribe this relation through a form of unspoken warfare; to re-inscribe it in social institutions, in economic inequalities, in language, in the bodies themselves of each and every one of us."[20]

The speech of survivors, then, is highly politicized. If "telling it like it was" threatens the status quo, powerful political, economic, and social forces will pressure survivors either to keep their silence or to revise their stories. If the survivor community is a marginal one, their voices will be drowned out by those with the influence and resources to silence them, and to trumpet a revised version of their trauma. Less marginal trauma survivors can sometimes band together as a community and retain a measure of control over the representation of their experience. Much of my work focuses upon the interaction between the survivor as individual, the community of survivors, and the wielders of political power.

Bearing witness is an aggressive act. It is born out of a refusal to bow to outside pressure to revise or to repress experience, a decision to embrace conflict rather than conformity, to endure a lifetime of anger and pain rather than to submit to the seductive pull of revision and repression. Its goal is change. The battle over the meaning of a traumatic experience is fought in the arena of political discourse, popular culture, and scholarly debate. The outcome of this battle shapes the rhetoric of the dominant culture and influences future political action.

If survivors retain control over the interpretation of their trauma, they can sometimes force a shift in the social and political structure. If the dominant culture manages to appropriate the trauma and can codify it in its own terms, the status quo will remain unchanged. On a social as well as an individual psychological level, the penalty for repression is repetition. In Daniel Goleman's words: "On the one hand, we forget we have done this before and, on the other, do not quite realize what we are doing again. The self-deception is complete."[21]

The Holocaust serves as a paradigm case, demonstrating the appropriation and codification of a traumatic event. Des Pres writes, "At some unconscious level, the image of the Holocaust is with us – a memory which haunts, a sounding board for all subsequent evil – in the back of the mind . . . for all of us now living: we, the inheritors."[22] What is "with us," however, is not the memory of the massive and complex set of historical and cultural events that comprised the Third Reich, but rather a distilled and reified set of images for which "Holocaust" has become the metonym. "Holocaust" is a signifier for, among other things, the Nazi genocidal campaign against the Jews; the reign of evil upon the face of the earth; and the rationale for the existence of the State of Israel. Drawn from religious terminology and spelled with a capital "H," the term Holocaust is set apart from descriptions of other man-made evils, such as slavery, genocide, and oppression. A proper noun, its uniqueness is emphasized every time it is named. Yet, as literary critic James Young observes, it is "ironic that once an event is perceived to be without precedent, without adequate analogy, it would in itself become a kind of precedent for all that follows: a new figure against which subsequent experiences are measured and grasped. . . . The process is inevitable, for as new experiences are necessarily grasped and represented in the frame of remembered past experiences, 'incomparable' experiences like the Holocaust will always be made – at least rhetorically – comparable."[23]

The force of the Holocaust as precedent and yardstick to measure trauma in contemporary U.S. culture, and the influence of the Holocaust survivor on the perceived legitimacy and interpretation of the statements of survivors of other traumas has never, to my knowledge, been discussed in print before. To seriously undertake such a project, we must disregard the cultural prohibition against profaning the sacred. We must demystify the Holocaust, reducing it, once again, to a series of historical and cultural events on par with other cultural and historical events and therefore undeserving of a capital "H," except as a sort of casual shorthand, as we speak of the Enlightenment, or the Renaissance. With Miriam Greenspan, I believe that "The view of the Holocaust as Sacred Event . . . goes along with a decided ignorance of the forces of fascism and anti-Semitism, not only as they existed in World War II Europe, but as they exist in the world today."[24] However unpopular, I consider it imperative to reduce the Holocaust from "holy object" to "something which happened in history"[25] if we are to understand, for example, exactly what George Bush meant when he called Saddam Hussein "another Hitler," and why this naming seemed to serve as a justification for going to war against Iraq.[26] How has the "Holocaust" been invoked and represented in the U.S.? What is the interaction between the Holocaust survivor and mainstream U.S. culture? What is implied when Holocaust survivor Elie Wiesel presents Hitler-invoking George Bush with a humanitarian award at the peak of Bush's war against Iraq?

As I have grappled with these questions, I have discovered that it is imperative to make a distinction between those individuals who have been traumatized in a particular way and those individuals who have not suffered such traumatization. I have also found it necessary to make distinctions between members of groups subject to systematic traumatization, and members of groups not subject to such persecution, as well as to account for movement from one group to another, or simultaneous membership in two or more groups. I have tried to create a coherent structure for analyzing different sociocultural patterns of traumatization and reassimilation, and to account for complex social relationships.

In a social system that supports the systematic oppression and persecution of a particular minority group (such as Jews in Nazi Germany), the victims of persecution have a limited set of available options. They may capitulate, which will result in continued suffering and perhaps the eventual death of all members of the targeted group if the intent of the oppressor is genocide. They may resist by appealing to existing legal, moral, or ethical structures in the dominant society (i.e., litigation, religious arguments) and use tactics such as passive resistance or nonviolence. They may respond with force – intending to change the power structure. Or they may attempt to escape the confines of the oppressive social structure, either by relocating to a less hostile environment or by "passing" as a member of a nontargeted group.[27]

Within a society, there may be several targeted groups, whose members are subject to traumatization in greater or lesser degrees. Targeted groups can and should be examined both in relation to the dominant group and to each other. In the United States, Jews are only one of several targeted groups. Though discriminated against, Jews do not suffer from violent racism or systematic economic oppression. Other targeted groups – women and racial minorities, for example – are at higher risk of traumatic assault.

Membership in the targeted group is determined on the basis of externally imposed definitions (i.e., race, class, gender, religious affiliation), which are created and enforced by dominant social groups, and which – once created – are often internalized by members of targeted groups and incorporated into their individual self-concepts. A characteristic of targeting is that persons falling within the dominant group's definition are subject to the same treatment, whether or not their self-definition includes membership in the targeted group. For example, Jews and Gypsies in Nazi Germany were targeted based on "blood" relationships defined by the Nazis and in the Nuremberg Race Laws. In the U.S. (both in the antebellum South and, in many states, into the 1960s) blackness was also determined by ancestry. Self-definition played no role in such social classification.

In a situation of ongoing oppression or involving the risk of traumatic violence, many members of a targeted group will be victimized (some repeatedly), while other members will escape physical harm. In such circumstances, the category of trauma "survivor" is problematic, since every traumatized member of an oppressed community is aware of the potential for repeated victimization. Where there is no safe refuge, the designation of "survivor" is always temporary and conditional. Jews and Gypsies in Nazi Germany existed in a state of ongoing oppression. Jews in America are no longer members of a community at risk. Soldiers were at risk in Vietnam, but veterans are not targets of systematic violence in the United States. Women and children in the U.S. comprise a community under siege.

Most readers will accept the notion that Jews and Gypsies are members of oppressed groups. Many others readers will be familiar with and supportive of feminist arguments that women and children also belong in this category. However, the mechanism by which soldiers are systematically exposed to traumatic assault and then reassimilated into U.S. society as veterans requires more explication.

During the Vietnam war, men from both targeted and untargeted groups enlisted or were drafted, and were sent to Vietnam. Those exposed to combat or other life-threatening events, and those exposed to the carnage resulting from combat were traumatized.[28] But combat soldiers, though subordinate to their military superiors and frequently at the mercy of their enemies, still possess a life-or-death power over other people. Much recent literature – popular, clinical, and academic – places the combat soldier simply in the victim's role; helpless in the face of war, and then helpless to readjust from the war experience upon his return home. Feminist critics should be quick to voice their disapproval of an interpretation so drastically at odds with reality. The soldier in combat is both victim and victimizer; dealing death as well as risking it. These soldiers carry guns; they point them at people and shoot to kill. Members of oppressed groups, by contrast, almost never control the tools of violence.

The fact that the "community" of combat soldiers exists only during wartime, and that these veterans of the U.S. war in Vietnam returned to a society that did not view them as a distinct, targeted group did not prevent them from voluntarily associating. American survivors of the Vietnam war formed a new, self-defined group – the Vietnam war veterans[29] – based upon their common traumatic experience. They identified themselves as distinct not only from civilians, but from veterans of previous wars, founding their own organizations and often refusing to join the large, "inclusive" traditional veterans organizations such as the American Legion and the Veterans of Foreign Wars.

Posttraumatic group identification is sometimes quite strong. However, over time it tends to deteriorate, especially when membership in the post-trauma group spans both targeted and nontargeted groups in contemporary society. Current group interests and status will increasingly take precedence over survivor group identification. As group cohesiveness diminishes, social and political pressures upon the survivor group begin to take their toll on members. This process can be traced in the history of Vietnam War veteran associations, which began with the formation of the radical Vietnam Veterans Against the War (VVAW) in 1967.[30]

As the number of American soldiers in Vietnam decreased in the early 1970s, membership in the VVAW (along with antiwar activism in general) waned. In the mid-1970s the shrinking VVAW was shattered by an ideological battle between radical and liberal members. After a contested election in 1978 and a lawsuit between feuding parties, the energies of both sides were exhausted. The liberal wing won the right to use the VVAW name, and the much diminished radical wing was granted the appellation VVAW-AI (Anti-Imperialist). Both groups were quickly overshadowed by the new Vietnam Veterans of America (VVA), founded in 1978 by Robert Muller. Since the late 1980s VVA has itself split into two organizations – Muller left VVA because he resisted its increasing conservatism and founded the Vietnam Veterans of America Foundation. This secession also initiated a lawsuit, which left the VVA with the bulk of the funding and pauperized VVAF. Today the VVA has more than 44,000 members, but it numbers far fewer Vietnam veterans than either the American Legion (750,000) or the VFW (500,000).[31] However they perceive of themselves, Vietnam War veterans do not function as a coherent, self-identified group with a distinct agenda, but have instead gravitated as individuals to identify with groups that best represent the interests of their particular combination of class, race, and gender.

The struggle for self-definition enacted throughout the history of Vietnam veterans' organizations is both reflected in and shaped by popular, political and scholarly discourse. Like the experience of the Holocaust survivor, the experience of the American combat soldier in Vietnam has been revised and codified – survivor testimony has been overwhelmed and revised by the dominant culture. Tom Cruise's character in Oliver Stone's *Born on the Fourth of July* completely overshadows (and defines) the "real" Ron Kovic. Today, one can purchase "The Vietnam Experience" for $14.99 an installment from Time-Life Books, Inc. Cultural theorist Timothy Luke writes:

> The packaging of ideological collaboration here is highly sophisticated, promising that, "If you were there, this is your story. If you weren't here's your chance to learn what it was really like. . . ." When such "history" can be purchased on a monthly installment plan from a corporate image factory, it signals the final colonization of its ideopolitical significance by the society of the spectacle. Stacked along the aisles of collective choice in its bright attractive packaging, next to the comparably priced and packaged "World War II" product, "the Vietnam experience" thus acquires new shelf life as another over-the-counter nostrum for young Americans anxious to keep their world safe for democracy.[32]

The Vietnam War has taken its place on the shelf beside "the Good War" as a noble chapter in U.S. popular history. And, as all such chapters must, it presents *the* normative Vietnam War "experience," implicitly informing the reader: "If you were there then this is your story – and if it isn't your story, you weren't really there."[33]

The shape of public discourse has changed a great deal since the late 1960s and early 1970s. Then, comparisons were regularly made between American soldiers committing atrocities in Vietnam, and *German* soldiers committing atrocities during the Nazi regime – critics of U.S. policy who invoked the phrase "war crimes" to describe U.S. actions in Vietnam were keenly aware of the echo of Nuremberg.[34] This exercise sounds shocking today in light of the "rehabilitation" of the Vietnam veteran, and our current tendency to define him as a victim, rather than an executioner, and it is worth paying attention to – especially since that comparison was sometimes made by the GI himself:

They wanted to call us heroes for serving the country. They offer us recognition and honor, even a national monument. Heroes for serving a country that burned down villages and shot anything that moved. Recognition for being the pawns and agents of a ruthless death machine. . . . Should we pin medals on the chests of the guards at Auschwitz! Should there be a cheering ticker-tape parade for the flight crews that dropped atomic death on Hiroshima and Nagasaki or fire-bombed Dresden! Perhaps we should build a monument to the nun-murdering troops of the Salvadoran National Guard or to the National Guard at Kent State.[35]

"Most American soldiers in Viet-Nam do not question the orders that lead them to raze villages and wipe out men, women and children for the 'crime' of living in Viet Cong-controlled or infiltrated areas," wrote Eric Norden. "To many critics of the war this 'new breed of Americans' bears a disquieting resemblance to an old breed of Germans."[36] Jean-Paul Sartre firmly stated that the Vietnam War met all of Hitler's criteria: "Hitler killed the Jews because they were Jews. The armed forces of the United States torture and kill men, women, and children in Vietnam merely because they are Vietnamese. Whatever lies or euphemisms the government may think up, the spirit of genocide is in the minds of the soldiers."[37] Even satirist Art Hoppe made the connection in a cartoon depicting a German psychiatrist counseling his patient – a participant in the My Lai massacre – to repeat three times a day: "I didn't know what was going on. These things happen in war. I was only following orders as a good American. Our soldiers are good American boys. The war is to save the world from Communism. Our leaders were wrong. The unfortunate victims were members of an inferior race."[38] In February of 1971, hundreds of Vietnam combat veterans gathered in Detroit to hold hearings on war crimes. The testimony of these Winter Soldiers was published in the *Congressional Record* on April 6, 1971, and filled over 100 pages. Similar hearings were held in other cities. All of these veterans admitted to committing or witnessing acts of atrocity, and several compared themselves or other Americans to Nazis.

In 1991 these anecdotes seemed surreal. U.S. soldiers were hailed triumphantly by the American public when they returned from war in the Persian Gulf in 1991, and the Vietnam veteran as icon is firmly established in the American heroic tradition. Comparisons between American soldiers and Nazis are now jarring and incredible. How has the rehabilitation of the image of the American soldier been accomplished? Why have combat veterans of the Vietnam War like poet, novelist, and peace activist W. D. Ehrhart been "drowned out by the cheerful cadences of prodigal sons on parade . . . in faded fatigues . . . [waving] to the cheering crowd."[39]

Historians Marvin Gettleman, et al., offer us one explanation. It was politically expedient, they assert, for the dominant U.S. political interests to attempt to rewrite history after the Vietnam War:

> ... [B]y the late 1970s, [the] national consensus of "No more Vietnams" was becoming a major obstacle for the US government, which was stepping up its intervention in Latin America, Africa, Asia, and the Middle East, preparing to reinstitute draft registration, and initiating the most colossal military buildup in US history. . . . [I]t was necessary to rewrite history once again. Hence, a new body of writings emerged (known by the collective term 'revisionism') which sought to return to the myths that had been dispelled by the knowledge we had gained at such a terrifying price.[40]

Gettleman, et al., do mention briefly that popular film productions and the mass media appeared to cooperate in the revisionary venture, but they offer us no explanation of the mechanism by which such a radical erasure of history was effected. Nor does their theory that powerful interests conspired to rewrite history account for the fact that even long-time liberals have been indoctrinated in the new history of the Vietnam War and the role of the U.S. soldier in Vietnam.

Peter Davies, journalist and champion of the students comprising the Kent 25 (injured students and relatives of the four students murdered by the National Guard at Kent State University on May 4, 1971), was able, in 1991, to equate the Kent State dead with the soldiers killed in the Vietnam War.[41] In this recent article Davies asserts that "there had never been any difference between these . . . victims of forces beyond their control, only what President Nixon had wanted us to see."[42] Davies' desire to see the soldier as victim is new – there is no hint of it in his 1974 speech, "Four Students."[43] At that time the combat soldier in Vietnam would more likely have been analogous to the murderous National Guardsmen of Ohio in the minds of most critics of the Kent State shootings, while the protesters would have resided in quite a different category – perhaps more closely aligned with National Liberation Front fighters or civilians in Vietnam. This creation of the larger category of "victims" (typical of post-1981 thinking) elides the category of Vietnam veterans and active duty servicemen who protested the war, and who actively defied the directives of Presidents Johnson and Nixon.

James William Gibson, in his well-documented analysis *The Perfect War: Technowar in Vietnam*, provides us with a useful analysis of the process of erasure and revision. Gibson notes that by the mid-1970s "no one wanted to talk about the war."[44]

> Somehow . . . even in news reports about Vietnam veterans, the war itself was never revisited. Debates around the dioxin Agent Orange and post-Vietnam stress-disorder cases made their official appearances in

claims for medical benefits or for special consideration in legal contexts. The war thus disappeared as a topic for study and political consideration and instead became dispersed and institutionalized in the complex of medical, psychiatric, and legal discourses. It was as if a new series of medical and judicial problems with no traceable origin had appeared in American society. Or rather, although it was acknowledged that Vietnam was the origin, once the word "Vietnam" was mentioned, the war itself was dismissed and discussion moved on to how an institution could solve the problem. . . . In this way the war became progressively displaced and repressed at the same time it was written about.[45]

Gibson, a sociologist, suggests that the structure of American society shapes our abilities to listen to or to disregard certain kinds of stories. We privilege those who inhabit the top of the "stratification system" because they hold "a virtual monopoly on socially accepted 'scientific' knowledge."[46] He draws on Foucault to explain that the testimony of combat veterans is "subjugated knowledge," and argues that combat veteran writing is marginalized because it is written as narrative, because one veteran's work can be isolated from another's, because it is often colloquial rather than formal, because it is obscene, because it is uncivil.[47]

As a society, we have effectively inhibited Vietnam veterans from speaking in terms other than those we have defined as acceptable, silencing those whose stories fall outside the boundaries of convention. Harry Haines, a scholar of communications and mass media and a Vietnam veteran, argues, "Administrative power offers a therapeutic position for Vietnam veterans, 'hailing' them as World War II heroes and demonstrating hegemony's ability to smooth over ideological contradictions, to make them seem natural and right. . . ."[48] Haines explains that Vietnam veterans are given a clear message, a new status produced for them by hegemony:

> The message identifies the veterans' burdens as "little solace," the lack of compassion and acceptance given to combat veterans by their countrymen once the war was lost. The lack of solace is further specified as a characteristic of Americans "unable to distinguish between" a generalized abhorrence for war and "the stainless patriotism" of Vietnam veterans. The contradictions of the veterans' firsthand experience, the war's "counterfeit universe" are explained as "philosophical disagreements" in the process of resolution. Where disagreement existed, a consensus is manufactured which attempts to integrate the Vietnam veteran with other veterans and to normalize the Vietnam war in terms of other wars. For the veteran, the price of reintegration is the revision of memory to coincide with hegemony's newly produced consensus. Many veterans are willing to accept these terms, a measure of their postwar isolation. Hegemony structures "the field of other possible

actions" open to some veterans, who bring their interpretation of Vietnam in line with prevailing interpretations. . . . In this way, Vietnam veterans may become . . . "fully paid-up members of the consensus club," the sign of the reintegrated society.[49]

The voices of warrior-poets such as W. D. Ehrhart and combat veteran survivors with similar messages are drowned out because they cannot be incorporated into the process that critic Michael Clark defines as the transformation of "individual experience into communal redemption":

> . . . [T]he evolution of the character of the veteran . . . suggests a more profound continuity between the dream and the memory than is apparent in the shifting winds of public taste and political doctrine. As the veteran's participation in the Vietnam war ceased being represented as an obstacle to his assimilation and started to appear as a moral corrective and strategic support for the social order, the historical contradictions that the war raised within the traditional forms of social coherence were transformed into psychological conflicts in the veteran's sense of continuity between his present position in society and his past actions in the war. . . .[50]

An individual is traumatized by a life-threatening event that displaces his or her preconceived notions about the world. Trauma is enacted in a liminal state, outside of the bounds of "normal" human experience, and the subject is radically ungrounded. Accurate representation of trauma can never be achieved without recreating the event since, by its very definition, trauma lies beyond the bounds of "normal" conception. Textual representations – literary, visual, oral – are mediated by language and do not have the impact of the traumatic experience. Chaim Shatan, psychiatrist and pioneer of trauma research, explains that the victim enters the catastrophic environment of trauma through the "membrane" that separates sense from nonsense, narrative from chaos, and "Reality is torn asunder leaving no boundaries and no guideposts."[51] There is, in this case, no substitute for experience – only being is believing.

The process of translation of traumatic experience into text is best understood in terms of Émile Beneviste's description of the dual semiotic and semantic functions of language. Beneviste argues that "the sign" must be recognized, while "the discourse" must be understood: "The difference between recognition and comprehension refers to two distinct faculties of the mind: that of discerning the identity between the previous and the present, and that of discerning, on the other hand, the meaning of a new enunciation."[52] Beneviste also notes that "two systems can have the same sign in common without being, as a result, synonymous or redundant; that is to say, the functional difference of a sign alone matters, not its substantial identity."[53]

Those who have passed through the trauma membrane are equipped with virtually the same set of signs as their nontraumatized peers. As Paul Fussell notes in his landmark study, *The Great War and Modern Memory*, the English language is "rich in terms like *blood, terror, agony, madness, shit, cruelty, murder, sell-out, pain* and *hoax*, as well as phrases like *legs blown off, intestines gushing out over his hands, screaming all night, bleeding to death from the rectum*, and the like. . . ."[54] Fussell believes that communication is hindered only because the audience refuses to listen, that we have "made *unspeakable* mean indescribable; it really means *nasty*."[55] The problem, however, is much more complex. Traumatic experience catalyzes a transformation of meaning in the signs individuals use to represent their experiences. Words such as *blood, terror, agony* and *madness* gain new meaning, within the context of the trauma, and survivors emerge from the traumatic environment with a new set of definitions. On the surface, language appears unchanged – survivors still use the word *terror*, non-traumatized audiences read and understand the word *terror*, and the dislocation of meaning is invisible until one pays attention to the cry of survivors, "What can we do to share our visions? Our words can only evoke the incomprehensible. Hunger, thirst, fear, humiliation, waiting, death; for us these words hold different realities. This is the ultimate tragedy of the victims."[56]

As it is spoken by survivors, the traumatic experience is reinscribed as metaphor. In Barthes' terms, such signifiers are polysemous, implying a "floating chain" of signifieds among which readers may "choose some and ignore others."[57] Barthes believes that "traumatic images are bound up with an uncertainty (an anxiety) concerning the meaning of objects or attitudes. Hence in every society various techniques are developed intended to *fix* the floating chain of signifieds in such a way as to counter the terror of uncertain signs. . . ."[58] Barthes is, I believe, wrong in his claim that readers may "choose" from a variety of meanings – there are meanings available to survivor–readers that are not available to nontraumatized readers. Furthermore, the ability to "read" words like *terror* may extend *across traumas*, so that the combat veteran of the Vietnam War responds viscerally to the transformed signs used by the survivor of the concentration camp since they mirror his or her own traumatic experience, while the nontraumatized reader will come away with a different meaning altogether.

Survivors have the metaphorical tools to interpret representations of traumas similar to their own. The representations may trigger "flashbacks" in the survivor–reader.[59] However, the reexperience of trauma in the reader will always be derived from the reader's *own* traumatic experience, and not from the read experience of the survivor–author. Like the survivor, the nontraumatized reader has at his or her disposal the entire cultural "library" of symbol, myth, and metaphor, but he or she does not have access to the meanings of the sign that invoke traumatic memory. The profusion of available images allows for a variety of readings, which are accessible in different ways to different audiences. Multiple meanings encoded in particular "loaded" signifiers (*blood, terror, murder*) characterize survivor writing, and distinguish it from other genres.

The writings of trauma survivors comprise a distinct "literature of trauma." Literature of trauma is defined by the identity of its author. Literature of trauma holds at its center the reconstruction and recuperation of the traumatic experience, but it is also actively engaged in an ongoing dialogue with the writings and representations of nontraumatized authors. It comprises a marginal literature similar to that produced by feminist, African-American, and queer writers – in fact, it often overlaps with these literatures, so that distinct subgenres of literature of trauma may be found in each of these communities. Theories that treat such marginal literatures are necessarily predicated on the critic's ability to discern an author's relationship to the group in question. Joan W. Scott's suggestions for an agenda that combines poststructuralist theory and feminism can easily be applied to a reading of literature of trauma:

> The point is to find ways to analyze specific "texts" – not only books and documents but also utterances of any kind and in any medium, including cultural practices – in terms of specific historical and contextual meanings. . . . The questions that must be answered in such an analysis, then, are how, in what specific contexts, among which specific communities of people, and by what textual and social processes has meaning been acquired? More generally, the questions are: How do meanings change? How have some meanings emerged as normative and others have been eclipsed or disappeared? What do these processes reveal about how power is constituted and operates?[60]

Only after we have contextualized the trauma can we separate the outside interpretations of "Other People's Trauma" (OPT) from the narratives of the survivors and successfully "read" the revisions of that trauma.

The critic of trauma literature must determine: the composition of the community of trauma survivors; the nature of the trauma inflicted upon members of the community; the composition of the community of perpetrators; the relationship between the communities of victims and perpetrators; and the contemporary social, political, and cultural location of the community of survivors.

The approach of most postmodern critics is inappropriate when applied to reading the literature of trauma. Postmodern critics have been concerned with the problematics of *reading*:[61] As professional readers, it is in their interest to put forward the argument that any text, properly read, can be "understood." Those among them who do not claim to be able to divine the author's intent simply claim that an author's intent is irrelevant. It's obvious that this ap-

proach won't work for the literatures of trauma. The act of *writing*, though
perhaps less accessible to the critic, is as important as the act of reading.

I am far from the first person to notice that the author's identity matters.
In 1939 Jorge Luis Borges penned an absurd ficcion – "Pierre Menard, Author
of *Don Quixote*" – in which he described the process by which Menard
recreated Cervantes' tale. Menard's imaginary novel is not, as Borges is quick
to note, a contemporary rewrite of the Spanish knight's adventure, but, word
for word, "*the Don Quixote.*" Borges' story is narrated by a literary critic, and
the centerpiece is the critic's comparison of two passages which, of course, are
the same word for word:

> . . . truth, whose mother is history, who is the rival of time, depository
> of deeds, witness of the past, example and lesson to the present, and
> warning to the future.[62]

"Written in the seventeenth century, written by the 'ingenious layman' Cervantes, this enumeration is a mere rhetorical eulogy of history," notes the
critic. Menard's version, he believes, has greater depth, though it is less fluent:

> History, *mother* of truth; the idea is astounding. Menard, a contempo-
> rary of William James, does not define history as an investigation of
> reality, but as its origin. Historical truth, for him, is not what took place;
> it is what we think took place. . . . Equally vivid is the contrast in styles.
> The archaic style of Menard – in the last analysis, a foreigner – suffers
> from a certain affectation. Not so that of his precursor, who handles
> easily the ordinary Spanish of his time.[63]

Though Borges' tale is fanciful, it suggests not only that the reader's interpretation of a work is affected by the his or her ability to contextualize, to cross
disciplines, to couple history and philosophy with literature, but that two
writers writing may pen the same words and tell entirely different stories. The
critic of literature of trauma may extract the moral that two people can
represent the same experience, using similar imagery and descriptive terminology and create literary works with entirely different meanings – meanings
which are located not in the words themselves, but in the interaction between
writer and text, between reader and text, between reader and writer.

The work of the critic of the literature of trauma is both to identify and
explicate literature by members of survivor groups, and to deconstruct the
process by which the dominant culture codifies their traumatic experience.
Survivors bear witness in a social, cultural, political, and historical context.
Their location within the complex network of communal relations deter-
mines the reception of their testimony and the interpretative and revisionary
pressures that will be brought to bear on their traumatic experience. Members
of opposing interest groups will attempt to appropriate traumatic experiences
while survivors will struggle to retain their control. The winner of this battle

over meaning will determine the manner in which the experience is to be codified.

Representation of traumatic experience is ultimately a tool in the hands of those who shape public perceptions and national myth. In contemporary U.S. culture, this battle over codification and appropriation of trauma is glaringly obvious when one examines the interaction between testimony and cultural representation of institutionalized sexualized violence against women and children. Rape, sexual abuse, and incest are woven into the fabric of contemporary American culture. Rapists are protected by a criminal justice system that demands that rape victims "prove" that intercourse was not consensual. Courts are unlikely to accept that intercourse was forced if the accused is an acquaintance of the victim, particularly if he is an ex-lover or boyfriend. In some states, wives are not allowed to bring charges of rape against their husbands unless they are legally separated.[64] Though most rapes are committed by men who are known to the victim, women who are raped by strangers are most likely to secure the conviction of their rapist.

Rape, especially acquaintance rape, is widely acknowledged to be an underreported crime. Rape victims are aware that the legal system does not work in their favor, and they fear the social, psychological, and personal consequences of prosecuting rapists. When women do report acquaintance rape, police frequently refuse to forward these reports for possible prosecution.[65] Prosecutors, in turn, systematically dismiss or downgrade acquaintance rape cases. And even if rape cases do make it to trial, juries tend to be prejudiced against the prosecution, and to be lenient with the defendant if they believe that the victim indulged in "contributory behavior" – including "hitchhiking, dating, and talking with men at parties."[66]

Men who sexually abuse children are also virtually immune from prosecution. Children lack the independence and power to bring charges against them. Some children are abused before they are even old enough to speak. Children who can speak, and who describe the abuse they suffer are frequently disbelieved. A significant part of the psychological establishment believes that young female children fantasize sexual interactions with their fathers or stepfathers, and that such fantasies are a part of "normal" development.[67] Prosecution of abusive men is difficult or impossible without corroborating evidence. The motives of wives or girlfriends who accuse their partners of sexually abusing their children are often questioned by civil courts, and their charges are looked upon with suspicion. And when abuse is found by the court, children are often placed in foster homes where they are often again abused by other male adults.

Incest is so rarely reported, and prosecution is so rarely effective that most incestuous relationships are finally ended by the victim when she becomes old enough, independent enough, and powerful enough to break away from her abuser. Some abused children may never live to reach that point: a 1983 study found that 38% of incest *survivors* had attempted to kill themselves.[68] We will never know how many children and young adults have taken their own lives to escape sexual abuse.[69]

Popular culture stereotypes reinforce the legal apparatus in protecting the men who rape women or sexually abuse children. Films, mainstream novels, and advertising reinforce the idea that women who say "no" mean "yes," and that children are willing partners in the sexual adventures of grown men.[70] Pornography, a $10 billion per year industry, obsessively focuses on rape as a pleasurable experience for the male rapist, and often casts female children in the role of the seducer.[71]

Women and girls are taught to believe that they provoke men into assaulting them, and that they will bring pain and humiliation upon themselves by dressing, speaking, or acting in a provocative manner. They are taught that there is a thin line between seduction and rape, and that it is their responsibility to keep men from crossing that line. But the demands of daily life, of child care, and of holding a job, make it impossible for women to entirely avoid being exposed and vulnerable. All women run the risk of being raped or assaulted.

Unlike the European Jew 40 years after the Holocaust, or the combat veteran returned from war, the American woman lives in fear of an enemy who stalks her today. Her enemy is free to assault her on the street, in her place of work, or in her own home. He may attack her once, or repeatedly. If she hides from him, he may find her. If she asks for the protection of the authorities, he may have the right to demand she be returned to his control. If she tries to press charges, he will be protected by a legal, political and social system that is biased against her. Sociologist Anthony Wilden has emphasized that "if there is one class of individuals who cannot rely on their community for self-defense it is women – and after them, teenage girls and children. The reason for that is that it is their own community that attacks them."[72]

All American women are threatened with violence, regardless of their race or class, just as all Jews were in danger in Nazi Germany. Money and connections can help only to a point: a woman jogging alone in Central Park after dark is a potential target whether she is an advertising executive or a welfare mother. More hue and cry may be raised by the press and citizenry when the victim is upper-class, and prosecution is more likely if she is white and her attackers are men of color. Regardless, the first question any court will ask is: "What was she doing alone down there at night?"

Often victims find themselves completely without support. Social and legal institutions, churches, and frequently even a victim's own family and friends may place the blame on her shoulders. Dr. Natalie Shainess, a psychiatrist who works with sexually abused children, suggests: "It calls to mind the problem of Jews in Nazi Germany: how many Germans would go against their own interests to help? What hope was there? Who would listen, who would believe?"[73]

In this hostile climate, what does it mean when women bear witness to sexual assault? To whom do they testify? Do they believe that men will hear them and go against their own interests, reduce their own power, in order to make the world a safer place for women? Or do they think that by speaking to their sisters they can organize against sexual assault, take power by force? Who is their audience? Do men read incest and rape narratives and, if so, for what purposes? How are women's stories of sexual assault packaged and sold? Ten years ago, it would have been impossible to begin to answer these questions. There simply did not exist a body of rape and incest testimony to examine. That situation has recently changed, mainly due to the increased activity of the feminist movement, which has created a small but supportive community within which women can safely tell their stories.

Consider the striking similarity between Audre Lorde's explanation for why she writes, and John Ketwig's inscription in the prologue of his narrative, . . . And a Hard Rain Fell. Lorde is a black, lesbian feminist and Ketwig is a white, male Vietnam combat veteran. Both of them express sentiments uncannily akin to Holocaust survivor Aharon Appelfeld. "The inability to express your experience," Appelfeld explains, "and the feeling of guilt combined together and created silence. . . . Not everyone remained within that isolation. The desire to tell . . . broke out and took on strange and different forms of expression. Since new words had not been invented, people made use of the old ones, which had served them before."[74]

"I write," explains Lorde,

> for myself and my children and for as many people as possible who can read me, who need to hear what I have to say – who need to use what I know. . . . I write for these women for whom a voice has not yet existed, or whose voices have been silenced. I don't have the only voice or all of their voices, but they are a part of my voice, and I am a part of theirs.[75]

Ketwig writes:

> I wanted my wife to know all I was feeling. I hoped someday my kids would read it and understand. . . . This story became a book simply because so many Vietnam vets pleaded with me to make it public. Many are still searching for words. Our families and loved ones have waited so long for an explanation of the enormous changes the war crafted into our personalities. . . . I don't want my children to see the world I have known.[76]

Literature of trauma is written from the need to tell and retell the story of the traumatic experience, to make it "real" both to the victim and to the community. Such writing serves both as validation and cathartic vehicle for the traumatized author. Des Pres reminds us, "Displacement is the goal of any story, in degree; all fiction aims to usurp the real world with a world that is imagined."[77] Desires for affirmation and release cross subgenre lines, manifesting themselves in writings by combat veterans, holocaust survivors, and rape and incest survivors. They are also manifested in the work of many feminist writers who are not specifically identified (either by themselves or others) as trauma survivors.

My goal is to present a coherent rendering of the relationships between individual trauma and cultural interpretation, using as my focus the Holocaust, the Vietnam War, and the phenomenon of sexualized violence against women. In order to do so, I must create a rich context for each trauma and its representations, and let nothing go without saying. Historian and literary critic Jonathan Morse notes, "On the page, history is present in every text, 'historical' or not."[78] We must seek complexity, rather than avoid it:

> Words that come out of history are complicated; they are cluttered with etymology and connotation. And that slows us down when we try to understand them. . . . But words that make up their histories as they come into existence leap at us unchaperoned. First they are in our leader's mouth, then they are in ours. It is a wonderful gift. We can hum along with the words passing through us; we can clap, we can jump. And as we respond to the music we make, we will feel ourselves coming into our being. We will be wrong, but we will believe that we know at last who we are.[79]

Our search for complexity begins with the paradigm case of the Holocaust, the *Ur*-trauma in the U.S. mindscape.

2

A Form of Witness

The Holocaust and North American Memory

Can we literally feel that *everyone* must remember the Holocaust? That there is something of import achieved in recounting the whole story to, say, primitive tribesmen in New Guinea?

– Jerry Samet[1]

In September, 1990, I took a walk down to the Vietnam Veteran's Memorial – the Wall – in Washington, DC. To enter the Memorial proper, visitors must pass by the literature tables set up on the paths leading to the Memorial and on the plaza in front of the Lincoln Memorial, where Vietnam veteran entrepreneurs and true believers pass out POW/MIA propaganda, hawk commercial products, and campaign against flag burning, peace, and Jane Fonda.[2] On this particular afternoon I paused before a booth that sold T-shirts. In addition to the usual "POWs Never Have a Nice Day" logo, I spotted a stack of new "Desert Shield" shirts that featured the legend "Desert Shield: Persian Gulf Pest Control" and a graphic depicting Saddam Hussein as a dangling spider with a man's head. When I asked about them, the fortysomething guy in combat fatigues behind the counter commented that the shirts were "hot," and that he was going to order "a lot more" from the "artist."[3]

I bought the T-shirt, and the next day I brought it along when I went to work.[4] My colleagues at the U.S. Holocaust Memorial Museum certainly found the shirt distasteful, and many commented on the striking resemblance borne by the caricature of Hussein's face to the "Jews" in Nazi antisemitic propaganda. A few noted that the phrase "Pest Control" resonated unpleasantly with Hitler's rhetoric in *Mein Kampf*, where the metaphor of vermin and insect infestation was invoked with great regularity and Hitler expressed his desire to exterminate [*vernichten*] the pest. Yet my suggestion that the Museum should issue an official statement condemning racist anti-Arab propaganda was met with no more enthusiasm than an earlier suggestion that the

Museum had an obligation to publicly comment upon President Bush's characterization of Hussein as "another Hitler." The U.S. Holocaust Memorial Museum, a congressionally mandated public institution supported by privately donated funds, refused to enter into any discussion of the Persian Gulf War, tacitly supporting U.S. policy and refusing to exercise its claim to authority over the meaning of the Holocaust in contemporary U.S. culture.

As cultural critics Jochen and Linda Schulte-Sasse note, "while Western political discourse has persistently likened Hussein to Hitler, its iconography likens him in significant ways to Hitler's Other, the 'Jew.'"[5] Images of the U.S. are equally confused. Bush portrayed himself as a glorious American Führer leading the country to deserved prominence in a "New World Order" (all that was "good" about Nazi Germany),[6] and at the same time the U.S. population was painted as the victimized "Jew," suffering at the hands of evil dictators and terrorists. Hussein is Hitler, we are Hitler, Hussein is the Jew, we are the Jew, and behind it all lies the metonym of "Holocaust."

"Hitler," "Jew," "Nazi," and "Holocaust" imply floating chains of signifiers in the Barthesian sense, each invoking a variety of signifieds. Every individual interpretive choice is the product of a dialogic heteroglossia – "Everything means, is understood, as a part of a greater whole – there is a constant interaction between meanings, all of which have the potential of conditioning others."[7] The resulting symmetry of competing interpretations resembles Rabelais' "grotesque body," a carnival environment "loud with many voices," promising "the closure which all monologism promises, its own monologism ultimately subverted by the heteroglossia of the collection as a carnival whole."[8] Each participant in the dialogue attempts to counter the terror of the traumatic image by "fixing" the signified, restricting its meaning and, thus, its implications.

The meaning of the "Holocaust" is not fixed in contemporary U.S. culture. Representations of the Third Reich in elite and popular media, the manner in which the Holocaust is taught in schools, the construction of the U.S. Holocaust Memorial Museum, histories produced by scholars, the interpretations advanced by theologians, the claims of politicians – all are sites of ideological struggle. It is my intent, in this chapter, to demonstrate that the critics who take the literature of the Holocaust as their subject are likewise engaged in the attempt to fix the meaning of the Holocaust. Each critic has a social and political agenda. The efforts of critics to promote particular definitions and interpretations of "Holocaust literature" are inextricably tied to the contest over the meaning of the Holocaust. Like the rhetoric of public debate, scholarly arguments are often emotional and usually charged, a "politics of the passions."[9]

Debate in the public arena is most visible when extremist groups such as the "Institute for Historical Review" assert that Jews have fabricated evidence of the Nazi's genocidal campaign in order to perpetrate the "Holocaust hoax" on the peoples of the world,[10] provoking impassioned responses from historians and survivors who point to the massive body of documentary proof and testimonial literature dealing with Nazi atrocity. Though not a single reputable historian supports the claims of the Institute for Historical Review, Holocaust-deniers have successfully kept themselves in the public eye by provoking a First Amendment argument of mammoth proportions over their tactic of publicizing their views by taking out ads in college and university newspapers.[11]

The struggle over the meaning of the Holocaust is complicated by the fact that the antagonists are simultaneously engaged in battle at several overlapping ideological sites. Though conservative Holocaust scholars such as Lucy Dawidowicz express their "shock" at the discovery of the political agenda underlying curricula designed by progressive Holocaust scholars,[12] their pose of offended innocence is both opportunistic and insincere. In an article which is, ostensibly, about teaching the Holocaust, Lucy Dawidowicz's words resonate with Alan Bloom's and Dinesh D'Sousa's when she claims that the subject of history

> is being squeezed out to make room for subject matter demanded by special-interest groups. Blacks have called for teaching about the role of blacks in American history and culture, and Hispanics, Native Americans, and women have followed suit, giving rise to what has irreverently been labeled "oppression studies." The original psychological rationale for these studies – that they would foster pupils' self-esteem – has now been superseded by an ideological rationale which preaches the equality of all cultures and attacks the "hegemony" of Western civilization and its "Eurocentric" character. In either case, the time and space that could be devoted to studying the murder of the European Jews shrink even more. And lobbying efforts by Holocaust survivors, which intentionally or not often reinforce the impression that the Holocaust is nothing more than the Jewish branch of oppression studies, cannot always compete with other more fashionable or better organized "causes."[13]

Dawidowicz believed that the study of "the murder of the European Jews" does *not* fall into the category of "oppression studies," although the misguided efforts of some survivors mistakenly reinforce that misconception. Rather, she asserted that "*the* primary lesson of the Holocaust" is that we ought to return to "the fundamental moral code of our civilization and of the three great religions whose basic text is the Jewish Bible." Her underlying critique is that the separation of church and state prevents "teaching moral standards as they are incorporated in the Ten Commandments (or even in just one commandment) . . . something is clearly wrong with both our system of education and our standards of morality."[14]

Dawidowicz has taken her stand against multiculturalism and "political correctness," the conservative demon. Her critique of Holocaust scholarship relates not only to the subject of the Holocaust as history, but to contested ground in a contemporary political debate between right and left. She claims that study of the Holocaust reveals certain universal truths that transcend the limits of individual "self-esteem" and base ideology – universal truths rooted in religious dogma. She reserves her strongest criticisms for the group "Facing History and Ourselves," a Boston-based Holocaust education project dedicated, in their own words, to "promote awareness of the history of the Holocaust and the genocide of the Armenian people, an appreciation for justice, a concern for interpersonal understanding, and a memory for the victims of those events."[15] Dawidowicz claims that Facing History is "a vehicle for instructing thirteen-year-olds in civil disobedience and indoctrinating them with propaganda for nuclear disarmament."[16]

Facing History explicitly delineates the goal of its curriculum:

> This curriculum must provide opportunities for students to explore the practical applications of freedom, which they have learned demand a constant struggle with difficult, controversial, and complex issues. The responsibility that citizens have for one another as neighbors and as nations cannot be left to others. This history has taught that there is no one else to confront terrorism, ease the yoke and pain of racism, attack apathy, create and enforce just laws, and wage peace but *us*. Information and experience in the political system can challenge the fear, the propaganda, the training in obedience and the lack of information that discourage active decision making about today and the future.[17]

Unabashedly ideological, Facing History claims that the study of the Holocaust supports their conclusions – that, in fact, proper understanding of the Holocaust *impels* one into progressive political activism. Both Facing History and Lucy Dawidowicz believe that study of the Holocaust provides access to universal truths, but they each argue for a different interpretation, a different truth. For Dawidowicz, the Holocaust stands as a vindication of traditional (Jewish) religious culture and conservative politics, and places the Jew at the center of the greatest tragedy in the history of the world. For Facing History, the Holocaust is an emblem of conservative politics run amok, the result of illiberal attitudes towards difference and the refusal of individuals to take responsibility for their actions. Rather than emphasizing the particularity of the Jewish victim, Facing History urges its audience to make a direct comparison between antisemitism in the Third Reich and racism in the United States, between Hitler's massive military build-up and our own nuclear arms race, between the apathy of German citizens and the apathy of U.S. citizens in the face of injustice.

But the struggle over the meaning of the Holocaust is not limited to a tug of war between the right and the left. In the contemporary political arena, it is complicated by the reactions of various groups to current events in the state of Israel, and by tensions between African-Americans and Jews in the United States – a product of the "post-consensus politics" described by cultural critic Kobena Mercer, in which a multiplicity of social and political agents have "pluralized the domain of political antagonism."[18] Mercer writes, "No one has a monopoly or exclusive authorship over the signs they share in common: rather, elements from the same system of signs are constantly subject to antagonistic modes of appropriation and articulation."[19] Thus, in the recent Persian Gulf War, members of the left argued among themselves over whether it was reasonable to equate Hussein (and, by inference, the Palestinians who supported Hussein) with Hitler.

A few Jewish members of the progressive political community have cautioned non-Jews that their application of the Holocaust metaphor to the Israeli/Palestinian conflict reflects a (perhaps unconscious) antisemitism. Orthodox rabbi David Landes ties leftist antisemitism to damaging representations of the Holocaust: "The Left's difficulty with the Jews is linked to its approach to the Holocaust."[20] According to Landes, Leftists "misappropriate" the Holocaust in three ways: erasing the specifically antisemitic character of the Holocaust; universalizing the Holocaust; and equating "Jewish Israelis with the Nazis, and Arab Palestinians with the persecuted Jews."[21] He also claims that Jews who adopt the leftist perceptions of the Holocaust are "self-hating." Though Landes admits that it is possible that "one can be critical of Israel without being a self-hating Jew,"[22] and further acknowledges that the label of "self-hating Jew" has been used to suppress dissent in the Jewish community, he goes on to claim that the term is not entirely meaningless. And those whom Landes specifically and emphatically identifies as self-hating are the Jews who

> . . . identify as Jews, but . . . simultaneously deny as an essential part of that definition: either peoplehood, religious culture, or the Jews' historical relationship to the land of Israel. The Israel/Nazi analogy relieves the self-hating Jews of this tension: they can be good prophetic Jews by opposing exclusivistic Jews, fanatical Judaism, and the "Fascist" Jewish state. The attack on the Jewish state thus gives them an explanation for why they are not involved in Jewish concerns and simultaneously allows them to claim that they are still connected to their Jewishness.[23]

Landes insistence on a "correct" representation of the Holocaust is tied to his social and political agenda – he wishes to build a progressive Jewish community that adheres to religious traditions and supports the continued existence of the state of Israel.

Jewish leftist Noam Chomsky has a different set of political and social goals than does Landes, and thus a completely different perspective on representations of the Holocaust. While Landes believes that the application of Holocaust metaphors to the current Israeli/Palestinian conflict is a great mistake, Chomsky identifies many self-proclaimed Zionists with the fascist regime of the Nazis, and equates persecuted Palestinians with persecuted Jews. Chomsky asserts that the American Jewish community is "deeply totalitarian," and that American Jews use accusations of antisemitism and the specter of the Holocaust to silence critics of Israel as part of a carefully engineered political strategy.[24]

> There is just no way to respond. If you are denounced as being an anti-Semite, what are you going to say, I'm not an anti-Semite? Or if you are denounced as being in favor of the Holocaust, what are you going to say, I'm not in favor of the Holocaust? I mean you cannot win. . . . Why not say I am in favor of the Holocaust. I think all Jews should be killed. That is the next thing to say. The point is that they can say anything they want.[25]

Chomsky strongly criticizes Elie Wiesel, whom he accuses of taking the position that "one must maintain silence in the face of atrocities carried out by one's favorite state."[26] He notes that Wiesel is far more popular in the U.S. than in Israel, and observes that it is "an interesting fact about American culture . . . that a man who puts forth this position can be regarded as a moral hero."[27] No one, least of all Chomsky, would argue with the assertion that his "agnostic" position on the Holocaust reflects his own political ideology. Chomsky is adamant in his insistence that the U.S. is an aggressive imperialist power bent on maintaining world dominance at all costs, a "violent terror state," supporting equally violent client states, including the state of Israel:

> The modalities of state terrorism that the United States has devised for its clients have commonly included at least a gesture towards "winning hearts and minds," though experts warn against undue sentimentality. . . . Nazi Germany shared these concerns, as Albert Speer discusses in his autobiography. . . .[28]

There were moderate and liberal American Jews who thought that the label of "Nazi" was best applied to Hussein's supporters. Though many progressive Jews were disturbed by a February 1990 press conference in Tel Aviv at which four prominent Israeli peace activists declared their support for the war against Iraq, others approved of their call for the elimination of Hussein's "genocidal" regime.[29] Novelist and well-known Israeli peacenik Amos Oz's assertion that a preference for sanctions over war amounted to "appeasement," struck a chord with moderate Jews like representative Stephen Solarz (D) of Brooklyn, New York, who wrote that although Bush's equation of Hussein and Hitler was "wildly overdrawn," the comparison was not entirely illegitimate: "But if there are fundamental differences between

Saddam and Hitler, there are also instructive similarities. Like Hitler, Saddam has an unappeasable will to power combined with a ruthless willingness to employ whatever means are necessary to achieve it."[30] Solarz and his Committee for Peace and Security in the Gulf had strong support from the liberal Jewish community, which closed ranks once the war began; some no doubt moved to join the prowar agitators by their perception of the antiwar movement as actively anti-Israel and covertly antisemitic. Jewish progressive John Judis claims, "Peace activists did not merely criticize Israel's government or policies; they blamed the Jewish state (as a previous generation had blamed Jewish bankers) for the ills of the world, including millennial conflicts between Arab peoples."[31]

Further complicating the question of representation of the Holocaust is the current tension between the African-American and Jewish-American communities. As Cornel West notes, the period in U.S. history during which Blacks and Jews were most strongly allied "depended on both sides' identifying with a form of universalism that did not highlight questions of identity. There is no going back to such a period. If there is going to be a renewed connection between these two communities, or even a sensible dialogue, it depends on our ability to remain sensitive to the positive quests for identity among Jewish Americans and African-Americans."[32] West points out that the division is not always clear – conservative Jews oppose both Blacks *and* liberal Jews on such issues as affirmative action and social welfare programs – but that it is most evident in the African-American critique of U.S. foreign policy:

> This critique coincided with the emergence of conservative forces in Israel after the 1967 and 1973 wars – first as a conservatizing influence in the Labor party, then as the triumph of Menachem Begin's rightwing coalition – and the increasing identification of Israel with an American foreign policy that was dominated by cold war preoccupations and a refusal to see anything good in Third World liberation struggle. This connection to American foreign policy made it easier for many Blacks to identify Israel as a tool of American imperial interests.[33]

As early as 1967, black intellectual Harold Cruse observed that American Jewish Zionists seemed to support a position of "anti-Jewish-integration-assimilation," while at the same time taking a "pro-Negro integration position and an anti-black nationalist position."[34] Black nationalists identify with the Palestinians in Israel, and see the Jewish Israelis as colonial oppressors. I have not come across black literature that equates Israelis with Nazis and Palestinians with Jews – rather, the Israeli government is repeatedly compared to the South African government, and both are accused of using brutal methods to oppress or enslave an indigenous population.[35]

Cruse, who is certainly an antisemite, articulates the perspective of a segment of the black community which believes that the Holocaust occurred, and that it was terrible, but that "for all practical purposes (political, economic and cultural) as far as Negroes are concerned, *Jews have not suffered in the United States*. They have, in fact, done exceptionally well on every level of endeavor, from a nationalist premise or on an assimilated status."[36] From this point of view, Jewish references to the Holocaust seem to be both gratuitous and manipulative – a false claim to sympathy and kinship:

> At the Village Vanguard, when [LeRoi] Jones and [Archie] Shepp were reminded of the six million Jews exterminated by Hitler, Jones replied to Larry Rivers, "You're like the others [whites], except for the cover story." Shepp added: "I'm sick of you cats talking about the six million Jews. I'm talking about the five to eight million Africans killed in the Congo. . . ."[37]

The black community is divided on the meaning of the Holocaust. Cruse, in his major work, *The Crisis of the Negro Intellectual*, was, after all, writing to protest what he saw as a black intellectual propensity to be overfond of Jews, to see them as natural allies and as partners in suffering. He was fighting a long-lived tradition in the black church, reaching back into the antebellum period, in which enslaved blacks likened themselves to the Jews under Pharaoh, and freedom was equated with the Promised Land – Harriet Tubman was not called "Moses" by accident. Among his contemporaries, Cruse criticized Lorraine Hansberry and James Baldwin for their alleged reliance on Jewish support, and he argued that the post-World War II American Jew bore no resemblance to the idealized Jews of black mythology.

Today, the spectrum of debate within the black community encompasses progressives such as Cornel West and bell hooks, and radical antisemites such as Louis Farrakhan. Farrakhan, a Black Muslim and a strong supporter of the Palestine Liberation movement, promotes the notion of a Zionist conspiracy. His views on the Holocaust come uncomfortably close to those of the Holocaust deniers. West and hooks, on the other hand, acknowledge the importance of the Holocaust both to Jewish people, and to outside observers. Though West argues against what he calls a "rootless" universalism, he does assume that there is a basis for black–Jewish alliance – presumably on the grounds that both groups share an understanding of persecution and oppression. hooks is more explicit, explaining that comparison of black and Jewish "holocausts" leads to important new insights for members of both groups.[38] There is no segment of the U.S. black community that supports the claims of conservatives like Dawidowicz or liberals like Landes to the "uniqueness" of the Holocaust, or to its overwhelming importance in world history. Black history – from the Middle Passage to the tribal wars of the African continent – seems to provide most African Americans with evidence of sufficient genocidal precedent and antecedent.[39]

The parallels between debate over the Holocaust and over the issues of multiculturalism and "political correctness" are not coincidental, nor is the fact that some of the most passionate arguments take place in the realm of literary theory. "Traditional" literary theorists face off against the new literary critics, who espouse a variety of interpretive strategies, including (but not limited to) poststructuralism, reader-response criticism, semiotics, cultural studies, and deconstruction. The last term, "deconstruction," has been adopted by conservatives as a catchphrase for a whole range of nontraditional criticism as well as the leftist political agenda this criticism is assumed to endorse. As Nina King observes in her analysis of the curricular wars at Duke University:

> [T]he deconstructionists regard language as a tricky, slippery medium that cannot be pinned down to a single fixed meaning. The critic's task is to demonstrate that trickiness and slipperiness in a given work, to show how meaning changes shape when the medium is carefully examined. "Meaning" and, by extension, concepts such as "truth" and "art" are viewed as relative – historically and culturally determined rather than fixed for all time.[40]

The notion that there is no single, "correct" interpretation of a text is deeply troubling to representatives of the political right. George Will complains that the "supplanting of aesthetic by political responses to literature makes literature primarily interesting as a mere index of who had power and whom the powerful victimized."[41] Though most new critics would hardly call literature a "mere" reflection of power relations, they would certainly acknowledge that power hierarchies are inscribed in (and describe) texts.

The claim of the new critics – that no objective standard of judgment exists – confounds conservatives, who find themselves desperately trying to conserve that which may never have been there in the first place. Tension between theory and doctrine is unavoidable, since doctrine rests upon a moral and ideological foundation that cannot bear too much questioning and it is the business of theory to question. When Terrence Des Pres detailed the three principles that comprise the set of "fictions" that "set limits to respectable study" of the Holocaust, he was both engaging in a critical act and a political protest, wrestling, in the words of Nancy Armstrong and Leonard Tennenhouse, for possession of the "key cultural terms determining what are the right and wrong ways to be a human being."[42] Des Pres claimed that Holocaust doctrine demands that one concede the following:

> 1) The Holocaust shall be represented, in its totality, as a unique event or special case or kingdom of its own, above or below or apart from history. 2) Representations of the Holocaust shall be as accurate, as exacting, as unfailingly faithful as possible to the facts and circumstances of the event itself, without change or manipulation for any reason –

artistic or literary reasons included. 3) The Holocaust shall be approached as a solemn, or even a sacred event, admitting of no response that obscures its enormity or dishonors its dead.[43]

Des Pres was a literary theorist, and he engaged the question of representation of the Holocaust from a critical stance. A Catholic, and an American, Des Pres could not stake his claim to knowledge of the Holocaust on personal experience. His struggle with Bruno Bettelheim, psychoanalyst, survivor, and Jew, over the right to define and interpret the Holocaust is worth examining in some detail, and I would like to pay particular attention to the following two essays; Bruno Bettelheim's "Surviving," which originally appeared in the *New Yorker* in 1976, and Terrence Des Pres' "The Bettelheim Problem," which was published in *Social Research* in 1979. "Surviving" was Bettelheim's response to the nearly simultaneous release of Lina Wertmüller's film *Seven Beauties* and Des Pres' widely excerpted and reviewed study of life in the concentration camps, *The Survivor*. Though Bettelheim does not mention it in the essay, *The Survivor* included a section which was very critical of Bettelheim's earlier psychoanalytic study of the camps, *The Informed Heart*, and much of "Surviving" is directed at discrediting not only Des Pres' scholarship, but at questioning his moral character. "The Bettelheim Problem" was Des Pres' response to "Surviving," and amounted to a bold attack on Bettelheim as both an academic and a survivor. Taken in context, these works provide a framework within which to examine the controversy over the definition of the Holocaust and the role of the survivor. The tensions between different literary critical strategies, between mythologization and medicalization, between personal testimony and "objective" analysis are all evident in the debate between Bettelheim and Des Pres, and are played out, again and again, in the works of critics of the literature of the Holocaust.

In *The Survivor*, Des Pres asserts that "serious study of the concentration-camp experience has been done almost exclusively from the psychoanalytic point of view."[44] The two studies he points to are Elie A. Cohen's *Human Behavior in the Concentration Camp* (1954) and Bruno Bettelheim's *The Informed Heart* (1960).[45] Both were written by Jewish survivors of concentration camps who were, before and after the war, engaged in the practice of medicine and psychiatry.[46] Des Pres' complaint is that the psychoanalytic approach is flawed at its heart, "misleading because it is essentially a theory of culture and of man in the civilized state."[47] Psychoanalysis is based on an assumption that behavior is symbolic, and Des Pres argues that human behavior in extremity is action stripped of symbolism, with only one level of meaning – survival at all costs.

Des Pres does not reject the foundation of psychoanalysis – that "the phenomenon of civilization, no matter how advanced or primitive, is based first of all on processes of sublimation and symbolization"[48] – but he claims that the state of extremity to which concentration camp prisoners were subjected reduced each of their actions to a life or death issue, stripped away the layers of symbol which protected them from confronting their "primal needs and crude necessities," and forced them into a state in which "at every moment the meaning and purpose of their behavior [was] fully known."[49] Des Pres rejects Bettelheim's claim that prisoners' behavior in the camps followed a model of regression to childlike behaviors and eventual identification with the camp authorities (parent figures) as prisoners' individuality and autonomy dissolved. It is Bettelheim's notion of autonomy that Des Pres most vehemently opposes, for in the circumstances of the camps, pursuit of that autonomy could only result in death:

> Heroism, for him [Bettelheim], is an isolated act of defiance through which the individual *as* an individual confronts death. . . . The act he celebrates is suicide. . . . What can "autonomy" at the cost of personal destruction amount to? . . . Bettelheim's argument comes down to this: "manhood" requires dramatic self-confirmation. . . . Insofar as the struggle for life did not become overtly rebellious, prisoners were "childlike."[50]

Furthermore, Des Pres claims that Bettelheim's analysis of the camps is shaped by his agenda: "to compare the survivor's experience with the predicament of modern man in 'mass society.'"[51]

In Des Pres' estimation, Bettelheim is interested in recuperating the (Judeo)Christian world view which rests on the principle that "survival in itself, not dedicated to something *else*" is both meaningless and ignoble.[52] For Des Pres, however, the survivor represents man in a pure state, stripped of the "style or fine language," "masks and stratagems" we use to cover ourselves and to conceal from ourselves our own mortality – all those layers we require psychoanalysis to excavate and clarify. Although Des Pres adds that "one does not have to survive the concentration camps in order to arrive at awareness of life's immanent value,"[53] he believes survivors have a "special grace." Our reluctance to listen to the words of survivors springs, in his estimation, from our terror of mortality and our inability to confront evil, "the demonic content of our own worst fears and wishes."[54] Survivors represent our deepest fears, they have descended into Hell and emerged transformed to remind us that the content of our nightmares can burst into the world and consume us. "The essence of survival is passage through death; this way of speaking may be metaphorical for us, but not for survivors. . . . And here especially we must not be misled by our reliance on metaphor: the survivor is not a metaphor, not an emblem, but *an example*."[55]

Des Pres' claims apparently disturbed Bruno Bettelheim deeply. The psychoanalyst was moved to publicly discuss the representation and interpretation of the Holocaust in both popular and high culture – film and criticism

– and to declare himself a qualified critic on the basis of his status as a survivor. Though Bettelheim notes in the short preface to "Surviving" that he was motivated to write his essay only by the "near universal acclaim"[56] with which Wertmüller's *Seven Beauties* was received in this country, and does not acknowledge his desire to respond to Des Pres, "Surviving" is obviously intended to answer (and perhaps to silence) the younger scholar.

Bettelheim begins by posing a question to the reader: Which of these two claims does Wertmüller support? – "Survive! No matter how. Survival alone counts!" or "There is no meaning to survival!"[57] The notion that she could be advancing both theses simultaneously – that the film might even take as its subject this contradiction – angers and disgusts Bettelheim: "If the latter is true, the film would make its urging and its warning a mocking of us – the observers who are pulled first one way, then in the opposite direction, as the ludicrous turns into horror, and the dreadful becomes farce."[58] He is intensely aware that Wertmüller's art has political ramifications, screened in a world where "we all live under the specter of Auschwitz and Hiroshima, atomic bombs and genocide, the concentration camp in its German and its Russian varieties."[59] Bettelheim is deeply disturbed that the current generation's fascination with the Vietnam war seems to coincide with their indifference to the traumatic events of their parent's generation, and his example of this indifference is Wertmüller's reduction of "the unspeakable horror of yesteryear"[60] into a farce.

Bettelheim perceives himself to be a guardian of the truth, and advances his essay as a corrective measure to the dangerous misinterpretations of the Holocaust offered by wrong-headed outsiders: "Why spoil the enjoyment of those for whom the gas chambers are a hoary tale, vaguely remembered, best forgotten? Out of such considerations, I would have kept silent but for my conviction that this film and, more important, most of the public reaction to it interpret survivorship falsely, in terms both of the past and of the present."[61] To Bettelheim, *Seven Beauties* stands as a justification of the acceptance of Fascism, both in past and present moments. To support his argument he psychoanalyzes Wertmüller, asserting that she consciously wishes to affirm "the goodness of man," while she is subconsciously fascinated by Fascism and machismo.[62] The result of this unconscious undermining of her own intended project is a film in which "only evil triumphs."[63] Once he has constructed this argument, he then applies it to the manner in which the "American cultural élite" read both Wertmüller's film, Albert Speer's memoirs, and "sympathetic biographies of Hitler," insisting that, "Nothing could be more dangerous than if disappointment with the obvious shortcomings of the free world and life in it should lead to an unconscious fascination with the world of totalitarianism – a fascination that could easily change into a conscious acceptance."[64]

Bettelheim believes that in order to be moral, all texts must present the clear message that one must "take a firm stand against evil, even if it meant risking one's life."[65] Films like Wertmüller's, which justify "evil by implanting a smug conviction that nothing could have made a difference and, by implication, that nothing would make any difference today," blur a line that Bettelheim would like kept clear: "evil is evil."[66] In the morality play suggested by Bettelheim, at least one "good" character must triumph, or, at worst, no "evil" character should survive beyond the last, triumphant act of autonomy that results in the death of the "good" character. Unlike *Seven Beauties*, Bettelheim's fictions would allow the audience to "truly embrace goodness as to fully reject evil."[67] Confusion is dangerous, ambiguity leads us to Fascism, absurdity threatens the foundations of our culture. In his estimation, merely viewing *Seven Beauties* degrades us as human beings.

Ten pages into "Surviving," after concluding his rousing indictment of Wertmüller, Bettelheim introduces the subject of Terrence Des Pres and his work. After commenting on the wide publication and the critical acclaim that Des Pres, like Wertmüller, has enjoyed, he comments that both artist and critic arrive at like conclusions: "the main lesson of survivorship is: all that matters, the only thing that is really important, is life in its crudest, merely biological form."[68] By beginning his discussion of Des Pres at the conclusion of his condemnation of Wertmüller, and then equating the two, Bettelheim clearly and immediately defines Des Pres as morally incorrect. Furthermore, both Wertmüller and Des Pres are accused of twisting the truth – "a much greater distortion than an outright lie" – weaving "misleading myths around the truism that one must remain alive."[69] Bettelheim interprets Des Pres' claim that survivors learn the value of life by passing through death as a call to struggle for survival by any and all means, "even those which until now have been unacceptable."[70] He then argues that while Des Pres as theorist articulates the lessons to "'live beyond the compulsions of culture' and 'the body's crude claims,'" Wertmüller as artist "gives these principles visible form and symbolic expression."[71] Together, they function to prepare the way for the triumph of Fascism.

Bettelheim places his own description of survival in the camps – survival through cooperation and moral behavior – against Des Pres' description of an environment where moral behavior often reduced one's chance of survival. Refusing to acknowledge the complexity of the world of the concentration camps, where the choice between "good" and "evil" was often blurry and indistinct, Bettelheim concludes that the "principles that Wertmüller and Des Pres present to us as guidelines for survival were in fact those by which the Nazis, and particularly the SS, lived, or at least tried to live."[72] In Bettelheim's estimation, both theorist and artist are Fascists, as are the audiences who praise their work, and it is his moral obligation to raise his voice in an "autonomous" act of protest, mirroring the heroic autonomy of the survivors he praises:

When a large and significant segment of those who speak for the American intellectual establishment seems ready to accept the most basic principles of Nazi doctrine and to believe the suggestion – presented in carefully camouflaged by convincing forms in *Seven Beauties* and Des Pres' critically celebrated book – that survivorship supports the validity of those principles, then a survivor must speak up to say that this is an outrageous distortion.[73]

Bettelheim points out that, ultimately, survival in the camps had almost nothing to do with the behavior of prisoners, and everything to do with the process of release or liberation. He divides the process of survival into two categories: day-to-day survival within the camp (in which a prisoner may in some small way be able to delay an inevitable execution), and rescue by an outside force. Bettelheim cautions, "Any discussion of survivorship is dangerously misleading if it gives the impression that the main question is what the prisoner can do, for this is insignificant compared to the need to defeat politically or militarily those who maintain the camps – something that the prisoners, of course, cannot do."[74] The impression, given by both the film and Des Pres' essays, is "that prisoners managed to survive on their own,"[75] thus avoiding the need to address larger questions. One of those larger questions, at least in Bettelheim's estimation, is the oppression of Soviet dissenters in the Gulags, to which Bettelheim refers several times throughout the essay. Bettelheim reminds us that we would not be able to hear the survivor testimony of dissident writer Solzhenitsyn if he had not first been freed by his captors, implying that our first duty is to liberate those who are still imprisoned.

The political landscapes painted by Bettelheim and Des Pres stand in stark contrast. Bettelheim depicts a world of clashing superpowers – first the Axis (Fascism) against the Allied Forces (Democracy), and later the Soviet Union (Communism/Fascism) against the U.S. (Democracy) – in which the agents of freedom battle the agents of oppression. He is profoundly disturbed by the fact that Des Pres colors us all morally culpable, as nations and individuals, with no clear distinction between good and evil, right and wrong – the Allied forces liberated the concentration camps and then incinerated Japanese civilians with atomic bombs; later the Soviet Union maintained a concentration camp system, while the United States waged a genocidal war on the people of Vietnam. Just as Bettelheim condemns Wertmüller for her insistence that good does not triumph over evil, that the whole world is a bordello, he condemns Des Pres for his failure to judge the behavior of survivors by an established moral code.

In his attack on Des Pres' assertion of moral ambiguity, Bettelheim uses language that is both emotional and highly charged. Des Pres' arguments are accused of being "scandalous," "incredibly callous," "utterly false," "spurious," and "untrue."[76] This is doubtless a response to the section of *The*

Survivor in which Des Pres attempted to undermine Bettelheim's privileged status as a survivor by publicly stating that Bettelheim had been in Buchenwald and Dachau only for a year, "at a time when prisoners could still hope for release, and before systematic destruction became fixed policy," and asserted that Bettelheim had traded both on the fact that "he was there and speaks with that authority," and on the early appearance of his first analysis of the camps ("Individual and Mass Behavior in Extreme Situations," 1943) to establish his position as *the* authority on the subject.[77] Des Pres challenged Bettelheim by declaring that Bettelheim's version of events "differs sharply from that of other survivors,"[78] and, in effect, called him either a liar or a fool for his "grave misrepresentation of basic facts" in Eugene Kogon's memoir, *The Theory and Practice of Hell*.[79] Des Pres accuses Bettelheim of being so obsessed with autonomy, "his concept of transcendental selfhood," that he is blinded "to collective action and mutual aid" among prisoners.[80] He claims that Bettelheim is rooted in "the old heroic ethic" – made obsolete by the machinery of mass destruction – and that by failing to embrace the necessary ambiguity of simultaneous resistance and acquiescence Bettelheim endorses a plan of action that is doomed to failure, and which will result in the ultimate destruction of all victims (including, presumably, the present generation, in the inferno of nuclear holocaust).

Bettelheim's response is to approach Des Pres from his unguarded flank. He reminds the reader that survivors lived by virtue of the fact that they were released by others, and follows by quoting some of Des Pres' most flowery and overblown prose descriptions of survivors:

> It will be startling news to most survivors that they are "strong enough, mature enough, awake enough . . . to embrace life without reserve," . . . What about the many millions who perished? Were they "awake enough . . . to embrace life without reserve" as they were driven to the gas chambers?[81]

Using his authority as a medical professional, Bettelheim reminds us of the many survivors who were psychically scarred by their experiences in the camps, who have been unable to overcome depression, nightmares, or full-blown psychoses. From this angle, also, he accuses Des Pres of outrageous foolishness for objecting "to the idea of guilt, the pangs of which are a most powerful motivation for moral behavior. . . . Des Pres writes that the average survivor should not and does not feel guilty, since guilt is one of the most significant 'compulsions of culture,' of which Professor Des Pres claims that the survivor has freed himself."[82] At this point in Bettelheim's critique, his deepest conflict with Des Pres emerges.

In *The Survivor*, Des Pres constructs the survivor as *example*: one who has passed through the Hell which for others exists only as metaphor. In the camps (Hell), survivors adopted a communal identity which, even after they were liberated, they never abandoned: "Survivors are not individuals in the bourgeois sense. They are living remnants of the general struggle, and certainly they know it."[83] Since the survivor is merely "remnant" rather than whole, the bulk of his or her identity is with the dead; in fact, the survivor has become a sort of speaker for the dead. As such, the survivor becomes "a disturber of the peace . . . a runner of the blockade men erect against knowledge of 'unspeakable' things."[84] Removed from the realm of "normal" humanity, Des Pres' survivor is a kind of mythic construct, a creature whose "special task" is to awaken our conscience. Guilt, which is a human emotion, thus has nothing to do with the survivors Des Pres constructs: "Survivors do not bear witness to guilt, neither theirs nor ours, but to objective conditions of evil."[85] Since psychoanalysis takes as its project the reintegration of the subject into society (a process that often requires "adjustment, acceptance, forgetting"[86]) its goals are antithetical to those of Des Pres, who wishes to preserve the survivor as outsider, frozen forever in the role of Hell's witness, a kind of Cassandra doomed to forever prophesy the past.

Bettelheim is dedicated to humanizing the survivor, to placing his or her psychological responses to trauma in the context of normal human response. He is also intent on clearly delineating good and evil, relying upon and reaffirming a traditional moral code for which the Holocaust stands as the most violent and terrifying breach. Both Des Pres and Bettelheim agree that the survivor who bears witness serves as an embarrassment to those whose lives have been untouched by atrocity. But for Des Pres, conscience is a "social achievement," resulting from the "collective effort to come to terms with evil, to distill a moral knowledge equal to the problems at hand. Only after the ethical content of an experience has been made available to all members of the community does conscience become the individual 'voice' we usually take it for."[87] In Des Pres' model, the survivor is destroyed as an individual, but can serve as a voice that redeems the collective through testimony, changing the moral order. For Bettelheim, conscience is always individual and "autonomous," and the survivor bears witness to the truth and value of a moral order in which life is not meaningless. He concludes "Surviving" by claiming that concentration camps taught survivors ("us") that:

> . . . miserable though the world in which we live may be, the difference between it and the world of the concentration camps is as great as that between night and day, hell and salvation, death and life. It taught us there is meaning to life, difficult though that meaning may be to fathom – a much deeper meaning than we had thought possible before we became survivors. And our feeling of guilt for having been so lucky as to survive the hell of the concentration camp is a most significant part of this meaning – testimony to a humanity that not even the abomination of the concentration camp can destroy.[88]

This final assertion rests solidly on Bettelheim's authority as a survivor, rather than as a well-established and respected psychoanalyst. By choosing to end in this manner, Bettelheim poses himself as an insider (one who knows) defending truth, and locates Des Pres and Wertmüller as outsiders (who can only surmise). Furthermore, he reminds us that he and other survivors will soon be dead, and that soon there will be no one left to correct the misapprehensions of the uninformed public. Bettelheim privileges one way of knowing (to have been "there") above all others, though as a scientist he simultaneously occupies the position and assumes the authority of objective observer. Neither scientist nor survivor, Des Pres is granted no position in the debate as Bettelheim construes it.

This dismissal doubtless infuriated Des Pres, who must have felt that his status as academic and literary critic gave him a right to discuss what are certainly literary texts. Bettelheim's assumption that his own credentials as survivor and psychoanalyst made him an expert on film and literary theory might have further irritated the younger scholar.[89] Des Pres' response was to publish what can only be called a nasty personal attack on Bruno Bettelheim entitled "The Bettelheim Problem." It might have been more accurately labeled, "My Bettelheim Problem," or even "Our Bettelheim Problem," since it addresses the question of authority over a subject (the Holocaust) in a particular social and cultural context, rather than some observed phenomenon in physics or mathematics. In this response to Bettelheim's 1979 book, *Surviving and Other Essays*, Des Pres takes on Bettelheim's claims of authority directly:

> The general view has long been that Bettelheim speaks from a privileged position, and he himself has fostered this attitude. He has always stressed his own "camp experience" as the basis for his authority in such matters. And by calling himself "a survivor of the camps" he suggests a kind of archetypal identity which might include any camp, Auschwitz, Treblinka, Belsen, from which survivors of the Holocaust emerged.[90]

The careful placement of quotations around the phrases "camp experience" and "survivor of the camps" calls into question the legitimacy of Bettelheim's claim of authenticity.

Authenticity is the subject of the essay. Des Pres argues that Bettelheim's credentials as a survivor are, at the very least, inflated and, at worst, outright forgeries. He rails at the critics who acclaim his opponent, the ones who, like the *New York Review of Books*, give Bettelheim "laudatory reviews," and accord him "absolute authority."[91] And he quickly establishes that Bettelheim has been criticized ("discredited") by other survivors, who themselves dispute the legitimacy of Bettelheim's self-declared survivor status. In his introduction, Des Pres pits the survivors, who "take exception to Bettelheim's assessment of their experience," against the "literary and scholarly community still largely [accepting] Bettelheim's position as the final word on men and women caught in extreme situations."[92] Thus, Des Pres aligns himself with the "real" survivors, against the bulk of his colleagues and peers who have accepted the word of the "false" survivor. The essay is staged as a conflict between "Bettelheim and other survivors" (one against the many) and between "eyewitness testimony and academic theorizing."[93]

Des Pres' Bettelheim is a monomaniacal control freak with a god complex: he has created his Orthogonic School for autistic children as a "uniquely self-contained world" – an inverse form of the concentration camps in which he was incarcerated by the Nazis – where he is able to engage in the "suspect practices" of "summoning . . . moral and emotional endorsement for his ideas by presenting them within the framework of his identity as a man who endured 'the camps' and as a sort of miracle worker with 'hopeless' children."[94] As he plays out his fantasies on helpless youths, Des Pres asserts, he "uses his special status in order to discredit people whose position questions or intrudes upon his own,"[95] and to claim that his critics are closet Nazis. Des Pres' indignation at Bettelheim's tactics is palpable, since he believes that Bettelheim is guilty of exactly the crimes of which he accuses Des Pres and Lina Wertmüller: "By arguing that prisoners identified with the SS, *Bettelheim* openly declares that survivorship supports the validity of Nazi principles."[96] The parameters of the argument are described in the following parody of an R. D. Laing "knot":

> Bettelheim: I am a survivor, so I know. Furthermore, I am a psycho-analyst, so I know that I know.
> Des Pres: I believe that only survivors know, but I do not agree with you. I know of survivors who do not agree with you. I think you are wrong.
> Bettelheim: You are not a survivor. Only those who are survivors know. Only survivors who are psychoanalysts know that they know. I am a survivor and a psychoanalyst, therefore I know, and I know that I know.
> Des Pres: You are not a real survivor. I agree with real survivors, and I do not agree with you.
> Bettelheim: I am so a real survivor, and you are a Nazi, whether you know it or not. If you were not a Nazi, you would agree with me.
> Des Pres: I am not a Nazi, you are. Real survivors think you are a Nazi, too.

Three pages into "The Bettelheim Problem," Des Pres resorts to the same kind of name calling Bettelheim employed in "Surviving": Bettelheim indulges in "characteristic" misuse of facts, "distortion" that is "pointed and cruel," and sustains a "blame-the-victim syndrome" that Des Pres compares to Hitler's own.[97]

Des Pres' most substantive complaint is that Bettelheim has misread him and others – perhaps deliberately – in order to bolster his own argument that autonomous acts of *resistance* were the only morally correct response to Nazi terror tactics. Des Pres claims that Bettelheim minimizes the efforts of those who struggled in the camp and ghetto underground, and that he fails to recognize the manner in which mutual assistance operated as resistance in the camp environment. While Bettelheim places emphasis on the inability of prisoners to free themselves, Des Pres underlines the manner in which prisoners "had organized themselves to *try*."[98] In Des Pres' estimation, Bettelheim's refusal to focus on "the struggle to survive" even in hopeless circumstances reduces him to making senseless and dangerous comparisons between "walking to the gas chamber" and "committing suicide."[99] Des Pres writes:

> There is something here entirely characteristic of Bettelheim: whenever he speaks of damage and destruction, he describes it in ways which make it appear as if the victims did it to themselves. . . . Being driven into the gas chambers was 'suicide.' Or of the dead: 'they had given up their will to live and permitted their death tendencies to engulf them.'[100]

Des Pres poses in ironic contrast to Bettelheim's demand for autonomous acts of resistance the psychoanalyst's own path to freedom: ". . . through money and political influence at the highest level, including a special invitation to come to America at a time when ships like the *St. Louis* were being turned away, he got out of the camps."[101] Such privilege places him, Des Pres argues, outside of the category of the common survivor and his "identification" with the experience of those survivors is "misleading" and "sad." If Bettelheim presumes to the role of literary critic, Des Pres is not averse at trying his hand at psychoanalysis.

Bettelheim has constructed a theory in which survival is "an act of individual self-assertion," Des Pres suggests, only because Bettelheim's own emotional needs are met by such a description. In Des Pres' opinion, Bettelheim's world view depends upon the assumption that he is superior to his peers, an uncommon prisoner and an uncommon man. Rather than describing the response of the common prisoner, Bettelheim reveals himself when he suggests that Jews interned in the camps identified with their Nazi oppressors. Why else, asks Des Pres, would Bettelheim focus so strongly on his "autonomous" act of defiance, which, after all, "entailed a crucial occasion on which Bettelheim managed to act in a way 'acceptable to an SS soldier,' a kind of behavior which 'did not correspond to what he expected of Jewish prisoners.'"[102] Why else would such contempt for the judgment of others run through his entire corpus of work, from studies of behavior in concentration camps, to behavior in the nuclear family? Des Pres carefully undermines our belief in Bettelheim's balance and even his sanity by excerpting passages from his works in which he compares, "without qualification, the predicament of the psychotic child with the situation of concentration camp inmates."[103] Some of these parallels are indeed outrageous, and Des Pres makes the most of them, commenting pointedly that

> Equating parents with "the death camps of Nazi Germany" is an extreme example of Bettelheim's habit of crossing worlds, an instance which shows forth the obsessive character of his vision and opens others of his well-known pronouncements to question.[104]

At the very least, it undermines Bettelheim's argument that Des Pres and Wertmüller are comparable to Nazis, since, as Des Pres is quick to note, the psychoanalyst cries "Nazi!" with all the consistency of the boy who cried "wolf!"[105]

After undermining Bettelheim's credibility, Des Pres attacks him for presuming to engage in literary or film criticism in such a naive and uninformed fashion. Bettelheim's tendency to "cling to the Romantic notion that the protagonist, simply by virtue of occupying center stage, carries the endorsement of the artist and audience"[106] is obvious both in his writings on *Seven Beauties*, and in the analysis of fairy tales that Bettelheim is famous for. Des Pres is also markedly upset by Bettelheim's tendency to use excerpts from the film to prove points about *The Survivor*, from which, as Des Pres notes, he never bothered to "quote a complete sentence or produce a concrete example of the Nazi doctrine he says the book embodies."[107] In the middle of the essay, Des Pres' frustration with the tendency of critics to bow in the face of Bettelheim's (to him) inexplicable authority is given full rein: he castigates a critic who has given Bettelheim's work a positive review in the *New York Times*, and, in the short section titled "Kalman/Kogon," Des Pres once again describes Bettelheim's misreading of Eugene Kogon's memoirs, and further ridicules the psychoanalyst for his lack of awareness (or suppression) of specific historical facts that not only undermine, but completely invalidate his argument.

Having painted Bettelheim as an arrogant, but ultimately pathetic clown, Des Pres can afford to be charitable in his conclusion, commenting that "Bettelheim's moral indignation seems so fervent and sound, his blunders . . . so vulnerable . . . his self-appointment and sense of vindication . . . so vigorous and unreflective that we cannot but wonder if in some fundamental way he does not see the unhappy and misleading statements that abound in his work."[108] Des Pres began his conclusion by claiming that he had "initially accepted Bettelheim's view," but it is clear by his final words that he (and by implication, the reader) has outgrown it. The psychoanalyst who claimed that in the concentration camps prisoners were subject to infantile regression, is himself painted as infantile in Des Pres critique, his authority reduced to the status of a tantrum, and his authenticity to a sad fantasy or an outright lie.

Though it appears on the surface that Des Pres' goal in "The Bettelheim Problem" is to usurp his "father's" power, any cursory reading of his larger body of criticism demonstrates that this is not the case. Des Pres, an outsider who concedes that only survivors can "know" the Holocaust, is merely substituting one authority figure for another. The "knower" who takes Bettelheim's place is the writer Elie Wiesel. In another essay, anthologized in the same collection as "The Bettelheim Problem," Des Pres asserts Wiesel's right to demand silence of everyone else (including other survivors) while Wiesel struggles to articulate the Holocaust on his own terms.[109] There is a profound contradiction between Des Pres' support of Wiesel's ability to speak for all survivors (and the dead) and his disqualification of Bettelheim, for certainly the trials of the fifteen year old boy in Auschwitz are no more representative of the whole than the tribulations of the adult psychoanalyst in Buchenwald. And while Des Pres condemns Bettelheim for the fact that all of his theoretical writings seem to represent an attempt to work through his concentration camp experience, he lauds Wiesel for the same tendency: "[W]hat makes Wiesel and his work outstanding has to do first with his unique position as a writer *and* a witness, and then with the fact that everything in his work relates directly or indirectly to that overwhelming event we call the Holocaust."[110]

Des Pres is engaged in an ongoing attempt to mythologize the survivor, and his praise of Wiesel is akin to the adoration displayed by mortals to their gods. Perhaps that explains why his denunciation of Bettelheim is so bitter – the psychoanalyst is more than a poor scholar; he is a fallen idol. This is not my construction – it is Des Pres' own, and it is most explicitly delineated in the introduction to *The Survivor*, where he notes that the Holocaust is a subject that one handles "not well, not finally. . . . Not to betray it is as much as I can hope for."[111] He uses "a kind of archaic, quasi-religious vocabulary," because he believes that "only a language of ultimate concern can be adequate to facts such as these."[112] Because he insists on observing the testimony of survivors through a filter of religious romanticism he is unable to construct a methodological framework that can hold a body of survivor testimony that is often contradictory, fallacious, and incomplete. It is not pure. It is not unified. It is not consistent. When faced with this dilemma, Des Pres' only recourse is to deny the "survivorhood" of the author of the problematic text.

Even though Des Pres admits that prisoners responded in different ways to the camp environment – some became *Muselmänner*, some committed suicide, some resisted dramatically, some collaborated, some endured – Des Pres cannot account for any diversity in survivor responses after the trauma has ended. His survivors are frozen in time, always already in the midst of the traumatic universe. Nor do they ever leave it; in Des Pres' analysis, the trauma is never "over" for survivors. Thus he does not acknowledge that there is a difference between experience within the traumatic universe, and the ways in which different people live out their lives after the traumatic event is past.

Even if Des Pres is correct in his assumption that on some level the trauma *is* always present in the life of the survivor, the form in which it is "not over" is still influenced by the interaction of a variety of personal, social and political forces that combine to create responses as diverse as, for example, those of Elie Wiesel, Bruno Bettelheim, Tadeusz Borowski, Jean Améry, and Primo Levi. Succumbing to his urge to designate survivor testimony as sacred, he neglects to note that testimony – by its nature – takes place after the fact. The act of writing means that one has survived, however briefly, to write. The possession of, and the ability to make use of, a pen and paper indicate at least a measure of the "civilized circumstance" that Des Pres claims extremity has stripped away.

Once he has accorded survivor testimony sacred status, Des Pres makes the mistake of assuming that simply because each survivor *claims* to speak for a collective whole, each survivor must have the same vision. He does not take into account the possibility that, since he or she was traumatized as a member of a group, the survivor might have a need to identify with that group and to portray his or her experience as representative of the group experience, whether it was or not. Des Pres disagrees with Bettelheim's interpretation of the "camp experience," and with his claim to speak for all survivors, yet he does not embrace the notion that there was a multiplicity of experience; instead, he claims that Bettelheim was "wrong" (and a "false" survivor), and that Wiesel is "right" (and a "true" survivor). This belief in the survivors' collective past, a "past identical for everyone who came through the common catastrophe,"[113] is one of the premises of Des Pres' argument, and serves as the rationalization for his idealization of the survivor as "a moral type."[114]

The reduction of the survivor from human being to "type" supports the central thesis of *The Survivor*, which is that survivors who "bear witness" to atrocity provide the catalyst for the "progress" of social conscience:

> Horrible events take place, that is the (objective) beginning. The survivor feels compelled to bear witness, that is the (subjective) middle. His testimony enters public consciousness, thereby modifying the moral order to which it appeals, and that is the (objective) end. Conscience, in other words, is a social achievement. At least on its historical level, it is the collective effort to come to terms with evil, to distill a moral knowledge equal to the problems at hand. Only after the ethical content of an experience has been made available to all members of the community does conscience become the individual "voice" we usually take it for.[115]

Des Pres describes the survivor as a specialized organ in the body politic. He or she is the instrument of transmission, the bearer of information ("truth")

that catalyzes a shift in the "moral order." In Des Pres' work, there is no sense
that this is a function of limited duration. This is not a stage through which
the survivor passes, but a permanent state. Des Pres' survivor is motivated to
bear witness on what can only be described as a biological level, an "involuntary reaction to extreme situations," and thus akin to "a scream." He writes:

> [P]erhaps it *is* a scream – a special version of the social animal's call to
> its group – and thus a signal of warning and appeal which on the human
> level becomes the process of establishing a record and thereby trans-
> mitting information vital for both moral and practical reasons. We learn
> what to fear, what to call evil and therefore what to call good, by
> absorbing the costly experience of others.[116]

There is a terrible confusion in Des Pres' analysis. On the one hand, he is
discussing a moral order of "good" and "evil" that transcends the physical
body and is lodged in some spiritual realm. The survivor, viewed from this
perspective, is an "example" that impels the receiver of testimony to participate in a life of "moral resistance" to evil. On the other hand, his description
of the "special nature" of survivors has a quasibiological foundation: in extremity man is stripped of the trappings of "civilization," and is thus somehow
purified of the "delicate, efflorescing extensions of selfhood which civilization
creates and fosters."[117] The prisoner's horror and revulsion at the conditions
under which he or she is forced to live is simultaneously an animal reaction
and the response of a civilized person to the violation of a cultural taboo. The
"scream" of survivors is both an involuntary physiological response and a call
to moral order. Our reaction to the survivor is automatic – the instinctive
response of a social animal to a warning of danger – at the same time that it
is an ethical judgment based on the "certainty" of eyewitness testimony. This
ambiguity is never resolved, in part because it is never fully acknowledged. In
the Preface of *The Survivor*, Des Pres informs us that survivor testimony
reveals "a world of actual living conditions, of *ways of life* which are the basis
and achievement of life in extremity." His conflation of "actual living conditions" and "*ways of life*," and of the "basis" and the "achievement" of "life in
extremity" prevent him first from recognizing, and then from solving this
problem.

   Bettelheim is caught in a similar trap. As a scientist, he desires to describe
the process of psychological adjustment to life in extremity, and then the
reintegration into "normal" society. However, he also desires a survivor who
can stand as a moral example. Unlike Des Pres, who takes a specific example
of atrocity and generates a universal theory, Bettelheim constructs a rather
neutral theoretical model, and then spends a great deal of time emphasizing
the uniqueness of the Holocaust. This places him in the rather difficult
position of both generating a model of reaction to extremity – which Bettelheim asserts has multiple uses, and which he employs in, for example, his

work with autistic children – and insisting on the historical specificity of the Holocaust. Thus he winds up defending the uniqueness of the Holocaust against all comers, from those who would judge it "an event deserving of most severe criticism but commonplace nonetheless."[118] Unsurprisingly, when faced with the arguments of those who believe other massacres, genocidal campaigns and physical assaults are comparable to the Holocaust, Bettelheim resorts to name calling: "These comparisons consciously or unconsciously take the side of the Nazis against that of the Jews, and this subtle siding with the Nazis is one of the most pernicious aspects of the attitude of all too many American intellectuals toward the extermination of American Jews."[119] Once again, Bettelheim combines his authority as a survivor and a psychoanalyst, claiming privileged knowledge of the Holocaust as well as an ability to judge both the conscious and subconscious motives of those who disagree with him.

Bettelheim and Des Pres represented two poles around which the first generation of Holocaust scholars and critics clustered. The decision to align oneself with either Bettelheim or Des Pres often seemed to have more to do with politics than with disciplinary affiliation: liberals tended to quote Des Pres, while conservatives tended to quote Bettelheim. Proponents of either school of thought uncritically embraced the contradictions their chosen man embodied, resting their arguments on the authority of the testimonial voice, and on the alleged ability of the critic to discern "meaning" in survivor narratives. It was not until the late 1980s that critical literature on the Holocaust – influenced by trends in contemporary theory – began to question not only the authority of that voice, but the notion that such a "voice" even existed. These new critics are the heirs of Bettelheim and Des Pres, and they cannot seem to escape the pitfalls of internal contradiction, of a criticism that wants, at once, to preserve the sanctity of survivor texts and to fit those texts into some coherent critical framework. The path of these arguments can be traced by looking at the progression exemplified by the following three works: James E. Young's *Writing and Rewriting the Holocaust: Narrative and the Consequences of Interpretation* (1988); Lawrence Langer's *Holocaust Testimonies: The Ruins of Memory* (1991); and Shoshana Felman and Dori Laub's *Testimony: Crises of Witnessing in Literature, Psychoanalysis, and History* (1992).[120]

Young begins his book as, explicitly, a second generation project: "This study began when I realized that none of us coming to the Holocaust afterwards can know these events outside the ways they are passed down to us."[121] Thus he shifts his focus from the traditional subject of those who study Holocaust literature – representations of the "horror of mass murder" – to a new question: "the narrative representation of events themselves" or "how historical memory, understanding, and meaning are constructed in Holocaust narrative."[122] Young underlines the interdisciplinary nature of his work, which he calls "literary historiography." He is careful not to link his project

to "contemporary theory and its often all-consuming vocabulary," but rather
to the critical impulse exemplified by Azariah de' Rossi, a Jewish historiog-
rapher of the 16th century. Despite his attempt to distance himself from those
(unnamed) recent critics who divert "attention from historical realities," he is
obviously and admittedly influenced by such scholars as Barthes, Jameson,
Eagleton, Foucault, Derrida and Hayden White.

Writing and Rewriting the Holocaust undertakes a dangerous project, and
Young moves to build immediate defenses against the charges he assumes will
be forthcoming. By employing contemporary critical techniques, he argues,
he will be able "to explore both the plurality of meanings in the Holocaust
these texts generate *and* the actions that issue from these meanings outside of
the texts."[123] Though he knows his tools can be used for "mere" deconstruction, he assures his readers that he is engaged in a project of "re-historicizing"
the Holocaust, rather than "de-historicizing" it. In order to begin his task of
re-historicizing, he delicately suggests that it is perhaps time for critics to give
up their roles as "guardians" of Holocaust texts, and to cease protecting and
privileging "texts like the Holy Scriptures and survivors' testimony from
'heretical' readings that undermine these texts' authority."[124] At the same time
that Young suggests that such "protection" is no longer appropriate critical
practice, he hastens to assure the reader that his own inquiries into the nature
of Holocaust literature are "pursued with care and tact" and "sensitivity."

Young attempts to bridge the gap between "testimony" and "interpretation," while at the same time remaining adamant that the testimony of the
survivor is still "privileged," though no longer "sacred." His strategy is to
separate the "authenticity" of the survivor narrative from its "authority as
'fact.'" He is exploring, in short, the attempt of survivors to fix the traumatic
events of the Holocaust in their texts: "Their impossible task is then to show
somehow that their words are material fragments of experiences, that the
current existence of their narrative is causal proof that its objects also existed
in historical time."[125]

> For Holocaust survivors who may have lived solely to bear witness and
> who believed they could bring the realia of their experiences forward in
> time through their words, the perception that their experiences now
> seem to dematerialize beneath the point of a pen becomes nearly un-
> bearable. . . . The more insistently a survivor–scribe attempts to estab-
> lish the "lost link" between his text and his experiences in the text, the
> more he inadvertently emphasizes his role as maker of the text, which
> ironically – and more perversely still – further undermines the sense of
> unmediated fact the writer had attempted to establish. Both the writer's
> perceived absence from the text and his efforts to relink himself to it
> thus seem to thwart – and thereby inflame still further – the testimonial
> impulse.[126]

What Holocaust testimony offers us, Young asserts, is "knowledge – not evidence – of events," the "conceptual presuppositions through which the narrator has apprehended experience."[127] Young sidesteps the Bettelheim/Des Pres contest of "my survivor is more authentic than your survivor" by claiming that "it is not a matter of whether one set of facts is more veracious than another, or whether the facts have been transformed in narrative at all." Rather, he argues, we must determine "*how* writers' experiences have been shaped both in and out of narrative."[128]

And this is the approach Young takes when he generates his defense of D. M. Thomas' controversial book, *The White Hotel.* Young details the controversy that appeared in the pages of the *Times Literary Supplement* in March of 1982, where critics charged that Thomas had lifted material from the text of Anatole Kuznetsov's *Babi Yar* in order to infuse his fictional work with "documentary authority." Young points out that the Kuznetsov work was also a novel, based "upon the verbatim transcription of yet another testimonial source ... the remembrances of the Babi Yar survivor, Dina Pronicheva. . . ."[129] Young also notes that the "interspersing of authentic witness with less authentic finds its place as a narrative technique in all kinds of Holocaust documentary literature, especially in the memoirs," and warns us that from "invoking the 'spiritual authority of authentic testimony' ... it is only a short step to fabricating it altogether within a text, whether it is called 'fictional' or 'nonfictional.' "[130] What Young is in fact attacking is the whole notion of documentary literature, with "its relentless insistence on denying its provisionality, not revealing it" – a denial that is "accomplished ingenuously by the unconscious internalizations of the ethos of one's tradition, or conscientiously by the writer on an ideological mission. . . ."[131] This is a profound and radical departure from the claims of authority voiced by Bettelheim and the acceptance of survivor authority promoted by Des Pres.

Young wishes to legitimate discussion of the Holocaust as metaphor, force the recognition that representations of events are always already mediated: ". . . even the Holocaust can never lie outside of literature, or understanding, or telling."[132] Furthermore, he insists that we engage the question of what the Holocaust itself has come to represent, acknowledging the irony of the fact that "once an event is perceived to be without precedent, without adequate analogy, it would in itself become a kind of precedent for all that follows: a new figure against which subsequent experiences are measured and grasped."[133] Young's point is that memory moves in two directions, shaping our interpretations of the past and the present: "Experiences, stories, and texts of the ancient past remain the same in themselves; but their meanings, their echoes, causes and effects, and their significance all changed with the addition of new experiences in the lives of these texts' interpreters."[134] This is indeed a slippery slope, and one that Bettelheim and Des Pres refused to set foot upon.

In a chapter devoted to exploring Holocaust imagery in the work of American poet Sylvia Plath – neither a Jew nor a survivor of the Holocaust – Young opposes the critics who attack Plath for her use of concentration camp and Holocaust metaphors, arguing for the legitimacy of using the Holocaust as "a figure, a universal point of reference for all kinds of evil, oppression and suffering," just as we accept the legitimacy of comparing "our lot with that of the Jews escaping Egypt, or the destruction of cities in wartime with that of Jerusalem in 587 BCE."[135] Language, argues Young, absorbs experiences, embodies them, and thus preserves them long after the "authentic witnesses" are gone.[136] Thus he moves from a focus on the survivor to a claim that language itself is a repository of memory – a radical departure. For if the survivor is the repository of memory, then memory is always an internal event, which can be represented only incompletely (only being is believing); but if language becomes the repository of memory, then the representations exist before and outside the individual, who then interprets his or her own experience with the representational tools at hand. In the latter case, no experience is "pure" or "true" since it is mediated by a kind of cultural library of symbols that limit and guide interpretation. Young concludes:

> [S]o long as we are dependent on the "vocabulary" of our culture and its sustaining archetypes, it may not be possible to generate entirely new responses to catastrophe. It may now be possible, however, to respond from within our traditional critical paradigms with self-critical awareness of where traditionally conditioned responses lead us in the world. . . . Critical reading can lead not only to further understanding of sacred and modern literary texts, but also to new understanding of the ways our lives and these texts are inextricably bound together.[137]

Where Young focuses on the manner in which the critic/reader is trapped by the representational structure that has been bestowed upon him by his culture, Lawrence Langer's *Holocaust Testimonies: The Ruins of Memory* attempts to define the complicated position of the testifying survivor:

> Testimony is a form of remembering. The faculty of memory functions in the present to recall a personal history vexed by traumas that thwart smooth-flowing chronicles. Simultaneously, however, straining against what we might call disruptive memory is an effort to reconstruct a semblance of continuity in a life that began as, and now resumes what we would consider, a normal existence. "Contemporality" becomes the controlling principle of these testimonies, as witnesses struggle with the impossible task of making their recollections of the camp experience coalesce with the rest of their lives. If one theme links their narratives more than any other, it is the unintended, unexpected, but invariably unavoidable failure of such efforts.[138]

Langer focuses on the repeated attempts of survivors to externalize their memories of the Holocaust in the tapes of the Fortunoff Video Archive for Holocaust Testimonies established at Yale University in 1982. He is suspicious of language, and believes that the "vocabulary" that Young describes confines those who have not experienced the Holocaust to inadequate and misleading representations since they are necessarily bound by traditional forms:

> [H]olocaust commentary gives birth to its own involuntary tensions: the habit of verbal reassurance, through a kind of internal balancing act, tries to make more manageable for an uninitiated audience (and the equally uninitiated author?) impossible circumstances. . . . Tributes are cheering; memorials are sad. Language often seems to be the fulcrum tilting us, as in this instance, away from one and toward the other.[139]

But neither are the survivors able to escape this trap, for the very telling of the tale implies a narrative structure that is counter to the traumatic experience it attempts to represent. To account for this paradox, Langer uses the categories he calls "common memory" (*mémoire ordinaire*) and "deep memory," (*mémoire profonde*) – drawn from Auschwitz survivor Charlotte Delbo's memoirs – claiming that survivors move back and forth between common and deep memory and employ (most often unconsciously) a sort of dual vision – "doubling" – to contain the contradictions of their past and present experience. Langer's interest, then, is in what he calls the "incoherence" of video testimony, which escapes the "*appearance* of form" (beginning, middle, end) given by a written narrative. Video narrative demands an "active *hearer*" – we must

> . . . suspend our sense of the normal and to accept the complex immediacy of a voice reaching us simultaneously from the secure present and the devastating past. That complexity, by forcing us to redefine our role as audience *throughout* the encounter, distinguishes these testimonies from regular oral discourse as well as from written texts.[140]

The "confrontation" between videotaped survivor narrative and active hearer "begins in separate narrative and ends in collective memory. . . ."[141] But the memory is inevitably incomplete, for the missing voices are always the voices of the dead, who can only be spoken *for*. In Langer's words, "Oral testimony is a living commentary on the limits of autobiographical narrative, when the theme is such unprecedented atrocity."[142] To explain the rupture, the failure of memory and language, Langer defines the Holocaust as "at once a lived event and a 'died' event: the paradox of how one survives a died event is one of the most urgent (if unobtrusive) topics of [Holocaust survivor] testimonies. . . ."[143] But Langer himself can't escape the paradox – the impossibility of representing the "died event" becomes apparent as he attempts to describe the survivor's doubled self using a critical terminology invented for this very purpose. The terminology – jargon, really – is as fractured and incoherent as the stories it proposes to define and contain: deep memory, common memory, anguished memory, humiliated memory, tainted memory, unheroic memory. Langer's active hearer is charged with the task of discriminating between these categories and unraveling the threads of memory within the survivor testimony – distinctions which the survivors are, in his estimation, incapable of making. Survivors, in Langer's descriptions, are confused, bewildered, unconscious, frustrated, silenced, or anguished. They speak the truth, but do not know what it is they are saying. Thus, it is left to the critical audience to interpret the survivor's narrative, to gloss the text; in fact, Langer's theory requires a critical audience for the whole story to be told, for only the informed audience is capable of hearing the silence, of explicating the revealing incoherence: "Testimonies resting unseen in archives are like books locked in vaults: they might as well not exist. We use books to expand consciousness; we must use these videotapes for the same purposes."[144] Langer charges the reader with the responsibility of "interpretive remembering":

> An underlying discontinuity assaults the integrity of the self and threatens the very continuity of the oral narrative. Perceiving the imbalance is more than just a passive critical reaction to a text. As we listen to the shifting idioms of the multiple voices emerging from the same person, we are present at the birth of a self made permanently provisional as a result of fragmentary excavations that never coalesce into a single, recognizable monument to the past.[145]

Langer's survivor is a multiple personality who can never know herself, who can only *be known* from the outside, by others, and who – having lived past the moment of her death – is not even a subject in her own self-constitution, but a vehicle for the subjectification of the those who did not survive the Holocaust: "The 'people who have perished' emerge as the real subject of the testimonies, while the circumstances of their death define the unheroic memory that tries to reclaim them, as it does the surviving self diminished by their absence and by its own powerlessness to alter their doom."[146] He continues: "This memory, and the loss it records, has meaning only insofar as it engages the consciousness of us as audience. Otherwise, it remains mere archival anecdote."[147]

Langer's conclusion will sound familiar to almost every critical theorist in feminist or in African-American studies:

> One of the unavoidable conclusions of unreconciled understanding is that we can inhabit more than one moral space at the same time – witnesses in these testimonies certainly do – and feel oriented and

disoriented simultaneously. Another is that "damaged personhood" is one of the inevitable prices we pay for having lived in the time of the Holocaust, *provided* we acknowledge our active role as audience to the content of these testimonies. Indeed, it would be more than ingenuous to contend that the sources of such personhood in the twentieth century must be confined to this particular atrocity alone. History inflicts wounds on individual moral identity that are untraceable to personal choice or qualitative frameworks – though the scars they leave are real enough, reminding us that theoretical hopes for an integral life must face the constant challenge to that unity by self-shattering events like the Holocaust experience.[148]

Langer proposes that there is an intersection between individual psychic trauma and history, that this intersection (and this injury) is not confined to the Holocaust and Holocaust survivors, and that the appropriate response to such an intersection is active involvement on the part of a *hearing* audience. The fact that there *is* no "healing" from the Holocaust, that the wounds (individual and communal) are permanent and unredeemable, serves as a reminder for all who are willing to pay attention that "the organizing impulse of moral theory and art" masks a painful complexity that is difficult or impossible to contain. It is exactly this complexity that feminist and African-American literary critics have been attempting to articulate, as early as W. E. B. DuBois defined the "veil" which divides African-American consciousness:

> . . . this double consciousness, this sense of always looking at one's self through the eyes of others, of measuring one's soul by the tape of a world that looks on in amused contempt and pity. . . . Two souls, two thoughts, two unreconciled strivings; two warring ideals in one dark body, whose dogged strength alone keeps it from being torn asunder.[149]

As feminist critic Barbara Johnson reminds us, "Unification and simplification are fantasies of domination, not understanding"[150] – an assertion with which Langer would doubtless concur. That Langer has arrived at these conclusions by himself, without apparent familiarity with either African-American or feminist critical works is testament both to the isolation in which white male critics tend to work and to the commonalities between the various literatures of trauma. Langer's focus on the survivor's voice places him in opposition to both Young and Felman/Laub.

Unlike Langer, Young insists that video testimony mediates a survivor's memories in a highly structured fashion ("unified and organized twice-over . . . once in the speaker's narrative and again in the narrative movement created in the medium itself"[151]), and thus that video texts allow viewers to "become witness not to the survivors' experiences but to the making of testimony and its unique understanding of events."[152] Young's audience is passive, analytic and judgmental – the text is contained safely within the filmic framework and, though it refers to and draws upon cultural representations, it does not transcend the medium; it does not demand interaction. Young favors trained professionals – whether they are literary critics or, as he describes in his chapter on video testimony, trained psychiatrists conducting interviews with survivors:

> Of all possible kinds of interviewers, trained psychoanalysts and thera-pists may well be the best qualified to elicit testimony. Trained to encourage narrative telling and interpretation, and through them in-sight into traumatic events, with a minimum of new psychic damage or further trauma, the psychiatrists who interview at Yale attempt as low a profile as possible.[153]

The combination of literary criticism and psychoanalysis has been irresistible to theorists dealing with the Holocaust, perhaps in part because it seems to allow them to transcend the contradictions embodied by Des Pres and Bettelheim and to resolve the tensions between literary critical strategies, between mythologization and medicalization, and between personal testimony and "objective" analysis.

Testimony: Crises of Witnessing in Literature, Psychoanalysis, and History is the result of a collaboration between Shoshana Felman and Dori Laub. Felman is a literary critic and Laub is a psychoanalyst who treats trauma survivors. There are seven chapters in the book – two by Laub, and the balance by Felman: the jointly written preface claims that their work has evolved "out of the encounter and the dialogue between these two professional perspectives, and between the mutually enhancing lessons of these different practices," and that these pieces "are . . . the product of this intellectual and conceptual interaction and of this continuous dialogue of insights, that has served both as the motivating and as the enabling force in the process of writing."[154] The key passage in this preface follows:

> As our ventures will bear witness to and as the concrete examples we narrate will show, the encounter with the real leads to the experience of an existential crisis in all those involved: students as well as teachers, narrators as well as listeners, testifiers as well as interviewers."[155]

The language chosen by Felman and Laub *is* the language of the survivor. They are not simply writing a critical study, they are "bearing witness" – the "encounter with the real" leads to an "existential crisis" for all involved. Whereas Bettelheim and Des Pres focused on the authenticity of the survivor voice, Young concerned himself with the process of representation, and Langer placed his emphasis on interpretation, Felman and Laub are entirely concerned with reenactment of the traumatic event in the psyches of those who "encounter the real." In this critical text, the survivor's experience has

been completely replaced by the experience of those who come in contact
with the survivor's testimony – an appropriative gambit of stunning proportions. We are treated to a new traumatic phenomenon: "the crisis of witnessing."

Felman's opening chapter, "Education and Crisis, Or the Vicissitudes of
Teaching," poses a series of initial questions:

> Is there a relation between crisis and the very enterprise of education?
> To put the question even more audaciously and sharply: Is there a
> relation between trauma and pedagogy? In a post-traumatic century, a
> century that has survived unthinkable historical catastrophes, is there
> anything that we have learned or that we should learn about education,
> that we did not know before? Can trauma *instruct* pedagogy, or can
> pedagogy shed light on the mystery of trauma? Can the task of teaching
> be instructed by the clinical experience, and can the clinical experience
> be instructed, on the other hand, by the task of teaching?[156]

There are a number of interesting assumptions embodied in this paragraph.
There is an equation of "crisis" to "trauma." There is an assertion that this is
"a post-traumatic century." There is the claim that certain historical catas-
trophes are "unthinkable." We expect, since this *is* a book about literary
criticism, psychoanalysis, and trauma, that the answer to these questions is a
qualified "yes" – which leads us to wonder exactly what is meant here by
"trauma," "pedagogy," and "clinical experience." All of these definitions go
without saying, all except the word "testimony," which is introduced in the
second paragraph and which is described first as the act "of bearing witness
to a crisis or a trauma,"[157] and, a short time later,

> as a discursive *practice,* as opposed to a pure *theory.* To testify – to *vow,*
> to *tell,* to *promise* and *produce* one's own speech as material evidence for
> truth – is to accomplish a *speech act,* rather than to simply formulate a
> statement. As a performative speech act, testimony in effect addresses
> what in history is *action* that exceeds any substantialized significance,
> and what in happenings is *impact* that dynamically explodes any con-
> ceptual reifications and any constitutive delimitations.[158]

But the act of bearing witness is not, in Felman's construction, the sole act of
the survivor; rather, it is placed in Freudian psychoanalytic terms, in the
framework of the *"psychoanalytic dialogue,* an unprecedented kind of dialogue
in which the doctor's testimony does not substitute itself for the patient's
testimony, but *resonates with it,* because, as Freud discovers, *it takes two to witness
the unconscious."*[159] In fact, Felman's analysis partakes of the worst sort of
psychoanalytic pomposity, evident when she describes the testimonial videotapes in the Yale collection as

autobiographical life accounts given by Holocaust survivors to volunteer, professionally trained interviewers, most of whom are psychoanalysts or psychotherapists. Within the context of these dialogic interviews, many of these Holocaust survivors in fact narrate their story *in its entirety* for the first time in their lives, awoken to their memories and to their past both by the public purpose of the enterprise (the collection and the preservation of first-hand, live testimonial evidence about the Holocaust), and more concretely, by the presence and involvement of the interviewers, who enable them for the first time to believe that it is possible, indeed, against all odds and against their past experience, to tell the story and *be heard*, to, in fact *address* the significance of their biography – to *address*, that is, the suffering, the truth, and the necessity of this impossible narration – to a hearing "you," and to a listening community.[160]

As French lesbian feminist critic Monique Wittig comments, the psychoanalyst sets him or herself up as the interpreter of the unconscious – only they "are allowed (authorized?) to organize and interpret psychic manifestations which will show the symbol in its full meaning."[161] Setting aside the problem of determining whether or not the subject of an interview has ever told his or her story before "in its entirety," and the impossibility of knowing when any survivor's story – even one recorded on videotape – is complete, we are still faced with a set of rather astonishing assertions about the role of the interviewer, whose mere presence somehow serves as an enabling force, bestowing on the survivor a sense of trust and self-confidence heretofore unattainable.

The appropriative nature of Felman's project becomes most evident in her discussion of the progress of the class on testimonial literature that she taught at Yale. As students were exposed to Holocaust testimonies, they felt increasingly – in Felman's words – "set apart," "obsessed," "at a loss, disoriented, and uprooted." In Felman's eyes, the dimensions of the "crisis" suffered by the class was "critical." After consulting Laub, she determined "that what was called for was for me to reassume authority as the teacher of the class, and bring the students back into significance."[162] She began by giving an address to her students in which she compared the dysfunction in the classroom to the rupture of language suffered by Holocaust survivors:

I will suggest that the significance of the event of your viewing the first Holocaust videotape was, not unlike Celan's own Holocaust experience, something akin to *a loss of language*; and even though you came out of it with a deep need to talk about it and to talk it out, you also felt that language was somehow incommensurate with it. What you felt as a *"disconnection"* with the class was, precisely, an experience of *suspension*;

a *suspension*, that is, *of the knowledge* that had been acquired in the class:
you feel that you have lost it. But you are going to find it again. . . .[163]

She believes that her course was a success, and she finds her proof in the fact
that her students turned in final papers that she describes as "an amazingly
articulate, reflective and profound statement of the trauma they had gone
through and of the significance of their assuming the position of the witness."[164] From here, she goes on to claim that the practice of teaching itself

> takes place precisely only through a crisis; if teaching does not hit upon
> some sort of crisis, if it does not encounter either the vulnerability or
> the explosiveness of a (explicit or implicit) critical and unpredictable
> dimension, it has perhaps *not truly taught*; it has perhaps passed on some
> facts, passed on some information and some documents, with which
> the students or the audience – the recipients – can for instance do what
> people during the occurrence of the holocaust precisely did with in-
> formation that kept coming forth but that no one could *recognize*, and
> that no one could therefore truly, *learn, read* or *put to use*.[165]

Not surprisingly, Felman sees parallels between teaching and psychoanalysis,
just as she sees parallels between testifying and psychoanalysis. In fact, the
three are often indistinguishable to her, as the following passage describing
her interpretation of events in the classroom clearly illustrates:

> When the story of the class – the story I am telling now – was for the
> first time, thus, narrated to the class itself in its final session, its very
> telling was a "crisis intervention." I lived the crisis with them, testified
> to it and made them testify to it. My own testimony to the class, which
> echoed their reactions, returning to them the expressions of their shock,
> their trauma and their disarray, bore witness nonetheless to the impor-
> tant fact that their experience, incoherent though it seemed, *made sense*,
> and that it *mattered*.[166]

Felman's hubris is mirrored by Laub's own – manifest from the first page of
his initial solo chapter, "Bearing Witness or the Vicissitudes of Listening." To
Laub, the one who listens to a testimony is "the blank screen on which the
event comes to be inscribed for the first time," and thus the listener "by
definition" must partake "of the struggle of the victim with the memories and
residues of his or her traumatic past," and "to feel the victim's victories,
defeats and silences, know them from within, so that they can assume the
form of testimony."[167] It is the listener, and not the survivor, who is the
"enabler" of the testimonial act; in fact, it is the "task" of the witness to be "the
one who triggers its initiation, as well as the guardian of its process and of its
momentum."[168] He makes no distinction between the primary trauma suffered by the Holocaust survivor and the sort of secondary stress suffered by

the testimonial audience, claiming that the listener "can no longer ignore the question of facing death; of the limits of one's omnipotence; of losing the ones that are close to us; the great question of our ultimate aloneness; our otherness from any other; our responsibility to and for our destiny; the question of loving and its limits; of parents and children, and so on."[169] The survivor herself has disappeared from the picture, reappearing only as a device for pushing the listener to self-examination, to allow him to participate in "the reliving and reexperiencing of the event."[170] Wittig views psychoanalysis as a reinscription of the victimization of the survivor:

> In the analytical experience there is an oppressed person, the psychoanalyzed, whose need for communication is exploited and who . . . has no other choice, (if s/he does not want to destroy the implicit contract which allows her/him to communicate and which s/he needs), than to attempt to say what s/he is supposed to say. They say that this can last for a lifetime – cruel contract, which constrains a human being to display her/his misery to an oppressor who is directly responsible for it, who exploits her/him economically, politically, ideologically and whose interpretation reduces this misery to a few figures of speech.[171]

Laub's description of the drive to testify is at odds with Langer's. For Langer, all testimony is inevitably failed testimony – the rupture in the narrative fabric cannot be "healed" by telling and retelling. Laub is a psychoanalyst, however, and it is his business to heal people – permanent wounds such as Langer describes are inconceivable; all trauma can be resolved in the process of the talking cure, however severe, however delayed. And in his view, *all* survivors are impelled to speech: "None find peace in silence, even when it is their choice to remain silent."[172] Laub is, in fact, unsure whether narrative precedes or follows survival: "The survivor did not only need to survive so that they could tell their story; they also needed to tell their story in order to survive."[173] Both Langer and Laub posit an active audience, but Langer's active hearer is responsible for formulating an interpretation based upon the recorded testimony of the survivor – the interaction is between *hearer* and *text* – while Laub's active listener is an interventionist, facilitating (even demanding) that the survivor herself revise her experience in collaboration with the listener/analyst who Laub seems to feel is at least an equal partner in the construction of the narrative. Laub's notion that no Holocaust text can be created without the participation of the interventionist listener is linked to his notion that the Nazis created a universe so completely destructive that one *"could not bear witness to oneself."*[174] Borrowing from Bettelheim, Laub asserts that the Nazi system "convinced its victims, the potential witnesses from the inside, that what was affirmed about their 'otherness' and their inhumanity was correct and that their experiences were no longer communicable even to themselves, and therefore perhaps never took place."[175] It is impossible to ignore how convenient this construction is for a psychoanalyst, who makes a living interpreting the thoughts and feelings of other human beings – in fact, what he has done is abridge the authority of the survivor to speak for herself, and appropriate that authority.

The coupling of Laub's personally appropriative interpretive strategy and Felman's tendency to appropriate the "experience" of the Holocaust leads to some remarkable conclusions, not least the complete exoneration of literary critic Paul de Man for his collaborationist political activities as a journalist in Belgium during World War II. Felman does not dispute the charge that de Man was a collaborator, but seeks to elaborate on his silence, which she argues comprises his testimony. Since it has become the business of these critics and analysts to interpret not only texts but silences, it is hardly surprising that it is the nature of de Man's *failure to speak* that Felman addresses:

> It is judged unethical, of course, to engage in acts that lent support to Germany's wartime position; but it is also judged unethical to forget; and unethical, furthermore, to keep silent in relation to the war and to the Holocaust. The silence is interpreted as a deliberate concealment, a suppression of accountability that can only mean a denial of responsibility on de Man's part.
>
> I will here argue that de Man's silence has an altogether different personal and historical significance, and thus has much more profound and far-reaching implications than this simplistic psychological interpretation can either suspect or account for.[176]

"No doubt . . . " Felman admits, " . . . the twenty-year-old Paul de Man made a grave mistake in judgment. . . ."[177] She argues that his decades-old silence on the matter does not compound his mistake, but rather (reaching for an analogy with Captain Ahab – de Man translated *Moby Dick* during the war – and a reference to Baudelaire) represents a sort of suicide –

> suicide as the recognition that what has been done is absolutely irrevocable, which requires one in turn to do something irreversible. . . . What appears to be an erasure of the past is in fact this quasi-suicidal, mute acknowledgment of a radical loss – or death – of truth, and therefore the acknowledgment of a radical loss – or death – of self; the realization that there can be no way back from what has happened, no possible recuperation.[178]

Since de Man was, as Felman admits, "a controversial yet widely admired and highly influential thinker and literary critic," and the Sterling Professor of Humanities at Yale, and the information about his collaborationist activities stayed hidden until after his death in 1983, it seems a bit of a stretch to claim that de Man had committed any sort of suicide whatsoever. Felman claims that de Man's later writing, which does *not* tell his story of the Holocaust, is *by virtue of that fact*, bearing "implicit witness to the Holocaust, not as its (impossible and failed) narrator (a narrator–journalist whom the war had dispossessed of his own voice) but as a witness to the very blindness of his own, and others' witness, a firsthand witness to the Holocaust's historical disintegration of the witness."[179] There is a wildly Orwellian quality to her argument – "he bore witness by virtue of the fact that he failed to bear witness" – that seems to escape the confines of logic and sense. If speaking is speaking, and silence is speaking, then what possible way is there *not* to testify? When is silence silence, and when is silence speech? And who is to determine the meaning of things except for Felman, the self-styled interpreter? On what ground does one stand to contest her interpretations?

For Felman, every "good" representation of the Holocaust is described as a vehicle for evoking the Holocaust "experience," from her own class, to de Man's silence, to Lanzmann's epic documentary on the Holocaust, *Shoah* (which she compares to the testimony of survivor Jan Karski): "I would now suggest that Lanzmann's own trip is evocative of that of Karski: that Lanzmann, in his turn, takes us on a *journey* whose aim precisely is *to cross the boundary*, first from the outside world to the inside of the Holocaust, and then back from the inside of the Holocaust to the outside world."[180] Felman, as is her habit, makes no distinction between real and metaphorical crossings. And that, in the end, is the danger of her work, and of its coupling with Laub's psychoanalytic musings. As we shall see, the appropriation of survivor experience and its reduction to metaphor is a crucial component of the process of depoliticizing the survivor and then medicalizing her condition. The movement from "sacred" survivor texts (Des Pres and Bettelheim), to "contextualized" survivor texts (Young and Langer), to appropriated survivor texts (Felman and Laub) is predictable and consistent across traumas, as I shall demonstrate in the case of the Vietnam War and the campaign of violence waged by some American men against the women and children of this country.

3

Between the Lines

Reading the Vietnam War

On March 1, 1991, President George Bush stood before the American Legislative Exchange Council and announced, in the wake of the Gulf War, "And, by God, we've kicked the Vietnam syndrome once and for all."[1] The next day he told U.S. soldiers, in a radio address to the U.S. Armed Forces stationed in the Persian Gulf region:

> Americans today are confident of our country, confident of our future and most of all, confident about you. We promised you'd be given the means to fight. We promised not to look over your shoulder. We promised this would not be another Vietnam. And we kept that promise. The specter of Vietnam has been buried forever in the desert sands of the Arabian Peninsula.[2]

Two days later, Bush addressed the Veterans Service Organizations with the following remarks:

> I made a comment right here at this podium the other day about shedding the divisions that incurred from the Vietnam War. And I want to repeat and say especially to the Vietnam veterans that are here – and I just had the pleasure of meeting some in the hall – it's long overdue. It is long overdue that we kicked the Vietnam syndrome, because many veterans from that conflict came back and did not receive the proper acclaim that they deserve – that this nation was divided and we weren't as grateful as we should be. So somehow, when these troops come home, I hope that message goes out to those that served this country in the Vietnam War that we appreciate their service as well.[3]

The Vietnam War, for which the country-name "Vietnam" has come to stand as a metonym, had, since the early 1980s been described as an "experience" – something one lived through. It was also described, in a competing metaphor, as a "syndrome" – something one was afflicted with. James William Gibson points out that it is conservatives who are most likely to employ the medicalized metaphor, focusing on the need to "get over" the Vietnam Syndrome as if "the war was just a normal part of growing up for a young nation, a childhood disease like chicken pox, which leaves behind some small scars but builds character."[4] In Bush's construction, the whole country has been struck ill with this disease, and the Gulf War is the prescribed (and successful) cure. National division causes psychic damage, and national unity heals it.

Liberals are more likely to adopt the "experience" label, which is consonant with their belief that our adventures in Vietnam were well-intended, but mistaken. As Gibson notes, the liberal construction of the war as "mistake and misjudgment," as proof that the U.S. was "capable of error," has been advanced by major media sources including *The Christian Science Monitor* and *The New York Times* since the mid-1970s.[5] Coupled with this admission of error is, of course, a rationalization: "Vietnam" was a "quagmire," a "swamp," a "morass," a "slippery slope," a "nightmare" that "entrapped" us, rendered our good intentions and rational powers useless, "lured" us into its depths. "Tragedy," notes Gibson, "is also a favorite, as if thirty years of American intervention in Vietnam were a Greek play in which the hero is struck down by the gods. In the face of the incomprehensible, absolution: fate decreed defeat."[6]

The struggle to fix the floating signifier of "Vietnam" is necessarily a contemporary political struggle – one in which the Vietnam War itself "became progressively displaced and repressed at the same time it was written about."[7] Both "experience" and "syndrome" metaphors are ahistorical: experiences are entirely subjective and emotional, and syndromes partake of the "objective" terminology of a "science" based in "natural law," and thus lie outside of history. They work in opposition to the documentary drive of the survivor, who wishes to preserve the historicity and specific details of the traumatic event. As we examine the movement away from history and toward myth, we may wonder, along with African American cultural critic Lisa Kennedy, if in fact history has "been murdered in order to prevent us, the collective body, from resuscitating it, exhuming it, performing an autopsy, doing whatever it takes to get it to bear witness to the atrocities and triumphs to which it's been privy."[8]

The competing drives to resuscitate history and to generate myth are exemplified by the struggle over the Vietnam Memorial Wall – the result of a massive effort by veterans to memorialize themselves. Arguments between conservative and liberal Vietnam veterans and their respective political supporters over the appropriateness of the severe black design (created by a young Chinese-American woman named Maya Lin) and the placement of a representational statue (sculpted by Frederick Hart) and an American flag at the site clearly delineated the lines of national debate. The ambiguity of the Vietnam Memorial Wall upset conservatives. All those names engraved on a flat, black surface would most likely fail to evoke the patriotic and heroic images upon which our national mythology is built. As Jan Scruggs noted, "Aesthetically, the design does not need a statue, but politically it does."[9] The metaphorical competition between liberals and conservatives are neatly summed up by Hart's and Lin's criticisms of each other's work:

> Hart: "I don't like blank canvases. Lin's memorial is intentionally not meaningful. It doesn't relate to ordinary people, and I don't like art that is contemptuous of life."
> Lin: "Three Men standing there before the world – it's trite. It's a generalization, a simplification. Hart gives you an image – he's illustrating a book."[10]

The Wall acted as a focal point for renewed public discussion and deliberation on the meaning of the Vietnam War. The dedication of the memorial in 1982 brought national attention to veterans' claims that they had been forgotten by their countrymen. In this period, as James William Gibson notes, "the Vietnam War became a major cultural topic. It was as if a legendary monster or unholy beast had finally been captured and was not on a nationwide tour."[11] "Welcome home" parades and the dedication of monuments honoring Vietnam veterans became common events across the country.[12] Seminars were offered at major universities. PBS affiliates released the 13-part series, *Vietnam: A Television History*. Two court cases – a class-action suit brought by veterans against the manufacturers of Agent Orange, and the controversial *Westmoreland vs. CBS* case – regularly appeared in the news.

This attention spurred an interest in the writings of veterans, and a number of publishers began to issue and reissue Vietnam War narratives: Avon had begun reissuing Vietnam War novels in 1978 and maintained its series through 1982; Ballantine published a new line of "Vietnam/Nonfiction"; Bantam focused on Vietnam in its War/Nonfiction series; and the Vintage Contemporaries (Random House) began reissuing Vietnam War novels. *The New York Times*, on August 4, 1987, claimed that the Vietnam War "has catapulted to the forefront of American culture."[13] In the same article, Philip Caputo called the phenomenon "Vietnam chic."

The first wave of popular postwar books and articles about the Vietnam War appeared after the publications of two major works of Vietnam War literature: Michael Herr's New Journalism piece, *Dispatches* (1977) and Tim O'Brien's novel, *Going after Cacciato* (1978). *Dispatches* was reviewed in such disparate forums as *The New York Review of Books*, *The Nation*, *Commentary*, and *Rolling Stone*. O'Brien's *Cacciato* was the winner of the National Book Award and also received a great deal of attention from reviewers and critics. Between 1978 and 1982, a steady trickle of reviews and critical essays found its way onto the pages of book review sections everywhere and even occasionally into scholarly journals such as *Criticism*. This trickle turned into a steady stream after 1982.

Seven important book-length studies on the literature of the Vietnam War have been written to date, all of them since 1982. Philip D. Beidler's *American Literature and the Experience of Vietnam* (1982) was published the same year that James C. Wilson's *Vietnam in Prose and Film* appeared. John Hellman's study *American Myth and the Legacy of Vietnam* followed Beidler and Wilson in 1986. Thomas Myers' *Walking Point: American Narratives of Vietnam* was issued in 1988. Susan Jefford's landmark study, *The Remasculinization of America: Gender and the Vietnam War* was published in 1989. Philip Melling's *Vietnam in American Literature* appeared in 1990, and Beidler's follow-up volume, *Re-Writing America: Vietnam Authors in Their Generation* was published in 1991. Like literary critical works on the Holocaust, these texts reflect both political and critical trends in the larger culture.

Beidler proposes a strong connection between classic American literature and the literature of the Vietnam War. Cooper, Melville, and Twain created heroes who "prefigured" the heroes in Vietnam War novels. Beidler asserts: "American writing about Vietnam, for all one's sense of the new and even unprecedented character of the experience it describes, often turns out to be very much in context . . . with regard to our national traditions of literature and popular myth-making at large. . . . [I]t seems almost as if our classic inheritance of native expression has prophesied much of what we now know of Vietnam, made it by self-engendering symbolic fiat part of our collective mythology long before it existed in fact."[14] Our classic literature embodies cultural myths, which then have an effect upon our understandings of current events, influencing the course of history.

Myth and actual events seem to be equally involved in generating "history" – for Beidler, a strangely retroactive process in which we revise our interpretations of the past as new cultural myths are generated, and thereby affect our future decisions and actions. This trend is reflected in Vietnam War literature, he says, in the emergence of "a certain identifiable centrality of vision." This centrality is rooted in the "understanding that just as the 'real' war itself so often proved a hopeless tangle of experiential fact and projected common myth, so a 'true' literary comprehending of it would come only as a function of experiential remembrance and imaginative invention considered in some relationship to near-absolute reflexiveness."[15] By weighing equally "real"[16] experience and mythic construction, Beidler collapses time and space, and gives Cooper's Deerslayer the same authority as Philip Caputo, veteran and writer of Vietnam War narratives. Beidler conflates the fictional characters of classic American writers, and the memoirs of real Vietnam veterans. Beidler's end goal seems to be the reduction of the war to "sign" – for him, Vietnam War literature is part of a continuing process of signification: the telling and retelling of the war inscribes it upon the nation's consciousness until "we have learned at what cost it was waged for everyone it touched then and now and beyond."[17] When the signification is complete the war will be

over: "Then we can say good-bye to it."[18] There is an urge to closure in
Beidler's analysis. When the war becomes sign (and therefore not-war) we
won't have to think about it anymore. It will, in Barthés' terms, "go without
saying."

James Wilson's perspective on the literature is at heart political rather than
literary: "One thing needs to be clear from the beginning. I am not concerned with a purely formalist analysis here; rather I am interested in this
body of literature and film for what it tells us about ourselves and our
culture. For these works reflect the difficulties we have in comprehending
the war; our evasions, our distortions, our denials. And yet, at the same time,
they reflect our limited successes too. The best of the Vietnam books and
films provide an invaluable record of the initial steps we have taken toward
facing the unpleasant truth of an unpleasant war."[19] He thinks it unimportant to connect Vietnam War literature to mainstream American literature, and prefers to point out the special features of the literature. "Almost
all Vietnam writers and directors," Wilson states, "share an apocalyptic vision" of the war's end. "The world born in Vietnam becomes a monstrosity
of senseless violence and random destruction. . . . Out of this collective vision comes a literature and a cinema of despair laced with death. . . . The
end, then, is physical annihilation, purely and simply."[20] An important feature of the literature is that "the Vietnam writers and directors imply the
destruction of human values and human morality."[21] To Wilson, this por-
trayal of annihilation and the destruction of values and morality are a metaphor for current American "cultural crises," taking "to an extreme the un-
reality, the discontinuity, and the loss of values that may characterize much
of our experience in America today. . . . "[22] The answer to the current cultural crisis is to listen to the words of the Vietnam veterans, rather than to
the politicians. We must confront the reality of the war in Southeast Asia,
and take responsibility for the crimes which our nation committed in the
Vietnam War, rather than succumbing to the rationalizations provided by
politicians, who describe the war as a "noble cause."

Beidler denies the existence of the "real" war, while Wilson is looking for
"reality." To Wilson, Vietnam War literature is a useful tool, a warning for
Americans: "If we try, we can save the next generation from being crucified
a decade from now in distant lands whose names we barely recognize now.
We can prevent another misbegotten war."[23] Wilson demands a political
awareness from both his writers and his readers; we read Vietnam War
literature in order to learn what not to do next time.

Hellman's study is closer in spirit to Beidler's analysis than Wilson's. He
is also concerned with the question of the continuity of classical American
cultural myths. Hellman claims that Vietnam War literature reflects a national
disillusionment with the frontier myth upon which we based our involvement in Vietnam, and that veterans "have presented a Southeast Asian land-

scape that overturns the meaning of the previously known landscapes of American myth."[24]

> The American mythic landscape is a place fixed between savagery and civilization, a middle landscape where the hero sheds the unnecessary refinements of the latter without entering into the darkness of the former. Ever-receding, this frontier gains its validation as a setting for the mythic hero because his killing makes way for the progress of the civilization advancing behind him. In the memoirs of the Vietnam War, however, the American hero has somehow entered a nightmarish wilderness where he is allowed no linear direction nor clear spreading of civilization, where neither his inner restraints nor the external ones of his civilization are operating.[25]

This disruption may, Hellman suggests, enable us to stretch our cultural perceptions enough to include the "reality" of the Vietnam "experience."

He charges artists with the mission of taking the American people "on their second journey through the Viet Nam war. In the best of their works, that meant finally moving back toward the realm of fantasy – of symbolic imagining – to discover the continuing dimensions of the war as a terrain of the American psyche. Having entered the Vietnam War as a symbolic landscape, Americans would through highly imaginative narrative art have to find their way back out to American myth, enabling them to journey again forward into history."[26] The contradictions contained within this argument are stunning: in order to understand the "reality" of the Vietnam War we must first properly fantasize it – reduce it to a "symbolic landscape." The function of the real event is the recreation of a symbolic event (myth) which, through some mystical turnabout, helps us to understand reality. Only then, says Hellman, will we be able "to journey again forward into history." As an example of these new American myths, Hellman gives us Lucas' *Star Wars* films. These represent "the first significant step in moving beyond the purgation of our old myths to the synthesizing of an energizing new myth of America, a dream in which Americans may secretly – even to themselves – re-experience the horror of the Vietnam self-discovery and emerge from it not only regenerated but transfigured."[27] His hope is that the assimilation of such myths into popular consciousness will make an opening for "a visionary politician or historian to restructure American history" according to the new pattern. "Then Americans will once again see themselves in a narrative that they can both believe and act upon."[28]

Star Wars is, in mythical terms, a standard offering; a space opera. Evil creatures are running the Empire, and bold space rebels (of various races, creeds, sexes, and colors) seek to oust them from power. Good guys are almost always of noble blood. God (in the transparent guise of The Force) is on the rebel side. Serious questions of social, cultural, and political import are foregone, and the credo of continuous action is embraced.[29] Does Hellman think that we should rewrite American history in such simplistic terms?

The answer lies in Hellman's assertion that "No nation can survive without a myth," and that the best myths lie somewhere between "a cynical 'realism'" and a "self-deluding fantasy."[30] He envisions a myth for America that embraces our uniqueness, and allows us to see ourselves as more than an "ordinary country":

> The United States certainly has had reason to feel a special obligation to the rest of the world. Its geography long left it remote from entanglement with other nations. It allowed the young nation to expand to frontiers easily defended and yet opening upon trade and commerce. It allowed the modern world's first republic to settle its major issues, develop its institutions, and form its character without interference. In the process, America became a nation identified, at its best, with possibility and freedom and progress. . . . We can see that the deeply flawed past, from which the nation began by declaring its independence, is truly our father. But we can also see that only a second failure, of nerve, would cause us then to draw back from the American frontier, from our own better dreams. . . . Perhaps from the landscape of our Vietnam failure, we can find a new determination to brave the opening expanse.[31]

In Hellman's eyes the best Vietnam War literature, and the best new American literature, will help us to reformulate a myth we can live with. Each element of Hellman's myth is, of course, historically inaccurate (as all vast generalizations are historically inaccurate), but what is important in his myth-making effort is the assertion that as a nation we can continue on the road to progress, the journey "forward into history." The Vietnam War, then, becomes a trial in a *Pilgrim's Progress* approach to American history; an episode in the development of the American character. Predicated on this artificial notion of progress, the search for meaning becomes compromised: the assumption of the "fact" of progress becomes the ground for the disqualification of all Vietnam War (and all American) literatures that do not support his thesis.

Thomas Myers borrows much from the arguments of Beidler and Hellman in his 1988 study, *Walking Point*. Fascinated by the interplay of history and myth in the generation of war literature, he insists that it is in this literary genre that "the leviathan of the national cultural paradigm" can "sound and surface."[32] War literature can serve as both a record of history and a cultural document "as it responds to the rending and reconstituting of national mythos."[33] The war novel illustrates three crises: historical, cultural, aesthetic. Myers believes that historical and aesthetic changes occur simultaneously, and that the response of the author to the uselessness of older American myths is to "light out for new aesthetic territory and begin anew,"[34] basing his new mythical constructions on the ruins of the earlier myths. Vietnam veteran writers resurrect the "secret history" of the war, and serve as conduits for the experience of the soldier. The metamorphosis of the raw recruit into the hardened warrior serves as metaphor for the process that deforms and then reshapes the American self-image.

Unlike previous critics of Vietnam War literature, Myers also admits that he has come face to face with a phenomenon that he does not fully under-stand: "With all its aesthetic restructuring, behind its many necessary trans-formations of the conventions of a specific literary tradition, there is in even the most powerful writing something that language cannot reach or explicate, an experience that words point toward but that only the reader's own creative energies can begin to trace."[35] But this observation is quickly abandoned and he takes up the task of the critic, examining various works, and generating prescriptions for the writing and reading of Vietnam War literature:

> The writers who have produced what are likely to be the most lasting documents of the war are those who have assessed and incorporated into their works the battle of words and images that transformed the war into something as much symbolic as real. To do battle in compen-satory history with the [war] managers' capacity for illusion and eu-phemism, the writer is required to first retrieve and then re-create the feelings, rhythms, and specific images that remained largely sequestered behind conveniently reconciled history and to place those components in opposition to the dominant text: in effect, both to reconstruct and to invent a historical debate. The failure of the managers to supply valida-tion for human sacrifice is the true American defeat in Vietnam, one that placed the responsibility for the retrieval of meaning firmly on the shoulders of each soldier, citizen, journalist, and artist."[36]

Myers, like Wilson, has an explicit political agenda. Like Hellman, he regards the mythmaking process as a crucial political tool (though his political ends seem closer to Wilson's than Hellman's). Myers (and Beidler and Hell-man) believes that the Vietnam War was "as much symbolic as real."[37] Like Beidler, Myers asserts that the war is not over until it is properly signified. The common assumptions of these four authors guarantee that they will come to similar conclusions – ones which are seriously flawed.

Susan Jeffords approaches the study of Vietnam War literature from a different angle. In *The Remasculinization of America: Gender and the Vietnam War*, the first major feminist treatment of Vietnam War literature and film, Jeffords claims that gender is central to American representations of Vietnam:

> [G]ender is not simply another of the many oppositions that mark Vietnam representation. It is the difference on which these narratives and images depend because it is *the* single difference that is asserted as

not participating in the confusion that characterizes other oppositions. While friends may be uncertain, enemies unidentifiable, and goals unclear, the line between the masculine and the feminine is presented in Vietnam representation as firm and unwavering. . . . [Gender] is what Vietnam narrative is "about." Gender is the matrix through which Vietnam is read, interpreted, and reframed in dominant American culture. . . . The unspoken desire of Vietnam representation, and its primary cultural function, is to restage "the Nam" (read: gender) in America.[38]

Hers is a carefully constructed argument that clearly illuminates the hidden agenda of the four male critics of Vietnam War literature. The American myths and traditions that Beidler, Wilson, Hellman, and Myers seek to reconstitute are specifically masculine in character. In Jeffords' terms, Vietnam War literature and other representations of the war, are "an emblem for the presentation of dominant cultural ideology in contemporary American society,"[39] and that dominant cultural ideology is patriarchal.

Jeffords explains that American myths of manhood may be reconstituted only if the war is incompletely and incorrectly remembered. Representations of the Vietnam War must first de-historicize the war, dislocate it from the realm of "the real." Once that reformulation is successfully accomplished, authority to interpret the war rests firmly in the (masculine) author's hands:

The position of the reader/viewer/soldier in Vietnam narrative is constructed by the (con)fusion of the status of fact and fiction. The resulting paralysis of response can then be overlaid by the "new" "facts" of the narrative: "they" become "we," the viewers and participants slide together. There are three stages to this process: denying previous concepts of fact, offering the narrator/author as authority/guide for the new definitions of fact, and having the narrator/author predetermine and occupy the reader's position. All work toward positioning the reader in a kind of paralysis in relation to textual interpretation.[40]

This power has been used, Jeffords argues, to effect a "'remasculinization' – a regeneration of the concepts, constructions, and definitions of masculinity in American culture and a restabilization of the gender system within and for which it is formulated."[41]

Jeffords' gender-based analysis provides a new and important critical perspective – one in which race and class issues also become visible. If, as she argues, the primary goal of Vietnam War representation is to redefine the differences between men and women, a strategy of these representations will be to elide the differences between men. In many Vietnam War narratives there is a strong emphasis on the idea that all men are equal under fire, that the bonds of brotherhood transcend race and class barriers. This deliberate emphasis on the brotherhood of man is also obvious in the critical literature, as Jeffords demonstrates when she takes John Hellman to task:

> Hellman speaks confidently of "our" views and "our" alienation, assuming a cohesive characterization for his speaking subject. But, as he shows, that subject is always and already masculine. It may speak of class, race, and technology, but it cannot speak of gender, cannot raise the question of women. Hellman assumes and accepts this masculine voice for his narrative of social change. The self "we" are to examine is only the self that masculinity projects, the self that is constructed by gender. In such a context, to speak of "our view of ourselves" and assume that this view encompasses all Americans is decidedly deceptive.[42]

The only way the reviewer of war literature could know whether the author's tale was authentic was if the reviewer had, at least vicariously, experienced war. By confirming the "truth" of the tale, the reviewer places himself in the club of men who have survived war. The women who review Vietnam War literature find themselves in an awkward position. They can choose to work within the framework generated by writers and the male reviewing establishment; they are, however, excluded from the club. Nevertheless, they too may speak admiringly of "realistic characters," "gruesome descriptions of combat, moving dialogue, and . . . effective recounting of the tension and the moral dilemmas of facing men in combat."[43]

Jefford's gendered reading of Vietnam War narratives enables her to challenge masculine interpretive strategies. She can clearly describe the manner in which the masculine perspective is universalized, and the way in which representations of the Vietnam War demand the immasculation of the female viewer/reader. Furthermore, the objectification of women becomes painfully obvious, both in narratives (where female characters have no purpose except the advancement of the masculine storyline), and in life (where male bonding can be effected over the body of a woman, as in gang rapes). This kind of feminist revision is extremely important, and our understanding of Vietnam War literature is deepened and enriched by her work.

It is tempting to let Jeffords have the final word on the question of gender and Vietnam War narrative, since she is so clearly correct. We could simply name Vietnam War narrative another pillar of the patriarchy and leave it at that, leaning on it now and again as a good example of the repression inherent in the system. Feminist literary critic Jacqueline Lawson's anthology, *Gender and the War: Men, Women, and Vietnam* (which contains essays by scholars Lorrie Smith, Nancy Anisfield, Renny Christopher, Susan Jeffords, Jean Elshtain, and representatives of the Redstockings Women's Liberation Archives, et al.) certainly takes that as its theme.[44] Such critical studies can provide us with a great deal of insight about male attitudes toward women, and toward feminists in particular, as well as suggesting new directions for future research and action.

Yet in an important way *The Remasculinization of America* exposes the weakness of traditional criticism without transcending its limitations. Jeffords examined the political and cultural implications of the construction of the Vietnam veteran as "victim." In doing so, she made the *representations* of Vietnam veterans the object of her work, transforming gender into the subject, and "disappearing" the human beings who had actually served in Vietnam. The incapacity of traditional criticism to deal with the literature of the Vietnam War is exemplified in its inevitable and total reduction of the war to metaphor. Jeffords, too, makes use of that reductive strategy, analyzing all Vietnam War representation – from Vietnam War narratives by combat veterans to popular television shows such as *Miami Vice* – in the same terms.[45] This method of analysis leads her to a strong understanding of the social and political uses of Vietnam War texts, and to an apt criticism of the currently acceptable practice of identifying the Vietnam veteran as a victim. But it also enables her to suggest that the literature of the war is "merely" representative of the larger issue of gender relations and masculine anxieties. Though Jeffords is more careful than any other critic to make a distinction between the "real" war and the literature which has come to represent it, she has left no room for a discussion of Vietnam War *literatures*, nor has she created a space in which to consider the possibility of a disparity between a writer's intent and an audience's interpretation.

The insights Jeffords offers are not paralleled by similar advances in Melling's and Beidler's later works. Melling is a British scholar who uses Puritan "spiritual autobiographies" as his model for reading Vietnam War literature: "At its simplest the American literary response to Vietnam articulates the nature and purpose of a devout mission and the extent to which individual experience supports the philosophy of the state in making that mission."[46] Melling's descriptions of the Puritan influence are almost religious themselves: "Puritanism is about the way selected people *live* in the world and the structures they create to make their world a safe and habitable place. It is about the way people *see* the world, their sense of Godliness, and the enemies that exist within it. Puritanism is about the way people *talk* about themselves in the world and convey their sense of faith to one another."[47] You could replace "Puritanism" with any "ism" and it would make exactly the same sort of sense: Judaism, Nationalism, Conservatism, even Communism if you removed the reference to Godliness. Melling is *for* Puritanism and *against* "the dead end of absurdity and the postmodern faith of a surrender to fragments."[48]

Melling's is an attractive construction, but it is based on a flawed assumption – that Puritan narratives lay the foundation for all future personal narratives by Americans. Historian Perry Miller, for whom the Puritans are a consuming interest, writes that though students of American culture "would have to commence with Puritanism," it is only one of many American traditions, which also include "the rational liberalism of Jeffersonian democracy, the Hamiltonian conception of conservatism and government, the Southern theory of racial aristocracy, the Transcendentalism of nineteenth-century New England, and what is generally spoken of as frontier individualism."[49] To these influences we must certainly add African American and American Indian oral traditions and Mexican American cultural influences. Melling's construction, however, excludes the voices of nonwhite minorities in his acceptance of the Puritan conception of the godly man in the wilderness, which leads him to conclude that the description of the bush in Vietnam as "Indian Country" is indicative of a benign sort of narrative continuity rather than a tradition of American racism. The sole moment where Melling attacks ethnocentrism (he doesn't use the word racism) is in reference to Michael Herr's Dispatches – a book that he insists, "despite the claims that have been made," is "not the grand postmodernist text."[50] Melling criticizes Herr because "for all the narrator laments the loss of the wilderness at the outset, he shows little interest in the lives of those who must bear that loss."[51] Melling seems to prefer those who demonstrate an outright hatred and fear for the wilderness and its inhabitants.

By asserting that the Vietnam War "provide[s] us with . . . an opportunity to re-examine those styles of life and art which are characteristic of Puritan New England," Melling ignores Perry Miller's warning that "it is dangerous to read history backwards, to interpret something that was by what it ultimately became, particularly when it became several things."[52] For example, Melling asserts:

One of the ironies of Vietnam is that the Puritanism that helped define the war as both subject and structure also provided the soldier with a way of explaining it to others. Puritan instruction and exegetical address came to the Vietnam veteran's assistance. It gave him a voice and provided him with the opportunity to testify to what he had seen and personally witnessed. The Puritanism that had contained the soldier in Vietnam – garrisoned him in with enclaves and enclosures – now provided the means by which he could realize his freedom.[53]

For Melling, "Puritanism" serves as an all-purpose explanation.

In his favor, Melling offers the suggestion that we examine the writings of Vietnam veterans in a larger context, that we connect them to other kinds of personal narrative, and that we refuse to accept without question the argument that Vietnam was "a place of exceptional strangeness."[54] Melling takes issue with James Wilson's assertion that we can never know the truth about the Vietnam War, and he admires Hellman because Hellman believes as much in the redemptive power of the "American tradition" as Melling does himself. He notices that Myers "defines the war in Vietnam as an exclusively

American affair,"[55] and he doesn't like Myers' postmodernist perspective because Myers, like other postmodernist critics, has "become fascinated with Vietnam as a place redolent with the modes of modern experience – innovation, ingenuity . . . at the expense of its moral or social contexts."[56] He takes issue with Beidler's notion that Vietnam "was a place with no real points of reference, then or now," because that allows "present-day questions like the impact of Vietnam on American foreign policy in Central America or the role of the Vietnam veteran in the 'Olliegate' scandal" to "be easily pushed to one side."[57]

Melling's argument with postmodernism is interesting. He dislikes it because the postmodernist critic "encourages the reader to ignore those novels that cannot be integrated into the absurdist or postmodernist canons of experience and to endorse a fictional experience that confirms the Americanness of the world in which we live."[58] Melling prefers "stories" with meaning – stories which he can relate to the confessional narratives of Puritan society. At root, it is the concept of relativism with which he is taking issue. He requires a moral center. And like most skilled Church Fathers, he can interpret any text in the context of his beliefs. Melling longs for a simpler time, fewer gadgets, less commercialism, an appreciation of the simpler things in life: "The search for sensation not only perverts history; it fragments and rearranges the human character."[59] His incorporation of both liberal and conservative viewpoints is not contradictory, for his vision is more utopian than political. He has idealized the Puritan community and he urges us to make that ideal a reality. Melling ends his books with a section on Robert Stone, who he praises for his criticism of the assumption "that the country has both a divine right and a public duty to the moral leadership of the free world" and for Stone's willingness "to expose the commercial considerations on which American adventurism has rested."[60] Stone serves as an illustration by which Melling can criticize the flaws of the Puritan culture (poor treatment of the Indian, the presence of economic self-interest, an emphasis on the accumulation of material goods) and then make the claim that both Puritans and Americans in Vietnam War narratives "live under the threat of physical attack from without and moral collapse from within. The dinginess of My Lai . . . provides an indication of the moral drabness of Puritanism."[61] The book ends with Melling, literally, declaring the "victory of the Antichrist."[62]

Cultures can certainly be studied from the outside as well as from the inside, but Melling seems to lack a coherent picture of American culture(s). He conflates the growth of religious fundamentalism in the Falwell tradition with Watergate and the election of Jimmy Carter and comes to the following conclusion:

> What happened in America after 1976 was that a mood of born-again spirituality was grafted onto a set of values that were secular and hu-

manistic. Born-again religion and the events of Watergate, combined
with mounting anti-institutional fervor, directly contributed to the
legitimacy of personal narrative and literary exploration of public history. Exposing the moral hypocrisy of power allowed the Vietnam
veteran to assume the role of an investigative writer and to speak with
increasing conviction.[63]

Somehow, in this construction, Melling neglects to mention the fall of Saigon
in 1975, the subsequent waning of the antiwar movement, and the fact that
the Vietnam Veterans Against the War had been active and visible since 1971
and by 1976 was already well into its decline. If by "investigative writers"
Melling means the first Vietnam War revisionists, then perhaps he is on to
something, for certainly all the books he mentions in this part of his study
(William Mahedy's *Out of the Night: The Spiritual Journey of Vietnam Vets*; John
Wheeler's *Touched With Fire: The Future of the Vietnam Generation*; John Steer's
Vietnam: Curse or Blessing; David Hartline's *Vietnam: What a Soldier Gives*) are
conservative renderings of the war and stand in opposition to the testimony
given by Vietnam veterans at the Winter Soldier Investigation in 1971. Melling's refusal to explore the implications of Winter Soldier and the first
publications by Vietnam veterans is an indication of either poor research
techniques or deliberate cover-up, since a strong argument could be made
that they match perfectly his description of personal narrative and testimony.
However, if he had included them, he would have undermined the progression of his own redemptive narrative, as well as introduced political controversy into his determinedly "literary" and "cultural" text.

Beidler's *Re-Writing America* is a clear sequel to his earlier work. He still
insists on reading the texts he discusses as merely one more revision of the
"American" story, relating each author and text he examines to a plethora of
others in what ultimately becomes a truly hysterical crescendo. Tim
O'Brien's personal narrative, *If I Die in a Combat Zone . . .* is described as a
"masterwork of the American tradition of the contemplative, an odyssey of
consciousness in the lineage of Shepard, Edwards, Woolman, Thoreau, and
Henry Adams . . . "[64] O'Brien's first novel, *Northern Lights,* invokes Hemingway.[65] His enterprise in the award-winning *Going After Cacciato* is like "Melville's own."[66] Caputo – that mediocre pop-trash novelist – is apparently even
more connected to the American tradition, as Beidler asserts that "the chief
American literary progenitor presiding over much of his writing is Ernest
Hemingway. . . . Other major American presences include Fenimore Cooper
and Stephen Crane. As might be predicted as well, his writings often owe
much to related moderns such as Robert Graves, Siegfried Sassoon, Joseph
Conrad, and Graham Green."[67] Caputo's best-selling personal narrative, *A
Rumor of War,* lies "in the distinguished modern memoir tradition of Robert
Graves, Farley Mowat, and William Manchester."[68] Winston Groom's pop-

ular novel *Forrest Gump* "embraces the distinctive tradition of southern literature" and reminds Beidler of Mark Twain, William Faulkner, Eudora Welty, Flannery O'Connor, Roy Blount, Jr., Dan Jenkins, Lewis Grizzard, Beth Henley, and Barry Hannah . . . all in one paragraph.[69] Poet and memoirist John Balaban is influenced by Eliot, Pound, Roethke, Thomas Nashe, Thomas Kyd, and John Milton.[70] Robert Stone's *A Flag For Sunrise* "appropriates emphatically the whole mythic provenance of the political novel of Dostoevsky, Conrad, Green, Malraus, Mailer, as well as that of the novel of ideas from Tolstoi, Stendhal, Melville, Mann, Faulkner, Joyce; and it accommodates them both in the same moment to the sharp, familiar unfamiliarities of neorealism in the various postmodernist styles of Vonnegut, Styron, Mailer, Pynchon, Heller, Didion, Hunter S. Thompson and Michael Herr," moving from "Dantean horror through Kafkan nightmare," while also bearing the influence of T. S. Eliot, Malcolm Lowry, Ernest Hemingway, Emily Dickinson, Walt Whitman, and Francis Scott Key![71] No doubt, quite an extraordinary book.

Beidler's project seems to be to prove that the pieces of Vietnam War literature he chooses to examine fit into the American literary tradition, and thus to force other critics to take them seriously. He never seems to have problems reading these texts, never criticizes or questions them, never has unanswered questions. Everything he reads fits into his theoretical model: Vietnam War novelists rewrite the Vietnam War by using a vocabulary of myth passed down to them by their literary forbearers. This can be done in a "basically conservative and revisionary" manner (by, for example, James Webb[72]) or in a style of "complex experimentalism" (by, for example, Larry Heinemann[73]).

It is only in his last chapter, "The Literature of Witness," which appears to be more of an addendum than an integral part of the book, that Beidler attempts anything new. In this final section, he compares the work of Gloria Emerson, Frances Fitzgerald, Robert Stone, and Michael Herr, claiming that they partake in the "great literary project of the postmodern . . . *writing itself*," and that somehow this is a project with a "new character."[74] He posits Emerson's and Fitzgerald's books as "exemplary feminist texts . . . which attempt to re-write our vision of that experience from within a specific critique of the essentially male structures of consciousness that shape it."[75] But Beidler revises the term feminist by stating that he means to use it "in a context of general definition that goes beyond any localized politics of sexuality toward issues of language, authority and power in their largest sense: feminist, then, in that as texts by women they elect not to center themselves within various established value and meaning systems of a dominant culture."[76] The appropriative ploy in which Beidler is engaged here is pathetically obvious as he admits that Emerson voices "an early and quick disavowal of interest in particular concerns of the domestic women's liberation movement,"[77] and there is nothing explicitly feminist about Fitzgerald's text at all. Neither does Beidler feel moved to refer to feminist theoretical works which might support his claims; his understanding of "feminism" is autodidactic and idiosyncratic. Since he has barely given gender a passing nod in his discussions of Vietnam veteran authors, it is significant that he has chosen to tack it on as a coda, like late-breaking news or some sort of errata. Furthermore, Beidler declines to link either of these women's texts to the American literary tradition he so appreciates, or to a tradition of feminist literature. Emerson and Fitzgerald are apparently *not* like Vonnegut, Styron, Mailer, Pynchon, Heller, Didion, or Hunter S. Thompson. Instead, Fitzgerald's text is related to Shakespeare's *The Tempest*, and

> the fullest achievement of her *Fire in the Lake* as text is its measuring of the human depths of the tragedy of Vietnam against the backdrop of one of the most utterly inhuman spectacles of language ever mounted, an orgy of American techno-macho-malewrite and malespeak sublimely unaware of its hidden dialectics of cultural arrogance and insistently fostering the hideous politics of its own cruel self-deconstruction.[78]

Given the body of Beidler's work, this is a sentence anomalous enough to defy belief. It seems to have fallen from the moon. His discussions of the work of Stone and Herr, however, fall back into a more predictable pattern, Stone is "the novelistic laureate of the post-Vietnam American soul,"[79] and Herr "stands in this largest double implication of 'witness' as participant and mythic interpreter and does so to the degree that the act of writing so defined becomes in fact as much a 'subject' of the text as any other it can claim."[80] Beidler's confusion in the midst of, and unfamiliarity with the terminology of a truly "postmodern" critical project is painfully apparent in this all but incoherent chapter, where he attempts to describe a "literature of witness" distinguished by "its dominant, even obsessive . . . identification of the true locus of the war and its cultural legacy as at once the landscape of historical experience and of collective national imagining."[81] If we take this chapter seriously, it seems to undermine the entire course of his previous project, which is to prove the existence of an "American" literary tradition into which the literature of the Vietnam War can be comfortably integrated, without the tensions (or "double implications") of the "witness."

All six critics discussed here come from strong literary backgrounds. Literary critics concentrate on symbol and image, on "reading" events rather than on reporting them. Literary critics, like the authors and readers of Vietnam War literature, (con)fuse fact and fiction. They also blur the distinctions between themselves and their readers. The critic/reader relation has three stages: 1) Previous concepts of fact are denied (e.g., other interpretations are wrong because . . .); 2) the critic becomes the authority/guide for the new definitions of fact; and, 3) the critic predetermines and then occupies the reader's position. To return to the Jeffords quote above, "All work toward positioning the reader in a kind of paralysis in relation to textual interpretation."

This assumed authority leads some critics to make rather remarkable claims. Wilson asserts that the war was an "illustration" of the destruction of American values.[82] This is one of the mildest critical offenses against the memory of those individuals who actually suffered and died in Vietnam. More disturbing are statements such as Hellman's, "the enduring trauma of Vietnam has been the disruption of the American story;"[83] Beidler's remark that "the 'real' war so often proved a hopeless tangle of experiential fact and projected common myth;"[84] and Myers' incredible claim: "The most perceptive observers knew that the real battle was being waged not in the new geographical landscape of men and machines, but within the terrain of collective imagination, an area where the surface images of the war became a mere light show that dissolved in the stronger illumination of persistent cultural realities."[85]

The unfortunate truth is that the Vietnam War was the work of no one's imagination. It was, rather, a devastating reality – a series of events taking place on a physical, as well as a symbolic, level. It may be true, as Richard Slotkin argues, that American symbolic perceptions of the world shaped American political and military policy during the Vietnam War, but that policy affected, and that action took place within a physical arena in which real people were killed and real property was destroyed.[86] Only in memory or in narrative can war be elevated to the level of symbol. Narratives are generated in order to explain, rationalize, and define events. The symbols which these narrators create are born out of the traumatic events of wartime. In order to understand the traumatic event in context, and to comprehend the existence of a literature of trauma, we must

> insist upon the simultaneous separateness and inseparability of material and discursive practices, of "actions in the world" and symbolic gestures. By meticulously tracing the ways they weave in and out of one another, powerful yet mutually dependent, we can throw significant light on processes by which they construct one another, the real of the social, indeed, meaning, itself. In doing so, we will gain a far more precise understanding of the ways social and linguistic difference take shape and power is deployed.[87]

It is this new kind of critical practice I wish to demonstrate in the next chapter, an analysis of the work of Vietnam veteran poet and memoirist, W. D. Ehrhart.

The Farmer of Dreams

The Writings of W. D. Ehrhart

The Farmer

Each day I go into the fields,
to see what is growing,
and what remains to be done.
It is always the same thing: nothing
is growing; everything needs to be done.
Plow, harrow, disc, water, pray
till my bones ache and hands rub
blood-raw with honest labor –
all that grows is the slow
intransigent intensity of need.
I have sown my seed on soil
guaranteed by poverty to fail.

But I don't complain, except
to passersby who ask me why
I work such barren earth.
They would not understand me
if I stooped to lift a rock
and hold it like a child, or laughed,
or told them it is their poverty
I labor to relieve. For them,
I complain. A farmer of dreams
knows how to pretend. A farmer of dreams
knows what it means to be patient.
Each day I go into the fields.[1]

W. D. Ehrhart was born in 1948 and grew up in the small town of Perkasie, Pennsylvania, outside of Philadelphia. In 1966, at the age of 17, he enlisted in the Marines, and was sent to Vietnam in February of 1967, where – after a short course in Vietnamese at a language school in Okinawa – he remained until February of 1968, serving as an intelligence assistant and later assistant intelligence chief in the 1st Battalion, 1st Marine Regiment. While in Vietnam he participated in more than a dozen combat operations, and was wounded in Hué City during the 1968 Tet offensive.[2] His poetry was first anthologized in 1972, and he has published a steady stream of poems, books, and essays since that time. Though he is not the most famous of the Vietnam veteran writers, he is certainly one of the most prolific and committed members of that group of authors who have produced more than one book or anthology about the American war in Vietnam. Ehrhart's role as writer, critic and editor and his status as one of the founders of the field of Vietnam War literature is recognized both by scholars and by his fellow authors

Ehrhart is thus a perfect subject for an attempt to test the theory of the existence of a literature of trauma against an existing body of work. We should be able to locate in his work the "basic wound" described by Chaim Shatan, and the "new, permanent, and adaptive lifestyle" that Ehrhart generates in response to trauma. We should be able to find evidence of a retelling process that rebuilds Ehrhart's shattered personal myths; of Ehrhart's response to liminality and alienation; of his identity with a community of survivors. The permanent transformative nature of the traumatic experience should be obvious: Ehrhart's journey from the normal world to the abnormal world of the war should lead him to perceive "a normalcy so permeated by the bizarre encounter with atrocity that it can never be purified again."[3] Furthermore the tension between the drive to testify, the impossibility of successfully conveying the experience, and the urge to repress the experience entirely should be a constant presence in his work. We should find examples of his efforts to contextualize his trauma, to connect it across history to other atrocities, committed at other times. Finally, we should find evidence of Ehrhart's struggle to prevent his own traumatic experience from being appropriated and incorporated into an American national myth that does not reflect his experience.

Because the theory of a literature of trauma is based on the reintegration *process* – a series of discrete events that occur over a period of time – we can reasonably assume that a chronological approach would provide us the clearest picture of his development. Shifts in theme, voice and subject can then be plotted along a time line, and the pattern of response to trauma would become apparent. This is no simple project, however, since there are several separate chronologies that must be maintained – there is an important difference between the intent of poetry written by a young man in 1971, and an older man's 1986 retrospection about poetry he wrote in 1971. Retellings appear at different stages, and it is essential to consider each retelling as a part of the larger process of revision. A clear example of the importance of this observation is given to us by Samuel Delany, in the introduction to his autobiography, *The Motion of Light in Water*.[4] At the age of 36 Delany was invited to submit a biography for inclusion in a book-length bibliography of his work. As a part of the biography he included the information that his father had died in 1958, when he was 17 years old. The editors of the book gently informed him that this could not be true, since, if he was born in 1942, in 1958 he could not have been seventeen. Delany comments:

> "My father died of lung cancer in 1958 when I was seventeen."
> "My father died of lung cancer in 1960 when I was eighteen."
> The first is incorrect, the second correct.
> I am as concerned with truth as anyone – otherwise I would not be going so far to split such hairs. In no way do I feel the incorrect sentence is privileged over the correct one. Yet, even with what I know now . . . the wrong sentence still *feels* righter to me than the right one.
> Now a biography or a memoir that contained only the first sentence would be incorrect. But one that omitted it, or did not at least suggest its relation to the second on several informal levels, would be incomplete.[5]

We must attempt, as critics, to search for truth, and to find it and judge it with more than one chronological yardstick.

Ehrhart's poetry was first anthologized in 1972, yet we know, by reading his later autobiographical writings, that the period between his discharge from the military and his first publication was not a barren one – in fact, some of the poems anthologized in 1972 appear to have been written as early as 1969 or 1970. These early works represent Ehrhart's immediate postwar response to his combat experience, and to the difficulties of adjustment to civilian life.

In 1972 three Vietnam veterans allied with the organization Vietnam Veterans Against the War gathered the poetry of other antiwar Vietnam veterans into an anthology. The purpose of this collective effort – consonant with the radical ideals of the time – was to urge readers into action, and to thereby encourage change: "If properly used, this volume should be dog-eared within a month."[6] Ehrhart was one of 33 poets featured in the volume. Seven of the eight Ehrhart poems in *Winning Hearts and Minds: War Poems by Vietnam Veterans* are short, imagist pieces, born of the combination of beauty and horror Ehrhart saw in the landscape of Vietnam, or the brutal suddenness of violence in war. "Viet-Nam – February 1967" and "One Night on Guard Duty" are descriptive poems, contrasting images of peaceful nature and destructive war machinery, or the confusing mixture of beauty and danger in weapons technology. "The Sniper's Mark" is written in the style of H.D. or William Carlos Williams, a vivid moment characterized by "A brainless savage flurry / Of arms and legs and chest / and eyes at once." A sense of emotional distance from the scene is underlined by the namelessness of the subject, his reduction to a "mark," a "brainless" and thus inhuman thing.

"Full Moon" ventures into interpretation when a soldier reflects, "Strange, in the bright moon / he did not seem an enemy at all." But the reflection is ended with an action – "I shot him" – and the title ensures that the moon, rather than the act of murder, is at the center of the poem. "Hunting" also attempts to move beyond mere representation, but though the narrator ventures to reflect "That I have never hunted anything in my whole life / Except other men . . ." he turns from the question; thus, the poem is not about the implications of the hunting of men, but represents instead the refusal to examine the implications of the hunting of men. "Fragment: The Generals' War" gives the impression that it is a nine-line excerpt from a bigger, as yet unrealized project. The shocking contrast between paper orders and real death is obviously at the heart of the poem, but the images have a curious lack of emotional impact. Ehrhart encases that real death in paper himself, beginning with the line "Paper orders passed down and executed," and signaling the conclusion with "Returned to paper. . . . " The only truly interpretive poem in the collection is "Christ," undoubtedly a self-conscious attempt to be "literary."

> I saw the Crucified Christ three days ago.
> He did not hang on the cross,
> but lay instead on the shambled terrace
> of what had been a house.
> There were no nails in His limbs,
> no crown of thorns, no open wounds.
> The soldiers had left nothing
> but a small black hole upon His cheek.
> And He did not cry: "Forgive them, Lord;"
> but only lay there, gazing at a monsoon sky.
>
> Today, angelic hosts
> of flies caress His brow;
> and from His swollen body comes
> the sweet-sick stench of rotting flesh.[7]

Ehrhart's Christ simply lies there rotting on Resurrection Day instead of rising and affirming man's salvation. Though melodramatic and contrived, this represents an early attempt to describe the manner in which his ideals were shattered in Vietnam.

One might liken this early period, where Ehrhart describes rather than interprets, to a state of posttraumatic shock. We have, in fact, a case of compounded shock – the trauma of war, and the trauma of reentering a world where the trauma of war is inconceivable. The incredible effort demanded from the writer who merely wants to *portray* the war pales in comparison to the dedication and fortitude required of the writer who wishes to somehow *explain* the event. He must first invent a whole new mode of speaking in order to articulate his subject: "The problem, one cannot repeat too often, is to create a language and imagery that will transform mere knowledge into vision and bear the reader beyond the realm of familiar imagining into the bizarre limbo of atrocity."[8] By the mid-1970s Ehrhart was at least partially successful in inventing a language that could bear his message.

In 1976 ten more Ehrhart poems were anthologized in a second collection of Vietnam War poetry, one which Ehrhart also coedited.[9] All but two of these poems appeared in Ehrhart's first collection of poetry, *A Generation of Peace*.[10] The two poems which did *not* reappear are significant, and the themes are reintroduced in Ehrhart's later writing. The first of these is "The Obsession," an early poem marking the chasm that seems to separate him from normalcy. His nightmare fears, memories of actual events in Vietnam, have become "irrational obsessions," and the woman he loves cannot understand them. This is his first clear articulation of one of the characteristic beliefs of the trauma survivor – that two realities can indeed occupy the same space. To his girlfriend's irrefutable and logical arguments he can only answer, "You were right. . . ." The final line of the verse suggests, however, that Ehrhart cannot fully accept the "rational" consensus view of reality; he has begun to assume the role of the "one-eyed seer," a man "possessed of a double knowledge; cursed into knowing how perverse the human being can be to create such barbarism and blessed by knowing how strong he can be to survive it."[11]

The second poem is entitled "Vietnam Veterans, After All." An awkward, passionate poem that takes as its subject the work of Vietnam veterans in the antiwar movement, this poem gives us an early indication that Ehrhart identifies with the community of these veterans, that he sees himself as one among many traumatized survivors of the war, and ties his fate to theirs. The words "we" and "our" are repeated nine times in a 24 line poem. Also clear in this work is an early suspicion that his alienation and separation from Americans who live outside of "his" community of veterans might be a permanent thing. The poem laments that even after "we" veterans had "harnessed our terrible knowledge" and become ". . . the soldiers / For peace," and even after the war had ended, there remained ". . . an awareness / An invisible hurt / A gaunt energy bearing / the rags of our dream."

The poems in *A Generation of Peace* are obviously those Ehrhart considered his most accurate representations and clearest interpretations. Reprinted from *Winning Hearts and Minds* are "One Night on Guard Duty," "The Sniper's Mark," "Hunting," "The General's War," and "Christ," most very slightly revised. Other poems, not previously issued, seem to be from the same period – perhaps they were not accepted or submitted for publication – but they have the same early, imagist quality of those first published poems. A few are notable for their introduction of what will turn out to be, for Ehrhart, recurring motifs.

"Souvenirs," is the first of Ehrhart's retellings of a deed that haunts him: his thoughtless destruction and looting of a Buddhist temple. A small cup symbolizes the thoughtless evil that men do as, in this short verse, the first lines resonate to the last:

"Bring me back a souvenir," the captain called
"Sure thing," I shouted back above the amtrac's roar
★★★
One vase I kept,
and one I offered proudly to the captain.

"Farmer Nguyen," "Sergeant Jones," and "Mail Call" are among Ehrhart's earliest attempts at portrait verse. Flat and representative, rather than moving and evocative, they still indicate a shift from mere reportage to empathy. "Farmer Nguyen" is Ehrhart's attempt to visualize the plight of the Vietnamese peasant. In "Full Moon" Ehrhart first recognizes that the enemy soldier has arms and legs and a head, that he is, in short, a human being. But just as "Full Moon" minimizes the impact of that realization by changing the subject, "Farmer Nguyen" dilutes the message by generalizing Farmer Nguyen (whose very name is the equivalent of the American Farmer John) into a sort of Vietnamese Mr. Everyman. "Sergeant Jones" is also representative: "The kind of guy the young enlisted men / admire: / he can hit a gook at 50 yards / with a fuckin' .45." He is symbolic of the values that young men adopted in Vietnam, values that are a natural outgrowth of John Wayne hero worship, but are clearly at odds with Christian ideals. "Mail Call," a poem about the now apocryphal "Dear John" letters soldiers received in Vietnam, creates a "story" about a death in Vietnam. Private Thomas, the point man "unscathed, unharried, though constantly exposed," is killed by the fact that his wife's attorney has mailed him divorce papers. Though perhaps the poem hints at the irony of committing suicide in a war zone, the enemy here is not the NLF, or NVA, or even the war, but the stateside wife. These poems are neither fully realized portraits, nor fully constructed narratives. But they are the precursors of Ehrhart's later writings – poems that embody fully realized human beings, and autobiographical prose that extends into full-length narrative.

Another early poem, "Time on Target," relates a soldier's response to the random artillery fire that often fell upon Vietnamese civilians. The poem's narrator remembers walking past "a woman / with her left hand torn away," a dead child beside her. Rather than allowing his narrator to feel sympathy or sadness, Ehrhart has his narrator say: "it gave us all a lift to know / all those shells we fired every night / were hitting something." The very callousness of this image jars us into a realization of the horror of war – Ehrhart's antiprotagonist forces us to define our own morality against his. The narrator is defined as outside the rules of "normal" morality, ethically ungrounded and subject only to the rules of war. Robert Lifton suggests that "atrocities are committed by desperate men . . . victimized by the absolute contradictions of the war they were asked to fight, by the murderous illusions of their country's policy. Atrocity . . . is a perverse quest for meaning, the end result of a spurious sense of mission, the product of false witness."[12] "Time on Target" points irrefutably to the corruption and evil fostered by the murderous illusions of American perception.

An early attempt at allegory, "The Rat," is an animal metaphor for the victims of military brutality: "flashing jagged teeth, / he squealed and shrieked. . . ." "His final glimpse of life / was the bottom of a cinderblock." It's tone evokes "The Sniper"; however, the death in this poem is dealt not by an invisible marksman, but by American soldiers who club a defenseless (though unattractive) creature to death. Ehrhart still maintains a careful distance from the event – though he acknowledges his complicity in the animal's murder, his symbolic rat is only a stand-in for real Vietnamese. "The Hawk and Two Suns," a poem about a napalm airstrike, similarly transfers the real deaths of real human beings to the realm of the signified. By invoking a mythologized hawk, he *represents* the destructive nature of the American military with the images of "burnt-black bodies and lungs / burst outward in frantic search of oxygen." His displacement of the victim into the realm of allegory or myth is characteristic only of this short period of Ehrhart's writing. It may have been a transitional stage, a step in the process of reintegrating and accepting his role as the bearer of evil news.

Support for the argument that this allegorical and mythical phase marks an important transition in the trauma survivor's effort to come to terms with his new social role can be found in the work of Lawrence Langer who suggests that the imagination of the trauma survivor "is never free to create an independent reality; it is circumscribed by the literal event, by the history of the horror, by the sheer mass of anonymous dead who impose a special responsibility on the writer's talent."[13]

> One of the main problems of the Holocaust writer is to find a secure place, somewhere between memory and imagination, for all those corpses who, like the ghost of Hamlet's father, cry out against the injustice of their end, but for whom no act of vengeance or ritual of remembrance exists sufficient to bring them to a peaceful place of rest.[14]

It is exceedingly unlikely that any writer could reach that secure place in one, or even several, steps. There may, in fact, be a kind of neverending process by which trauma survivors, like Xeno's arrow, can only cut the distance between themselves and peaceful rest by half each time, placing the final destination eternally out of reach.

By the time of the publication of *A Generation of Peace*, Ehrhart's repertory had expanded; he handled effectively both the horrific images inhabiting his memory and imagination, and the theme of his alienation from his own emotions and from others. "The One That Died" is a poem about callousness, about the necessity of repressing emotion in order to survive. "The Next Step" works similarly to create the image of a reality fraught with danger and uncertainty. "The Ambush" clearly illustrates Ehrhart's frustrations with the limitations of language – fragmented, oddly punctuated, it reflects the confusion of a world where one is always "waiting to come to an end" while at the same time "things remain as they were."

The first word in "The Ambush" is "illusion" – there is a terrible inability to distinguish the real from the unreal at a moment when an error can mean death. "One of the basic premises . . . of this genre is the absence of a sense of any larger order to which the suffering of the individual can be related." Like the Holocaust survivor, the soldier in the war suspects "that he has been abandoned, forgotten and, even before his death, banished from the land of the living."[15] This feeling of banishment is reflected in "Another Life," a poem that makes the separation between the childhood world of traditional moral values and the new world of the war explicit as Ehrhart's narrator reclines against a paddy dike: "I close my eyes / and struggle to recall / another life."

The Vietnam veteran's separation from the "normal" world is not relieved by a simple return to the United States. Seen through the savage filter of the war, day-to-day existence in an unchanged America is bizarre and shocking. The survivor, unable to reconcile his present and his past, becomes a "disturber of the peace." Ehrhart finds himself in this position immediately upon his arrival in San Francisco airport, on a flight from Vietnam. In "Coming Home," images of a busy airport contrast with his recent memories of ". . . corpsmen stuffing ruptured chests / with cotton balls. . . . " It is as if his disruptive nature is immediately apparent to "normal" people. He innocently asks a young woman to join him for a soda: "She thought I was crazy; / I thought she was going to call a cop." Her rejection becomes emblematic, appearing again and again in Ehrhart's later writing, whenever he recalls the anguish and disappointment of his homecoming.

"Imagine," another homecoming poem, describes the unbridgeable gulf between the veteran and the civilian as a returned soldier tries to answer a question about the war. Ehrhart evokes an apocryphal image in the Vietnam War mythology – the inevitable moment an insensitive listener asks a soldier: "had he ever killed?" Such a query defines the distance between the survivor and the civilian. Those who have survived an existence in extremity, in an institution "which through threat and force attempts to reduce its members to nothing but functions in the system," understand that there may be no way to live except to come to terms with evil:

> And although this imperative opens the door to every manner of hypocrisy and lie, and therefore becomes a permanent occasion for cor-

ruption, it cannot be avoided. The luxury of sacrifice – by which I mean the strategic choice of death to resolve irreconcilable moral conflicts – is meaningless in a world where any person's death only contributes to the success of evil.[16]

Taken in the context provided by "Imagine," the poem "Guerrilla War" can be understood as a rationalization, an explanation for American brutality in Vietnam. "It's practically impossible / to tell civilians / from the Vietcong" and they all might be dangerous: "Even their women fight; / and young boys, / and girls." "Guerrilla War" pulls back from analysis, and a full acceptance of complicity, with a glib summation: we couldn't tell the difference. The implication is that if one *could* have told the difference, the war would have been fought differently. In its own way, it represents a wish for a "real" war, a "good" war, like World War II. The importance of this poem is in its reflection of Ehrhart's own ambivalence, of his failure to accept completely his own responsibility for the actions he committed in Vietnam. It is a transitional poem, one which indicates an awakening, but a not yet complete dedication to the task of bearing witness.

Poems explicitly dealing with the issue of responsibility do appear in *A Generation of Peace*. By their subject matter and relative polish, we can assume that they were written later than most of the other poems in the collection. "Old Myths" embodies a youth's disillusionment with the dreams of his childhood. His attic study, once filled with mementos of his achievements (described in the opening line as "Citations, medals, warrants of promotion" (foreshadowing their military equivalents) is now ". . . cluttered with old clothes / and broken toys and boxes." He has abandoned the room because "I've lived the myth, and know / what lies are made of." Such breaks with the past are not clean, Ehrhart's narrator admits, as even the older, wiser man finds in himself "traces of an older pride." In a moment of great insight he reflects: "I guess old myths die hard."

Though many of these early poems are bitter and cynical, "A Relative Thing" seems to be one of Ehrhart's first truly angry poems. The voices of the betrayed patriot, callous soldier, and bitter veteran give way to that of the committed activist when the narrator warns:

Just because we will not fit
into the uniforms of photographs
of you at twenty-one
does not mean you can disown us.

We are your sons, America,
and you cannot change that.
When you awake,
we will still be here.

His activist stance is accompanied by a newly self-conscious attempt to portray the soldier's relationship to the Vietnamese people. Unlike his earlier poem, "Farmer Nguyen," Ehrhart's "Making the Children Behave," and "To the Asian Victors" make no attempt to appropriate or objectify Vietnamese experience. Instead, "Making the Children Behave" contrives a startling role reversal:

> Do they think of me now
> in those strange Asian villages
> where nothing ever seemed
> quite human
> but myself
> and my few grim friends
> moving through them
> hunched
> in lines?

Though Ehrhart's narrator calls the Asian villages "strange" and says that "nothing ever seemed quite human" but himself and his companions, the language of the poem makes it quite clear that it is the soldiers who move through those villages "hunched" like horror movie monsters. The final stanza reinforces the idea that the Vietnamese, far from being inhuman, are people who have children and take part in the communal activity of storytelling as Ehrhart asks:

> When they tell stories to their children
> of the evil
> that awaits misbehavior,
> is it me that they conjure?

Ehrhart has become his own childhood nightmare; a theme also reflected in "To the Asian Victors," where the narrator admits: "In school, as a child, / I learned about Redcoats – / I studied myself, / though I did not know it at the time." "To the Asian Victors" establishes the distance between the veteran and his civilian peers:

> Looking back
> at the pale shadow forever
> calling at dusk from the forest,
> I remember the dead, I
> remember the dying.

> But I cannot ever quite remember
> what I went looking for,
> or what it was I lost
> in that alien land that became

more I
than my own can ever be again.

The Vietnam veteran inhabits a land peopled with the dead. Vietnam War
novels and poems by veteran writers are filled with ghosts – ghosts whose
demands are often more real and more urgent than the needs of the living.[17]
"It is not an exaggeration, nor merely a metaphor, to say that the survivor's
identity includes the dead."[18]

The final selection from A Generation of Peace, "To Maynard on the Long
Road Home," is dedicated to a friend killed in a motorcycle accident. The
narrative style of the first two stanzas is reminiscent of Frost's "Swinging
Birches," or "The Death of a Hired Hand" – restrained, nostalgic, under-
stated, and filled with the same kind of landmarks, dialogue, and place names
that pepper Frost's verse. Though the fact that Maynard survived Vietnam
only to die on an American highway might seem ironic to some, Ehrhart clues
us that the accident has martial overtones. Maynard dies because he has no
"helmet" on. He is "struck / and hurled sixty feet, / dead on impact." Thus,
along with the narrator, "we know better" than to believe Maynard's death has
nothing to do with the Vietnam War. Maynard is dead because he, like the
narrator, has "lost" something in the war. The curious fact is not that Maynard is dead, but that Ehrhart is assumed to have survived:

I show my poems to friends now and then,
hoping one or two might see
my idealistic bombast
in a new light:
the sharp turns of mood, anger
defying visible foundation,
inexplicable sadness.
How often they wonder aloud
how I managed to survive –
they always assume the war is over,
not daring to imagine our wounds,
or theirs, if it is not.
I think of you,
and wonder if either of us
will ever come home.

The theme of homecoming is repeated, not only in Ehrhart's poetry, but
in the poetry, fiction, and nonfiction of most, if not all, Vietnam veterans.
Such a homecoming as they might wish for is always unreachable, because it
is based on returning not only to a place, but to a time where they were
innocent of war – the pretrauma state. What we find in these poems is a
graphic illustration of the survivors' plight:

In psychological terms, the victory over destruction often gets translated into its opposite – the prolonged distress of an unwanted, unearned life. In moral terms, the survivor frequently feels himself indicted for unspecified but unforgivable crimes. . . . In literary terms, the memoirist finds himself beset by a double burden, then: that of recollection, which is painful enough, but also that of psychic restoration and moral reconciliation, which may be simply impossible. The first forces him back into his most discordant, nightmarish experiences, which he must try to order into some kind of patterned narration simply to appear credible to his readers; the second lacks not only an inherent order but any apparent *meaning*, and certainly is without any inner logic or secure metaphysical implications. Yet, despite these difficulties, the memoirist must get his story told . . . to commemorate the dead and make his own life-after-death somewhat more manageable.[19]

I have concentrated so heavily on Ehrhart's early poems because they seem to lay the foundations for subjects treated again and again in his poetry, his fiction, and his essays. As his poetry begins to expand beyond the subject of the Vietnam War, the themes treated in his early work appear and reappear in altered form. "The Last Day," from *Rootless*[20] (1977), is not explicitly a war poem, and would most likely not be read as one by someone not familiar with the larger body of Ehrhart's work. Yet his final stanza, "The sun climbs in the east; / still the streets and roads / are empty. No one moves; / each is locked forever / in a dream," articulates quite clearly the sense of separation from the world, the confusion of reality and dream that was first articulated in his early Vietnam War poetry. "Geese," from the same collection, is a poem about lost love and abandonment. The images of a world forever changed by the absence of the unnamed object of the poem – "All that day the colors / slowly drained from the world . . . The people lost their faces, / appearing only as bland shapes/at the end of long tunnels" – are close to the alienation and despair of Ehrhart's first post-Vietnam poems. The inarticulable "loss" described in "To Maynard . . . " could be the same as that described in "Geese":

All this was a long time ago;
but the wind still blows from the north
and the frost on the walls remains.
The colors have not returned, nor the leaves
nor the faces nor the blue sky.
And I do not wonder any longer
when they will.

Ehrhart also attempts, in the *Rootless* period, to connect his evolving perception of American misjudgment and wrongdoing in Vietnam to larger political issues, drafting poems like "Bicentennial," "Empire," and "To Those

Who Have Gone Home Tired." In the latter poem, he makes an earnest effort
to place his perceptions of the war in a context which includes the Kent State
massacre, the My Lai massacre, the dropping of the atomic bomb on Hiroshima, police brutality, capitalism, the destruction of Native American culture, repression in South Korea, and damage to the environment – an example
of a survivor's desperate attempt to contextualize his suffering. Ehrhart's
developing political consciousness, and his new insistence on the responsibility of the individual to resist such evils is clearly articulated in his conclusion:

> After the last iron door clangs shut
> behind the last conscience
> and the last loaf of bread is hammered into bullets
> and the bullets
> scattered among the hungry
>
> What answers will you find
> What armor will protect you
> when your children ask you
> Why?

Ehrhart opens a dialogue with a North Vietnamese soldier in *Empire*,[21]
published in 1978. In "Letter to a North Vietnamese Soldier Whose Life
Crossed Paths With Mine in Hue City, February 5th, 1968," Ehrhart takes
one more step in the direction of locating the enemy within himself, as he
speaks to the unknown NVA soldier whose rocket fire almost killed him in
Vietnam. His hope for the future is rooted in the idea that the NVA soldier
lives, and will remember the war:

> remember where you've been, and why,
> And then build houses; build villages,
> dikes and schools, songs
> and children in that green land
> I blackened with my shadow
> and the shadow of my flag.

Ehrhart's alienation is at this time so complete that he is not sure he is grateful
to be alive, and sure that he is not grateful to live in an America where
". . . we've found again our inspiration / by recalling where we came from /
and forgetting where we've been." "*Do better than that*," he urges the unknown
soldier, and we are unsure whether he means that the soldier should build a
better world, or take better aim next time, or both.

In the same year that "Letter to a North Vietnamese Soldier" was published, Ehrhart reviewed Michael Herr's *Dispatches*.[22] Though impressed with
Herr's style and talent he feels a deep uneasiness with Herr's glorification of

the common soldier, expressing distaste for his "combination of poignant sympathy and wrongheaded blindness."[23] The omission of the Vietnamese viewpoint strikes him as outrageous – a not surprising reaction, considering Ehrhart's own recent writings. Most of all, he despises Herr's unabashed love of combat, his exhilaration at survival in a war zone:

> Like so many of us, Michael Herr went to Vietnam in search of his initiation into manhood. The really sad part is that he thinks he found it. For all the superficial differences, *Dispatches* is just another paean to men-at-war, a glorious–grisly–romantic tribute to the ultimate insanity. It is a tragic injustice to the men he obviously loved and admired and pitied, for in its stock portrayal of war, it does its part to ensure that there will always be young men stacked in body-bags waiting to come home.[24]

To Ehrhart, Herr's flashy New Journalism style merely masks the reinscription of old myths of manhood. He takes the greatest offense at Herr's claim to equal authority with the "grunts" in the field, pointing out the contradiction between Herr's insistence upon his submersion in war and his ability to retire to the safe and comfortable hotels of Saigon. What Ehrhart fears is an appropriation of his privileged position as witness; that an unworthy claim to historicity will be honored above his own, and that false testimony will be accepted as "the real war" by an ignorant public.[25]

As Alvin Rosenfeld explains, it is difficult to fathom the depths of a survivor's commitment to bearing witness:

> When . . . the task of not only recording but also interpreting, judging, and ever again suffering through the agony falls to a living writer . . . then we are no longer talking about acts of sympathetic imagination but about something else, something that we do not have a name for and hardly know how to grasp. The nightmare, in a word, is never-ending, and repeats itself over and over.[26]

The survivor sees always with two sets of eyes, and in one set – on an endless loop – play the horrors of war, terrible memories superimposed on the most commonplace events.

The duality of the Ehrhart's vision is reflected even in poems that do not specifically deal with the Vietnam War. In "Going Home with the Monkeys" (from *Rootless*) Ehrhart clearly expresses his inability to escape the curse of double vision, a situation that can make daily life almost intolerable. These "shadows," as he calls ". . . the beggar on the corner, / a headline, a siren, a dream / of green palms in moonlight" are ever present:

> They are the shadows of everything,
> except what we are,
> and what we have done.

And they never seem to get
any closer.

And they never leave us alone.

Between 1978 and 1980 Ehrhart's poems about the world outside the war
were fully realized. These works deal with the questions of interpersonal
relationships, man's relation to nature, and the process of aging, and they all
reflect Ehrhart's preoccupation with making sense of the world – the impassioned search for reason that trauma survivors must undertake if they elect to
live sanely in the present. In "Turning Thirty"[27] Ehrhart writes:

And just like that these
thirty years have come and gone;
and I do not understand at all
why I see a man
inside the mirror when a small
boy still lives inside this body
wondering
what causes laughter, why
nations go to war, who paints the startling
colors of the rainbow on a gray vaulted sky,
and when I will be old enough to know.

His sense of personal responsibility haunts his political poetry, from "Letter
to the Survivors"[28] (a poem explaining the sequence of events that lead to
nuclear war), to "High Country,"[29] (which links the Vietnam War to American aggression in Central America). Ehrhart explores the way in which life
goes on in a world full of pain and trouble, and the ways in which truth and
falsehood are uttered and understood. He is aware that the shape of public
history influences foreign policy, and is concerned that his pain and suffering
not be misinterpreted by an ignorant public or a manipulative political administration:

The Invasion of Grenada

I didn't want a monument,
not even one as sober as that
vast black wall of broken lives.
I didn't want a postage stamp.
I didn't want a road beside the Delaware
River with a sign proclaiming
"Vietnam Veterans Memorial Highway."

What I wanted was a simple recognition
of the limits of our power as a nation

to inflict our will on others.
What I wanted was an understanding
that the world is neither black-and-white
nor ours.

What I wanted
was an end to monuments.[30]

He fights the process of historical simplification, the myth of American good
intentions gone bad in Vietnam, the urge to reduce the Vietnamese to an
immoral other:

> What most of us can't deal with – can't even begin to conceive of, in fact
> – is the vision of the United States as a force of evil in the world every
> bit as malignant as that arch-villain, the Soviet union. Such a notion
> runs against the very fabric of self-perception. It is too hideous to
> imagine. . . . And so we turn away from that terrible vision and seek
> solace in books . . . which offer us a less painful way of explaining the
> havoc we sow in the world.[31]

"The Teacher," an early poem about a subject that continues to preoccupy
Ehrhart, voices Ehrhart's passionate desire to shock an unconscious world
awake. "Hardly older than you are now," he writes to his students at Sandy
Spring Friends Schools in 1978,

I hunched down shaking
like an old man
alone in an empty cave
among the rocks of ignorance
and malice honorable men
call truth.

Out of that cave I carried
anger like a torch
to keep my heart from freezing,
and a strange new thing called
love
to keep me sane.

. . . .

I swore an oath to teach you
all I know –
and I know things
worth knowing.[32]

Education becomes one of Ehrhart's passions, a duty to a younger generation:

"If our children are to help us build the kind of world they deserve, they must known what kind of world they live in, and how we got where we are. All of us must be teachers. It is not an option. It is an obligation."[33] Despite his dedication, Ehrhart often feels an overwhelming sense of the futility of his mission. Protecting the youth of America from exploitation and unnecessary suffering may not be possible. This hopelessness may spring from the struggle simply to articulate the evils he wishes these youngsters to avoid, a problem linked to the impossibility of fully conveying the traumatic experience:

> I could tell you all sorts of horror stories. There was the entire class of first- and second-year college students I had in 1977, none of whom had ever heard of Dean Rusk, much less who he was or what he had been a part of. There was the girl I taught in 1979 who, when confronted with five Vietnam poems in a high school English class, blurted out, "Do we have to read these, Bill? It's so depressing." There was the boy who, in the midst of my 1982 history course on the Vietnam War, asked me when I was going to tell them "the other side," oblivious to the fact that "the other side" is all he's been hearing since the day he was born. . . . I'm so tired of paddling against the torrent that most days I wake up not knowing how I can possibly pick up the paddle even one more time. . . . Nothing I do will make any difference, but to do nothing requires a kind of amnesia I have yet to discover a means of inducing. The dilemma leaves me much of the time feeling like a failure at everything I do.[34]

This is the heart of the survivor experience: *Nothing I do will make any difference, but to do nothing requires a kind of amnesia I have yet to discover a means of inducing.* The traumatic past places the burden of bearing witness on the survivor, but the day-to-day demands of posttrauma existence force the survivor to make the act of bearing witness at best a part-time occupation:

> My wife and child deserve something better than sleeping bags and canned sardines. I've got bills to pay, a rotting back stair that needs to be fixed, a hamper perpetually full of dirty clothes, and a widowed mother who'll break her neck if she tries to change her own storm windows. I've got a classroom full of 15-year-olds who'll eat me alive the first day I come into school unprepared. I can't even find the time to keep up with my own writing, let alone to go out and change the world.[35]

Despite the discouraging refusal of the world to change for the better, and the emotional difficulties that sprang from his traumatic combat experience, Ehrhart seems, by the early 1980s, to have settled into a consistent style. He sounds stronger, grounded, self-assured:

> I know we are running out of time. We absolutely must set aside our

vision of the world as we would like it to be, and deal with the world as it is, set realistic goals, and go after them one step at a time. That is the only way we have any chance at all of building a world as we would like it to be – the world of our visions that we all so desperately want to bequeath to our children's children.[36]

Though his vision is always double, he has made some sort of peace with the view: "I am a teacher now; I live alone. / I am anchored to this world / by all cold necessity / holds sacred: water, salt / the labored rhythms of breathing." ("Again Rehoboth"[37]) He has thought long enough and hard enough about the nature of violence and evil to declare that man-made violence is different from the violence of the earth: "St. Helens is the throat of Mother Earth, / and the violence is Her song – / and there is no sadness in it."[38] He has also come to believe that the fight against the violence and evil of human beings is a necessity, and that he must commit himself to the struggle, despite his urge to ". . . own a house, raise a family, / draw a steady paycheck" ("Matters of the Heart"[39]). And he has found hope as well as despair in the next generation, in his students, in the children of friends: "Be what you are," he tells a small child whose mother has died, "Be a candle. / Light the awful silence with your laughter."[40]

This small hope grows into a larger hope: that he will not always have to be alone. The survivor, destined always to see the world through two sets of eyes, knows better than anyone else that his experience can never be conveyed to those who have not lived through it. Yet those who, like him, have survived, are often too damaged to feel love or to return it, and many find the presence of other survivors too sharp a reminder of a past they have chosen to repress or ignore. A survivor's salvation, suggests Ehrhart, can be found in rediscovering the capacity to love.

In 1980 Ehrhart wrote an essay entitled "The Long Road Home to Intimacy," in which he reflected on the difficulty he had maintaining relationships with women:

> I think it comes back to the feeling that I am, somewhere deep inside, essentially a bad person: Certainly I must be to do what I did – a convoluted but insistent logic. Therefore, if a woman gets to know me well enough, eventually she'll discover what I already know about myself – whereupon she'll reject me. But if I don't allow myself to get too close, I won't be left staring at myself in the mirror with all those unanswerable questions.[41]

As this essay might suggest, much of Ehrhart's post-1980 poetry deals with the search for companionship, his struggle to imagine a love relationship that can provide him with peace and security, a safe harbor.

"Channel Fever,"[42] published in 1982, is a radical revision of the Circe myth, a new myth for a man who has chosen not to be a warrior:

When I cast off in my small boat
with its one sail white and yellow
brilliant in the sunlight, I thought
I heard the sea calling in a soft song
sweet as any mermaid sings to sailors
in their dreams. I disappeared after it
into that vastness searching, searching.

Circe, as described in the story of Ulysses' voyage, was a powerful sorceress and the daughter of the Sun. She lived on the Æan Isle, in a palace surrounded by wild animals who had been tamed by her magic, and who had once been men before she had changed them with her magic into beasts. Ulysses sent out half his crew to forage the isle, and Circe captivated them with her charm and hospitality before turning the lot of them into pigs – all except one crew member who escaped to tell Ulysses the tale. Thus warned, Ulysses came to her palace and dined with her, but did not fall under her spell. In fact, he overpowered her and threatened her life. She begged for mercy, which he granted after she restored his men to their original forms, and then she entertained him and his crew in opulent style until someone reminded Ulysses that "a man's gotta do what a man's gotta do," and, in the words of Thomas Bulfinch, "he accepted their admonition gratefully."[43] Thus reminded of his manly duties, Ulysses set sail for the horizon after being instructed by Circe on how to avoid falling prey to the Sirens, who lured sailors to their death with their beautiful songs.

Ehrhart's sailor, a Ulysses without a crew, finds himself delirious on an ocean that supports his boat and provides him with food but does not nurture him, "tearing the tattered remnants of my clothes, / shouting at stars, fighting to keep / from pitching myself headlong into the sea." Where Ulysses sees danger, Ehrhart sees salvation – Circe's summons, and her invisible hand on his helm, is merged with the Siren's song, a call for men to put away arms, to accept peace and vulnerability. One has the sense that Ehrhart's Circe has the power not to transform men into beasts, but to change beasts into men. Margaret Atwood, revising the same myth, spoke in Circe's voice when she asked Ulysses, "Don't you get tired of saying Onward?"[44] Atwood's Circe stands against the mythology of masculinity, and wishes only to be able to use her power to promote peace. But Ulysses still cannot be persuaded to renounce his sword: "Circe's power is not sufficient to transform her lover's story without his consent. . . ."[45] Ulysses must transform himself, and it is this transformation, from warrior to lover, that Ehrhart struggles to effect.

The Outer Banks & Other Poems, published in 1984, is dedicated to Ehrhart's wife, Anne "with whom I discovered the Outer Banks and with whom I constantly rediscover, even in a world apparently terminally mad, the joy of living." Divided into three sections, The Outer Banks opens with a prose-poem entitled "The Dream." The poem, the only entry in the first section of the book, opens with a party scene: Ehrhart and his friends – friends from every period in his life – mixing together and having a great time:

> All of a sudden the door bursts open. No, it's been kicked in; it's
> all splintered around the latch. Eight or ten men in combat gear
> swagger in. They're wearing green jungle utility uniforms, flak
> jackets, and helmets. It's a squad of Marines. Hey, what is this?

It's an attack, of course, and Ehrhart watches in horror as friends are murdered, raped, and tortured. Despite his anguish, there appears to be nothing
he can do to stop it – despite his screaming the Marines pay no attention to
him, never notice him:

> I run down the hall crying, but something catches my eye, and I
> stop abruptly. I'm standing in front of a full-length mirror. I'm
> dressed in combat gear. There is a black M-16 rifle in my hands.
> The barrel is smoking.

After over a decade of writing poetry, Ehrhart is still obsessed by the notion
that he is the embodiment of his worst fear. Even in this volume, dedicated
to his wife, he places first the poem that must alert us all that he is capable
of destroying that which he most loves. A poem in the second section of the
volume, "A Warning to My Students," seems to continue the story begun in
"The Dream":

> "It's all right," she says;
> she strokes my head;
> "It's just a dream."
>
> And she's right, too:
> these days, for me
> it's just a dream
>
> because the next time they come looking
> for soldiers, they won't come looking
> for me. I'm too old;
> I know too much.
>
> The next time they come looking
> for soldiers, they'll come looking
> for you.

Despite the violent opening imagery of *The Outer Banks,* and the tensions and
anxieties invoked by poems like "Surviving the Bomb One More Day" –
". . . waiting / in the eerie fog of half-awake / for the final slap of the blast"

– Ehrhart's verse portraits are gentle and loving. He writes of the innocent courage of a young girl on a Wyoming ranch,[46] the tender faithfulness of Senator Everett Dirksen to his wife,[47] "... the light that cannot fade ..."[48] because a friend still lives on in his memory, forever young. The most optimistic poem in the collection is dedicated to Brady Shea, an adventurous friend who perished in a climbing accident:

> Later still, Daniel's letter
> said you fell from a mountain in Colorado –
> but I know you must have reached the peak
> and climbed straight up from there.[49]

The astute reader will notice that Ehrhart invests a great deal of his hope and faith in those who are already dead and gone. He does, occasionally, even suggest that the death of the subject is the source of his emotional investment:

> Funny, how I managed to survive
> that war, how the years have passed,
> and how I'm thirty-four and getting on,
> and how your death
> bestowed upon my life a permanence
> I never would have had
> if you'd lived.[50]

The idea that another's death might bring life is disturbing only outside the context of a literature of trauma. Ehrhart's early poem, "To Maynard ... ," written in a previous stage of adjustment to the traumatic experience, clearly states that there is no hope to be found in Maynard's death, and that, in fact, there is really no difference between Maynard's death and Ehrhart's life: "I wonder if either of us / will ever come home." Both men are dead in this poem – the writer and the subject – and Ehrhart's only amazement is at the fact that nobody notices. The elegies of *The Outer Banks* demonstrate a shift in Ehrhart's perspective – he has noticed that there is a difference between his life and other peoples' deaths. In fact, "... the light that cannot fade ... ," dedicated to Carolyn Sue Brenner, a friend killed the summer after they graduated high school, can easily be read as a revision of "To Maynard. ..." Compare the first stanza of each poem:

From "To Maynard ...":

> Biking at night with no lights
> and no helmet, you were struck
> and hurled sixty feet,
> dead on impact.
> The newspapers noted the irony:
> surviving the war

to die like that, alone,
on a hometown street.
I knew better.

From ". . . the light that cannot fade . . .":

Suzie, you picked a hell of a time
to teach me about mortality.
I was in North Carolina then,
talking tough, eating from cans,
wearing my helmet John Wayne style –
and you were suddenly dead:
a crushed skull on a pre-dawn road
just two weeks shy of college,
and me about to leave for Vietnam.

"To Maynard . . ." opens with the graphic and cold "facts" of death, and suggests that the accident may have been preventable, that Maynard's death may have been in some sense his choice because he insisted on "biking at night with no lights / and no helmet." The description of his death evokes images of wartime violence, and the last five lines of that stanza reinforce this notion, placing Ehrhart (a fellow warrior) in a position of privilege in relation to "the newspapers," and implying that he has "the real story." Ehrhart knows the truth, and the truth, quite simply, is that both Maynard and he were really killed in Vietnam, and the only choice left is how long it's worth the effort to maintain the physical body.

". . . the light . . ." begins very differently, stating clearly that Ehrhart is the student here. In addition, Suzie has no implied control over the manner of her death, she is "suddenly dead;" not even a person anymore, but "a crushed skull on a pre-dawn road." And in this poem, it is Ehrhart who wears the helmet, who takes the effort to protect himself from what he thinks is danger, to protect himself from his own death. That macho ideal is, however, a fiction, a "John Wayne" image that does not protect him from what he now recognizes to be the real danger: the death of someone he cares about.

The emotional scars a survivor bears are the deaths of others – a survivor, by definition, never dies himself. One of the psychological coping mechanisms quickly developed by those who live while others die around them, and those who live in constant anticipation of death, is an emotional barrier, a refusal to feel anything at all. Consonant with this denial is an identification with the dead, an inability or refusal to distinguish between life and death that is reinforced by the suppression of human emotion. Ehrhart's poetry of this later period reflects the breakdown of these coping mechanisms, and his ability to once again fully experience the range of human emotion is epitomized in his poetry, especially those poems that reflect upon his relationship with his wife:

... Whether we shall be together
or alone in death, I have no way of knowing;

but I know the weight, and how it feels
to pass the night without you.[51]

Renouncing his authority as a dead man, Ehrhart chooses life and uncertainty.

He is, however, still apparently unable to envision trusting living persons other than his wife, and reserves his celebrations of friendship and love for those safely in the grave, or those who he will likely never meet again – static relationships, which no longer have the power to threaten his security. Instead, Ehrhart locates the source of his pleasure in nature, and his most profoundly joyous feelings are invested safely in the beaches and estuaries of the Outer Banks, in the beauty of the Potomac River, in "the moonless night sky above New Mexico."[52]

In the same period that Ehrhart was writing the poems in *The Outer Banks*, he must have been working to finish his autobiographical novel, *Vietnam-Perkasie*. Of this novel, Ehrhart writes:

> This book is not fiction in the traditional sense; virtually every incident included, to the best of my knowledge, did take place. Neither is the book autobiographical memoir: liberties have been taken with the sequence of events, the speaker's participation in some of them, and the characterization of certain individuals.
>
> I came to this form through a succession of rewrites over several years. It seemed to me, as I worked on the book and began to seek a publisher, that at this late date a strict memoir by a bit-player in the Vietnam War would be a barren venture. But I am not yet ready, literarily or emotionally, to treat Vietnam as fiction. I chose, therefore, to combine a narrative of my own direct experience with, to a limited degree, other information I had acquired into as readable and compelling a book as my abilities would allow. [53]

Ehrhart's inability "to treat Vietnam as fiction" is a result of his intimate relation to the war, and the profound and shattering effect that the experience of combat had upon his system of beliefs. The war was fiction *before* he experienced it; now, though, he recognizes the great gap between traditional fiction and his own reality, and the experiential chasm between his readers and himself. He will not cater to their desires and expectations by treating his traumatic experience as fiction. This attempt to undermine the ideal of fiction itself (sustained illusion) and to deconstruct the idealized war by questioning the foundations of both memoir and novel makes this narrative, like many Holocaust narratives, subversive, and disturbing. In order to grasp this literary paradigm:

[W]e must understand the revisionary and essentially antithetical nature of so much of Holocaust writing, which not only mimics and
parodies, but finally refutes and rejects its direct literary antecedents.
The *Bildungsroman,* as Lawrence Langer has demonstrated, is one of
these. . . . [T]he traditional pattern of successfully initiating a young
boy into social life and his own maturity is altogether reversed. . . .
[O]ne sees not only the reversal of a familiar literary pattern but also a
repudiation of the philosophical basis on which it rests. Wiesel defined
that for us precisely when he concluded that "at Auschwitz, not only
man died, but also the idea of man." With the crumbling of that idea,
all narrative forms that posit the reality of *persons* – rational, educable,
morally responsible beings – are undermined and perhaps even invalidated. Yet such personal memoirs of the Holocaust . . . necessarily
depend upon the traditional means of memoir, autobiography, and
Bildungsroman, even though the stories they relate rewind the process of
growth *backwards* – from life toward death.[54]

Ehrhart's narrative follows this process of reversal quite faithfully. Where the
traditional *Bildungsroman* tells the story of a callow youth who must come to
manhood after enduring the initiation rituals of adolescence, Ehrhart's main
character is most fully realized as a moral being in his childhood, and his
"trial" of combat is clearly no initiation rite – he is destroyed by war, fragmented instead of made whole, reduced to aimless wandering, and unable to
regain his moral bearings. At the conclusion of *Vietnam-Perkasie,* the protagonist is fully infantilized, dissolving in the warm water of the womb.

Vietnam-Perkasie begins with an incident familiar to those who have read
Ehrhart's earlier poetry: a brush with death in Hué City in 1968 when a rocket
fired by an NVA soldier hit the governor's mansion, where Ehrhart was
resting between bouts of house-to-house fighting during the Tet offensive
("Letter to a North Vietnamese Soldier"). The focus, in this retelling of the
story, is on Ehrhart's own dislocation from the world of normality. The novel
opens with the sentence, "All I wanted was a cup of coffee," and the concluding paragraph of that first chapter drives home the point that "normality"
was not only permanently out of reach for the combat soldier, but that his
survival depends on his ability never to "forget completely everything he's
ever learned about staying alive, plop himself down in a big easy chair like it
was his own kitchen back on the block, shrug his shoulders, and try to fix a
nice cup of coffee."[55]

In the classic manner of what has become known as "the Vietnam War
novel," Ehrhart takes us through a short review of his childhood, his enlist-
ment in the Marines at seventeen, and a classic boot camp experience. At
graduation from boot camp, he stands in formation, "barely able to contain
the pride struggling to get out of me in a mighty shout."[56] "Old Myths," one

of Ehrhart's earliest public poems, foreshadows the disaster implicit in such pride and the reader flinches at the deadly innocence of boyhood, knowing that an older man will write: "I've lived the myth, and know / what lies are made of." But a refusal to privilege the viewpoint of the older man marks the entire text of *Vietnam-Perkasie*. Ehrhart deliberately constructs a relentless, blow-by-blow account of the trauma of war with the clear intent of immersing the reader in his experience: *this* happened, and then *that* happened, and it looked just *this* way. Rejecting the option of creating an older and wiser narrator, Ehrhart accepts the challenge of recreating the war *as he lived it.* He desires that the readers live, rather than re-live, the experience with him and that they will sustain some of the same damage to their belief system as he did in the war.

Instinctively, he understands that no one who has not himself been there can encompass horror. But he rejects, in the writing of *Vietnam-Perkasie,* the notion that no matter how well he tells his story, no matter how honestly and brutally he relates the facts, the audience will never stand with him, survivors together. He refuses to accept that reading is never a substitute for being.

Vietnam-Perkasie stands on its own as a survivor testimony of the Vietnam War. The work holds up less well as a novel – Ehrhart's prose skills are not yet as polished as his poetic voice. *Vietnam-Perkasie*'s greatest value to the critic writing on the literature of trauma lies, however, in its articulation of certain events which, to Ehrhart, have become symbolic of his experience of the war. Most notable among these is the image of his destruction of a Buddhist temple, first articulated in the poem "Souvenirs." In that poem, the event has already been converted from actual to symbolic – the two vases stolen from the altar of the ruined shrine represent his innocence (offered up to the captain), and his callousness and ignorance (kept for himself). Prose, however, does not lend itself to such graceful and elegant delineation. Instead, the sloppiness and randomness of the devastation is sandwiched in between the discovery of a Viet Cong tunnel, and a conversation about the treacherousness of the Vietnamese people. The temple is destroyed almost incidentally, the offhand obliteration of a sacred and aesthetically pleasing structure by a group of brutal boys intent on dismantling something they don't understand. The vase is handed to the Captain with the comment, "You wanted a souvenir, sir. Here it is. Genuine Buddhist vase. Duty free. No waiting. Get 'em while they last." In this retelling, it is quite clear that the symbolic value of the vases was evident only in retrospect. The tragic message in the story is that the younger Ehrhart never conceived of those vases as meaning anything at all. This revision could also be read less pleasantly – by emphasizing the younger Ehrhart's unconsciousness of evil, the author invokes Christ's plea, "forgive them, Lord, for they know not what they do."

There are also appearances *in Vietnam-Perkasie* of the now amply documented hostility many combat veterans bear towards women. Ehrhart's out-

rage and disbelief when he receives a "Dear John" letter from his girlfriend
Jenny during his eighth month in Vietnam is peculiarly vivid – as if that
violation is somehow more real and more devastating than any death he has
witnessed or caused. This is the first incident in the war which has made
Ehrhart question whether life is worth living, and it takes place back in the
World.

The last half of the novel is filled with anger, and this anger is frequently
directed not at enemy soldiers, not at idiot officers, but at Jenny, or at other
women who reject or disappoint. Even his idyllic relationship with his Danish
lover Dorrit ends in tragic despair when Ehrhart reads in *Stars and Stripes* that
she has been raped and murdered. It is the death of this woman, not the death
of some comrade in combat, that convinces Ehrhart of the insanity of war, and
finally drives out of him all feeling but pain. And in the final scene of the
novel, Ehrhart, after masturbating, passes out in the shower, his sanity and
identity dissolving in the stream of warm water, after being rejected once
again by Jenny.

Klaus Theweleit, in his study of fascist mentality, refers again and again to
the images of women as flowing water:

> A river without end, enormous and wide, flows through the world's
> literatures. Over and over again: the women-in-the-water; woman as
> water, as a stormy, cavorting, cooling ocean, a raging stream, a waterfall;
> as a limitless body of water that ships pass through ... woman as the
> enticing (or perilous) deep, as a cup of bubbling body fluids; the vagina
> as wave, as foam, as a dark place ringed with Pacific ridges; love as the
> foam from the collision of two waves, as a sea voyage ... love as a
> process that washes people up as flotsam ... where we are part of every
> ocean, which is part of every vagina. To enter those portals is to begin
> a global journey, a flowing around the world. He who has been inside
> the right woman, the ultimate *cunt* – knows every place in the world that
> is worth knowing ... *the* ocean that covers two-thirds of the earth's
> surface and all its shorelines, the irreproachable, inexhaustible, anon-
> ymous superwhore, across whom we ourselves become anonymous
> and limitless, drifting along without egos, like ... God himself, im-
> mersed in the principle of masculine pleasure.[57]

Unlike the fascist, who fears such dissolution, Ehrhart seeks it desperately,
longing to wash away the evils he has witnessed and committed in the
cleansing female sea. The impossibility of realizing this desire is driven home
every time a woman "fails" him – Jenny cannot "save" him from Vietnam,
Dorrit can save neither Ehrhart's life nor her own. Yet the younger Ehrhart
clings to the idea that women are his salvation, like a drowning man clings to
a floating spar – if only a young woman will sit down with him and drink a

Coke, he will be able to make it home, back to the world, to be safe. When a woman who looks like Dorrit refuses his offer to buy her a Coke, Ehrhart's response is to mutter, "Goddamn bitch," a phrase which applies both to the stranger and to Jenny, who "Couldn't even wait a lousy goddamned year. I'm puttin' my life on the line, and she's out flyin' around in private airplanes and goin' to proms."[58] Ehrhart's conflation of the two women, and his anger at them, is indicative of the common tendency of survivors to seek a justification, an outside enemy upon which they can heap the blame and condemnation that they fear they themselves deserve.

Ehrhart abandoned his unrealistic vision of dissolution in the sea of feminine salvation by the time he published *Marking Time* in 1986.[59] (The manuscript was originally, and more accurately, titled *Passing Time* and has since been republished under that name. At the request of the author I will refer to it by that title.) "Channel Fever," the opening poem in Ehrhart's 1982 collection of the same name, indicates that although the poet has set to sea in search of salvation, his true happiness awaits him in the form of a woman on land, a grounded woman rather than a flowing river. In this spirit, Ehrhart dedicates *Passing Time* to his wife: "For Anne, who was waiting on the beach, and for all the people who kept me afloat until I reached her." The Ehrhart depicted in the text of *Passing Time,* however, is not nearly as wise as the Ehrhart who wrote the dedication to the book, and the protagonist is still caught up in the search for the mythical healing female. Much of the action in the autobiography actually takes place on a ship, an oil tanker called the SS *Atlantic Endeavor,* where Ehrhart has chosen to "pass time" while he sorts out his life. *Passing Time* begins and ends with a card game played out with his friend Roger, an engineer. Ehrhart always wins, and Roger always responds by throwing the deck of cards out the porthole window – an object lesson that Ehrhart never seems to learn.

In fact, the entire autobiography is about Ehrhart's inability to learn lessons. The book fully articulates the liminal space inhabited by the survivor who still cannot integrate his wartime experience with his life in the postwar world. Better written, and more self-consciously literary than *Vietnam-Perkasie,* this text deliberately introduces and abandons Ehrhart while he is still at sea, watching and listening in vain for the singing mermaids he will never find. Salvation, the reader is told before the book even begins, is to be found on the shore. Ehrhart follows a path walked earlier by Elie Wiesel, whose first book, an autobiographical memoir entitled *Night,*[60] took place entirely in the hellish world of the Holocaust, but whose later work was concerned with the posttrauma world of the survivor.

He is less concerned with how one survives *in* the camp . . . than with how one survives afterward, having left part of oneself behind. The problem does not end with liberation – it only begins. His version of survival stresses keeping alive the *dead,* not the living, to find a way of enabling the victims to enter and remain in the consciousness of those who shared with them the Holocaust ordeal, but managed to escape its fatal snare. This is the first step in a sequence that continues when both kinds of "survivors," the living and the dead, combine with the memory and intelligence of the reader, who slowly discerns how *their* merged existence can alter the substance of his. Gradually the scope of the challenge widens, until we find ourselves facing one of the great unsettled dilemmas of our time: how to cope with the wasted lives of millions in a culture already witnessing a waning reverence for the individual human life.[61]

The protagonist of *Passing Time* has relinquished the need to force the reader through the traumatic experience, and relies instead on a technique of retrospection, seeking to explain rather than to recreate. Ehrhart's battle to make a place for himself in a now alien world is interspersed with scenes from his comfortable life on the ship, which act as a counterpoint to his feeling of being a freak or a pariah. Early in his reminiscences he dismisses his anger at Jenny's rejection – which had served as the pivotal point in *Vietnam-Perkasie* – with the phrase, "Suckers like me in every war," his flippant and unconsidered remark indicating that though the emotions have grown less intense, he has not yet entirely accepted responsibility for his own feelings. In a paragraph closely following that dismissal, he says that the postwar world seems like a dream, and that at times it is hard to remember the differences between dreams and reality: "I'd be walking along across campus half expecting to wake up at any moment and discover Wally and Hoffy and Gravey in single file up ahead of me . . . all of us strung out at long intervals to minimize casualties. . . . "[62] Like Wiesel, Ehrhart "inhabits two worlds of truth, but has not yet found a means of repairing the broken circuit that keeps them apart."[63]

Memories from Vietnam weave in and out of his reminiscences about college, about his relationships with women, about his political education. Once again, his relationship with a woman, his girlfriend Pam, is used to demonstrate how far the distance between combat veteran and civilian actually is. "What's the worst thing you ever did?" asks Faye, a friend of Pam's.[64]

> Good God! How could I answer a question like that? I got up from the bed and walked over to the window of Pam's room, gazing out over the broad rolling campus – so beautiful, so peaceful, so far removed from anything real. What did these people know about anything? The lawyer's daughter. The doctor's daughter. (p. 56)

And, knowing they will never understand, he tells them the story of the worst thing he ever did, which is, of course, far worse than they can imagine or forgive. To overcome their rejection he claims to have invented the story, and he says, to overcome Pam's fears, "You've felt these hands in action, kid. . . . Are these the hands of a man who could do something like that?"[65] She is comforted, but Ehrhart, and the reader, know that the same hands are capable of both comforting and killing. The dual nature of Ehrhart's hands reflect the dual nature of his perceptions, the difficulty he has distinguishing reality from dream. We can hear strong resonances from other works of survivor literature:

> In [Elie Wiesel's] *The Accident,* the memory of atrocity corrupts the anticipation of love, infecting the sentiment that once overcame all obstacles to human intimacy. "You claim you love me," complains Kathleen to the narrator, "but you keep suffering. You say you love me in the present, but you're still living in the past. You tell me you love me but you refuse to forget." The form of the disputation, the reduction of complex inner anguish to apparently simple verbal formulas, should not deflect our attention from the gravity of the argument. "Anyone who has been there," replies the narrator, echoing a charge that reverberates beyond the specific locus of the Holocaust, "has brought back some of humanity's madness. One day or another, it will come to the surface." The narrator's inner world is saturated by such suffocating gloom that Kathleen would find it intolerable were he to express it. He knows that survivors must not give other men and women "the sour taste, the smoke-cloud taste, that we have in our mouth." But this leaves the narrator shrouded in a gloom that not even the act of love can pierce.[66]

Though Ehrhart's anger at political and social structures has been clearly expressed in his poetry, up until this point the anger he chose to express in his prose was directed almost entirely at individuals who had done him a personal injustice. The American invasion of Cambodia, described in Chapter 17 of *Passing Time,* brings Ehrhart to the first conscious realization that the Vietnam War is important to him on more than a personal level. Though he tries to study, images of Allied soldiers liberating France, small Vietnamese children being battered by a barrage of c-ration cans hurled by soldiers, the murder of a Vietnamese peasant, and (not surprisingly) his destruction of the Buddhist temple, all run through his head The impact of these memories, bursting through the barrier of repression and alienation, are overwhelming and in a moment of completely characteristic projection he strikes out at Pam, slamming into her with a clenched fist:

> Pam's eyes were the same eyes I'd seen in a thousand faces in a hundred villages, staring up at me in mute hatred as I towered over her, my whole body still cocked, ready to explode again. And this time there was

no rifle, no uniform, no Sergeant Taggart barking orders, no mines, no snipers, no grenade ready to explode, no juggernaut momentum of a vast military bureaucracy out of control and bogged down in human quicksand, not a single excuse with which to defend myself. (p. 92)

Coming face-to-face with his own brutality and capacity for evil, with humanity's madness come to the surface, Ehrhart is shocked into action. He believes that his liminal state has been resolved, that he is ready for action: "It was time to stop the war. And I would have to do it."

Action, however, does not necessarily provide resolution, though it did, in this case, get Ehrhart back his girl: after an impassioned confession of his sins she takes him back in sobbing reconciliation. Not surprisingly, the relationship doesn't last – it falls by the wayside, a victim of Ehrhart's newfound dedication to the antiwar movement. The unstable nature of his enthusiasm is pointed out by a wiser, once again liminal Ehrhart in a shipboard scene: "Boy, she really stuck it to you, huh?" asks his friend Roger. "Oh, it wasn't her fault," replies Ehrhart casually, as they play cards. "She was just a kid – and I was one wired-out head case. God knows what she thought she was in love with."[67]

Just as women are the focus of agony in *Vietnam-Perkasie,* so they continue to be the source of and the resolution to pain in *Passing Time.* Though Ehrhart, as a college student, has lost his idealism he cannot displace his desire:

It was a constant battle between my near-obsessive fear of sleeping alone and my battered sense of self-respect. I did not care to trust anyone the way I had trusted Jenny or Pam. Even Dorrit, my beautiful Danish faerie queene, had failed me in the end, persuading me that I had to go back to Vietnam and then dying a horrible death in a back alley in Hong Kong. I wanted desperately and I didn't want at all, and I didn't know how to cope with it.[68]

The image of the woman in the San Francisco Airport haunts him – both the dream of a pleasant moment spent over a soda, and the reality of her whitened face and her fear. His anger at women has now been partially transferred to another set of betrayers – the politicians who sent him to Vietnam, and the unfeeling civilians who cannot appreciate the hell he has gone through.

The one-two punch of rejection is delivered first in a bar scene, when Ehrhart is taunted by the customers for his counterculture appearance, and then, on the very next page, when the revelations of the Pentagon Papers are published in the *New York Times.* Furious, he drives madly across Canada:

Maybe I would even stay there. What was there to go home to? A bunch of turds who'd stolen or shattered every dream I'd ever believed in. A bunch of pigs trying to beat my brains out. A bunch of rummies in a bar who weren't worth the filthy paper I flushed down the toilet. Fuck em all. I'd rather be a fur trapper.[69]

It is only after this cathartic outburst that the older Ehrhart, the Ehrhart on the SS *Atlantic Endeavor,* can begin to teach his friend Roger about American political history, lecturing articulately and assuredly on imperialism and racism. Read this, he says, pulling out a copy of *Bury My Heart at Wounded Knee,* and read this, handing Roger a copy of Bernard Fall's *Street Without Joy.* The reader is reminded of that early angry poem "For Those Who Have Gone Home Tired," with its passionate insistence that all evils are connected to each other.

Another, though quieter, resolution is reached when Ehrhart goes on a camping trip with a close friend from the war. After hearing of the death of a boyhood friend, another Marine Corps veteran, in a motorcycle accident (see "To Maynard . . ."), and deciding that "the war had claimed another casualty," Ehrhart grows afraid. "God, I wanted to *talk* to someone," he writes. So he locates Gerry through his parents, and arranges a meeting, seeking solace in another survivor. The effort to make a postwar connection to Gerry is a failure; Ehrhart discovers over a weekend camping trip they have little in common: "There was nothing between us but the fire and the marshmallows and the war" – not enough to sustain a relationship, and not enough to offer him the hope of salvation.[70]

Still desperate, in a fit of what can only be termed insanity, Ehrhart joins the Marine Corps Reserves. It begins with an urge to embarrass the Corps, to pick up a promotion to staff sergeant looking like a hippie freak. Instead, he finds himself uncannily attracted to the idea of rejoining the military and, justifying his urge with the excuse that he needs the money and that the Vietnam War hadn't been the fault of the Marine Corps, Ehrhart becomes a soldier again. His enthusiasm lasts about 15 minutes, and he panics and resigns. The incongruous nature of this episode is never explored, and we are left with the feeling that the older Ehrhart understands it as poorly as the reader must. Equally unclear is Ehrhart's motivation in signing a contract to teach riflery at a kids' summer camp, and then refusing to fulfill it. He sees the connection between the evil of the Vietnam War and the act of teaching children to shoot, but there is no indication that he understands why he might have the *inclination* to join the military, or to teach children to shoot. Perhaps the question is too frightening to consider.

At the conclusion of *Passing Time,* the oldest Ehrhart (who is neither the Ehrhart of the flashback, nor the Ehrhart who remains on the ship) suggests that he will find his salvation in poetry, in the mission of bearing witness to the world. This possibility is apparently beyond the young Ehrhart's grasp, who quotes the entire text of "A Relative Thing" to an appreciative audience.

He is embarrassed and uncomfortable with the depth of his own emotional response to it, and reacts to this unprecedented exposure of self by immediately sabotaging his own happiness and success, destroying his relationship with a woman who loves him. After he betrays her, he looks at her and sees in her eyes the reflection of his other evil actions, conflating, in a remarkable passage, the women he has wronged with the peasants whose lives he destroyed in Vietnam:

> Her eyes burned. They were the same eyes I'd seen the day I'd tried to knock Pam Casey's head off, the same eyes I'd seen on the faces of the Vietnamese peasants whose lives I'd routinely made so miserable. I could hardly believe what I was seeing, or the pain that I had inflicted. Was there no end to what I am capable of? [71]

His punishment for committing the crime of thoughtlessly wounding another is, once again, abandonment, but it is an abandonment he himself has contrived, both to prove his unworthiness and to ensure that he suffers for it. Still sure that unhappiness is his deserved fate, he carefully sets the scene for righteous retribution, and encourages his lover to voice the words he most fears to be true: "You are the cruelest, most coldhearted bastard I've ever known." Her final words echo Ehrhart's deepest fear and deepest desire: "I wish you were dead."[72]

After destroying any possibility that life in the World could remain bearable, Ehrhart, free at last, takes the option of retreat and finds on the *Atlantic Endeavor* a kind of world outside the world, a quiet space for reflecting and collecting his thoughts, for growing older and wiser. Though we leave him, at the end of the book, still passing time, we are sure (though he is not) that this is only a transitional period. We know better (as the older Ehrhart knows better than the younger) when we hear him say:

> What did I want or need or care about back there on the beach? Out here, I had wonders in the deep, and the thousand mermaids, and the hearts of infinite Pacifics, the moon's wide river, gulls soaring low between the waves, and the gliding schools of porpoises. They could have their crazy world full of dreams and wars and broken promises. Out here, I had a world unto myself. What else did I need? I could go on sailing forever. I could sail forever. Or at least till the mermaids married me. And that would be long enough.[73]

We have read, as the younger Ehrhart has not, the inscription on first page of *Passing Time;* we know that the journey he must make begins not when he heads to sea but when he turns his face again to shore, and that the love he seeks is not to be found in mermaids' songs.

Ehrhart's struggle to faithfully portray his own shattering experiences – to create texts that reject the device of an omniscient narrator, to refuse to let his readers know more than he knew at the moment of which he writes – demands a strong sense of purpose and great self-discipline. His position as the bearer of witness gives him a great deal of authority as both an interpreter and a critic of the writings of other Vietnam combat veterans.

Keenly aware of the difficulties of the long journey toward peace, he demands that other Vietnam veteran writers live up to the same standard of brutal honesty he upholds in his own work. Philip Caputo's first Vietnam War novel, *Indian Country,* issued in the same year as Ehrhart's *Passing Time,* comes in for some heavy criticism in a *Philadelphia Inquirer* review written by Ehrhart. The problem with *Indian Country,* he suggests, is the same problem that haunted Caputo's "highly regarded" memoir, *A Rumor of War,* published almost a decade before: "Ten years later, *Indian Country,* Caputo's fourth book and third novel, suggests that he is still in the grip of war, torn still between fascination and repulsion, exhilaration and sadness, tenderness and cruelty." Ehrhart argues that Caputo has not yet renounced the mythology that war makes a man, "that war is still the greatest experience a young man can have, the exhilaration, fascination and tenderness of war being a fair trade for its repulsiveness, sadness and cruelty." Such a viewpoint is, for Ehrhart, an intolerable affectation – especially in the work of one who should know better. Ehrhart, firmly convinced that his youth was destroyed, and his growth to manhood delayed, by the trauma of war can only conclude: "If you think Caputo is right, you will probably find this book more attractive than I do."

More than anything else, Ehrhart believes that people *must* take responsibility for the evils they commit. Even those evils they commit in ignorance. In a 1989 *Philadelphia Inquirer* editorial entitled "Who Will Apologize for Vietnam?"[75] Ehrhart describes the blindness of his trust in the government, and the agony that his mistake has cost him: ". . . more than a decade of nightmares and alcohol and self-loathing; a white-hot fury, shapeless and unpredictable, that seared anyone who came too close; a loneliness profound as the silence beyond the stars. And I was lucky." He claims, however, that he was *both* a victim and a perpetrator, that he had to come to terms with his complicity and his guilt. "I can live with myself," he says, though, he implies it often isn't easy. But he cannot comprehend those men who, responsible for the decisions that led to and prolonged the war in Vietnam, seem completely untraumatized by it: "I have often wondered how these men live with themselves. How do they get up each day and look themselves in the eye? . . . I'd like to believe that these honorable men didn't just walk away from the wreckage they created without a second thought. I'd like to believe they have nightmares too." Why is it, he seems to demand, that some men's mistakes cost them everything, and other men's mistakes seem to cost them nothing at all?

In 1987, Ehrhart published still another book of prose, *Going Back,* which he also dedicated to his wife Anne, and to his infant daughter Leela. *Going Back* was written after a 1985 visit to Vietnam, a mixture of diary, travelogue, and sketches that describe Ehrhart's impressions of a Vietnam at peace. Face to face with his past, in the person of Mrs. Na (who appears in a poem in his collection *Winter Bells*), Ehrhart confirms that the man he is today is inseparable from the man he once was, and that what he wants – forgiveness – is nothing he can ever have; not from others, and not from himself. Ehrhart soon concludes:

> I do not want to be here. . . . I have been telling myself for months that I'm not expecting anything, that I'm wide open to whatever may happen. Now I have to realize that I've arrived with all sorts of expectations and extra baggage. It's embarrassing, mortifying. I have been lying to myself for months – for years. It is hard for a man of 37 to have to come to terms with his own foolish romanticism.[76]

Ehrhart's prose is cleaner now, and his language is more relaxed than it was in *Passing Time*. He writes fluently, mixing vivid description with personal and political history. Perhaps because he is more comfortable with himself, he seems to have less need to ensure that the reader sees the world as he sees it, less investment in our opinion. He writes a few of his older poems into the text, juxtaposing them against his contemporary assessments – they benefit from the context. He carefully gives each Vietnamese he comes in contact with a name and a face, conscientiously respecting their humanity and making amends, we suspect, for the less thoughtful treatment dealt out on an earlier visit.

A great deal happens in *Going Back* that Ehrhart does not understand. One of the strongest features of the book is its refusal to interpret, to appropriate the voice of the Vietnamese, to report falsely. A Vietnamese interpreter named Loan is scolded by an old woman:

> "What was that all about," we ask. Loan just shakes her head. She is pale, visibly shaken, her eyes full of tears. Did the old woman think we were heathens? Russians? Americans? Did she think Loan was a prostitute and we her clients? Was she just plain crazy? What *was* that all about? But Loan will not tell us.[77]

Thoughts of Anne are woven throughout the text of the book. He misses her, and worries about her: "This would have been Anne's and my first Christmas together in our first real home after a succession of cramped apartments. So there she is, alone in an empty house. And here I am, alone in an empty hotel room half a world away."[78]

It is no surprise that Ehrhart chooses to describe a reconciliation with Buddha towards the close of *Going Home*. His preoccupation with his destruction of the temple has been a feature of his writing since the war, and the desire for closure is natural. Denied the forgiveness of Mrs. Na, Ehrhart can seek the more easily attained peace of the Pagoda of the Sleeping Buddha, where he bows before the statue and places incense in a painted vase – a vase which no doubt reminds him of its stolen mates. The bitter truth that he cannot assuage the pain of the Vietnamese, just as he could not end the war, is symbolized in his tearful parting with two young Amerasian girls: "I'll miss you," is all that Ehrhart can say, "Take care of each other."[79] Finally, he concludes:

> At least in Vietnam today, no one is dropping bombs or burning villages or defoliating forests, and what is taking place is not being done in my name or with my tax dollars, and no one is asking me to participate. It is their country, finally, and it is their business what they do with it. The Vietnamese have burdens of their own to bear; they have no need and no use for my anguish or my guilt. My war is over. It ended long ago.[80]

This strong assertion of closure was merely the hope of the moment and not a lasting truth. This is obvious even in the text of the introduction to *Going Back,* which was no doubt composed well after Ehrhart's pronouncement that his war is over: ". . . Vietnam has remained a permanent condition of my life – as much a state of mind as a geographical location, the turning point, the place where I first began to see and think and learn and question."[81]

Ehrhart's next book of poetry, much of it written in the wake of his trip to Vietnam, reflects an awareness that the war lives on within him, and that it may be passed on to his children, and down through the generations. *Winter Bells* was published in 1988 and is again dedicated to Anne and his young daughter Leela. It begins with a love poem, another Siren's song, in which his wife's voice summons him back from terrible memories:

> Who would have thought a single
> voice could change the nature of the world
>
> or my unnatural fear
> of short days and a long life?
> Woman with voice like a carillon
> pealing the cold from my bones.[82]

Though the trauma of the past, here represented by the cold, is always present, he has, through his ability to love and be loved, moved farther away from despair. The nightmare no longer comes first; it need not preface the volume, or have a section of its own: in *Winter Bells* it is integrated into the text as Ehrhart has integrated it into his life. And from his new position of strength Ehrhart can carefully evaluate the impact of the Vietnam War on others – veterans, the families of MIAs, the Vietnamese – and place it in the context of his own decision to pursue life and love, rather than death and hate.

He renounces rationalizations and justifications for the war in "POW/MIA,"
writing sadly:

> God forgive me, but I've seen
> that triple-canopied green
> nightmare of a jungle
> where a man in a plane could go down
> unseen, and never by found
> by anyone.
> Not ever.

He rejects the false comfort of "welcome home" parades, and refuses to be
one of ". . . the sad / survivors, balding, overweight / and full of beer, weep-
ing, grateful / for their hour come round at last," and asks instead "What fire
will burn that small / boy marching with his father? / What parade will heal /
his fathers wounds?"[83] And he can say, to fellow Vietnam veteran and fellow
poet Bruce Weigl, "take care of your beautiful life, / and trust me. The long
flight, / the long hump into the gathering night, / what do they matter? / We
will walk point together."[84] The poem dedicated to Weigl is one of Ehrhart's
few poems to the living, and represents the willing extension of trust and faith
embodied in *Winter Bells*. He writes, now, one after another, poems addressed
to real people: Mrs. Na of Cu Chi District and Nguyen Thi My Huong of
Ho Chi Minh City have replaced the faceless "Farmer Nguyen."[85] A visit to
Nicaragua in 1986 inspired "Adoquinas," a poem about a single old man who
fought for the revolution, and "Nicaragua Libre," dedicated to the freedom
fighter Flavio Galo. The final two poems in the volume, "Why I Don't Mind
Rocking Leela to Sleep," "What Keeps Me Going," and a third poem, "Some
Other World," published in *Z Miscellaneous* in 1987, represent the transfer of
his hope from an amorphous "next generation" to his own daughter, Leela,
and his ambivalence about her chances of happiness:

> From "Why I Don't Mind":

> What I want for my daughter
> she shall never have:
> a world without war, a life
> untouched by bigotry or hate,
> a mind free to carry a thought
> up to the light of pure
> possibility.

> From "What Keeps Me Going":

> She sucks her thumb, rubs her face
> hard against the mattress, and begins

again the long night dreaming
darkness into light.

From "Some Other World":

And I'm wishing this moment
could last forever; I'm wishing
the things that trouble my dreams
could be kept outside like the wind.

Ehrhart's development as a poet and autobiographer can be attributed to
his talent and his hard work. To stop the analysis there, and to simply call him
a good writer, however, would be a grave injustice. It would be as ridiculous
and false as calling Primo Levi merely a fine storyteller. Ehrhart laments, in
1989, "At thirty-nine, already I'm a marked man," unable to convince publishers that his "love poems, cold poems, poems / about my mother in a
house alone / for the first time in forty-four years"[86] are just as good, just as
important as his poems about the Vietnam War. Publishers, I suspect, miss the
point that *all* of Ehrhart's poetry has passed through the fire of the war, that
the literature of trauma is defined by the experience of the poet rather than
the nominal subject of the poem. Ehrhart's good poems and his bad poems,
his poems about war and his poems about his wife, are all part of a larger work
– the interpretation of the traumatic experience, and the integration of that
experience into a posttraumatic existence. Critics miss the point, too. Ehrhart
complains that "of the few reviews my poetry has received, almost all focus
exclusively on the obvious 'Vietnam poems,' ignoring completely or paying
only passing lip service to the large number of my poems not obviously
connected to the war."[87]

Since the publication of *Winter Bells,* Ehrhart has continued to produce
poems, to teach, and to write prose. The problem with any study of a living
author – particularly as young an artist as W. D. Ehrhart – is that any analysis
is out-dated even before it is printed. I consider this a beginning, rather than
an ending – ongoing work on a survivor–poet who has reached maturity, but
who has yet to find his limits. His latest poems reflect a growing focus on
living subjects, and include many poems about Central America (he visited
Nicaragua and El Salvador in the mid 1980s), contemporary Vietnam, and the
intersection between the personal and the political. He has also continued to
produce critical works, anthologies, and fiction. In 1993 he was the recipient
of a Pew Grant, which will doubtless serve as the foundation for a great deal
of new writing. He has also completed a new memoir, *Busted: A Vietnam
Veteran in Nixon's America* (University of Massachusetts, 1995), which takes
place after he is thrown off the ship where he works, "busted" for smoking
marijuana. In the coming decades it is my hope that we will have a growing

body of Ehrhart's work to examine, a tribute to the ongoing process of healing and growth. "The journey from version to vision to revision seems endless."[88]

The profound dislocation of combat, the confusion of perpetrator and victim, power and powerlessness, create in the survivors of war a duality of perception characteristic of trauma survivors. Their choice – to close their eyes to the horror of the past and deny their own experience, or to attempt to integrate the traumatic experience into the banality of everyday life – is always difficult. Many survivors simply succumb to their inability to escape the traumatic landscape and choose to die rather than endure. Some few, like Ehrhart, refuse both to repress the past and to renounce the present; they take as their responsibility the impossible task of bearing witness both to what we are, and to what we could be. For these authors, writing is not simply a therapeutic task, and the war is not simply "good subject material": bearing witness is a sacred trust, and the product of a life of hard work. These men and women are the guardians of history, the voices of Cassandra, the "farmers of dreams."

> I no longer believe that I can change the world. I no longer believe that even all of us together are going to change the world. But I do believe we have to keep trying. . . . *I* have to keep trying because it is the only way I can live with myself, knowing what I know. It is the only way I can live with my wife, who believes in me more than I believe in myself. It is the only way I can live with my daughter, who will inherit the world I give her.
>
> I'll tell you my darkest fantasy: when they drop the big bomb on the oil refineries of South Philadelphia, I want to have time to take my daughter in my arms and hold her tight and whisper into her ear, "Kid, I'm sorry about this. I did the best I could." That's it. That's all I ask for. Looking around at the world today through rational eyes, that's all I reasonably *can* ask for: the time to say it, and the knowledge that what I am saying is true, that I did the best I could.[89]

5

There Was No Plot, and I Discovered It By Mistake

Trauma, Community, and the Revisionary Process

The difference between a war story and a fairy tale is
that a fairy tale starts with "Once upon a time ..."
and a war story starts with, "This is no shit. ..."

Traditional literary interpretation assumes that all symbols are accessible to all readers – that the author and the reader speak a common language. Critics' inability to recognize the inaccessibility of the survivor's symbolic universe seems to lead them to dismiss the "real" war and its devastating effect on the individual author. They replace the war with a set of symbols – metaphors of "experience" or "syndrome" – which denote instead an internal crisis of the "American character." This problem is rooted in the conflation of two very different, but constantly intersecting, kinds of myth: national and personal.

National (collective) myth is propagated in textbooks, official histories, popular culture documents, public schools, and the like. This myth belongs to no one individual, though individuals borrow from it and buy into it in varying degrees. Beidler's "cultural myths," and Hellman's, Melling's, and Myers' "American myths" are collective myths that comprise our concepts of what "America" and "American character" are. National myth, as these writers suggest, can be gradually revised as new elements are introduced into the public discourse and old ideas become outmoded. A major upheaval can introduce new ideas and images that are adopted into the popular consciousness. For example, the replacement of the horse by the automobile gradually made the traditional cowboy hero obsolete (now a beloved though outdated relic of the American past) and spurred the development of new heroes who drove cars. The hard-boiled detective who became a popular hero in the

1920s and 1930s has his roots in the lone cowboy hero of earlier years, and his predecessors date back to 17th century pulp literature. It is national myth that Susan Jeffords so competently takes as her focus.

Personal myth is the particular set of explanations and expectations generated by an individual to account for his or her circumstances and actions. Psychologist Daniel Goleman suggests that personal myths take the form of schemas – assumptions about experience and the way the world works. What information an individual absorbs and interprets is determined by the schemas operating in a particular situation. Schemas frequently operate at the level of the unconscious, and it is inevitable (and in fact, it is their *purpose*) to automatically skew perceptions of events. The misinterpretation of much of what goes on around us is frequently useful as a coping strategy, if a properly interpreted event threatens important, foundational schemas. This process results in the "trade-off of a distorted awareness for a sense of security," and Goleman believes that this is an organizing principle of human existence.[1]

Grand revision of a personal myth must always spring from a traumatic experience, for the mechanism that maintains those foundational schemas will automatically distort or revise all but the most shattering revelations. Chaim Shatan, a psychiatrist who works with Vietnam combat veterans and other survivors of trauma, describes this drastic uprooting of belief as the "basic wound" that creates a new, permanent, and adaptive lifestyle.[2]

The conflation of national and personal myth by traditional critics of Vietnam War literature is supported by their universal failure to make the distinction between literature by combat veterans and literature by nonveterans. Though a nod is always given to the value of veterans' writing (which gives us the "real" flavor of the war as it reveals the "secret history"), the universal tendency of these critics is to ultimately compare and contrast on the same terms Graham Greene's *The Quiet American,* Lederer and Burdick's *The Ugly American,* and Norman Mailer's *Why We Are in Vietnam* with combat veteran Philip Caputo's *A Rumor of War,* O'Brien's *Cacciato,* and Kovic's *Born on the Fourth of July.* Whether, like Beidler, a critic believes that most Vietnam War literature is written by veterans or, like Hellman, that veterans play only a small role in the process of revising American myth, he never considers the possibility that there might exist *literatures* (rather than a *literature*) of the Vietnam War.

War literature by nonveterans can be critiqued in the same manner as other genre literatures. These works are the products of the authors' urge to tell a story, make a point, create an aesthetic experience, to move people in a particular way. Nonveteran literature is, in short, the product of a *literary decision.* The war, to nonveteran writers, is simply a metaphor, a vehicle for their message – just as the war is a metaphor in the eyes of literary critics such as Wilson, Hellman, and Myers.[3] The "real war" about which they write *is* the war of symbols and images.

For combat veterans, however, the personal investment of the author is immense. *Re*-telling the war in a memoir or describing it in a novel does not merely involve the development of alternative national myths through the manipulation of plot and literary technique, but the necessary rebuilding of shattered *personal* myths. To understand the literature of these veterans, we must embrace critical strategies that acknowledge the peculiar position of the survivor–author. It is not possible to generate such strategies solely from the field of literary criticism; rather, the critic must expand her horizons and move into the realms of psychology and sociology, acknowledging the specific effects of trauma on the process of narration. Some progress has already been made in this direction, notably by Eric J. Leed and Gerald Lindeman.

Leed's *No Man's Land: Combat and Identity in World War I* (1979) suggested a new subject for interdisciplinary study – "the transformation of personality in war" – and provided scholars with a new methodological approach. Stating first that his book was neither military history, literary analysis, nor psychohistory, Leed proposed a theory of transformation that incorporated both psychological examination of human response to wartime trauma and the examination of the effect of cultural myth upon human reaction to war. Borrowing concepts from psychiatry, anthropology, history, and literary criticism, Leed began to discuss the First World War as a "modernizing experience":

> [The First World War] fundamentally altered traditional sources of identity, age-old images of war and men of war. The Great War was a nodal point in the history of industrial civilization because it brought together material realities and "traditional" mentalities in an unexpectedly disillusioning way. . . . [T]he disillusioning realization of the inherent similitude of industrial societies and the wars they wage . . . eviscerated, drained, and confounded the logic upon which the moral significance of war and the figure of the warrior had been based.[4]

Leed makes good use of an anthropological theory which was articulated by Arnold Van Gennep: "Van Gennep divided rites of passage into three phases: rites of separation, which removed an individual or group of individuals from his or their accustomed place; liminal rites, which symbolically fix the character of the "passenger" as one who is between states, places, or conditions; and finally rites of incorporation (postliminal rites), which welcome the individual back into the group."[5] Leed claimed that liminality was the condition of the front soldier in World War I, and that, rather than passing into the postliminal phase upon his return, the war veteran continued to be a "liminal type": "He derives all of his features from the fact that he has crossed the boundaries of disjunctive social worlds, from peace to war, and back. He has been reshaped by his voyage along the margins of civilization, a voyage in which he has been presented with wonders, curiosities, and monsters – things that can only be guessed at by those who remained at home."[6] The theory of liminality describes a process of symbolic production based on the traumatic experiences of those entering the transition, or liminal, state. But the symbols generated by liminality are readable only to those familiar with the "alphabet" of trauma; what they represent is not common knowledge. Symbols which commonly represent a particular idea may be drastically transformed within the mind of the liminal type. For example, the symbolism inherent in the Holocaust survivor poet's description of a bakery's bread oven is entirely different than the same invocation by a nonsurvivor.

In Leed's estimation, the normal difficulties experienced by the World War I veteran on his return to peacetime society were intensified by the front soldier's perception that those on the home front had benefited monetarily from his suffering – that capitalists had made profits on the war, and that civilians had suffered little or no privations. To support his argument, he points to the organization of veterans' groups around issues of restitution, benefits, and bonuses.[7] The "comradeship" of which veterans spoke was a comradeship of victims, an emotional tie that became the focus of fond memory when the soldier returned to peacetime society and found himself unable to identify with what he found there: "Many ex-soldiers ritualized their liminal status, their position between the front and the home. . . . These men 'worked' their war experiences to maintain themselves on the peripheries of society."[8]

Calling World War I "the first holocaust," Leed asserts that it was destined to lead to World War II: "Those who had internalized the war, its peculiar relationship between victims and victimizers, the liminality that it imposed upon combatants, were destined to play a significant part in this repetition. For many could not resolve the ambiguities that defined their identities in war and resume their place in civilian society without acknowledging their status as victims."[9] World War I provided a crushing blow to the "fictions" by which they lived their lives.

Gerald Linderman advances a similar argument in *Embattled Courage: The Experience of Combat in the American Civil War* (1987), emphasizing the internal changes undergone by the men who experience combat. He rarely distinguishes between Union and Confederate soldiers, insisting that the psychological and sociological effects of combat were roughly equivalent in both groups. Linderman divides his book into two sections, the first of which – "Courage's War" – describes the expectations and ideals of the men who joined the Union and Confederate armies. The second section – "A Perilous Education" – deals with the increasing disillusionment and anger of these soldiers when they found the war was not at all like the one they had imagined. Though he does not use the same terminology as Leed does, his characterization of veterans' liminality is similar.

After the Civil War, combat veterans returned to a society that held notions about war that the soldiers knew, from hard experience, to be outdated (if, indeed, they had ever had any validity). But the new truths soldiers had discovered were out of place at home: "Killing once again became homicide; foraging was again theft, and incendiarism arson. Even language was a problem: Camp talk had to be cleaned up."[10] In order to cope with the demands and difficulties of everyday life, soldiers had to rewrite their war experiences; smoothing over the difficult parts, revising the unpleasantness:

> While forgetfulness worked to efface painful experience, soldiers construed bad memories in a way that smoothed their departure. When they were able to discuss the problem among themselves, soldiers ordinarily did so under a rubric – "Time heals all wounds" – revelatory of their assumptions. . . . Disturbing memories were to be kept to oneself, not to be aired publicly to relieve the sufferer and certainly not to correct public misapprehension of the nature of combat."[11]

Like Leed, Linderman believes that the soldier who remembered correctly would have been forced to acknowledge his role as a victim of a government and a social order that had exploited him. Linderman and Leed also agree that the veteran had a strong role in supporting and encouraging American involvement in a subsequent war. Participating gratefully in commemoration efforts, Civil War veterans benefited from and supported the revival of American interest in martial matters: "Although they remained 'men set apart,' their separation had been granted public recognition and their estrangement elevated to civic virtue."[12] Even veterans who had earlier been antiwar and alienated began to take part, and encourage, this martial spirit. This revision was so complete that by 1898 the nation enthusiastically applauded the start of the Spanish-American War. The old values were reestablished: "Civil War veterans had become symbols of changelessness – but only by obliterating or amending an experience of combat so convulsive of their values that it had for a time cut the cord of experience."[13]

These two important studies point us in a new direction, urging us toward an understanding of the personal revision process and its interaction with historical myth. Though they confine themselves to the discussion of the experience of the combat soldier, they describe a reaction to trauma that is not limited to men at war. Recent work in psychiatry suggests that we can make a connection between the trauma of soldiers and the trauma of other persons subjected to severe stress. Studies on Post Traumatic Stress Disorder (PTSD) have shown that similar symptoms may be found in large percentages of traumatized populations, including Holocaust, Atomic bomb, rape, incest, prison camp, refugee camp, and natural disaster survivors.[14] Trauma is a transformative experience, and those who are transformed can never entirely return to a state of previous innocence. According to Lawrence Langer, "The survivor does not travel a road from the normal to the bizarre back to the normal, but from the normal to the bizarre back to a normalcy so permeated by the bizarre encounter with atrocity that it can never be purified again. The two worlds haunt each other. . . ."[15] "After Auschwitz," wrote Elie Wiesel, "everything brings us back to Auschwitz."[16] A careful study of the works of literature produced by trauma survivors points to a certain uniformity of experience and unanimity of intention that transcends the particular incidents described.

One of the strongest themes in the literature of trauma is the urge to bear witness, to carry the tale of horror back to the halls of "normalcy" and to testify to the people the truth of their experience. "In one sense, all writing about the Holocaust represents a retrospective effort to give meaningless history a context of meaning, to furnish the mind with a framework for insight without diminishing the sorrow of the event itself. Knowledge of the past cannot be exorcised. . . ."[17] To be a survivor is to be bound to the dead, to impose upon oneself what Robert J. Lifton calls "an impossible standard of literal recreation of 'how things were,' a kind of sacred historical truth, which leads . . . to what might be called the documentary fallacy; or else a need to glorify the dead and deny them the dignity of their limitations."[18]

This universal drive to testify is articulated by writers across traditional genre lines. Wiesel asserts, "I never intended to be a philosopher or a theologian. The only role I sought was witness. I believed that, having survived by chance, I was duty-bound to give meaning to my survival, to justify each moment of my life. I knew the story had to be told. Not to transmit an experience is to betray it. . . ."[19] He is echoed by Vietnam veteran writer Larry Lee Rottmann, who stated for the record at the Winter Soldier Investigations:

> There is a question in many people's minds here. They say, "Well, why do you talk now? Why do you come here and tell us these things that happened two, three, maybe four, five years ago? . . ." I'm here, speaking personally, because I can't not be here. I'm here because, like, I have nightmares about things that happened to me and my friends. I'm here because my conscience will not let me forget what I want to forget.
>
> I didn't want to talk about it when I first got back, you know, I didn't want to talk about it at all. . . . But it gets to the point where you have to talk to somebody, and when I tried to talk to somebody, even my parents, they didn't want to know. And that made me realize that no matter how painful it was for me, I had to tell them. I mean, they had to know. The fact that they didn't want to know, told me they had to know.[20]

Jill Morgan, a victim of childhood sexual abuse, explains her desire to speak out in similar terms:

A close personal friend (male) has asked me repeatedly, "Why do you have to rehash it? It happened. It's over. Now forget it and go on." Only by owning myself and my past, by affirming and confirming my innocence in the whole, sordid drama can I rest and feel comfortable with myself.

If my survival is to be meaningful at all to me, it must be because it gave me the strength to fight, the will to survive and the empathy to reach out to other women.[21]

Each of these authors articulates the belief that he or she is a storyteller with a mission; their responsibility as survivors is to bear the tale. Each one also affirms the process of storytelling as a personally reconstitutive act, and expresses the hope that it will also be a socially reconstitutive act – changing the order of things as they are, and working to prevent the enactment of similar horrors in the future.

But the task of the traumatized author is an impossible one. For if the goal is to convey the traumatic experience, no second-hand rendering of it is adequate. The horrific events that have reshaped the author's construction of reality can only be described in literature, not recreated. Only the experience of trauma has the traumatizing effect. The combination of the drive to testify and the impossibility of recreating the event for the reader is one of the defining characteristics of trauma literature: "Could it be surmounted? Could the reader be brought to the other side? I knew the answer to be negative, and yet I also knew that 'no' had to become 'yes.' . . . One had to break the shell enclosing the dark truth, and give it a name. One had to force man to look."[22]

Caught forever in this liminal state, the survivor comes to *represent* the shattering of our *national* myths, without being able to shatter the reader's individual *personal* myths. And it is those personal myths that support and uphold the most widely accepted national ones. No grand restructuring of national myth can be accomplished without a concurrent destruction of the personal myths that words simply cannot reach. Terrence Des Pres describes the survivor as "a disturber of the peace": "He is a runner of the blockade men erect against knowledge of 'unspeakable' things. About these he aims to speak, and in so doing he undermines, without intending to, the validity of existing norms."[23] But the impact of the survivor's strongest message – that his traumatic suffering was seemingly without purpose, arbitrary, outside the framework of meaning – simply cannot be absorbed by the reader, whose framework of meaning remains essentially intact. This paradox leads John Hellman to assert

"Getting used to" moving through the perils of time without the assurance of luck, without the conviction of a special grace conferred by a special geography, is precisely the function of the literary and cinematic narratives which American artists have produced in response to the Vietnam experience. The stories through which we have retaken the

Vietnam journey ... have presented a Southeast Asian landscape that overturns the meaning of the previously known landscapes of American myth. These narratives purge us, forcing the reader or viewer to reexperience, this time self-consciously, the tragic shattering of our old myths. This process may prepare the culture to accept a significant alteration of our view of ourselves and of our world, a new mythic interpretation of our historical experience that will intelligibly include the experience of Vietnam.[24]

Survivors never "get used to" losing their sense of meaning; they are forever changed by it. Many are transformed into liminal figures who must remain, like ghostly Cassandras, on the fringes of society. Some manage to become postliminal by repressing or revising their experiences (though this is seldom a completely successful tactic, since the revelatory nature of their experience has shown them the inadequacy of "normal" concepts of meaning in the world). Expression, in the form of narration, is frequently a step on the journey towards becoming postliminal, towards rewriting the traumatic events that severed their connections to the rest of society. Nonsurvivor readers and viewers cannot "retake" a journey through a Vietnam that they have never actually visited, and thus cannot "reexperience" a "tragic shattering" of old myths. I cannot emphasize too strongly the fact that *the personal myths of the reader are never "tragically shattered"* by reading. Only trauma can accomplish that kind of destruction. The revision of national myth occurs only as far as the changes made *do not interfere with non-survivors' basic conceptions of themselves.*

The inability to communicate trauma is evident in the preoccupation of trauma authors with the limitations of language. Once again, this preoccupation is evident across traditional genre lines:

> The word has deserted the meaning it was intended to convey – impossible to make them coincide. The displacement, the shift, is irrevocable. . . . We all knew that we could never, never say what had to be said, that we could never express in words, coherent, intelligible words, our experience of madness on an absolute scale. . . . All words seemed inadequate, worn, foolish, lifeless, whereas I wanted them to be searing. Where was I to discover a fresh vocabulary, a primeval language? The language of night was not human; it was primitive, almost animal. . . . A brute striking wildly, a body falling; an officer raises his arm and a whole community walks toward a common grave. . . . This is the concentration camp language. It negated all other language and took its place. Rather than link, it became wall.[25]

In his first novel, *Close Quarters*, Vietnam combat veteran Larry Heinemann inscribes his protagonist's deep sense of alienation, the barrier that language cannot surmount:

> I have traveled to a place where the dead lie above the ground in rows and bunches. Time has gone somewhere without me. This is not my country, not my time. My skin is drawn tight around my eyes. My clothes smell of blood. I bleed inside. I am water. I am stone. . . . I have not come home, Ma. I have gone ahead, gone back. There is glass between us, we cannot speak.[26]

For at least 20 years, the subject of language as a limitation on the expression of woman's thought has been a topic of discussion in feminist circles.[27] It may be that a partial explanation for the silence of women is that such a large percentage of us have survived the trauma of rape, incest, or battering. Our stories may not be incoherent or inarticulately told, but simply inconceivable – as the stories of other liminal types are inconceivable. Patterns of violence against women are far from recent developments – statistics such as those provided by the Los Angeles Ad Hoc Committee on Rape (one out of three women over the age of 14 in Los Angeles County will be raped sometime during her lifetime[28]) pale in comparison with previous episodes, such as the European witch hunts. Those campaigns persisted for almost 400 years, resulting in the burning of some nine million women.[29] A continuing history of gynocidal persecution may well have resulted in the current perception that male language cannot encompass our experience:

> We know only the language of these folks who enter and occupy us: they keep telling us that we are different from them; yet we speak only their language and have none, or none that we remember, of our own; and we do not dare, it seems invent one, even in signs and gestures. Our bodies speak their language. Our minds think in it. The men are inside us through and through. We hear something, a dim whisper, barely audible, somewhere at the back of the brain; there is some other word, and we think, some of us, sometimes, that once it belonged to us.[30]

Dworkin's assertion is similar to Sidra Ezrahi's observation about the transformation of the German language by the Nazi system, "whose syntax, style, and symbolic associations were profoundly and abidingly violated by what came to be known as 'Nazi-Deutsch,' the perverse rhetoric that signified the collective actions of the National Socialists."[31] Ezrahi argues that the ideology of Nazism extended it to "every area of cultural expression," literally taking over the language. Preoccupied with the maintenance of written records, yet determined to conceal the actions of the state from the outside world, the Nazis "created a complex of verbal acrobatics which subsequent generations of linguists would strive painstakingly to sort out."[32] Much German postwar writing, she claims, is "an attempt to purge, through subtle parodies, and ironic reversals of traditional literary modes and forms of speech, the language and the literature of their implication in the crimes of Nazism."[33]

Paul Fussell suggests that it is the death of metaphor that embodies the distance between the language of the survivor and that of the nonsurvivor reader.[34] Alvin Rosenfeld suggests that all previous critical schools are useless in the critique of Holocaust literature since

> the conception of man, or world view, embodied in psychoanalysis or dialectical theory or theories of aesthetic autonomy had almost no place in the ghettos and camps, which were governed by forces of an altogether different and less refined nature. As a result, it would seem a radical misapplication of method and intentions to search through literary accounts of Auschwitz or the Warsaw Ghetto for covert Oedipal symbols, class struggle, revealing patterns of imagery and symbolism, mythic analogies, or deep grammatical structures. Auschwitz no more readily reduces to these considerations than does death itself.[35]

Each of the traumas discussed has as its victims a certain group of persons definable by characteristics of race, sex, religion and/or geographical location. If the members of a persecuted group define themselves as a community, bonded by their common misfortune, and see their individual sufferings as a part of a common plight, then (and only then) will the urge to bear witness be present. If a trauma victim perceives herself as suffering alone, and has no sense of belonging to a community of victims, she will remain silent, imagining that her pain has no relevance to the larger society. She will likely come to believe that she has, in some way, brought her suffering upon herself. The internalization of blame for the evils that befall one is difficult to escape even when the notion of community exists;[36] it is all but impossible to avoid when one feels no connection with a community of victims. The community of Holocaust victims, the community of combat survivors, and the community of rape and incest survivors are very different in composition, and thus the work of bearing witness is quite different within each of them.

Holocaust survivors see themselves most clearly as members of a community of victims:

> Firsthand accounts of life in the concentration camps almost never focus on the trials of the writer apart from his or her comrades, apart from the thousands of identical others whose names were never known. Books by survivors are invariably group portraits, in which the writer's personal experience is representative and used to provide a perspective on the common plight. Survival is a collective act, and so is bearing witness. Both are rooted in compassion and care, and both expose the illusion of separateness. It is not an exaggeration, nor merely a metaphor, to say that the survivor's identity includes the dead.[37]

Des Pres claims that the task of survivors is the awakening of conscience in the greater community, and that the testimony of survivors bears witness to "objective conditions of evil" that will naturally arouse the sympathies of ordinary people.[38] He assumes that the terror and mass murder visited upon the community of victims is irregular, and distinguishably evil, that all good people everywhere would object to such acts if only they were aware of their commission. Holocaust victims are both a part of the community of victims, and of the greater community of good people to whom they can appeal.

Ezrahi counters that only some Holocaust literature locates "the individual within the historical and valuational continuum of the community of which, in his extremity, he still remains a part, even if the whole no longer exists and even if his own life is fractured beyond repair."[39] Other Holocaust writers were "cast adrift by the Nazis from the sources of . . . life's continuity" and became existentialists, "placing the exposed self at the center as the irreducible source of meaning, and viewing biography as the limit of history."[40]

The testimony of those who continued to perceive of themselves as members of a greater community could recreate a historical vision, "anchoring the meaning of life of the self in the fate and the cultural resources of the group."[41] The testimony of those cast adrift was fragmented, and could create no greater meaning for their suffering. For example, the Jew who perceived of himself as a German first, and only incidentally Jewish would see his persecution in terms of an assault on his personal myth (self-definition), while the Jew who saw himself first as a Jew – a people with a history of persecution – might envision his sufferings as a chapter in the martyrology of his people. Each Jew might testify, but the community to whom they testified would be quite different. Furthermore, the testimony of each Jew would be interpreted by different audiences in different ways.

Survival literature tends to appear at least a decade after the traumatic experience in question.[42] As the years pass and the immediacy of the event fades into memory the process of revision begins to occur in the mind of each survivor. The dislocation of trauma, which removed meaning from the world, is gradually replaced by new stories about the past that can support a rewritten personal myth. The survivor's perception of community is a crucial element in the shaping of her new myth. To the Jew with a strong feeling of community with other Jews, testimony becomes a rallying cry, leading to the pledge, "Never again!" The previously assimilated Jew, with little sense of belonging to the Jewish community,[43] may identify with the greater community of "good people" whom Des Pres describes, and tell her story to appeal to the conscience of the world. For some, the Holocaust serves as a justification for the creation of the state of Israel, and thus takes its place in the greater story of Jewish history. Survivors can make sense of their sufferings by creating a historical context.

Without a sense of community power, testimony is useless. Testimonials have as their premise a sympathetic listenership with the power to prevent the recreation of such traumatic experiences in the future. Martin Buber stated that "'testimony without acknowledgment' may paralyze the will,"[44] inhibiting action and speech. Buber angrily responded to Ghandi's assertion that nonviolent protest tactics would eventually allow the Jews to prevail over German Nazis, insisting that the sort of sacrifice Ghandi suggested was useless in a society that condoned atrocity, a martyrdom "thrown to the winds." Natalie Shainess makes connections across traumas when she ties the silence of the abused child to the silence of the Jews in Nazi Germany: "Why doesn't she tell her mother? Why doesn't she run away? Why doesn't she go to the police? It calls to mind the problem of Jews in Nazi Germany: how many Germans would go against their own interests to help? What hope was there? Who would listen, who would believe?"[45]

The need for a powerful community within which, and to which, one can testify is evident in the scarcity of testimony by victims of rape, incest, and other forms of sexual abuse. Less than 10% of the rapes that occur in America are reported; abused women know that their stories will not be listened to. Though generally acknowledged by the psychiatric establishment to be victims of severe trauma, and suffering in numbers that would seem to indicate a distinct pattern of abuse, women who have been raped rarely testify publicly to their experiences. This is due in large part to the special context of women's trauma. For many other trauma victims there exists a "time before" and a "time after:" a greater social structure in which the commission of crimes against the community is considered improper. Atrocities against women are grounded in a system that supports them, which in fact encourages crimes against women:

> In the traditional professional approach to dealing with violence, the legal system and the police in effect aided and abetted the woman-beater. Moreover, medical and social services were powerless, in fact, to provide even short-term or intermediate solutions to the problem of spousal violence. . . . A woman either was sent back home or went to stay with relatives. Whichever she chose, she remained vulnerable, easy to find, and thus a defenceless target for pressure and attack by her aggressor. The result was that she was forced to withdraw legal charges, resume her role as wife and mother and try to swallow her anger and bury her fear.[46]

Louise Wisechild, who testifies to incest, insists: "Incest is not separate from other abusive messages in our social culture. I couldn't write about incest apart from what I was told as a girl-child growing up in the 50s and 60s. The religious attitudes of my childhood, the myths surrounding the 'normal' family and my experience at school helped keep the incest a secret. These messages reinforced the self-hating images I saw in my internal mirror. In addition, each member of my family had a role in the dynamic of secrecy."[47] The victim of violence against women has no preatrocity consciousness, and interpretation of the event occurs in a mind which, at some level, *expects* atrocity and has been prepared for it since birth. Internalizing blame is a natural consequence of growing up in a dehumanizing system. We know that it is common for the victim of even unexpected trauma to feel responsibility for the event.[48] How much easier is it to accept responsibility for an event when one has been raised listening to the insistent repetition of the phrase, "If it happens, it's your fault; you were looking for it"?

Those few women who do testify about atrocities have a strong sense of community, chiefly with other women who they see as potentially powerful enough to have an effect on the social, political, and economic structures that support sexual abuse. Louise Thornton believes that the testimony of a few abused women will reach other such women, unlocking "the power of the spoken or written word for the thousands of additional women who never told anyone."[49] Ellen Bass, writing in the same anthology, claims:

> In this book, survivors of childhood sexual abuse use the power of speech to transform, to fuse secret shame, pain, and anger into a sharp useful tool, common as a kitchen knife, for cutting away lies and deception like rotten fruit, leaving the clean hard pit, that kernel of truth: These insults were inflicted, are inflicted, now, every day. The repercussions are deep and lasting. The will to survive is strong, the tenacity and beauty of survival inspiring. We are not alone. We are not to blame. We are innocent, innocent and powerful, worthy of our healing fury, self-love, and love for each other.[50]

The most important factor in women's decisions to testify to atrocity is the feeling of sisterhood, of connection to other women, and the hope that the community of women will be strong enough to prevent the commission of atrocities in the future.

Unlike women and Holocaust victims, combat soldiers were physically removed from the communities with which they identify, and relocated to a new and foreign environment where previous notions of self were rendered useless. Basic Training is designed to traumatize the recruit, to systematically strip him of his civilian identity. The development of a new set of personal myths is required:

> The recruit brings with him to Basic Training a set of values, beliefs, and expectations about his rights as an individual member of society. He has taken for granted a whole framework of supporting cultural factors, a conception of himself and his achievements which reflects the status he has been accorded in his past social environment, and a set of defensive maneuvers which have served him well in dealing with con-

flicts, failures, and other personal adversity. The early weeks of training are characterized by physical and verbal abuse, humiliation, and a constant discounting and discrediting of everything in which the recruit believes and everything which serves to characterize him as an individual.[51]

According to Peter Bourne, the three goals of Basic Training are to destroy the soldier's civilian identity, to force him to acknowledge and accept discipline from the military, and to convince him of the validity and justice of the military system.[52] Armed with this revised perspective on life, the recruit is sent off to battle, believing that he has earned the right to join the masculine ranks of the warrior. Once in combat, however, disillusion sets in, beginning the process of alienation so eloquently described by Leed and Linderman. Ideas of valor and heroism are undermined by the randomness of death in combat. The failure of the social myths upon which the soldier's personal myths are based is the result of immediate, and traumatic experience. The soldier enters the liminal state and becomes a man without a community outside of the war. He has, like the Holocaust survivor, gone beyond metaphor: "Once there is a wedding of the symbolic world of language and the nonsymbolic world of physical experience, the realities of the war become 'things to think with', to fantasize with, to apply in action within political and social contexts."[53]

The acts soldiers commit in battle are comprehensible only in a world defined by war: the killing of human beings, the burning of homes, the defoliation of land. In "Beyond Atrocity," Robert Lifton argues that much violence can be done by men desperate to define their world in a coherent manner. He calls atrocity "a perverse quest for meaning, the end result of a spurious sense of mission, the product of false witness."[54] At My Lai, for example, soldiers fired upon men, women, and children because they equated them with the enemy: "they were finally involved in a genuine 'military action,' their elusive adversaries had finally been located, made to stand still, and annihilated – an illustration, in other words, that they had finally put their world back in order."[55] But the "order" of war cannot be assimilated into the order of civilian life, and the combat soldier returning home cannot recall his wartime experiences without negating the national myth. The soldier who desires to bear witness against his own crimes in war, and against the crimes of his nation, speaks to a community that does not wish to hear his story. Additionally, he knows that to speak is to condemn himself; to confess to crimes for which he should be punished under civilian law.

Langer relates the story of the SS doctor at Auschwitz who protested the Nazi policies of selection for the gas chamber, and who refused to participate in the process. The infamous Dr. Mengele explained to the reluctant executioner that the sentence of death had already been passed on all Jews, and that gas chamber selections merely determined who should live for a short time longer. The doctor was persuaded, and cooperated. When the war was over and he was to be arrested, this doctor killed himself. Langer suggests that the reason for his suicide lay in his inability to face

> a traditional world of justice, where categories like "guilt," "punishment," and "responsibility" resumed their former ethical force. Since his earlier behavior suggested that he had never entirely repudiated these categories, we can assume that his suicide is partly a response to the total collapse of a system that had (in his case) so tentatively supported his compromised spirit. His death may have been an acknowledgment of how badly he had used the area of inner freedom that was available to him in spite of external pressures.[56]

The combat soldier, too, is faced with the reestablishment of the "traditional world of justice." He must suspect that his actions must ultimately be judged according to the rules of the society to which he will return.

The process of psychic numbing is frequently an effective coping or delay mechanism for men who are not ready to acknowledge the enormous gap that has opened between their society's expectations and wartime realities. Vietnam veteran Al Hubbard describes the process:

> Sacrificing a portion of your
> consciousness so *you* won't have
> to deal with
> Being there
> and
> building mental blocks
> so *you* won't have to deal with
> *having been there*.[57]

But the veteran who is incapable of successfully repressing his combat experience will be disturbed by the intrusion of memories of wartime actions into civilian life. This double vision is troubling, intolerable for some, including Rottmann and the 99 other Winter Soldiers who testified to witnessing or participating in war crimes in 1971. Also in 1971, some one thousand Vietnam veterans gathered in Washington, D.C. and hurled their medals over the White House fence, protesting the continuation of U.S. involvement in Vietnam and the needless deaths of tens of thousands of Vietnamese and Americans.[58] The testimony of these men was given at tremendous personal cost: their condemnation of the American policy in Vietnam contained an implicit criticism of their own complicity in acts of brutality and atrocity. "There's not so much charm in war stories, you know," said Christopher Soares, a Lt. Cpl. in "G" Company from February to April of 1969. "But at

times you have to tell war stories because what happened to you in Vietnam
is always on your conscience. . . . There is so much you have to get rid of in
your mind. Sometimes I just stay up half the night and cannot go to sleep
because my mind bleeds from hell when it goes back to Vietnam."[59]

At the same time, testifying to crimes can be a purgative experience – the
confession that purifies the soul and prepares it for readmission into the house
of God. By evaluating his acts in light of reestablished social and moral norms,
the soldier can contextualize his experience: "I was bad then, but I'm good
again now." Once he repents his crimes, and suffers punishment, he is free
to rejoin contemporary society a sadder and wiser man.

> The new American soldier, as I see it, is a person who has come to a
> point in his life where he's rejected violence – he's seen too much of it.
> He's been so much a part of it. He's learned about how and to what
> extent human beings can really torture one another. So now, he's
> thinking about the future, about his own kids, about the other people
> who haven't been born yet, and how the last thing in the world he could
> wish for would be for them to go through what he's been through. He's
> got eyes that are set really deep, because he's cried a lot. I think he's cried
> a lot in shame, for the year, maybe two years of his life in which he
> killed, in which he raped the countryside, and I think that's a shame he's
> going to live with for his whole life. And that's a really incredibly hard
> road, I think, for the new American soldier because he has to accept the
> fact that he spent a portion of his life doing these things.[60]

When Sgt. Jim Weber left Fort Polk and went to Vietnam, he was a good
soldier, trained to fight and kill. He believed in the American cause. But his
attitude changed immediately when he witnessed the beatings of Vietnamese
children: "And from there on, it was all downhill and, man, like I was a great
American, and I think I still am a great American, you know."[61] Obviously,
Weber's notion of what makes a "great American" has undergone some drastic
restructuring. This restructuring places Weber's definition of the "great
American" in conflict with the tenets of national mythology: national mythology supports a war which Weber's great American would oppose. If Weber
were a lone voice, a man without a community, he would soon be drowned
out by the multitude, and his new mythology would go unnoticed.

But there is a community of combat survivors; or rather, there are multiple
communities. One kind of community is composed of men who have rejected, repressed, and revised most of their war experiences until the parts that
they can recall seem to be consonant with the greater body of national myth.
These men belong to the VFW, the American Legion; they support traditional
patriotic ventures; they back U.S. policy in Central America; they "support
the troops" in the Gulf War. They mirror, in short, the community of Civil

War veterans Linderman describes in *Embattled Courage*; veterans such as Oliver Wendell Holmes, Jr.:

> In combat, twenty years earlier, he had undergone severe disillusionment. He had grown weary of such words as "cowardice," "gallantry," and "chivalry." . . . In May 1863 he had prayed that he might lose a foot in order to escape a return to combat, and a year later . . . he had feared that battle's "terrible pressure on mind and body" was pushing him toward insanity. He finally resigned his commission, prior to the end of the war, because he no longer thought it a duty to serve. By 1885, however, the war of 1864–65 had largely departed from his consciousness. . . . He installed his sword and regimental colors above the mantel in his study. . . . In public addresses he exalted unquestioning faith and obedience to command as the hallmarks of the true soldier. . . . "War, when you are at it, is horrible and dull," he told the Harvard graduating class of 1895. "It is only when time has passed that you see that its message was divine. . . . For high and dangerous action teaches us to believe as right beyond dispute things for which our doubting minds are slow to find words of proof. Out of heroism grows faith in the worth of heroism."[62]

The members of another veterans' community do not seek to valorize their deeds in war, nor to rewrite the history of the war so as to make their presence there more honorable. These combat veterans attempt to come to terms with their experience by undertaking the task of rewriting *national* mythology so that it conforms to the basic tenets of their revised personal myths. Gathering in groups as diverse as Vietnam Veterans Against the War, Vietnam Veterans Against the War (Anti-Imperialist), Veterans for Peace, Vietnam Veterans Foreign Policy Watch, the Smedley Butler Brigade (a group of veterans who attempted to bring food and medical supplies to Nicaragua), Veteran's Vietnam Restoration Project, Veterans Peace Action Teams, and the renegade VFW post in Santa Cruz, California, these men and women work towards changing our conception of the American character. They believe, like writers of trauma literature (which many of them are), that if they can only *make us see* what they have seen, we too will be changed: We too will see *as they see*.

The imperative of most critics of literature of trauma is to define their positions as outside readers. No matter how empathetic the critic (if she is not herself a survivor) the trauma of the author becomes, upon translation into text, merely metaphor. The shattering of individual myth and the transformation of the protagonist did not happen to the reader; it can only be described and studied from without. Crucial, then, is the ability to consider the author as *survivor*, to bring to bear the tools of sociology, psychology and psychiatry, – an understanding of *trauma* – to the task of reading the literature of survivors. If we begin here, we can start to examine the process of writing as an act of personal revision, and then ask the important questions: "What fundamental changes in the author's personal myths have occurred? How do these affect the author's conception of national myth? How is this public revision of personal myth perceived or utilized outside of the marginal community that supports it? How does it change the national myth?" When trauma is written as text, it transcends the bounds of the personal. It becomes metaphor; yet, when such texts are read, they are once again personalized, assimilated somehow by the reader. How do readers interact with texts of trauma? How are the texts revised and adapted so that the reader can incorporate them into personal myth systems that do not include traumatic experience?

If we recognize the importance of the traumatic experience in the life of the writer, we are led to make critical distinctions between texts. This distinction is already a basic tenet of feminist literary criticism, which has foregrounded the nature of the text – "For feminists, the question of *how* we read is inextricably linked with the question of *what* we read."[63] We must carefully distinguish between texts written by the survivors of a particular trauma, and texts by writers who describe or detail traumatic situations they have not experienced. We must also seek to understand the meaning of the storytelling process to an individual writing after a traumatic experience.[64]

The basis for any interpretation of the literature of trauma is, therefore, an underlying theory that explains the human need to tell stories. Cognitive scientists Ann Weber, John Harvey, and Melinda Stanley claim, in their essay "The Nature and Motivations of Accounts for Failed Relationships," that people form accounts about failed relationships for six basic reasons:

1. *Preserving and protecting self-esteem.* Accounts provide "retrospective excuses" that masquerade as the past. By "reframing" their performances, storytellers can present themselves in "a more acceptable, socially approvable way."
2. *Emotional purging.* Storytelling allows people to detach from bad relationships or disturbing events by distancing and objectifying them, putting the pain and grief of the past behind them.
3. *Taking control of the past.* By generating their own version of events, storytellers can recreate the event so that previously uncontrollable forces are no longer mysterious. "We can after all retrospectively understand and make sense out of an experience that at the time must have seemed very senseless and ridiculous. A very painful experience can in retrospect be seen as one that has provided a valuable lesson or important moral."
4. *The search for closure.* "The importance of closure cannot be underestimated in terms of psychological comfort. . . ." Though life rarely provides neat endings, storytellers can use stories to provide what real

life cannot. In fact, storytellers may find their invented endings even more satisfactory than the events upon which their tales are based.

5. *Ongoing attributional activity.* We do not just decide to tell stories when an event is over. Storytelling is an ongoing process; we are always involved in telling the story of our lives. The process of revision, emendation, and addition is unending.

6. *Stories are ends in themselves.* Constructed out of memories and desires, stories take on their own separate existence. They can become important to the storyteller *as stories*, and may take any one of many forms: explanations, rationalizations, popular fictions, etc.[65]

The most important suggestion that cognitive science has to offer us is that every story has at its heart the *pursuit of goals*, i.e., there are purposes for telling the story. "In order to count as an acceptable story one must first establish a goal state, an end-point, or an event to be explained. . . . As adults we scarcely tolerate stories without established end-points, and these end-points are typically suffused with value."[66] The goals determine the selection of a story's events, reducing the candidates for inclusion to a manageable number.[67] It is essential for us to make the distinction between the relevant and the irrelevant because we are constantly deluged with an unmanageable amount of information. We include only the elements of a story that seem "relevant" to our purposes. Most of this process is automatic and unconscious.[68] Holocaust survivor, author, and critic Aharon Appelfeld supports this argument in his essay "After the Holocaust," in which he notes, "While the survivor recounts and reveals, at the very same time he also conceals."[69] He notes that all testimonial literature ought to be read with "caution," and with the understanding that survivor testimony "is first of all a search for relief. . . ."[70]

The goal of telling a story can be to hide information as well as to share it. As anthropologist Gregory Bateson explains, people have many mechanisms to avoid assimilating disturbing information:

> They are self-corrective against disturbance, and if the obvious is not of a kind that they can easily assimilate without internal disturbance, their self-corrective mechanisms work to sidetrack it, to hide it, even to the extent of shutting the eyes if necessary, or shutting off various parts of the process of perception. Disturbing information can be framed like a pearl so that it doesn't make a nuisance of itself; and this will be done, according to the understanding of the system itself of what would be a nuisance. This too – the premise regarding what would cause disturbance – is something which is learned and then becomes perpetuated or conserved.[71]

There is a sort of subconscious but intentional ignorance in operation in human beings. We do not notice a great deal of what we do not want to notice. What is disturbing can be ignored until (and often well after) it becomes dangerous to continue to ignore it. Bateson explains, "I, the conscious I, see an unconsciously edited version of a small percentage of what effects my retina."[72]

What happens when a traumatic event forces someone to "re-cognize" a disturbing reality? There is a transformation, a change in the terms of representation – even a revision of what constitutes an "event," both in perception and in storytelling. The chasm between those who have experienced trauma, who have been "disturbed," and those who have not is vast. Umberto Eco, in *The Name of the Rose*, sums up the problem in his portrait of traumatized youth: "'There was no plot,' said William, 'and I discovered it by mistake.'"[73]

Those of us whose perceptions remain essentially undisturbed must become aware of our tendency to filter out unpleasant realities. We would often prefer to generate comforting myths about traumatic experiences, rather than acknowledge the arbitrary nature of life. Holocaust scholar Terrence Des Pres, so perceptive in his understanding of the depth of the traumatic experience, cannot come to terms with the idea that the suffering of the Jews held no great meaning, and in a 1988 essay he regrets that, "Some of our best commentators . . . have declared outright that the Holocaust is without meaning, that it allows for no redeeming grace. . . ."[74] But another Holocaust scholar, Lawrence Langer warns us against generating comforting stories where the evidence does not, in fact, support our efforts: "When we use words to make us feel better, we cannot expect them simultaneously to help us *see* better. . . ."[75] To understand the trauma of the Holocaust (and, I will argue, in order to understand all man-made trauma[76]), Langer claims we must set aside our stories of the world, particularly our myths about survival. "The challenge before us is to move beyond the heroic enhancement of survival theories to the unheroic diminishment of men and women who are soiled by the situation they find themselves in, whether they live *or* die."[77]

The clearest point of access for untraumatized readers to the writings of survivors is through an understanding of clinical analysis of the effects of trauma on survivors. Reactions to specific traumas, including Holocaust, combat, rape, and incest, have been studied, catalogued, and discussed by the psychiatric establishment. Interest in the subject of trauma is so great that the psychiatric community supports organizations, such as the Society for the Study of Post Traumatic Stress, which are devoted entirely to understanding human response to trauma. The medical and psychiatric literature on trauma (especially war-related trauma) dates back more than 100 years.

Early theories of war-related trauma assumed that a traumatized soldier suffered a temporary inability to function brought on by an inherent weakness in his character or constitution. The innate "flaw" in the soldier explained why only certain men seemed to suffer "shell shock" or "battle fatigue" after combat. Much of the work on war-related trauma was done by military physicians, whose interest was in curing the symptoms of combat fatigue and sending a soldier out into the field to fight again. The growing popularity of Freudian psychiatry emphasized the idea that a man's reaction to combat trauma was determined by his character, and introduced the idea that early childhood experiences might have been responsible for his susceptibility to shell shock.[78]

Contemporary medical studies of trauma are no longer universally rooted in Freudian theory. Most begin with the observation that trauma places extraordinary stress upon an individual's ordinary coping mechanisms. While life is full of minor stresses that initiate defensive processes, major stresses (such as brutalization and threat to life) overcome an individual's normal defensive mechanisms.[79] The assessment and comparison of clinical pictures of survivors of traumatic events has enabled psychiatrists to construct a relatively clear picture of the symptoms specific to Post-Traumatic Stress Disorder (PTSD) – which replaced terms such as shell shock and battle fatigue, and thus acknowledged the connection between war-related trauma and other traumatic experiences such as rape, incest, incarceration in concentration camps, etc.[80]

In 1980, the American Psychiatric Association (APA) formally acknowledged the existence of "PTSD" in *Diagnostic and Statistical Manual of Mental Disorders III*. According to the APA, PTSD is a series of symptoms that follows a trauma "generally outside the range of usual human experience."[81]

> The characteristic symptoms include autonomic arousal, which is often manifest in panic attacks or startle reactions; a preoccupation with the traumatic event in the form of nightmares, flashbacks, or persistent thoughts about the trauma that intrude into everyday affairs; and a general dysphoria, a numbness that takes the meaning out of life and makes it hard to relate to other people. In [some] cases . . . the symptoms manifest themselves after a latency period of several years or . . . alternate with apparently asymptomatic periods that, on closer inspection, turned out to be periods of denial.[82]

Official recognition of PTSD was granted by the (mainly male) APA in response to public outcry about the disorder in Vietnam veterans (most of whom are also male). But the "unveiling" of PTSD is useful to feminist critics, who have searched for new ways to understand and interpret women's experience and its inscription in women's literature. Rape and incest are considered to be causes of PTSD, along with combat, violent crime, internment in POW or concentration camps, industrial accidents, and natural and man-made disasters.[83]

The large number of American women who have reported diffuse sets of anxiety-related symptoms have often been treated in an offhand manner by the medical profession as a whole. Women complaining of problems which psychiatrists now recognize as symptoms of PTSD have historically been treated with tranquilizers ranging from laudanum (an opiate) to Valium and other drugs, or dismissed as neurotics or hysterics. The medical establishment generally ordered them to come to terms with their femininity by getting married, having children, and learning to be a better mother.[84] The naming of PTSD as an illness acknowledges the often traumatic nature of women's experience. It provides us with a new analytic tool for the study of women's psychology and history.

Critic Alice Jardine argues that "struggle" is the characteristic that necessarily differentiates the feminist text from all others: "The *inscription* of struggle . . . whether written by a man or a woman – it was this that was found to be necessary. The *inscription of struggle* – even of *pain*."[85] Jardine suggests that the *struggle itself* marks a feminist endeavor – though a struggle's result might certainly be an antifeminist text. The inscription of struggle and pain is essential in much feminist literature, which is an indication that it may also be examined as literature of trauma. The struggle and its painful nature may be necessary precursors for the new knowledge that makes feminism possible. All feminist writers, in Jardine's estimation, have suffered, and then have struggled to express, trauma.

Can it be that *all* feminist literature is based in trauma? Perhaps not, but it is certainly a proposition to take seriously. Trauma has played a formative role in the lives of many, if not most American women. The relative number of women who have been traumatized far exceeds the number of men who have survived combat, or even the number of men who wore military uniforms during the Vietnam War era. As far back as 1973, the FBI estimated that in the U.S., a forcible rape occurs every 10 minutes.[86] It is generally acknowledged that official statistics are low, and authorities estimate that between 70 and 95% of all rapes go unreported.[87] Thus, *actual numbers* of sexual assault on females of all ages may reach half a million or more a year, or at least one every two minutes.[88] A 1988 study, administered on college campuses, found that 1 in 4 female respondents had been victims of rape or attempted rape. The survey noted that rape was "more common than left-handedness or heart attacks or alcoholism."[89] For women living in urban areas such as San Francisco, New York, or Chicago, the chance of being raped in their lifetime may be as high as 1 in 3.[90] When the APA states that the trauma which causes PTSD is "generally outside the range of usual human experience," it is clear that "usual human experience" means usual *white male* experience.

The most comprehensive study of incest and sexual abuse of young women suggests that 38% of American women have had at least one experience of incestuous and/or extrafamilial sexual abuse before reaching the age of eighteen.[91] These experiences involved actual sexual contact with a child. If broader definitions, which included attempted contact and exhibitionism, were applied, 54% of women age eighteen and under have been incestuously abused. These figures, combined with the statistics on rape of adult women, present a horrifying picture of a society where violence against women is the rule rather than the exception.

Literature of trauma is written from the need to tell and retell the story of the traumatic experience, to make it real both to the victim and to the community. Such writing serves both as validation and cathartic vehicle for the traumatized writer. Des Pres reminds us, "Displacement is the goal of any story, in degree; all fiction aims to usurp the real world with a world that is imagined."[92] Desires for affirmation and release cross subgenre lines, manifesting themselves in writings by combat veterans, holocaust survivors, and rape and incest survivors. They are also manifested in the work of many feminist writers who are not specifically identified (either by themselves or others) as trauma survivors.

Black poet and playwright Ntozake Shange has explained that her writing is based on her personal attempts to deal with a particular problem or issue. Catharsis, she claims, is at the heart of her writing:

> Obviously, I think it's important not to abort an emotional breakthrough. . . . Aborting emotional breakthroughs allows one to keep one's decorum at all moments. Our society allows people to be absolutely neurotic and totally out of touch with their feelings and everyone else's feelings, and yet be totally respectable. This, to me, is a travesty. So I write to get at the part of people's emotional lives that they don't have control over, the part that can and will respond. If I have to write about blood and babies dying, then fine, I'll write about that.[93]

Catharsis is also crucial to the healing of combat veterans with PTSD. Egendorf, Lifton, and other psychologists and psychiatrists insist on the importance of the reclamation of emotion in the process of overcoming the alienation characteristic in the disorder:

> Based on impressions from our research, a significant minority of Vietnam veterans have had moments of enlightenment, conversions, and other crucial points at which they turned traumatic experiences into sources of renewal. A review of Veterans' writings yields a similar impression. Most memoirs and novels deal with the war experience or with unsettling, if not traumatic, homecomings. A few accounts, however, focus on the struggles of healing, demonstrating that some portion of the veterans population knows what it means to turn suffering to joy.[94]

The theme of drawing together fragments into a whole is found again and again in the literature of trauma; re-piecing a shattered self. "I write," said Adrienne Rich, "for the still-fragmented parts in me, trying to bring them together. Whoever can read and use any of this, I write for them as well."[95] The metaphor of fragmentation is at the core of Vietnam veteran Stephen Wright's award-winning novel, *Meditations in Green*: "I had an amber vial then (50 DIAZEPAM Take As Required) in which I kept my fragments, my therapy. . . . I gathered lost cinders of shrapnel that rose surfacing in the milky pool of my thigh like broken bits of sea coral."[96] Each piece of shrapnel represents the surfacing of some repressed memory or idea. This is the true therapy, and it is fitting that Wright's protagonist places the fragments in a vial which once held anxiety suppressants.

Do not be taken in entirely by the similarities of theme in feminist literature and literature by Vietnam veterans. There is a crucial difference between the trauma of warriors and the trauma of rape and incest victims – due to the peculiar position of power of the warrior before, during, and after his traumatic wartime experience.

Soldiers, though subordinate to their military superiors and frequently at the mercy of their enemies, still possess a life-or-death power over other people. Victims of rape and incest experience violent injury but they are rarely in a position to do violence themselves. Much recent literature – popular, clinical, and academic – places the soldier simply in the victim's role; helpless in the face of war, and then helpless to readjust from the war experience upon his return home. Feminist critics should be quick to voice their disapproval of an interpretation so drastically at odds with reality. The soldier in combat is both victim and victimizer; dealing pain as well as receiving and experiencing it. Soldiers carry guns; they point them at people and shoot to kill.

"Soldier as victim" representations depend upon the invisibility of the soldiers' own victims, namely Vietnamese soldiers and civilians. These representations must also provide a convincing victimizer for the soldiers, e.g., inept or evil commanding officers, back-stabbing politicians, a traitorous Fourth Estate, or a callous and hostile American public. The purveyors of this myth have successfully peddled their wares to the moviegoing public in the form of violent retribution films (e.g., *Rambo*), as well as sensitive coming-of-age stories (e.g., *Platoon*). Many of the most popular Vietnam novels also reflect this attitude. James Webb's *Fields of Fire* blames the victimization of soldiers upon the antiwar movement, personified by effeminate intellectuals and faithless women.[97] John Del Vecchio's *The Thirteenth Valley* describes soldiers as mere pawns in the games of nations, fighting for their lives against nameless "enemies."[98] The general acceptance of this revision is apparent in public praise for the "healing" effect of the Vietnam War Memorial wall in Washington, D.C. – which includes the names of the American soldiers killed in Vietnam and excludes the names of any Vietnamese soldiers or civilians. It is further evident in the proliferation of belated and apologetic "homecoming parades" sponsored by cities and towns all over the U.S. in the months following the dedication of the memorial. These marches wed the idea that Vietnam veterans deserve honor for their patriotic sacrifice to the notion that they have been victimized and deprived of their due.

Despite his vulnerable position, a crucial aspect of the soldier's reality in Vietnam was the knowledge of the power he wielded. He had firepower, the power to bring death raining down in the form of bullets from his gun, fragments of his hand grenades, explosions from the mines he had set, and airstrikes called in to drop napalm, white phosphorus, and high-explosive bombs. Many personal narratives and novels feature a moment of epiphany, when the protagonist describes this realization of his godlike power over life and death and glories in it:

> He felt like Jehovah Himself, sitting on the bluff, calling down fear, death, and destruction on the poor dudes in the valley. . . . Between explosions he could hear the poor dumb fuckers on the other side going nuts, calling for their mothers, pleading for medics, cursing and shouting and trying to get their shit together. . . . "I love it!" he half-shouted over the crash of incoming shells. "Artillery is a beautiful thing once you learn to appreciate it."[99]

Women, by contrast, almost never control the tools of violence. Their traumatic experience – rape, incest, battering – is the most extreme form of the oppression visited on them by a society that generally reduces them to victims. Therein lies the most important difference between the trauma of the warrior and the trauma of the woman victim. Women view their trauma as a natural extension of powerlessness. Warriors are forced to realize the vulnerability of everything they have ever considered powerful.

The Western male consensus has been that power comes from the barrel of a gun. A vital American myth is that the good guys with guns beat the bad guys with guns. But in Vietnam, surrounded by their weapons, soldiers learned that guns and guts were not enough.

Again and again in Vietnam novels, the protagonist/narrator emphasizes the impossibility of distinguishing "friendly" civilians from National Liberation Front partisans. The soldier's desire to survive leads him to see all Vietnamese as the enemy, and to take the offensive whenever he has the opportunity. But violence is useless when everyone is your enemy. There is simply no place to hold and defend.

This situation reverses traditional notions of power. Americans had technology and firepower at their disposal but the real power lay with the Vietnamese Communists. The Vietnamese enemy could pick the time and place of a battle and then blend into the landscape. They were at home, could distinguish friend from foe, and, most important, know when they were safe from attack. The Americans could only be an alien and unwelcome presence in the landscape of Vietnam.

Individual soldiers reacted to this shock not with the self-condemnation and resignation of the victim, or with the anger of the oppressed, but with a deep sense of betrayal. *This was not the way it was supposed to be.* Narratives and novels by combat veterans emphasize the profound shock of the soldier's realization that their expectations about war were simply not compatible with reality.

Ron Kovic, a marine who was paralyzed from the chest down in Vietnam, described the trauma of shattered expectations in his memoir, *Born on the Fourth of July*. Kovic frequently used the third person to tell his own story, perhaps because the revelations were less painful when so distanced. In one instance, he writes about the accidental murder of one of his own men:

> I killed him, he kept thinking, and when I wake up tomorrow, he thought, when I wake up tomorrow it will still be the same. He wanted to run and hide. . . . He would wake up with the rest of them the next day. He would get up and wash outside the tent in his tin dish, he would shave and go to chow. But everything would not be all right, he thought, nothing would be all right at all. It was starting to be very different now, very different from what he had ever thought possible.[100]

"What we call traumatic responses," asserts Egendorf, "are the new strategies we concoct after being shocked into realizing that life doesn't play by our rules. When we can no longer pretend that life confirms our favored identity, we take on a negative version of our old self."[101]

Feminists have discussed similar transformations. Many early texts focused on women's need to overcome negative self-images generated by the inability of the individual woman to live up to an impossible social standard.[102] Much feminist work in the 1960s was directed at overcoming our culturally inculcated negative self-image, reclaiming anger and proclaiming our self-worth. We learned that even if we bought the myth of the "good girl," our favored identity would be betrayed at every turn. Conforming to traditional feminine roles was no protection against male violence, and stepping outside those roles was sure to bring trouble. We found that gender and power relationships were closely related, and that gaining power meant redefining ourselves *as women*.

Powerlessness, in Western culture, is most often equated with the feminine. Women are subject(ive); men are object(ive). To be a man is to be strong, in control of one's destiny; to be a woman is to be weak, to need guidance, to need protection.

Gender roles, though based on sex, are not necessarily determined by it. A man can lose his "manhood" if he is forced into submission, as black men were oppressed under slavery.[103] The soldier temporarily loses his manhood in boot camp. He is disempowered and thrust into a subordinate role, at times literally called a "girl" or a "pussy," until he completes the rites that win him a place in the community of soldiers, purged, apparently, of the last vestige of effeminacy.

But the soldier in Vietnam found himself in a traditionally "feminine" role. He was powerless against an enemy who struck whenever and wherever he wished. This second attack on manhood caused most combat soldiers to retreat even further from any indications of "femininity" in their own characters. They repressed emotions other than anger, avoided close relationships that involved caring or nurturing, and cultivated a callous attitude toward the feelings and humanity of others. This alienation was encouraged by the military system, which had established a training program geared to enhance combat effectiveness by reducing intimacy and grief of soldiers: "Both anti-grief and anti-intimacy were expressed by calling men who cried, or showed other signs of mourning, 'girls,' 'women,' 'ladies,' or 'hogs.' Men who showed intimacy to each other were often called 'fags.'"[104]

Soldiers valorized the trappings of masculinity, prided themselves on how "hard" they were, and articulated their alienation in the repetition of the phrases "it don't mean nothin'" and "there it is." Corporal Joker, in Gustav Hasford's powerful novel *The Short-Timers*, embodies the depths of the soldier's alienation, self-hatred and pain:

> Doing my John Wayne voice, I tell the squad a joke: "Stop me if you've heard this. There was a Marine of nuts and bolts, half robot – weird but true – whose every move was cut from pain as though from stone. His stony little hide had been crushed and broken. But he just laughed and said, 'I've been crushed and broken before.' And, sure enough, he had the heart of a bear. His heart weighed half a pound. . . . The world would not waste the heart of a bear, he said. On his clean blue pajamas many medals hung. He was a walking word of history, in the shop for a few repairs. He took it on the chin and was good. One night in Japan his life came out of his body – black – like a question mark. If you can keep your head while others are losing theirs perhaps you have misjudged the situation. Stop me if you've heard this. . . ."[105]

As feminist critics we must certainly not make the mistake of simplifying the soldiers' response to trauma. Women, after all, react to pain and oppression on many levels (and some of our reactions are contradictory). There is no reason to think that soldiers are less complex. It seems safe to assume that at the same time that the repression of the feminine was a denial of the soldiers' disempowered position, the bonding of soldier to soldier ("brotherhood") served as a method of creating community in a hostile world. Philip

Caputo wrote of the "intimacy of life in infantry battalion, where the communion between men" is more profound than any between lovers:

> It does not demand for its sustenance the reciprocity, the pledges of affection, the endless reassurances required by the love of men and women.... [I]t was a tenderness that would have been impossible if the war had been significantly less brutal. The battlefields of Vietnam were a crucible in which a generation of American soldiers were fused together by a common confrontation with death and a sharing of hardships, dangers, and fears. The very ugliness of the war, the sordidness of our daily lives, the degradation of having to take part in body counts made us draw still closer to one another. It was as if in comradeship we found an affirmation of life and the means to preserve at least a vestige of our humanity.[106]

The brotherhood of which almost all vets speak, the bond that holds the men who served in war together, is an uncanny reflection of the feelings of sisterhood often described by feminists. For soldiers, and later for veterans, this bonding was a way of coping, of creating a safe place in a hostile world, turning to each other for understanding and support. Given the state of gender relations in Western culture, Caputo's confession that the relationship he had with his men in wartime was more profound than any relationship he has ever had with a woman is unsurprising. What *is* fascinating about Caputo's claim is his description of men sharing tenderness and intimacy. Degradation and powerlessness seem to be the forces active in generating and shaping the relationships between soldiers. Men who are not under severe stress rarely form strong bonds of affection, or reach toward each other for emotional support. The act of caring functions as "the means to preserve ... a vestige of our humanity."

Not only did veterans face some of the same problems of poor self-image and perceived powerlessness as women traditionally face, some also recognized that healing would involve some new understanding of masculinity and femininity. It is no accident that the self-therapy rap groups begun by Vietnam veterans in the late 1960s were modeled on the consciousness-raising groups of the women's movement. Egendorf comments:

> We had come home weary, wanting to be taken care of, and women were no longer waiting as they had before. Many of the women we met – on campuses, in demonstrations, and through friends – were locked in battles of their own, campaigning for new rights, against exclusive male prerogatives.... Although we needed women more than ever, and feared them more as well, we looked to them for leadership in a way

that would have been unthinkable a short time before. We had the women's movement as a constant example, with their use of consciousness-raising groups as a major organizing tool. In the way we described them, the veteran rap groups were clearly inspired by women's groups. . . .[107]

While women were working on reclaiming anger and learning to assert themselves, Vietnam veterans were working hard at discovering within themselves the capacity to be gentle, supportive, and caring.

I do not mean to suggest that Vietnam veterans were intent on revising gender roles; nor do I intend to argue that these veterans are or were feminists. One need only read the literature of the Vietnam War to be convinced that veterans are no more likely to have enlightened attitudes about women than are any other class of men. I do want to point out, however, that the process which these men were going through on the way toward social reintegration is similar to the process of feminist consciousness-raising. That similarity is born, I assert, out of the commonality of trauma.

Teresa De Lauretis insists that the redefinition of the boundaries of the political is at the heart of the difference between feminism and other modes of critical thinking. Feminism "defines itself as a political instance . . . a politics of experience, of everyday life, which later then in turn enters the public sphere of expression and creative practice, displacing aesthetic hierarchies and generic categories, and which thus establishes the semiotic ground for a different production of reference and meaning."[108]

The mixing of personal and political is also a crucial aspect of the narratives of Vietnam veterans. But for the veterans who write these narratives (white males, for the most part) the trick is in mixing the political with the personal, rather than the other way around. Unlike women, American men have never been herded out of the political sphere; it is, in fact, their natural environment. For soldiers, Vietnam War trauma was exacerbated by their sudden, uncomfortable realization of just how personal politics could get. Their own politics (or some other white man's) had forced them into facing the strong possibility of death or terrible injury. The radical nature of this understanding is evident in the words and actions of Vietnam veterans who decided to protest against the war.

Using personal experience as political condemnation, some veterans began displaying their wounded bodies at antiwar rallies, rejecting the medals and commendations of the military, and publicly testifying to atrocities they had witnessed or committed in Vietnam.[109] These men were attempting to retell the past, "to inscribe into the picture of reality characters and events and resolutions that were previously invisible, untold, unspoken (and so unthinkable, unimaginable, 'impossible')."[110] Through bitter experience many

Vietnam veterans now know that the man with a gun can be painfully weak. Some veterans, in their journey toward healing from the war, have begun to understand the drawbacks of a society based upon the use of violent, coercive power.

Integration of the personal and political for men seems to involve a displacement of the locus of power. "Healing," states Arthur Egendorf, "occurs through an alternative expression of power, one that creates empowerment."

> To empower means to enhance another's power, something that happens as others come to see themselves as competent, as not missing anything essential, as already intact. Bringing people to this view is possible only if we already see them that way. Empowerment begins and ends with seeing others as already able and whole.[111]

In Egendorf's construction, healing is both personal and political – it involves individual psychological work as well as *social* work. Political activism is an essential component of the healing process – the recovering trauma survivor seeks *change*.

The first psychologists and psychiatrists to urge recognition of the psychological effects of traumatic stress on the Vietnam veteran population were, like Egendorf and Chaim Shatan, themselves activists, often associated with the radical Vietnam Vets Against the War and "were characterized by critics as 'crackpot, self-serving psychologists and psychiatrists who were probably all against the war anyway and were only looking for a surefire way to get some money out of the Veterans Administration.'"[112] It is ironic that the misrepresentation of these pioneering psychologist-activists would provide an accurate prediction of the post-traumatic stress industry which was to develop, mostly funded by money from the Veterans' Administration. Richard Fuller attributes the successful institutionalization of post-traumatic stress syndrome directly to the Watergate affair, which ushered in a new set of liberal Congressional representatives who eventually influenced the Veteran's Administration. Fuller explains, in 1985, that there are

> 55 members of the House who served in the military during the Vietnam era. Within the context of the "New Politics" in Congress, they banded together to form a coalition to isolate those issues of most concern to Vietnam veterans and to pressure the authorizing committees on these points when momentum seemed lax. As a group they represent a formidable force of influence for the legislative activity of the Veterans Affairs Committees in the House and Senate. Readjustment counseling and post-traumatic stress disorder became one of their top priorities.[113]

In addition to Congressional influence on the Veteran's Administration, the

demographic pressures exerted by Vietnam veterans began to influence traditional veterans organizations. President Carter fell in step with the liberal rhetoric and helped establish the Veterans Readjustment Counseling program:

> The media blitz which accompanied the opening of the 91 Storefront
> Counseling Centers, charged with the responsibility for dealing with
> post-traumatic stress disorder, was unprecedented in recent VA. his-
> tory. This positive attention surprised both proponents and detractors
> of the program. Vet Centers became a rallying point for Vietnam vet-
> erans across the country. Politicians jumped to cut the ribbons at
> Center openings. . . . The Centers and the program had identified an
> entire patient population that the Veterans Administration had not
> previously known to exist.[114]

The American veterans of the Vietnam War were recreated in a new image:
that of the "patient." The broad application of the PTSD diagnosis is evident
in the *Report of Findings from the National Vietnam Veterans Readjustment Study,*
which claims that "over the course of their lives, more than half . . . of male
theater veterans and nearly half . . . of female theater veterans have experienced clinically significant stress-reaction symptoms. This represents about
1.7 million veterans of the Vietnam War."[115]

Though we may be confounded by angry activist Vietnam vets marching
in the streets and hurling their medals back at the government that awarded
them, we are quite clear on what to do with "patients" – we place them under
the care of experts and we "treat" them, with therapy or drugs. We continue
the therapy until they are "healed." Dr. Charles Figley, the founding editor
of the *Journal of Traumatic Stress,* and a powerful force in the Society for
Traumatic Stress Studies, which was founded in 1985, describes the process:

> [A] trauma victim is a person who, in the process of recovering and
> working through the traumatic experiences struggles to make sense out
> of the memories of the traumatic event. Recovery is to eventually accept
> them and be able to face the possibility that something else like it may
> happen again. A trauma *survivor* is one who has successfully worked
> through and made peace with his or her traumatic memories.[116]

In contemporary, institutionalized forms of treatment for PTSD, the crucial
components of "recovery" are the decision to relinquish anger and to accept
the status quo. Making "peace" is learning to accept the world as it is. The
successfully "cured" posttraumatic stress patient is no revolutionary. Clini-
cians have a vested interest in the revisionary process by which a victim
recreates and reinterprets his or her memories until they take a manageable
form. For a clinician, the patient who cannot make peace with his or her
memories represents a failure of the psychotherapeutic process. The alter-

native view – as put forward by, for example, Lawrence Langer – is that the creation of the traumatized victim represents a *failure in the world*.

The conservatism of the current consensus on PTSD treatment promoted in the establishment psychiatric community is most obvious when we contrast its insistence on the doctor/patient dichotomy and its emphasis on interpretation and prescription with the radical antiexpert stance of the pioneers of the early veterans' rap groups. Lifton claims that when he and other professional therapists became involved with the consciousness-raising workshops of the veteran's antiwar movement

> . . . there was an assumption, at first unspoken and later articulated, that everybody's life was at issue; professionals had no special podium from which to avoid self-examination. We too could be challenged, questioned about anything – all of which seemed natural enough to the veterans but was a bit more problematic for the professionals. As people used to interpreting others' motivations, it was at first a bit jarring to be confronted with hard questions about our own and with challenges about the way we lived. Not only was our willingness to share this kind of involvement crucial to the progress of the group, but in the end many of us among the professionals came to value and enjoy this kind of dialogue.[117]

Lifton cautions us as early as 1976 that the "radical" possibilities of the early rap groups could easily be turned to conservative functions, that instead of creating "alternative institutions," they could be absorbed by existing institutions: "In this and other ways the rap group experience seemed to me a mirror of psychohistorical struggles of considerable importance throughout the society."[118] Bearing witness is always a double-edged sword. The rap group provided a forum in which the testimony of individuals could be reinterpreted and revised into a consensus testimony of victim–survivors, but as Lifton reminds us, the particular revision generated depends entirely upon the social and historical context in which it is generated.

I do not for a moment wish to dismiss the serious psychological and physiological effects that traumatic stress induces in those who survive it. Rather, I would like to briefly explore the manner in which those effects have been interpreted and represented to the society at large, and to the traumatized individual – interpretations and representations that are self-reflexive, so that "science" and popular culture become impossible to distinguish from one another. I take as my example a psychology text, *Vietnam: A Casebook*, edited by Jacob Lindy and published as Volume 10 in the prestigious Brunner/Mazel Psychosocial Stress Series (1987). Though this volume is intended as "a clinical book written for mental health professionals" it is strikingly and immediately infused with metaphor and literary allusion, beginning with its introductory sentence: "Vietnam intrudes as a recurrent nightmare searing the American consciousness."[119] In the second sentence we are told that "we resemble Faulkner's characters in *The Sound and the Fury*," locating us within an existing story. And lest we fail to grasp the primacy of the narrative venture, we are clearly instructed in the second paragraph that this text is:

> A story . . . in the here and now of two people constituting a therapeutic dyad, of their struggle to comprehend, to find mutual metaphor, and to communicate their understanding to each other. This is also the story of powerful happenings in the lives of young men, of political and military events now 12 to 15 years past. And finally it is a scientific venture – one which sets out to measure differing components of post-traumatic stress and to test the relative efficacy of a given method in the treatment of this disorder in survivors of war trauma.[120]

Though the storytelling venture is quite explicit, it seems also to thoughtlessly incorporate the stock elements that comprise the normative, pop culture interpretation of the Vietnam War "experience" – enemies who were indistinguishable from "friendlies"; women combatants; booby trapped children; the hostility of the antiwar movement. Nowhere in this casebook is there any evidence that the psychologists involved in working with Vietnam veterans are interested in exploring the limitations of their own knowledge of the war, or in asking themselves the question: How do we know what we know about the Vietnam War?

The therapists who record the cases in this book make common reference to book and movie plots as clues to understanding their patients:

> As Abraham's [pseudonym for the vet] tale unfolded, I felt a kinship with the narrator in Joseph Conrad's *Heart of Darkness*, who became increasingly and then passionately curious in his pursuit of the enigmatic and elusive Mr. Kurtz. Conrad shows us that to find a "Kurtz" and to know him is to plumb the depths of the human soul, the other's as well as one's own, though the journey be hazardous and uncharted. I glimpsed the horror and despair behind Abraham's vacant look. I wanted to know and understand this man and his story.[121]

Abraham's therapist assumes that Abraham has a "story" – that there's a plot to his life which is somehow comparable to the plot in Conrad's novel. Furthermore, the linkage between Conrad's *Heart of Darkness* and Abraham's Vietnam War experience is almost certainly a product of the therapist's familiarity with Coppola's film, *Apocalypse Now*, which revises Conrad's novel and stages it in Vietnam and Cambodia, uniting Conrad's text and the Vietnam War forever in the imagination of the American viewing public. Coppola's revision of Conrad's novel finds its parallel in the therapist's revision of the "real" story of Abraham – the therapist's ability to "read" Abraham's experience is limited by the framework within which he chooses to interpret it. What he sees in Abraham's eyes is "the horror" of Marlon Brando, playing Kurtz, as directed by Coppola interpreting Conrad, who wrote the fiction upon which this interpretive tree took root. Unaware of the existence of these filters, the psychiatrist assumes that his access to Abraham is unmediated.

Another therapist commences his case history with a reference to Steinbeck's *East of Eden*:

> In *East of Eden*, Steinbeck's Cyrus advises his sensitive son, Adam, to become a soldier.... Yet Cyrus chooses not to let his other, more aggressive son, Charles, go into the military.... Although I doubt there were any carefully discriminating Cyruses, Vietnam had both its Adams and its Charleses. My patient was an Adam....[122]

This kind of typecasting limits the ability of the therapist to actually see and hear the patient, allowing him or her to rely, instead, on a kind of shorthand, on the ability to "read" the patient as if the existence of a life story with a plot was actually possible. And plots are not drawn only from classics such *Heart of Darkness* or *East of Eden*, but also from pop culture books and films specifically about the Vietnam War. In still another case history, a therapist explains how he uses Cimino's *The Deerhunter* as a therapeutic tool:

> After meeting with him [Vietnam veteran "Vince"] for only a few sessions, I found that the powerful message of Michael Cimino's *The Deerhunter* became a reality to me. Ongoing knowledge and understanding of Vince brought to mind all of the movie's central players, characters who demonstrate both immediate reactions to overwhelming combat experience and those devastating aftereffects which we classify as PTSD. The metaphor of the movie became a most useful one in furthering Vince's understanding of his Vietnam experience.[123]

By rereading his Vietnam War experience through a preexisting, "approved" text, Vince is urged to revise his self-image so that it fits *The Deerhunter*'s plot. The idea that a therapist would be willing to replace Vince's confusion and anguish with Cimino's completely fantastic vision is incredible on its face, and its implications are chilling. As memory is progressively revised to imitate art, a process similar to petrifaction takes place, in which "reality" is gradually replaced by symbol. In Vince's case, this petrifaction is so advanced that the therapist is moved to compare Vince's traumatic memory of shooting a Viet Cong woman (which, when reenacted, seems to produce further violent impulses), to the actions of the character of Nick (played by Christopher Walken) in *The Deerhunter*:

The potential "compulsion to repeat" reminded me of the character of Nick in *The Deerhunter*, who at the war's end was continually playing Russian roulette, putting the revolver to his head as he had been forced to by the enemy earlier in the war.[124]

In the therapist's eyes, Vince's urge to "stick a gun" in another person's face is equivalent to the "compulsion" of the fictional character, Nick, to risk his own life in endless games of Russian roulette – even though the make-believe Nick's actions are entirely contrived in order to carry out Cimino's plot line. This sort of "therapy" fails to distinguish between psychological impulse and plot device, and forces the patient to rearticulate his experience within popularly accepted genre formats. That the patient may already be looking for answers within these genre formats only exacerbates the problem:

> It was still early in the therapy when Vince and I began to use the movie *The Deerhunter* as a way of approaching his intense fear of mutilation and death. In an unconscious effort to master his unresolved war trauma, he had been, almost perversely, drawn to movies and television shows about the Vietnam War and war in general. He had seen *The Deerhunter* on several occasions and knew the movie well. He had never, however, translated its central message into an explanation which could be helpful to him.[125]

Such reliance on genre conventions also leads to glib interpretations, or "readings" of the patient's "story" based on the therapist's assumption that film and other pop culture artifacts provide access – apparently without mediation – to the traumatic experiences of war:

> The Russian roulette scenes [in *The Deerhunter*] not only shock, they revolt us. As we live through these events with celluloid heroes, we either face the terror of war or we tune it out. Yet this terror is just what Vince and thousands of other combat veterans have been through on many occasions, and often for extended periods. I pointed out to Vince that the war and the enemy were as unrelenting and barbarous as the vicious guard in charge of the roulette game, that he, like the prisoners, was frequently one shot or one inch away from mutilation and death, and that the tension of being so close so often was essentially unmanageable and needed discharge. This movie, I said, explained some of what he had been doing since the war.[126]

As Michael Anderegg notes in his introduction to *Inventing Vietnam: The War in Film and Television* (1991), "Cinematic representations, in short, seem to have supplanted even so-called factual analyses as *the* discourse of the war, as the place where some kind of reckoning will need to be made and tested."[127] The truth of this is brought home with stunning clarity in the passage quoted above, in which a legitimate and respected psychotherapist unselfconsciously articulates, for an audience of his professional peers, the belief that a dramatic film can serve as both model for and explanation of the thoughts and actions of a flesh and blood human being.

The Deerhunter, described by John Hellman as a film that "presents Vietnam as yet another historic projection of an internal struggle of white American consciousness,"[128] is firmly rooted in the conventions of the Hollywood western. Its hero, Michael (Robert DeNiro), critic Leonard Quart argues, belongs to "a long tradition of literary and cinematic heroes – from Bumppo to Dirty Harry – who live according to an individualist code which has its roots in a mythicized past."[129] The therapist's confusion of life and artifice seems incredible until one remembers the foundation of the psychotherapeutic model – the talking cure – which is interpretation of the "story" told by the patient. The limitations of psychoanalytic theory become clear as we examine its failure to account for atrocity – a problem most fully explored by Klaus Theweleit in his ground-breaking study of fascist thought, *Male Fantasies* (1977). Theweleit writes that most psychoanalytic theories fail even to address the subject of atrocity, and that those theories which do attempt to engage the problem of "irrational" acts of violence and persecution do so by recreating those acts as "representative" or symbolic:

> The problem here is that, too often, fascism tends to become representational, symbolic. In the commonplace attenuated version of psychoanalytic theory that most of us have unthinkingly accepted, fascism is "really" about something else – for example, repressed homosexuality. Fascist murder becomes a misdirected way of getting at that "something else" – a symbolic act, if not a variety of performance art.[130]

The violent and traumatic acts described by the patient are always interpreted by the psychotherapists who pen these case studies, as representing "something else."

Part of the problem lies in the therapist's own difficulties in wrestling with and coming to terms with the patient's "story." Sarah Haley, a pioneer in the field of posttraumatic stress studies, explains that she had a very difficult time coping with the stories told to her by "Mark," a Vietnam veteran with a high combat history and a severe case of PTSD:

> As a therapist who had evaluated, treated or supervised the treatment of nearly 100 combat veterans and who felt she had "heard it all," I was not prepared for the descent into psychic hell that awaited me. As in Philip Caputo's *Rumor of War*, I felt myself being dragged, kicking and screaming for release down every jungle trail, burned out village, and terrorizing night patrol until the thin line between control and its loss, between combat killing and murder/atrocities, had been crossed. The veteran's

combat nightmares, night terrors and startle responses which had
plagued him since his return from Vietnam and which he had heretofore told no one were alive and shared in the treatment hours. I came
to dread those hours, to have sleepless nights before them, and often an
episode of crying or dry heaves following them.[131]

Haley's distress is clear, but in her case history she details the process of
therapy in a manner strongly reminiscent of a classic love story, reworking
Mark's experience and her interactions with him along romance genre lines.
Mark is "handsome." As the healing process progresses, he leaves behind a
destructive "sadomasochistic" marriage, and transfers his affections to his
therapist – a hopeless love in the romantic tradition. Finally (though the
transformation is poorly described), Mark returns to sanity, and, his eyes
"clear," he presents his new (proper) love object to Haley, presumably for her
blessing, and goes forth into the world, healed.

The move from interpretation to appropriation of a veteran's story is
apparent in the work of at least one psychotherapist featured in the Lindy text.
The therapist treating Abraham confessed to a wish-fulfillment male-bonding
fantasy which, in its contours, strongly resembles the manner in which most
male critics of Vietnam War literature enter the discourse by virtue of their
masculinity, and thus become vicariously "one of the boys." After concluding
a therapeutic relationship with Abraham, the therapist remarks:

I, too, felt sad knowing I might never see Abraham again. A fantasy
entered my mind. It was sometime in the future. A war was going on
and Abraham and I were comrades in arms, fighting together under
dangerous and precarious circumstances. We sustained and supported
each other. Somehow, I knew, we'd both come through all right and
remain buddies for life.[132]

The "successful" conclusion of therapy seems to require that the myth of the
warrior is reinstated – at least in the mind of the therapist, and perhaps at the
expense of the patient.

Revision of veteran experience to conform to the requirements of popular
culture mythology (from which many psychotherapists seem to derive their
understanding of the Vietnam War) requires a suspension of judgment on the
part of the therapist that often moves beyond the absurd and into the realm
of the obscene:

As therapy progressed, I began to see that Vince's "senseless" killings [in
Vietnam], sometimes of innocent people, had grown out of desire for
revenge and a need to discharge unmanageable tension. . . . Once Vince
began to understand his own rage and his desire for vengeance, he not
only could see why he had participated in these actions but could begin
to forgive himself. And my helping him develop that understanding let

him see that I too understood and that therefore other people would as well.[133]

Just as the Vietnam War depicted by Cimino in *The Deerhunter* "is a charnel house where good guys struggle with bad ones to survive, rather than a war determined by social ideology, Cold War politics, and nationalism,"[134] the Vietnam War described by the therapist exists only in terms of the subjective experience presumably survived by the veteran patient – a subjective experience mediated first by the patient's ability to describe the events of the war, and then by the interpretive structure of the therapist. Only in a completely depoliticized environment – one in which no critical inquiry was possible – could Vince's status as a Vietnam veteran entitle him to unconditional "forgiveness," even for acts of " 'senseless' killing." This same suspension of judgment is manifest in the comments of Marshall's therapist, who explains away an incident in which his patient stands up, points his finger at his therapist's forehead, and exclaims: "Click. I just walked up to that five-year-old child, pointed my revolver at his head, and blew it off. Then I sat down and continued with my lunch. There's no way you will ever understand that."[135] Instead of dealing with the fact that his patient has murdered a five-year-old-child, the therapist maintains his "composure" and answers:

> I said I had listened to many Vietnam veterans; that I understood how children could be dangerous; that in this kind of guerrilla warfare, as absurd as it may have sounded, such actions against children were sometimes necessary for survival. . . . In response to the tacit question Marshall asked in pointing the gun ("Are you one of us?"), I needed to answer very specifically, "Yes, I am."[136]

The sympathy these therapists have for their combat veteran patients is quite clear, and it resonates strongly with the sympathy (and the sense of superiority) demonstrated by Dori Laub in his discussions of his Holocaust survivor patients. But the suspension of judgment requires that we recreate the survivor as no more than a victim, a pawn without agency, caught up all unwilling in a vicious game of Russian roulette. The political nature of such "stories" of victimization is most apparent if we place a Nazi SS trooper on the therapist's couch. How many American therapists would hastily urge him to forgive himself? How many would, in response to his "tacit question," answer, "Yes, I am one of you."

The problem here is not in the therapeutic *mechanism* (the *process* by which a patient and therapist work together to assist the patient in becoming self-conscious) but in the therapist's failure to recognize the inherent biases of his or her interpretive structure. These therapeutic strategies are supported by an ideological structure and a political agenda that go without saying and are often unconsciously absorbed by the therapist who does not trouble himself to ask the question: "How do I know what I know about the Vietnam war?" A different set of ideological assumptions might lead to the creation of a therapeutic environment in which the goal was to urge the patient to radical *action* (to *change* the world), rather than to urge him or her to accept the status quo. This alternative perspective is suggested in the next two chapters, which deal with the feminist community's response to the testimony of rape and incest survivors.

6

We Didn't Know What Would Happen

Opening the Discourse on Incest and Sexual Abuse

We didn't exactly expect the world would say, "Oh. Glad you told us. We'll just cut that out." We didn't know what would happen. But (watch out, world) we were going to give it our finest try.[1]

– Louise Armstrong

On October 23, 1990, in a speech delivered at the Republican fundraising breakfast in Burlington, Vermont, George Bush countered the cries of anti-war protesters ("No War for Oil!") by explaining that U.S. intervention in the Persian Gulf was not motivated by economic interests. Instead, he claimed, it was the result of a chivalric impulse to put a halt to "the rape and the systematic dismantling of Kuwait," an event so terrible it "defies description." The metaphor of rape runs consistently through Bush's speeches on the war, braided neatly into his references to Hussein's similarity to Hitler, and the need for the United States to move past the "Vietnam syndrome." It is not the rape of the bodies of Kuwaiti women to which Bush refers, but the rape of the body politic, the foreign invasion (penetration) of a prostrate and femi-nized Kuwait by the brutal Iraqi military who are themselves an extension (an organ) of the demonic Hussein.

The evocation of rape as justification for use of force against an enemy "other" (particularly as justification for vigilante action) is an American tradi-tion so entrenched it barely needs to be described. One might nod in the direction of the early American captivity narratives (describing the expe-riences of white women abducted by Native Americans) and gesture at the literature of hysteria emanating from the American South (depicting an insatiable and lascivious black masculinity ever in search of virginal white maidens to despoil) and tip a cap to the anti-Japanese propaganda emanating from the pens of the patriotic press during World War II, but one would be just barely scratching the surface of a preoccupation with rape metaphor so firmly embedded in the national psyche that it almost always goes without saying.

Bush's speeches on Kuwait contain a litany of accusations of "rape, pillage, and plunder," and "unspeakable atrocities" that evoked a knee-jerk response in his U.S. audiences.[2] We respond to the notion of the violated "body" of Kuwait, but we did not expect to hear her voice. The story of the raped female body is quite literally assumed to be "unspeakable." Rape was originally conceived of as a crime against property – women were presumed to belong to particular men (fathers, brothers, husbands) who had an interest in their reproductive life and financial worth – and the raped woman was always spoken *for*. At issue in a rape case was a woman's lowered value (as "damaged goods") and the loss of face suffered by an owner who could not protect (or who could not control) his property.[3] The claim that women have a right to be protected from rape as *persons* is a recent development in Western history. The notion that female voices are worthy of being heard and evaluated on their own merits, rather than dismissed out of hand, is also relatively new. The testimony of rape survivors undermines the basis of rape-as-property-violation metaphors (in which category one must include Bush's reference to Kuwait – a country in which we appear to have strong economic interests), and is thus both threatening and politically subversive. Testimony of sexual abuse survivors differs from the other survivor testimonies examined in this book in an important way: The women who bear witness to these atrocities are still at risk, as all women are at risk, in contemporary America. As sociologist Anthony Wilden explains: "The ever-present threat of male violence against women is a ruthless assault on women's freedom to think and do and be as they are and run their own lives. The threat of rape makes growing up a recognition of subordination and life a state of siege."[4]

The feminist movement of the 1960s and 1970s created an atmosphere in which it was possible for some women to begin to talk about sexual assault among themselves, and to begin to connect that assault to political, racial, economic and social issues within the framework of the patriarchal system in which they lived. Susan Brownmiller's pioneering work, *Against Our Will: Men, Women and Rape* (1975) clearly articulated the connection between sexual assault and political, racial, and economic oppression.[5] Three years later, the first mass market volume of incest narratives was published – Louise Armstrong's *Kiss Daddy Goodnight* (1978).[6] There are thousands of Holocaust narratives, and hundreds of Vietnam War narratives, but when I began my research on the subject of sexual abuse testimonial literature in 1989, I was able to turn up fewer than a dozen autobiographies that could be defined as self-conscious sexual assault narratives.[7] Now the situation has changed: dozens of these narratives and shelves of self-help books are published by survivors and their supporters every year.

The first editions of incest and rape narratives were published in the mid to late 1970s and the early 1980s. They were a product of the feminist consciousness which was fostered by the women's movement, and their appearance marked a new stage in the production of personal narratives by American women. The narratives of female sexual abuse survivors bore witness to the fact that violence was perpetrated systematically and regularly by American men upon American women in a society that supported the oppression and subjugation of women.

The women who contributed to and edited the early sexual abuse survivor narratives were dedicated to revealing the atrocities committed in our midst. Determined to break the silence that shrouded incest and rape, they believed that if they spoke out, women all over the country would become enraged and empowered, and would move to challenge the laws and social conditions that protected sexually abusive men. Courageous and hopeful, they gathered together in small groups to talk to each other, to participate in writer's workshops, and to publish their testimonies. They operated under a dual burden – first they needed to convince their audience that sexual abuse was a widespread and pressing problem; only then could they successfully testify to their personal experience as a sexual abuse survivor.

Like most of the participants in the women's movement, the active members of the sexual abuse survivor communities were predominantly white and middle class. Their narrow perspective, combined with the thoughtless racism and ethnocentrism of much feminist activism of the period, resulted in a movement in which white women were overrepresented. When the first anthologies of sexual abuse survivor testimony appeared, narratives by women of color were ignored, decontextualized or appropriated. Though this was arguably not the intent of the anthologizers, their exclusion of women of color as *speaking voices* served to reinscribe patterns of discrimination already present in the culture, marginalizing or "disappearing" the testimonies of these women at the same time they contributed to a "whitinizing" or deracializing of the "normative" sexual abuse narrative.

When this book was completed in 1994, there was, to my knowledge, only one book-length example of sexual assault literature by a woman of color – Carolivia Herron's *Thereafter Johnnie* (1991) – a book which I believe it is worth a short digression to introduce to the reader, since the reception Herron's novel received was in part determined by the foundation laid by the (white) feminists who comprised the activist community of sexual abuse survivors. *Thereafter Johnnie* is based in Herron's own emerging memories of childhood incest. It is the first novel of an already accomplished scholar. By the age of 43, Herron was an associate professor at Mt. Holyoke, a Bunting Fellow at Radcliffe College, a fellow at both the Beinecke Library and Folger Shakespeare Library, a Fulbright Fellow and the director of the Epicenter for the Study of Comparative Epics at Harvard. Her edited collection of the letters of black abolitionist Angelina Grimké came out the same year as *Thereafter Johnnie,* published by Oxford University Press. After her novel was released, reviews reported that Herron's three-volume work, *African-American Epic Tradition* was forthcoming.

Despite Herron's status as an African-Americanist scholar of epic tradition, and despite her explicit claim that *Thereafter Johnnie* was based on "a classical epic structure of twenty four books," few reviewers made the connection between Herron's work and an African-American literary tradition.[8] The glaring exception to this rule was a careful and thoughtful essay by *New York Times* writer John Bierhorst, a folklorist and student of myth, who, in the one page allotted him, compared Herron's work to a range of traditional literature, from Genesis and Revelations, to the Odyssey and the Grail narrative, and to African-American folk tales such as "The People Could Fly," and spirituals like "This Little Light of Mine."[9] A few other critics superficially compared Herron's novel to classical epics, either favorably or poorly, but none entertained the notion that *Thereafter Johnnie* might mark a serious attempt on the part of an African-American lesbian survivor of childhood sexual abuse to revise the mythology that contributed to her oppression.

While examining the reviews of *Thereafter Johnnie,* I found myself turning again and again to Mary Helen Washington's essay about Gwen Brooks' autobiographical novel, *Maud Martha.* Washington suggests that the trivialization of Brooks' novel – despite her renown as a poet – was due to the fact that

> [I]n 1953 no one seemed prepared to call *Maud Martha* a novel about bitterness, rage, self-hatred and the silence that results from suppressed anger. No one recognized it as a novel dealing with the very sexism and racism that these reviews enshrined. What the reviewers saw as exquisite lyricism was actually the truncated stutterings of a woman whose rage makes her literally unable to speak.[10]

Reviewers of *Thereafter Johnnie* did focus on Herron's "lyricism," whether they saw it as contrived and "grandiose"[11] or "swirling and terrifying."[12] But in 1992, the notion that a novel by a black woman writer is about "bitterness, rage, self-hatred and the silence that results from suppressed anger" is common enough to go without saying. What surprised the reviewers of *Thereafter Johnnie* is the apparent "universality" of Herron's tale, which Richard Eder called "a story for our times about a black family so exceptional as to have a story that might as well be that of a fashionably troubled upper-middle-class white family."[13]

Herron explicitly locates her work in a continuum of testimony to atrocity, bearing witness to the crimes of rape and incest:

I am . . . a representative of 10 to 20 million people in this country – the adult survivors of childhood sexual abuse. . . . We aren't hiding any-more that we are victims. I think people should be asking why any culture or people would want to hide such a thing. . . . We're going to keep talking until you believe.[14]

But she is also located in the continuum of black women writers described by bell hooks:

. . . cultural production can and does play a healing role in people's lives. It can be a catalyst for them to begin the project of self-recovery. That's how many readers experienced Alice Walker's novel *The Color Purple*, and Toni Morrison's *The Bluest Eye* and/or *Beloved*. Certainly two books that really set me thinking about the ways in which black people can approach the issue of self-recovery are Paule Marshall's *Praisesong for the Widow* and Gloria Naylor's *Mama Day*.[15]

In an interview with *Washington Post* reporter Donna Britt, Herron said, "There is a connection between this text and my own life," and explained that she was engaged in the process of "converting life into art," and that "art has saved my own life." The conversion of life into art is often the explicit task of the African-American author, and Herron, as both literary critic and creative writer, has self-consciously drawn upon the traditions established by generations of African-American storytellers, and particularly upon the texts produced by black women writers who, in the words of Susan Willis, "en-vision transformed human social relationships and the alternative futures these might shape."[16]

Mainstream reviews of *Thereafter Johnnie* steadfastly refused to connect the work to the traditions of African-American women writing, *despite* Herron's acknowledged interest and expertise in the African-American epic. Sally Emerson, of the *Washington Post* compares Herron's work (unfavorably) to James Joyce's distinctly Anglocentric epic *Ulysses*. Richard Eder of the *Los Angeles Times* remarks that Herron draws upon a Biblical or "mystical tradi-tion" without reference to a single other author to which her work might be compared.

Mary Helen Washington describes the invisibility of the black woman in the 1950s using as her example critics' failure to connect *Maud Martha* to a black, female literary tradition. Her critique can as easily be extended to include the reception of Herron's novel, which was published in 1991: "Not one of these reviewers could place *Maud Martha* in the tradition of Zora Neale Hurston's *Their Eyes Were Watching God* (1937), Dorothy West's *The Living is*

Easy (1948) or Nella Larsen's *Quicksand* (1928)."[17] Nor, apparently, can they place *Thereafter Johnnie* in such a tradition, or even make the connection between Carolivia Herron and other contemporary black women writers such as Alice Walker, Toni Morisson, Toni Cade Bambara, Paule Marshall, Gayl Jones, or Gloria Naylor. But neither is Herron placed into the tradition of *white* feminist writers such as Marge Piercy, or Margaret Atwood, or Doris Lessing. Instead, she is isolated, discussed as though her work were a minor disturbance in the drawing room.

Michelle Wilson reminds us that defining a "tradition" is an exclusionary practice:

> ... to define a "tradition" that integrates black female critical voices is to be forced to confront the way in which such voices have been systematically excluded from previous notions of "tradition." It is, in other words, a "tradition" of speaking out of turn. The reasons for this are not inherent in the nature of black women, but are, rather, structural; they derive from the "outsider" position we tend to occupy in critical discourse.[18]

Women of color suffer under the conditions of both sexism and racism, and for that reason they may not view sexual assault as *the* traumatic event which shaped their lives. The sexual assault of a woman of color is inextricable from her assault as a *black woman*, a *latina*, or an *Asian woman*. The refusal of women of color to focus solely, or even primarily, on sexual assault reflects an awareness of the complex and interrelated character of race, gender, and class oppression. As Angela Davis explains, "rape is frequently a component of the torture inflicted on women political prisoners by fascist governments and counterrevolutionary forces. In the history of our own country, the Ku Klux Klan and other racist groups have used rape as a weapon of political terror."[19]

White women, particularly white middle- and upper-class women are threatened primarily by white men. Black women are threatened by black men; they are also threatened by white men. Since antebellum days, white men have considered access to black women's bodies their privilege by virtue of their status as white *and* as male.[20] (White women, while they participate in the oppression of women of color, do not rape them.) Race and gender oppression combine to place black women in a double bind. If they speak out against rape and focus on gender issues they may begin to alleviate the problem of sexual abuse. At the same time, they contribute to the oppressive stereotype of the black male rapist. If they do not speak out, they will continue to be raped and assaulted by the men of their own community. (Though I use black women as an example, the problem is equally complex for other women of color.)

Women of color participate in the shaping of literature of trauma, but we must not make the mistake of thinking that they enter into the discourse on the same terms as white women. Women work in separate traditions that reflect their particular social, political, and cultural locations. Our oppression as women, though universal, is not identical. This fact has not, unfortunately, been recognized by most of the editors and publishers of sexual assault narratives.

Perhaps it was this blindness that allowed the women who wrote and published the early sexual abuse survivor literature to believe that all they needed to do was to speak out against atrocity for it to cease. If these sexual abuse survivors had looked to the precedent set, for example, by African-American testimonial literature, they might have realized that testimony signals the *beginning* of a long process of struggle towards change, rather than effecting the change by itself. Instead of making connections between their own drive to testify to atrocity and the long tradition of antiracist and antisexist testimonial literatures that preceded their movement, they fell into the trap that some survivor communities cannot seem to escape: They insisted that their oppression was at once unique *and* universal.

The early examples of sexual abuse survivor literature are both personal and documentary. Published in the early 1980s, these testimonies are directed both at a large audience ignorant of the extent and devastating impact of sexual abuse upon women and children, and to a smaller audience intimately familiar with the details of their own personal experiences of sexual abuse, but unaware that they share their pain and anger with many other women.

Early sexual assault narratives were frequently published by feminist presses, which suggests that the audience was understood to be predominantly female, largely feminist, largely white, and that it contained a number of lesbian and/or consciously women-oriented readers. Because the majority of readers were women, it was likely that many – if not most – of them were also survivors of sexual assault. Reader and writer, in this case, belong to the same community. This community exists in more than simply an abstract sense. Many writers and editors of sexual assault narratives conduct self-help workshops for other survivors of sexual assault, or work with them as therapists, or teach writing courses aimed at helping other women to express their thoughts and feelings about the traumatic assaults they have survived. A number of the writers are also lesbians and women-oriented women – they have explicitly chosen the community of women over the traditional nuclear family.

Sexual abuse survivor literature, like other literatures of trauma, is produced as the result of an ongoing process. Thus, each work informs the next and comments upon the last, shaped by and in turn shaping the genre. Early works by sexual abuse and incest survivors were extremely influential, and many later works by sexual abuse survivors refer back to them either implicitly or explicitly. This is one reason why the white and middle-class orientation of the "essential" incest experience constructed by the first published testimonials was so important in shaping later perceptions. Though the decision of a few brave survivors to speak out was indeed revolutionary, it was at the same time exclusionary; a double-edged sword

Louise Armstrong's remarkable *Kiss Daddy Goodnight,* was the first mass-market publication that declared outright that its subject was incest and that its author was a survivor. Since many later sexual abuse survivor narratives refer back to Armstrong's work, it is important to examine *Kiss Daddy Goodnight* in some detail. Armstrong, whose father was a journalist of some note, sets the tone for later discussions of incest by emphasizing the remarkable nature of a crime which is committed by "normal" men in "normal" (i.e., white, middle-class) families.

The first chapter of *Kiss Daddy Goodnight* is entitled "My Father, Me." As the title suggests, Armstrong views herself and her father as connected identities, and indicates that he is the primary, and she the secondary entity. She also hints that *Kiss Daddy Goodnight* is the story of disillusionment and separation: "During my early school years, I held an almost belligerent belief in the magical powers of fathers – all direct personal evidence to the contrary."[21] The next sentence, a new paragraph, opens with the observation: "Other girls' fathers were shadowy figures." In this way, Armstrong immediately defines the difference between her father and "other" fathers, and at the same time underlines the peculiarity of her assumptions since other girls' fathers lived with their families and Armstrong's own father was not a daily presence in her life until she reached the age of eleven.

By beginning her first chapter with a discussion of her illusions about her absent father, and the "unnatural" condition of being raised by a single working mother, Armstrong establishes the sudden reentry of the father as a disturbance in the normal pattern of life, as well as an event fraught with expectation. The actual event of his return is glossed over. Armstrong instead focuses on a trip he took alone with her to New Mexico when she was twelve years old. On this trip, he began to crawl into bed with her and fondle her breasts. She explains: "In completely unformulated discomfort, I wriggled away and feigned sleep. I wanted my mother. I flew home alone."[22] She never mentioned the event, and quickly repressed it. This section ends with her decision to accompany her father on a trip to Pennsylvania a few years later: "At this time, I must say, I did not remember the New Mexico trip in its particulars. I simply didn't."[23]

The Pennsylvania weekend is the next focus. A sophisticated fourteen-year-old, Armstrong is excited to accompany her father, a famous newspaper correspondent. He purchases her clothes, features her in publicity photographs, takes her to dinner (they converse in French), and talks to her about her sex life "like grown-ups." During the course of the evening, Armstrong claims:

I knew what was in the air. A will-he, won't-he charge. But did I know
what was in my mind? What I wanted? No. Or at least I didn't know
then the important thing in my mind, which was that (at fourteen) I
wanted to be held – by my daddy. The way six-year-olds are.

Nevertheless, what I got in the end, just as I was finally, definitely,
decidedly in my own bed and drifting off to sleep, was oral rape.

But surely, at fourteen, I should have been capable of escaping, of
preventing that. . . . And I would have been, too, you bet, if I hadn't so
carefully preserved a portion of my kid-self, wrapped nicely in tissue
paper. That portion which held as tightly to a belief in the magical
powers of fathers as to a stuffed animal.[24]

As she introduces the scene of sexual abuse, Armstrong raises the questions
that will concern her, and the reader, throughout the text. Do female children
seduce their fathers? Was she at least partially responsible for her father's
attack? The last sentence of the quote is a reference to the opening sentence:
she was deluded, a child clinging to a mistaken belief in "the magical powers
of fathers."

Only now does Armstrong attempt to explain her decision to directly
address the subject of incest. "It was time," she writes, "to face up to the fact
that incest is not an American social taboo. Sexual abuse is frequent and
generally goes unpunished. Talking about incest is the taboo."[25] At the end of
the chapter, Armstrong describes exactly how she intends to go about breaking this taboo: "It was time to take a journey among other women who'd had
an incest experience. It was time to talk."[26]

She decides, first, to talk to her mother, who replies, "You know, dear –
I never did trust that man." A few days later her mother phones her back and
says, "You know, after all – when you get right down to it, I suppose it goes
on fairly often. I suppose, really, it's a matter of control. And – I guess – some
men just have more control than others."[27] Though her mother does not grow
angry at her, or cry and scream, Armstrong is dubious. The chapter ends with
her comment, "Still, I was uneasy. As it turned out, I was right to be."[28]

Her uneasiness with her mother's assessment is reflected in the title of the
second chapter, "It's Natural." "Why did he do it?" Armstrong asks, wondering if "all little girls try out their charms on their daddies," and if "all daddies
are tempted to respond."[29] She discusses the subject with several male friends
and acquaintances. One man explains that he believes that his adolescent
daughter is testing him: "She's testing me to see if she's really a woman. And
she's finding out that she is." He admits to being aroused by his daughter, and
says that he has now become cautious about coming into physical contact
with her: "I don't think it would be fair to her to suddenly change the
relationship. That would be a rejection. But I'm just more aware that I'm the
adult. I'm in charge of whether I control myself, control the situation."[30]

Other men echo this assessment, claiming that their daughters behave seductively when they become adolescents. She concludes "It's Natural" with a rejection of the "naturalness" of incest. The claim of seduction might hold up if men only had sexual relations with their daughters after they reached adolescence, but many female children are assaulted well before that time. We remember, though Armstrong does not remind us, that the first time her father assaulted her Armstrong was a preadolescent, in New Mexico.

Armstrong placed an ad in papers and journals which read: "I am a woman writer doing a first-person, documentary book on incest. I am looking for others who have had an actual or near actual incest experience to participate in my 'forum.'. . ." Responses from many women convinced her that incest often began when the child was quite young, and at least occasionally when the child was still an infant. Her horror at this discovery was not matched by psychiatrists or health professionals:

> . . . [A]s I began to talk to psychiatrists and to poke around in the literature on incest, I began to feel like a witness at the tribunal called by the Red Queen. With a few reassuring exceptions, "they" seemed to feel that our survival was proof that we got what we wanted. And our failure to survive was proof that we were defective merchandise to begin with.[31]

Professionals often based their assessment on a paper entitled "The Reaction of Children to Sexual Relations with Adults," published in the 1930s. She quotes from the survey:

> The most remarkable feature presented by these children who have experienced sexual relations with adults was that they showed less evidence of fear, anxiety, guilt or psychic trauma than might be expected. . . . The probation reports from the court frequently remarked about their brazen poise, which was interpreted as an especially inexcusable and deplorable attitude and one indicating their fundamental incorrigibility. . . . [C]ertain features in our material would indicate that the children may not resist and often play an active or even initiating role.[32]

Since the title for the chapter is taken from the above quotation, "Their Brazen Poise," the reader assumes that Armstrong is most troubled by the implication that incest is a consequence visited upon girls who do not behave in a properly ladylike fashion. The idea that incest is both a punishment visited upon female children, and a contact which they secret desire (perhaps because they are bad) is reinforced by the Freudian notion that young girls, desiring their fathers, fantasized about having sexual relations with them. Armstrong notes that "Freud, himself, after all, had a daughter," and that he had a vested interest in denying the reality of the stories of sexual abuse related to him by many female patients.[33] Her feeling that the professional community simultaneously discounted and diminished the traumatic impact of incest is summed up in her following conversation with one psychiatrist:

> "Incest," he said, "occurs at the onset of puberty."
> "But," I said, "so many of the women I'm hearing from – for them it began at four, five, six."
> "Did you call me as an expert?" he said. "Or did you call me to argue?"[34]

Armstrong is dedicated to proving the "experts" wrong. *Kiss Daddy Goodnight* is an impassioned and furious work, and Armstrong's honest admission that her writing is personally therapeutic does nothing to diminish the documentary impact of the book. In fact, it serves quite well as a case in point for many of her arguments about the nature of incest. Armstrong quotes Maddi-Jane Stern, director of Social Services at the Philadelphia Center for Rape Concern:

> Those women who are functioning members of society – where the incest has gone underground – have a tremendous need to resolve it. A tremendous need to go back and expose it to their fathers "Why did you do it? What was going on? Mother, why didn't you stop this?" There are feelings of guilt. A lot of our survivors come to us unable to express their anger at their fathers. They do a lot of justifying on all scores and really internalize a lot of their guilt. There is a lot of anger there, and once that starts to surface, they want to confront. . . . But the point at which I feel they're getting well is the point at which they say, "I want to talk to my father." Not, "I want to kill him." But "I want to talk to him. I want to find out why."[35]

Kiss Daddy Goodnight conforms to Stern's model of healing, as Armstrong goes through the process of questioning her father's motives, relating her discussions with her mother about the incest, and sharing her anger at a society that does not provide a support network for incest survivors.

Armstrong, as she so quickly admits, has succumbed to feelings of guilt and responsibility for her father's incestuous acts. In order to overcome her internalized guilt feelings, she must first establish that incest is real and damaging, and that it is inflicted on protesting children by powerful and dominating fathers. By relating tales of incest told to her by other victims, she can create a framework within which to examine her own experience. Therefore, much of *Kiss Daddy Goodnight* is devoted to reporting what Armstrong refers to as "The Grisly Details."

> It was in a brown metal bed, [says Anna] and we had the lamps, the old bed lamps. And he was lying on it this way. Spread-eagle. His pants

were open. And he made me go down on him. And I was crying. And I kept crying. I was about thirteen.[36]

[Pamela:] What he would do is I would lie on my stomach on a pillow and have my pants down. And he would be on top of me. And just rub his penis back and forth. . . . And then he would ejaculate, but it would be onto a handkerchief or something. . . . I wouldn't allow myself to feel. He would do whatever he wanted. I would just cry during the whole time and say, "I hate you! Leave me alone. I hate you, I hate you, I hate you!" . . . and he would say, "Shut up. Shut up." And he would do it until he was satisfied.[37]

[Maggie:] And I remember him showing me pornographic pictures. And making me sit on a chair with my left leg over the arm with no clothes on and masturbate. It was totally foreign. . . . And having him say, "You say this. I want you to say that. Now I want you to say it this way and then do this and do that." . . . And then he would do cunnilingus. . . . The hate, the hate was a living thing. . . . At six years old.[38]

Armstrong is determined to place the blame for incest squarely upon the male relative who inflicts the abuse. Approximately a quarter of the way through the book she inserts a chapter entitled "Mother's Fault," in which she cautions readers not to fall back on the age-old tactic of blaming the mother for her husband's or lover's behavior:

Suddenly, I noticed, authorities were springing up full-blown to pronounce on us; to explain the dynamics of each member of a family involved in the mischief of incest. And to lay it all on mom.

Here we are, world, five minutes into a conversation you've refused to have for a million-odd years, and we've already developed bromides and buzzwords. Things to recite in the dark. . . . Mothers are "inadequate." (Also, "passive," "cowardly," "domineering," and "manipulative.")[39]

Placing the responsibility on mothers, Armstrong claims, is analogous to blaming young girls for being seductive. In neither case do men have to face the consequences of their acts, and in neither case is a modification of male behavior called for.

Two of the points Armstrong makes in *Kiss Daddy Goodnight* have been echoed and expanded upon in later survivor narratives: The damaging and life-altering effects of incest on young female children, and the role of masculine power in the incest relationship. Armstrong believes that incest is a traumatic event which changes a girl's life forever. In her chapter "The Psychic Center Violated," Armstrong interviews June, who was incestuously abused by her stepfather from infancy. June married a man who battered her and her children. She feared her male children, and felt she could not control them. She was afraid of her own emotions when she was around her infant daughter, because she had strong urges to beat and torment her. June's second husband was also physically abusive to her and her children. She explains that because of her experiences she can't deal with her feelings, and is unable to respond to anything beautiful or pleasant: "There's a deadness there. Where I should feel." In answer to Armstrong's question she says that child incest "destroys you." When Armstrong asks whether she sees herself as a survivor, she answers:

> Oh, I'm a survivor. I don't look at myself as being maimed because each day is gonna be a new day. I know my kids have been touched and scratched up. They may carry that through their lives. But they, just like me, have to take the day and mold it. And it can be done. And it's OK, whatever has happened. Because you can try to erase it.[40]

Despite June's optimism, the reader is left with the overwhelming impression that her childhood incest experience has changed June's life forever, and not for the better.

In her search for an answer to the question "Why do men sexually abuse their children?" Armstrong is inevitably drawn into a discussion of masculine power. Fathers, she argues, are powerful and their decision to sexualize their relationship with their children is not without consequences. "Once you've eroticized the relationship, broken down the dividing lines between parent and child," Armstrong asks, "where are you going to renegotiate the boundaries?"[41] Her conclusion is that "when you sexualize a child to fulfill your adult, male needs, you are socializing her to subjection."[42] In an interview with Armstrong, incest survivor Jill comments:

> How does it go that a man can take advantage of a woman? Why does he feel he can take advantage of a two-year-old or a five-year-old or a seventeen-year-old or an eighty-nine-year-old? Why? It's because the society says that men are better than women, and that if a man wants something he is entitled to it, and the women have to nurture men and take care of men.[43]

The dominance pattern apparently manifests quite early in men, since older brothers frequently assault younger sisters. Attacks by male siblings seemed quite similar in character to attacks by fathers, step-fathers or other older male relatives. Armstrong records an interview with Barbara, who was assaulted by her brother:

> I was six. He would have been twelve, thirteen. I remember it being terrible, painful, burning. . . . Even then, though, I knew it wasn't right. I didn't know what it was. I knew it was not right because of the fact that he said I couldn't say anything. . . .[44]

Both adult male relatives and siblings appear to be aware of, and to play upon, the young girl's fear of retaliation (many men threaten that they will kill children if they "tell"), and on the fact that admitting one is a victim of sexual assault is humiliating, frightening, and likely to bring on blame and punishment.

Men also sexually assault male children. Armstrong emphasizes that the assaults of young children, whether male of female, are quite similar in nature. She places the emphasis on the unequal power relationship between adult and child, and the exploitation of a child's weakness for an adult's sexual gratification. The male survivors she interviews sound very much like their female counterparts. David, who was abused by his father, explains:

> I got very resentful and felt very abused. Sort of mutilated, if you know what I mean.
>
> That sort of feeling began when I was nine, tenish. I began to feel different. Like I knew my friends' parents weren't doing the same things to them. I mean I didn't ever mention it. It wasn't something to just drop casually into the conversation in the play yard. But I would just feel kind of bad about it.[45]

Armstrong concludes that "Implicitly, and explicitly we give men permission in this society to exploit others to soothe their sexuality."[46] Sexual abuse of children is merely one way in which men take advantage of that permission.

The final two chapters of *Kiss Daddy Goodnight* are entitled "Bad Thoughts," and "Recipe. Getting on with It." Both chapters are short, reflective, and highly personal. In "Bad Thoughts" Armstrong explains that she survived by immersing herself in practicing the piano. Music provided her with a reasonable and ordered world, and a way to repress her unpleasant experiences. She became emotionally numbed, talented at avoiding unpleasant situations, and an expert liar. At seventeen she left home and avoided further contact with her father, but she continued to be haunted by the memories and the effects of his abuse. She concludes that there is "no recipe" for curing her pain, and that the thought of the abuse makes her "Sad. Very sad." The last sentence of the chapter reads: "You don't have to like it. You just have to live with it. Like a small, nasty pet you've had for years."[47]

The title of her last chapter seems to directly contradict the conclusion of "Bad Thoughts." "Recipe. Getting on with It" focuses on Armstrong's mother. The first page records a kitchen-table conversation in which her mother relates her fears and hesitations about Armstrong's decision to write a book about incest. The final two pages of the chapter, and of the book, consist of a letter addressed from Armstrong's mother to Armstrong:

> . . . I was born into a period when people did not reveal their personal problems. . . . What would the world think of a girl who had an incest experience? Of me, the mother?
>
> But during these last months my feelings changed. What triggered

that? Maybe letters from among the many she received. Letters amazingly open, from all kinds of women, from everywhere. . . . I came to
realize that if it weren't for women who were willing to open up, to talk,
we'd still be hiding our maimed children.

My respect for these women is boundless. And for my daughter,
whom I'd have been tempted to dissuade from writing this book . . . I
have the utmost admiration.[48]

The contrast between the opening and closing of the text is dramatic. A book
that begins with the chapter "My Father, Me" ends with the words: "Mom?
Thanks."[49] Armstrong has depicted a journey from self-destructive identification with her masculine abuser to successful acceptance of healing acknowledgment from her newly supportive sister/mother. Her adamancy throughout the work that the blame for sexual abuse should fall squarely upon the
abuser is consonant with her own need to regenerate her image of her mother
and, thus, of herself. In Armstrong's world, men abuse power and women and
children suffer from it.

The word is Armstrong's weapon. She believes that building a community
of women to bear witness to incest will break the power of the patriarchy.
Rehabilitating her mother is a necessity, for all women must stand united
against sexual abuse.

Our work of the moment is not to criticize Armstrong's arguments, but
to understand the context in which she has chosen to testify. *Kiss Daddy
Goodnight* broke the silence that surrounded incest and child sexual abuse, and
suggested for the first time that sexually abused women might identify with
a distinct and credible community of fellow survivors. Armstrong's testimony
was acknowledged. *Kiss Daddy Goodnight* was a successful book and evoked
positive response from many readers. Her work had a real and lasting effect
upon the self-perception of many sexually abused women.

Four and five years after the publication of *Kiss Daddy Goodnight,* the first
anthologies of sexual abuse survivor literature appeared. Both of the texts
discussed here, *Voices in the Night* (1982) and *I Never Told Anyone* (1983) were
edited and compiled by women who were, or worked closely with, incest
survivors. A comparison of these anthologies is informative. Packaging and
presentation combines with choice of authors and subjects to produce a
particular "look" and "feel" for each book. Aimed at different markets, each
anthology bears witness to incest in a distinct and identifiable way.

Voices in the Night, was born out of a lesbian writer's group to which both
editors – Toni A. H. McNaron and Yarrow Morgan – belonged. Reflecting
the concerns of these writers, this anthology is strongly woman-oriented, and
many of the entries reflect a clear feminist consciousness and a distinct lesbian
voice.

I Never Told Anyone, published by Harper and Row, is aimed at a more general audience. Although frankly feminist in its politics and also the product of a women's writing group, *I Never Told Anyone* is more restrained than *Voices in the Night,* and the former is preoccupied with establishing the *authenticity* of its voices. It includes a number of excerpts from the previously published works of well-known women writers, such as Billie Holiday, Maya Angelou, Kate Millet, and Honor Moore. Four of the 33 women whose stories are featured in *I Never Told Anyone* are explicitly identified as lesbian (*Voices in the Night* features 16 explicitly identified lesbian voices out of a total of 37 writers).

The editors of these anthologies act as filters through which the testimony of survivors passes; they can transform the act of bearing witness into a revolutionary challenge or a conciliatory bow. The editors create a context and shape it for the audience. Ellen Bass and Louise Thornton may have been under some pressure by Harper and Row editors to "sanitize" their presentation of incest, or at least to package it in a form which would mitigate the hostile responses of potential mainstream readers.

Cleis Press, the publisher of *Voices in the Night,* describes itself as a "women's publishing company committed to publishing progressive books by women." Their unabashed declaration of feminist sentiment is reflected in their graphic design decisions – bright blue for the anthology's cover, the title – *Voices in the Night* – printed in large orange letters in a black box. Underneath the main title, in slightly smaller black letters, is the subtitle "Women Speaking About Incest." The back cover announces:

> *Voices in the Night* is the silence-breaking book read in incest survivors' groups, and in women's studies courses on women and violence, the family, psychology and literature. This is the tool used by therapists and women's advocates in shelters for battered woman and rape crisis centers. *Voices in the Night* is the simple powerful telling of a story that must be told.[50]

Excerpts from favorable reviews are also printed on the back cover. The reviews were published in *Medical Self-Care, Off Our Backs,* and *Mom . . . Guess What* – all organizations that would be familiar to feminists and active members of a lesbian community.

Without looking beyond the cover, we can see that *Voices in the Night* is intended for an audience of incest survivors and feminist readers. The volume is described as "a tool" that is used by professionals who deal with sexually abused women. Its therapeutic value lies in its mere existence – the volume serves as an example of breaking silence. A "story that needs to be told," *Voices in the Night* is not aimed at enlightening the general public, or even at raising the consciousness of the average woman. Instead, it is a work which is aimed at a community struggling to define itself.

Inside the front cover there is a table of contents listing the entries in the anthology, which are not arranged in any apparent order. A short preface follows, listing the "Women we wish to thank. . . ." Each editor states her appreciation to her own therapists and incest counselors. In less than half a page the editors have established the woman-oriented perspective of the anthology, and their own authority to speak as incest survivors.

The introduction begins in a single voice, and the first word is a qualifier:

> Though incest may occur in every third woman's life, there has been virtually no attention paid to it in writing until the last two or three years. Even now, books are few and tend to be either "studies of" or one woman's story. Rather than add to this literature, we have collected pieces written by a number of women. These have the immediacy and potency of direct expression together with the form and distance that come from writing a poem or letter or short story or journal entry.[51]

It is no accident that this volume opens with a statistic. Statistics are woven throughout incest and rape literature, used again and again to show, to prove, to demonstrate irrefutably that sexual abuse is *real*, that women suffer from it in large numbers, that it is not just some irrational woman's fantasy. But while many other books on sexual abuse footnote their statistics and rely on them to provide an explanation for their interest in the subject, Morgan and McNaron go on the offensive. They simply state that incest is a widespread problem and then ask the question, "Why has there been no attention paid to this phenomenon?"

For the incest survivor, the simple acceptance of the reality of her problem, expressed by McNaron and Morgan, must have come as a profound relief. This anthology generates an environment in which the survivor does not have to prove her case, but can focus on sharing her pain and suffering with her sisters. The survivor is not a subject to be studied. Instead, she is one in a multitude of voices raised to affirm her suffering. And that is, apparently, how the anthology came to be created. As McNaron and Morgan explain, several women in a writer's group discovered that they were in the company of other incest survivors. This mutual recognition stimulated a search for other survivors. They placed notices in newspapers, bookstores, and journals in the hopes of contacting other women who were interested in writing about their experiences as sexual abuse survivors, and were pleased with the number and quality of responses. That the editors view this anthology as part of an ongoing process is clear: "We see this book as one of many such anthologies. Every woman who can share her experience with this ugly reality surely gives increased permission to others still frozen in their terrorized silence."[52]

Writing is therapeutic both for the author and for her readers. Echoing Louise Armstrong, Morgan and McNaron believe that speaking out is the answer. However, Armstrong does not reach her conclusion that sexually abused women must join together and form a community until the *last* chapter of *Kiss Daddy Goodnight,* indicating that this revelation came at the end of a long journey. Morgan and McNaron, perhaps because Armstrong has led the way, choose to *begin* with that premise.

The contradictions inherent in bearing witness to a wrong that the larger society refuses to acknowledge are manifest in this short introduction. A woman who internalizes the blame for the abuse which she suffers is terribly self-destructive. Yet speaking out may also fail to bring relief since "women speaking, the oral telling of truths, have also been treated as a kind of silence in our culture."[53] The authors believe their book represents an attempt "to redefine the parameters of our world," creating a space in which women's pain can be heard and attended to. Such an attempt, they admit, is hampered by the patriarchal power structure, which deprives them of the right to speak and resist.

At this point, the unified voice of the editors diverges into two voices, "I, Yarrow" and "me, Toni." Yarrow explains that her incest experience and her therapy have led her to make the connection between individual acts of incest and the social and political structure of society. Most striking among her observations is her claim that incest put her "in a stance of 'other' in relation to [her] family and the outside world."[54] She was split off from her family and the outside world, just as she was alienated from her body and her emotions, and from all women ("being a woman was synonymous with being an object to be used and abused"[55]). Yarrow's description of her otherness is significant on two levels. It suggests that she suffers the sense of alienation from self and community that trauma survivors often report: numbness and distancing are both frequently reported symptoms of PTSD. It is also important on a symbolic, or metaphorically level. Feminist scholar Vivian Gornick suggests:

> In every real sense woman . . . is an outsider, one in whom experience lives in a metaphorical sense, one whose life and meaning is a surrogate for the pain and fear of existence, one onto whom is projected the self-hatred that dogs the life of the race . . . the wildness, grief, and terror of loss that is in us will be grafted onto her, and the strength of those remaining within that circle will be increased . . . that is what power and powerlessness are all about; that is what inclusion and exclusion are all about; that is what the cultural decision that certain people are "different" is all about; if only these . . . blacks, these Jews, these women will go mad and die for us, we will escape; we will be saved; we will have made a successful bid for salvation.[56]

Toni finds herself in a different position. "My issues are with my mother," she explains, "contrary to most of the women in this collection and to almost all available literature on the subject of incest." Even in a community of outsiders she is an outsider. She connects this abuse to her subsequent alcoholism and to both her attraction to and terror of her female lovers.

These personal revelations are followed by the claim that all incest, whatever its form, has the effect of generating self-destructive behavior in survivors:

> What begins as a way to endure the madness being inflicted upon the victim becomes at some point a force over which she no longer has any control. The behaviors most often "chosen" are alcoholism, and/or drug abuse, prostitution and/or sexual promiscuity with relationships unaccompanied by cash payments. The repetitive choosing of abusive relationships whether to friends and lovers, husbands or lesbian partners. . . . Victims need to be shown that they were trained for abusive relationships by their fathers, brothers, uncles, grandfathers, more distant relatives.[58]

But breaking self-destructive patterns and placing the blame on the abuser are extremely difficult in a culture based on a patriarchal structure that condones incest: "Incest is an early and very effective behavioral training in powerlessness and subservience. By beginning to speak about it, we begin to threaten its continued, unacknowledged presence."[59]

Like Armstrong, Yarrow disagrees with the opinions of male "experts." Men, she believes, do not want to change a system from which they reap the benefits of power and dominance. Thus, the attempt to alter reality must be made by women. The first step in creating the new reality is to believe in "our own lives and the lives of other women as more accurate than literature, social proscriptions, statistics."[60]

The testimonial process that Morgan and McNaron describe is familiar to a reader of the psychiatric literature on PTSD. By translating overwhelming and anxiety-producing memories into language, McNaron and Morgan believe that women begin to transform their painful experiences into more manageable stories. The writing and rewriting process allows women to manipulate imagery and generate metaphors for their suffering, reframing their problems in a useful and creative manner.[61]

Morgan and McNaron feel compelled to defend these writings from the charge that they are examples of mere "confessionalism." Male critics, they say, have too frequently insisted that when literature does not fit established "universal" (i.e., masculine) standards, that it has no artistic value. Instead, they affirm their commitment to women's artistic work as "healing, enriching and affirmative . . . "[62] "Incest," they write, ". . . will surely be found distasteful to male-oriented critics or reviewers or publishers. It will be a rare man who can be 'objective' about a group of poems and prosaic pieces which at some level accuse him and his fellows of being child-molesters – this time, their own child."[63]

There is no doubt that these women regard themselves as members of a traumatized community. Dedicated to bearing witness to incest, they seek the support of other women to publish and review their work, and they provide a support network for other incest and sexual abuse survivors. Writing about incest is an important part of a larger therapeutic process, at the same time it advances a larger political agenda. To eradicate incest, these women believe that they have to change the world. To change the world, they must first come together and speak to each other:

> To tell orally is the first step, and in the incest program I, Toni, went through, the power of saying my story . . . cannot be overstated. Similarly, to witness while the other women told there confirmed me as "like" them not in surface details, but in basic feelings, reactions, and most of all, in the necessity for silencing our own voices. . . . To write those same stories as narrative is a second and huge step because we put form around what has seemed so chaotic, we make public to strangers the most intimate truths about ourselves. . . . When we write a poem or letter or story about the impact or center of that narrative, we take a third leaping step – we dare to make art out of our female experience – to fly in the face of all expectations for what is acceptable in such forms.[64]

There are 37 separate works anthologized in *Voices in the Night,* ranging from short poems to essays. The first piece, entitled "Et Cum Spiritu Tuo," by karen marie christa minns, is a poem that begins:

> I want to tell you something   I want
> to tell you something
> that I've never told before . . .[65]

minns' is the first "voice in the night." Her poem begins the process of telling and re-telling, envisioning and re-visioning that is so graphically portrayed in this anthology. "Et Cum Spiritu Tuo" intersperses minns' emotional and personal commentary with statistics and quotes from the psychological literature on incest. She uses a normal typeface for her first-person voice and places the third-person voice in italics, indenting it slightly. Her structure generates two voices – inner and outer voice – and recreates the internal struggle of the incest survivor to articulate her pain and rage:

> "This is fucking," he says
> his tongue an eel in your ear, whispering, snaking
> its way deep into the brain
> where it will live for years
> "This is fucking."
>
> > *"A common experience in the victim is to leave the body – to tune out –*
> > *to experience out-of-the body consciousness. Results and symptoms of*

incest occurrences include: distance, feeling different from one's peers,
isolation, dislocation, inability to connect."

"58% under the age of ten."

I want to tell you what it is like. . . .[66]

The desire to "tell you what it is like" runs through *Voices in the Night,* the
invisible thread that holds everything together. Cygnet cries:

Now from the mouth you stuffed
those nights
when I was two, three, four, five

. . . .

now from my mouth I spit these words[67]

Terry Wolverton entitles her performance piece "In Silence Secrets Turn to
Lies/Secrets Shared Become Sacred Truth," and invites us:

to enter into this space, where secrets are spoken,
to share your secrets
by writing them in my notebook.[68]

"Secrets shared," Wolverton concludes, "become sacred truth."[69] Yarrow
Morgan echoes her: "I crack the frozen air: / haltingly   I remember, /
haltingly   I speak."[70] Toni McNaron writes to her mother:

I take our tangled strands,
lay them gently side by side,
and write this plain song whose forbidden key
eases the pain, replaces the noise
that kept us from each other.[71]

The words which close the volume speak directly to the words which opened
it. "I want to tell you something," wrote karen marie christa minns. Yarrow
Morgan, clear on what she wants to say, concludes the volume with the
reason why:

I tell you because I know,
I tell you because I will not be silent,
I tell you because I will not be silenced.[72]

All the women featured in *Voices in the Night* have felt the driving urge to
testify. Their writings of hope and recovery are most frequently addressed to
each other – sister survivors, mothers, women friends and lovers.

The rage and hatred of the women in *Voices in the Night* is directed at their
abusers, to whom they also bear witness. "Old father / fearsome liar / listen

to me well:" writes Cygnet. "my mind forgot / my body remembers / how we rehearsed night by night."[73] McNaron, one of the few women abused by a female relative, writes furiously to her mother:

I raise my phantom knife
and bring it down, down into your fat flesh
I cut stomach, breasts, and thighs
to shreds, you hear me? shreds
so die, damn you, die;
no use to write before me
smiling through your well-kept teeth[74]

Donna Young describes her decision to survive at all costs, "For without breath you cannot live / to Avenge yourself."[75] Joanne Kerr corresponds with her stepfather:

I have lied to my own mother for years. Why? To protect *you*! Pretty absurd, isn't it? Mother and I have suffered because of your cheap indulgence, petty lying, stupidity, all of which is part of the incest game which places blame, guilt and insanity on the victim – me! – instead of on the adult male aggressor – you!

I want you to understand how terrifying and horrible that experience was for me. Remember? Remember?[76]

Kate Muellerleile Darkstar accuses her brother: "Rapist, killer, abuser, traitor, brother. . . . How I hate the shitty things your depraved humanhood did to me. YOU'RE JUST LIKE YOUR FATHER. . . . I hated your sloppy, slimy kisses on my mouth – I hated your body on top of mine – I hated your hands on my yet undeveloped chest – I hated you. I hate you still. . . ."[77] Ran Hall rages:

he is a man
man is a cock
and a cock will fuck
he is man is a cock
and a cock hates
he is a man and man hates me
and anything that is part of me – woman
free from his cock hates free women

. . . .

lies as love
as truth, as natural
as protection

as need, as sharing
and giving, the face of hatred
shoves its way through
the face of hatred is a cock
cock is man[78]

Because *Voices in the Night* is directed to an audience of women-identified
women, Morgan and McNaron make no effort to soften the accusations
which women survivors direct at the men who abused them, or at men in
general. Though it is true that not all men abuse women, it is also true that
all but a very few sexual abusers are men. Lesbian separatism as a reaction to
male sexual abuse is not so different in nature and intent from the refusal of
many Jews to deal with Germans or to purchase German products after World
War II. Though not all Germans murdered and enslaved Jews, most Jews
were murdered and enslaved by Germans (or those acting under German
orders), and even those Jews who were not directly affected (such as American Jews) understandably identified with their oppressed brothers and sisters.
The frank antipathy which many of the contributors to *Voices in the Night* feel
for men is remarkable only because it is expressed in the midst of repression
and attack. They are quite as isolated as the German Jews who spoke out in
rage and hatred against Hitler in 1937. That these writers connect their incest
experience to a larger political, social and economic system which oppresses
women is unarguable. "T" states the case quite clearly:

> I believe incestuous sexual assault is another of the vicious forms of
> initiation practiced on girl children to teach us our subservient place in
> the patriarchy. I know that only by talking to each other, sharing what
> has happened to us, trusting our dreams and memories can we open this
> assault to each other and bring it to an end. . . . Not until mothers and
> daughters can grow into a healing of our crimes against one another and
> then turn toward the true enemy with united forces – once again the
> matriarchs and the amazons – will we be able to win back our world and
> care for each other and the earth as sisters and Lesbians free from male
> domination.[79]

The message of oppression and struggle inscribed in *Voices in the Night* is
made powerful because of its apparent universality. *All* women, the authors
make clear, suffer the injuries inflicted by the patriarchy. McNaron and
Morgan, by refusing to take the editorial privilege of contextualizing each
selection, create a book where all voices carry the same authority. We speak
for each other, they seem to suggest, and each speaks for all in her own way.

Though the effect of such an assertion is undeniably strong, it can be
misleading. *Voices in the Night* identifies gender difference as the foundation
upon which political, social and economic analyses of incest should be based.

Racial difference is entirely and unselfconsciously ignored. The single, glaring exception is a short story called "Black Girl Learn the Holiness of Mother-hood," by Susan Chute.

The title of the Chute story emphasizes the primacy of race in this incest tale, and, if we have missed that clue, the first paragraph also begins with the words "Black girl . . . " There are, in fact, ten paragraphs in the story and five of them begin with those words, including the first and the last paragraph. Chute begins:

> Black girl comb her dry wiry hair; pull it back in a ponytail jus by her right ear. Black girl look inta her chocklut face, steal a dab of her mamma's rouge, rub it deep on her cheek. Black girl makin her lean face full and ready.[80]

Chute's protagonist is an eleven-year old girl who believes that she is ugly, and that her blackness is a part of what makes her ugly. Changing her baby sister's diaper she notices that "her shit the same color as . . . the chocklut face she wuz fussin over seconds ago."[81] She wonders, at the same time, "who decided diapers should be white." Chute leaves her protagonist nameless, simply a "black girl," until the end of the third paragraph when her mother calls to her and names her Willa. Willa's self-consciousness about her black-ness is inseparable from her self-consciousness about her femaleness.

Willa is talking about more than simply gender oppression when she warns her younger sister Lana to be quiet and stop crying because "There gonna be things hurt worse than you hurt right now." Lana, whose white diaper has been changed, is sprinkled with white powder to make her smell good. This is no accident either. The colors Chute uses in the story are black, brown, white, gold, red, orange, and purple. Gold represents her father's prominent position in the society – his gold teeth flash when he delivers a sermon in the church. Red is the color of blood; red, orange, and purple are the colors of the labia and of flowers at a funeral.

It is not until the fifth paragraph that the reader is given any indication that Willa's life is any different than any other black girl's. Chute describes her in the kitchen, how she "wink & giggle wid Daddy, while she think, 'I do more than mamma here.' Black child Willa wonder, 'Do he know it's mamma's rouge?' "[82] Willa worries that her father is only pleased with her because her mother is pregnant again and "no good for mucha anythin now." The women are apparently interchangeable for Willa's father; he will turn to one when the other is "no good."

At church, Willa and her mother sit in the back holding the babies at evening services during a funeral for "the white lady" who used to sing in the choir. As Willa marvels at the flowers she reflects, "Bet her mamma wouldn't get that many when she die. Willa thinkin of the pure cold skin of the white mamma & the delicate petals of the lilies & then she thinking of Lana's live warm shit like her own hot brown face which she cover now wid rouge."[83] Blackness, a quality that Willa shares with her mother, disqualifies them both from consideration as either beautiful or worthy of special attention, while the white woman, by virtue of her whiteness, will go "to bliss in heaven & streets & castles made a solid gold."

Chute makes a bitter connection between the gold that belongs to white people because they are white, and the gold that flashes in Willa's father's mouth: ". . . her daddy open his mouth & show her his golden teeth, sayin it wuz god's personal gift to him, and god spoke to him through the gold in his mouth, and that wuz how he preach."[84] Reflecting on this outrageous claim the girl child Willa remembers "how many times she touch those teeth wid her tongue an it feelin smooth & cold & bitter. She fraid god gonna talk wid her tongue coverin the gold sometime, and daddy not gonna know what god is sayin to him."[85] In a single paragraph Chute graphically outlines the betrayal of black women by a black man who has sold his soul for white gold and white approval. If we have not gotten the message by now, Chute ensures that we grasp its implications in graphic detail:

> Her daddy up there still preachin but Willa not lissnin now. She watch-
> in a spaghetti sauce stain on daddy's suit, thinkin, "It the same color as
> the first nite when he touch me & the blood trickle & he call it the RED
> SEA OF MOSES & say god be very pleased cos we wuz luvin people.[86]

Willa's father's hypocrisy is unveiled in no uncertain terms – the spaghetti stain and Willa's blood have exactly the same symbolic value. Both are spilled by his carelessness. His god, the one who speaks to him out of the gold in his mouth, is the father of lies and rationalizations, the god of deception.

Willa's revelation comes after she hears her father say that the dead lady "a good mama." The funeral flowers, "all white & orange & purple & red coverin & climbin the walls" smell so strongly they almost cause her to faint just "like when her daddy fill her deep inside, makin her body jerk & shake." She watches her mother sing in the church and marvels that "her mamma's teeth shinin white & brighter than daddy's gold as her mamma sing, 'Steal away, steal, away, steal away to Jesus.' "[87] The depth of her betrayal becomes clear as she realizes her mother's simultaneous complicity in her own oppression and transcendence of it. The universal betrayal of all women by all men up to the very level of God, the Father is made clear. This realization is insep-arable from her understanding that, as a black woman, she will never be as valued a servant or sex object as a white woman:

> Black girl know now. She understandin bout death. She know the dead
> white mamma goin far away to the heavenly kingdom where she run
> her tongue in the mouth of the Lord, fulla bitter golden laughter. Then

that mamma be filled wid Jesus till she ache & shake. Cos Jesus probly
need lovin like all daddy.[88]

The inclusion of a single self-consciously black "voice in the night" has a
the chilling effect on the Yarrow and Morgan anthology. It effectively ends
discussion about race while at the same time appearing to address the subject.
McNaron and Morgan promote the idea that though there are differences
among individual women and groups of women, we are all the same *as women*.
Unfortunately, the women we are all the same as appear to be almost entirely
white and middle class. This problem has been thoroughly explored by
Elizabeth V. Spelman in her book *Inessential Woman: Problems of Exclusion in
Feminist Thought* (1988). Spelman argues that the feminist movement has too
frequently adopted the position that, though differences between women
exist, "it is not white middle-class women who are different from other
women, but all other women who are different from them."[89] The decision
to include a black voice implies the power to exclude them. As Spelman says,
"Welcoming someone into one's own home doesn't represent an attempt to
undermine privilege; it expresses it."[90]

Spelman suggests that feminists must consider race, class, ethnicity, gender, nationality, and other identifiers as inseparable, and argues for a feminist
theory that is encompassing rather than exclusive:

> The idea that gender is constructed and defined in conjunction with
> elements of identity such as race, class, ethnicity and nationality rather
> than separable from them helps explain why gender ought to be studied
> in connection with every academic discipline and not only in women's
> studies departments. If we really could understand gender in isolation
> from race and class . . . gender would be less important than it actually
> is in our lives. For one thing, as long as we think both that gender
> identity is describable without reference to race and class (and is ex-
> perienced and understood independently of them) and that feminism
> is centrally about gender and sexism, whatever else it might be about,
> then studies of race and class, racism and classism, have to remain
> peripheral to feminism. On the other hand, if gender is neither ex-
> perienced nor describable independently of race and class, then race and
> class become crucial to feminism.[91]

If Spelman is correct, and I believe she is, then the Morgan and McNaron
anthology perpetuates the myth that "womanhood" is white middle-class
womanhood, and that black or brown womanhood is merely a variation on
the theme, rather than a kind of womanhood in its own right. Chute's story
is therefore presented as a variation on a theme, rather than an entirely new
composition. Eliding issues of race and class may be convenient for white
women survivors of sexual abuse, for they can then more easily see them-

selves as members of a larger community of survivors composed of *all* abused women. But it is a great disservice to women of color who are perhaps tired of hearing white feminists talk about racism and sexism as "something experienced by some women rather than something perpetuated by others: racism and classism are about what women of color and poor women experience, not about what white middle-class women may help to keep afloat."[92]

Unlike *Voices in the Night,* which is printed in bright colors to attract attention, *I Never Told Anyone* is somber – the black cover is simply printed with a graceful serif typeface. The title is printed in white, as are the names of the editors. Beneath the main title, the subtitle, "Writings by Women Survivors of Child Sexual Abuse" is printed in red. The back cover explains:

> *I Never Told Anyone* is a deeply moving collection of first-person accounts of child sexual abuse. Here are stories and poems written by women of all ages and circumstances of the abuse they suffered either as young girls or as teenagers. In these compelling and poignant "life-refined" writings, we hear the long-repressed voices of sexually abused children. We learn of their fear, anger, pain, and love, and of their struggles to come to terms with the silence that allowed such abuse. Writing with courage and honesty, these women tell of experiences ranging from the most subtle overtures to repeated abuse. Introduced by brief biographies that place each woman in a past and present context, these pieces reflect a wide diversity of experience and emotional response and offer a powerful testament to all survivors of sexual abuse.
>
> As a complement to the writings, Ellen Bass, both a well-known poet and experienced counselor, has written a moving essay that places child sexual abuse in a broad social context and speaks in a special way to readers who have shared this experience. The book concludes with a comprehensive listing of treatment and prevention programs and bibliography of suggested reading and audiovisual materials. *I Never Told Anyone* not only recounts and illuminates; it offers real hope for change – and healing.

Excerpts from favorable reviews by Susan Griffin and Rod McKuen are included on the back cover. Griffin is undoubtedly quoted because of her well-deserved reputation as a feminist theorist concerned with issues of rape and domination. McKuen, interestingly enough, is included because of his status as fellow survivor; in his words, "a long-ago victim."

These anthologies serve as an illustration of the very different ways women's stories of survival can be packaged. The Morgan and McNaron book is boldly titled *Voices in the Night.* The voices are active and assertive, calling out loudly in the darkness. The message in the title is reinforced by the strong subtitle: *Women Speaking About Incest.* Speaking is also active, forceful. These women are speaking out in concert, and they will continue talking until they have been heard. In contrast, the Bass and Thornton anthology is titled *I Never Told Anyone*. Passive and introverted, the first-person voice isolates the survivors from each other, and suggests that the act of breaking silence is both frightened and furtive, a whisper rather than a shout. The subtitle continues in the passive voice: *Writings by Women Survivors of Child Sexual Abuse.*

While *Voices in the Night* is packaged as a "silence-breaking book" useful in feminist therapy, *I Never Told Anyone* is a "deeply moving collection," which is "compelling and poignant." The reader is invited to learn of the "fear, anger, pain, and love" of these women "and of their struggles to come to terms with the silence that allowed such abuse." *I Never Told Anyone* is presented to the reader as a fascinating, emotionally involving look at the painful lives of other people – in terms not too terribly different from those which are used to sell romance novels, war novels, and other works of literature that allow readers to live vicariously.

Even a soft-sell presentation cannot strip away the dangerous implications of women writing about incest. The reader is informed that each story is safely contained within an editorial framework, a process which places "each woman in a past and present context." The presentation of Ellen Bass as a qualified professional who will place "child sexual abuse in a broad social context" further reassures us that the matter is under control. But just in case we are still worried, her work will speak "in a special way to readers who have shared this experience," and point these damaged individuals to the "comprehensive listing of treatment and prevention programs" and "suggested reading and audiovisual materials" included in the text of the book. This is a far cry from the Morgan and McNaron's straightforward claim that "*Voices in the Night* is the simple powerful telling of a story that needs to be told."

I Never Told Anyone features a Foreword, a Preface *and* an Introduction at the front of the book, as well as a listing of treatment and prevention programs, a bibliography, and notes on the editors at the back of the book. Altogether, these mediating sections take up 88 pages out of a total of 278 pages. If we include the editors' introductions to each selection (an additional 25 pages), we find that more than *forty percent* of the anthology is composed of editorial "contextualizing." (*Voices in the Night* has 24 pages of commentary, out of a total of 187 pages, less than thirteen percent.)

These sorts of calculations do not provide us with any reliable index of how good or bad an anthology is. Rather, they suggest a particular set of *narrator–interpreter* relations. The Personal Narratives Group of the University of Minnesota argues that the production and dissemination of personal narratives is grounded in power relationships, and that both ethical and factual questions are involved in the process of packaging women's personal narratives for public consumption.[93] As feminist scholars, they take the following position:

In positing the centrality of the interpretive act, we recognize the possibility that the truths the narrator claims may be at odds with the most cherished notions of the interpreter. Personal narratives cannot be simply expropriated in the service of some good cause, but must be respected in their integrity. What are the rules governing their interpretation? Certainly the essays [included in the volume *Interpreting Women's Lives*] have not provided simple answers, but many do suggest the need to recognize both the agenda of the narrator and that of the interpreter as distinct and not always compatible. And they once again remind us that feminist scholars, by simply criticizing the distortions inherent in disciplinary criteria for validation, have not released us from all institutional constraints upon our own use of these stories or from political agendas that shape our interpretation of them.[94]

We must recognize that the extensive editorial interpretation surrounding the pieces in the Bass and Thornton anthology reflect both a particular set of institutional constraints upon their use of these incest stories, and a particular political agenda that shapes their interpretations of them.

The institutional constraints are quite clear – mainstream publishing houses will not publish books they cannot successfully market. Thus, Thornton and Bass are required to seek a larger audience than the community of self-consciously feminist, woman-oriented incest survivors. There is a reason that incest testimony does not appeal to a larger market. In fact, a defining characteristic of incest is the fact that no one wants to talk about it or hear about it. To overcome this obstacle, Thornton and Bass – and the Harper & Row marketing department – must somehow make incest narratives seem both safe and appealing. Without a doubt this is a difficult task. The marketing department appears to have taken the soft-sell approach. These stories are human stories, "deeply moving," full of the stuff pathos is made of: fear, anger, pain, love, struggle. The adjectives used in the back cover blurb are not so different from those used to sell other sad and painful tales. The Bantam paperback edition of Elie Wiesel's *Night* describes his story as "penetrating and powerful," "personal," "terrifying," "shocking" and "unforgettable."[95] As the large publishing houses have learned, Other People's Trauma *sells*.

Thornton and Bass have a more difficult task than the marketing department. The marketing department is responsible for selling the book to the public. Thornton and Bass first had to sell the book to a publisher. To mediate the essentially subversive message of these narratives by survivors of child sexual abuse, Thornton and Bass contain them within a structure which is both analytic and therapeutic. They divide the narratives into four categories: 1) "Survivors of Sexual Abuse by Fathers;" 2) "Survivors of Sexual Abuse by Relatives;" 3) "Survivors of Sexual Abuse by Friends and Acquaintances;" and 4) "Survivors of Sexual Abuse by Strangers." The first two categories each contain seven selections, the last two contain nine and ten selections respectively.[96] The number of entries in each category apparently do not reflect the statistics on child sexual abuse, which show that forty-seven percent of sexual abusers are members of children's own families, an additional forty percent are known to the children, and only eight to ten percent of the abusers are strangers.[97] Bass and Thornton downplay the frequency of abuse by family members, and heighten the emphasis on assaults by strangers, diluting the challenge to rape and abuse mythology that these narratives raise. Furthermore, they divide victims into categories based on the identity of the abusers, rather than on the nature and impact of the abuse. Our perspective is shaped and determined by the manner in which information is structured.

The book's therapeutic structure places abused women within the framework of mental illness. By making it clear that child sexual abuse had dramatic effects upon its victims, and by advocating that women seek counseling, advice, and support from professionals and therapy groups, Bass and Thornton create the impression that the survivors are weak, harmless and "sick" – no threat to the status quo. Thornton and Bass emphasize that women need "healing." They do not mention that many women survivors of child sexual abuse also believe that they need revolution.

Clearly, Thornton and Bass are both committed feminists determined to bring the words of incest survivors to the public's attention. Their success in publishing I Never Told Anyone is the result of hard work and dedication – even a strongly mediated message about incest cannot be gotten across without a tremendous amount of effort. It is possible they weighed the benefits of mass-market publishing against the drawbacks of softening their message, and decided that the survivor narratives would transcend the limits imposed by the market if only they could be read. The result, however, is an anthology that frequently compromises the integrity of the personal narratives, reducing and softening their impact on the reader, while at the same time creating the impression that, within each category, all incest experiences are somehow alike. The latter is accomplished, like an uncomfortable fit in a glass slipper, by a little judicious toe and heel trimming.

I Never Told Anyone opens with a Foreword by Florence Rush, identified on the cover as the author of The Best Kept Secret. The first words of her Foreword are, of course, "I Never Told Anyone . . . " and she follows them with the question, Why? Quickly answering herself, she writes:

> They never tell for the same reason that anyone who has been helplessly shamed and humiliated, and who is without protection or validation of personal integrity, prefers silence. Like the woman who has been raped, the violated child may not be believed (she fantasized or made up the story), her injury may be minimized (there's no harm done, so let's

forget the whole thing), and she may even be held accountable for the crime (the kid really asked for it).[98]

Rush immediately de-genders the subject, explaining "they never tell for the same reason that *anyone* . . . ," arguing the universal nature of abuse, yet the only comparison she can come up with is a woman who has been raped. The responses she suggests – "she fantasized," "there's no harm done," "she asked for it" – are traditional male responses to female accusations of sexual abuse.

Rush goes on to describe the damage incest does to an abused child: lost self-esteem, the internalization of shame, repression of emotions. Once again, though she uses the female pronoun, Rush tries to suggests the universal nature of "the child's" response: "When the offense remains hidden, unanswered and unchallenged, the sexuality, the very biology of the offended child, becomes her shame."[99] This last sentence really makes no sense at all. "Biology" is all-encompassing and that is certainly not what Rush means. "The child" is not ashamed of her elbows or knees, or the way she metabolizes her food. "The child" is ashamed of her sex, of her female identity, and of the biological functions she associates with her sex – menstruation, orgasm, arousal. Why is Rush, an articulate woman, deliberately speaking in these fuzzy and inaccurate universals?

Diane Russell, who conducted the most extensive study on incest to date, explains that some mental health professionals and researchers are "ideologically uncomfortable" with the idea that the preponderance of sexual abusers of children are male:

> In a cultural climate where feminists have called upon men to relinquish certain traditional modes of behavior, the fact that it is primarily men who commit sexual abuse bolsters feminists' arguments and may thus create defensiveness in those who oppose feminist thinking. Some people find the problem of sexual abuse an easier cause to promote when it is not entangled in "gender politics." Political support for issues of general "human" concern is much easier to mobilize than support for issues that appear to benefit one social group more than others – particularly when that group, women, is a stigmatized one of lower status. . . .[100]

Having established the universal nature of child sexual abuse, Rush seems to abandon it with great relief in the third paragraph of her Foreword, and to launch more enthusiastically into a feminist analysis of the abuse of female children. "In the beginning of our Western civilization," she explains, "the female, along with a house, ox, and ass, was man's property. Specifically, she was a sexual property. . . ."[101] Her second explanation of the reason why incest is "the best kept secret" is much more sophisticated than her opening thesis:

The sexual abuse of little girls is predicated upon their presumed inferiority. A little girl can be used sexually because she is property, or
because she is biologically imperfect, or because she is an enticing, sexy
temptress. Simultaneously defined and degraded by her sexuality, she
is constrained within a foolproof system of emotional blackmail. If she
is violated the culturally imposed concept of her sexuality renders her
culpable. Any attempt on the part of the child to expose her violator also
exposes her own alleged inferiority and sexual motives and shames her
rather than the offender. Concealment is her only alternative.[102]

Women, she goes on to argue, have more power than little girls, and are able
to refuse to accept inferior status. By "pointing a finger at our abusers" women
are made to "feel better about themselves because at last they have the courage
to tell their stories."[103] She concludes: "The lesson to be learned from this
testimony is to believe in and to protect the integrity of our children and to
break the silence that endangers them."[104]

Her analysis, though hopeful, is somewhat confusing. First of all, it cannot
encompass the sexual abuse of male children by older male relatives. Though
four times as many girls as boys are abused, the sexual abuse of male children
is far from uncommon, and the abuse of male children is often more severe
and of longer duration than the abuse of female children.[105] Second, it suggests that all women have to do is speak out about incest and abuse, "break
the silence that endangers them," and the male power structure will crumble.
Rush's analysis does not adequately account for the difficulties historically
faced by groups who seek to overthrow the rule of those who oppress them.
Sensible folk would not claim that if only black slaves in antebellum America
had spoken out against slavery and protected their children from slaveholders,
they could have freed themselves. In The Wizard of Oz, Glinda the Good
informs Dorothy that she had the power to leave Oz all along: "All you have
to do is click your heels together and repeat three times, 'There's no place like
home.'" Unfortunately, there are no magic slippers for oppressed peoples.

Thornton's Preface is less idealistic than Rush's Foreword, and makes
fewer claims on behalf of the speaking subjects. Perhaps this is because of her
experience in compiling the writings published in the volume. Like Voices in
the Night, the Thornton and Bass book grew out of a women's writing
workshop. At one session of the workshop (led by Ellen Bass), Jude Brister
read a story about an incestuous experience. The story had such a strong effect
that Bass and several participants decided to edit an anthology of incest
writings. These women made the decision to include writings by women who
had personally experienced childhood sexual abuse, and they agreed to broad-
ly define the term "sexual abuse" so that it encompassed any incident in which
"an adult or near-adult takes away the child's right to exclusive ownership of
her body."[106] Thornton carefully acknowledges that boys are also sexually

abused, and includes mention of two particular instances where that occurred, but she does not include those stories in the anthology though she
expresses the "hope that the experiences of men who have been sexually
abused as children will also be told."[107]

Male survivors of sexual abuse are not the only missing voices. When they
reviewed the submissions to the anthology they looked for "clear, strong,
distilled writing, 'life refined,' as Gwendolyn Brooks says about her poetry.
We hoped to find writers who would take an experience as horrendous as
being sexually abused as a child and, like Picasso with the bombing of
Guernica, turn it into a work of art."[108] The editors had a set of definite
aesthetic standards they wished their writers to meet. Though they also
wished "to help give the sexually abused child a voice," they seemed to
exclude from consideration survivors of sexual abuse whose work was not
"good" enough, as well as those who were politically opposed or simply
incapable of turning the narrative of their childhood sexual abuse into an
aesthetically pleasing work of "art."

Thornton's final point is that "telling" offers a kind of absolution for the
survivor: "In this telling she can reclaim her innocence. She *is* innocent. She
has *always* been innocent. Both the burden of the crime and the crime itself
are lifted from her shoulders. She can tell."[109] Despite this brave assertion,
many of the women published in this anthology have used pseudonyms,
indicating that their courageous act of bearing witness to sexual abuse did not
set them free. Thornton's failure to acknowledge this fact makes her unable
to ask a very important question: Which women are set free when they testify
to an experience of sexual abuse?

Her implicit belief that the range of possible experience of sexual abuse is
the same for all women is underlined when she quotes a fellow editor: " 'It
doesn't matter if you live in the city or in the country, if your family is
together or apart, if you're black or white, rich or poor; any child is vulnerable.' "[110] That some women are more privileged *to speak* than other women
is simply not considered. Echoing Rush, Thornton says:

> The women in these pages have transformed themselves, like phoenixes
> rising from the ashes, through their own words. Ideally this anthology
> will unlock the power of the spoken or written word for the thousands
> of additional women who never told anyone.[111]

For her, it is our refusal to speak out, to testify to abuse, that has kept us in
chains.

Ellen Bass begins her introduction where Thornton's Preface leaves off.
Entitled "In the Truth Itself, There is Healing," her essay celebrates women's
decision to speak the truth about sexual abuse. Divided into several subsec-
tions and making extensive use of footnotes and bibliographic citations, Bass'
essay appears more "professional" than the previous two introductions. She

discusses the extent of child sexual abuse, quoting statistical evidence to support her case, and accuses many members of the therapeutic establishment of tolerating and even advocating the sexual use of children. Claims that incest is harmless or beneficial, she argues, are absurd:

> When a man sexually uses a child, he is giving that child a strong message about her world: He is telling her that she is important because of her sexuality, that men want sex from girls, and that relationships are insufficient without sex. He is telling her that she can use her sexuality as a way to get the attention and affection she genuinely needs, that sex is a tool. When he tells her not to tell, she learns there is something about sex that is shameful and bad; and that she, because she is a part of it, is shameful and bad; and that he, because he is a part of it, is shameful and bad. She learns that the world is full of sex and is shameful and bad and not to be trusted, that even those entrusted with her care will betray her; that she will betray herself.[112]

A particularly interesting subsection of the Introduction describes Bass' interaction with a man who advocated sexual contact between adults and children. Entitled "A Good Excuse," the subsection introduces an anonymous critic, a "self-defined psychologist and sex researcher" who challenged Bass's claim that all child–adult sex was effectively abusive. Thornton and Bass met with the man and spoke with him for two hours. Bass describes the meeting as "frustrating and deeply disturbing." In her eyes, this man was completely unconscious both of his own sexist attitudes ("he referred to girls as prick teasers") and his desires to revise his sexually frustrated adolescence by sleeping with the thirteen-year-old girls who were denied to him in his youth. Bass was completely unable to communicate her feeling that, though he claimed the children "initiated" sexual contact with him, he had deceived himself "in pretending that their actions are autonomous, unrelated to what they sense we want of them."[113] She concludes, "Louise and I left the interview feeling we had said little of what we had really wanted to say and that very little of that had permeated his construct of how he wanted sex to be."[114] In this particular case, at least, "telling" was completely ineffective, failing even to make Bass feel better.

The possibility that "telling" might not solve the problem of sexual abuse is also suggested by Bass' own attempt to tie contemporary child sexual abuse to the history of women's oppression. She mentions arranged marriage, *suttee*, foot binding, genital mutilation, clitorodectomy, infibulation, witch burning, and rape, explaining that these horrors were perpetrated by men, whether or not women were involved in the process. Chinese women bound their daughters' feet because that was the only way to ensure their survival in an economy in which unappealing, large-footed women remained unmarried and thus faced starvation. Bass compares contemporary mothers who refuse to confront their daughters' abuse to the Chinese foot binders, failing to realize that by doing so she fatally undermines her argument that women can put a stop to child sexual abuse by just saying no. In a culture in which, as Bass documents, all our institutions including movies, magazines, art, advertising, and literature sanction child molestation, a woman testifying is a voice in the wilderness.[115]

Though it is never articulated clearly, this all boils down to one problem: men. Men do terrible things – to other men, to women, to children, to the biosphere. Why do they do it? Bass believes that they do it because they are ignorant:

> He does not know why. He does not know his own mind or his own body. He is a stranger to himself. And because he does not know himself, does not feel himself, he has in effect given himself up. There is no self to withstand the onslaught of messages he receives from his culture, encouraging him to abuse children.[116]

This is a weak theoretical construct. Who controls the creation of cultural messages? Does she believe that the men who project these cultural messages don't know what they want either? Does Bass believe that there are no men who know their own minds and still desire to abuse and oppress other people? And if men don't know their own minds, can we claim that women do? Do women know the minds of men well enough to claim that men don't know their own minds?

In Bass' world, men may not know their own minds, but women must doubt what they know:

> Working on this anthology has brought me into conscious struggle with the twisted, deep-rooted images of myself as a sexual female that I have absorbed from my environment through my life. Distorted, disturbing images I have suppressed have barged into my consciousness, upsetting me, forcing me to confront how I have been warped.[117]

Bass' confusion leads her to draw some strange conclusions. Like gonzo journalist and combat correspondent Michael Herr, who concludes his surrealist journey through the Vietnam War with the chant "Vietnam Vietnam Vietnam, we've all been there," Ellen Bass is reduced to muttering, "I was not sexually abused. Yet I was sexually abused. We were all sexually abused. . . ." But Herr and Bass are driven to share their versions of traumatic experience precisely because we have *not* all been there. The profound differences between those who have been sexually abused and those who have not been sexually abused are obscured by Bass' desire to universalize their pain. She ignores the special nature of survivor testimony when she claims that, male and female alike, "We are all wounded. We all need healing."[118]

The problem with placing male and female wounds on the same plane is quite obvious if we simply refer back to the statistics with which Bass opened her Introduction. Ninety-seven percent of child molesters and rapists are men. Ninety percent of sexually abused children are women. From this angle it's a one-question IQ test: Who needs healing and who needs restraint? Bass argues for a "restoration of consciousness where the rape of children – as well as the rape of women, of forests, of oceans, of the earth – is a history. . . ."[119] "Restoration" implies that this kind of consciousness existed in the first place, and Bass, in her own historical overview, never suggests that we once existed in this state of grace. In the final analysis, Bass places her faith in a mythology of spiritual transcendence, based on little but hope and desire.

Despite the thickness of the wrappings, the drive to testify in the writings of incest and sexual abuse survivors still shines through in the anthology itself. Jude Brister's child character Carrie wins respite from her battle with her father over her right to her own body, and retires to her own bed in triumph. Maggie Hoyal describes a child fighting back after her father rapes her, her brave outcries: "*No, get off me! Get off me!*"[120] A mother comes to the rescue of an abused child in Jean Monroe's "California Daughter/1950."[121] As in *Voices in the Night,* there are those writers who describe in graphic detail the abuse they suffered. R.C. writes:

> My father is crying and telling me to be good. He pulls down my pajama bottoms and tries to put something too big inside my vagina. I think about shitting. How this is almost like shitting. Only it's not coming out of me and it is not quite the right place. I am terrified that my father is crying. I won't mind the hurt if it will make him stop crying. The big thing won't go in, though, and I am still crying. He stops and tells me I must love him. I lie still and puts that big thing into my mouth. He is holding my nose. I can't breathe. He won't stop and I feel guilty for fighting it. He needs me. My mouth fills with stickiness and I am throwing up all over.[122]

And there are authors who rage and accuse, as Marty O. Dyke does in "Yeah I'm Blaming You":

> Yeah I'm blaming you
> You prickhole prick fuck flap jack
> I'm blaming you
> And I'm blaming you *good.*
> Yeah I'm telling you
> You're full of shit, your "innocence"
> I despise
> All the drivel snivel slime grime semen-webbed
> Words deeds
>
> . . . .

I KNOW
SHE KNOWS
WE KNOW
WHAT YOU DONE
AND YEAH I'M BLAMING YOU,
You prick fuck flip fuck dick duck. . . .[123]

Six of the entries in *I Never Told Anyone* were excerpted from full-length books or longer works. One of these is Yarrow Morgan's "Remember," which appeared in its longer form in *Voices in the Night*. Another is Jean Monroe's short story, "California Daughter/1950," which won the Martha Foley's Best Stories award in 1976 and was published in complete form in *Aphra* magazine that same year. A third is excerpted from a cycle of poems by Lynn Swenson, and the fourth is a short chapter from Kate Millet's *Flying*. All of these voices have inevitably been compromised in the excerpting process, but none suffer more than the last two by Maya Angelou and Billie Holiday. Both *I Know Why the Caged Bird Sings* and *Lady Sings the Blues* are black women's autobiographies, rooted in traditions of black women's literary and oral culture, and deeply concerned with issues of race and gender. Strongly black-identified in their writings and their art, both artists have served as role models for other creative black women. Yet Thornton and Bass carefully sidestep the issue of race.

Neither the introduction to Angelou's, nor Holiday's narratives mentions the fact that either woman is black. An ignorant but observant reader might guess that Angelou is African-American, since she is described as the northern coordinator for the Southern Christian Leadership Conference, but such a conclusion is difficult to confirm, particularly since Bass and Thornton describe her as "one of the few *women* members of the Directors Guild. . . ."[124] It would be reasonable to assume that if Angelou is black, her race also makes her one of the few *African-American* members of the Directors Guild. The emphasis on her status as woman, and the complete disappearance of her race indicate either a conscious or unconscious decision on the part of the editors to "disappear" the question of race in their text.

In the introduction to the excerpt from Holiday's autobiography, Holiday is described as a woman "inspired by recordings of Louis Armstrong and Bessie Smith," who "began to sing professionally in a Harlem nightclub." Again, those familiar with black history and music would identify Holiday as a black singer, but for the uninitiated, conclusions might be difficult to draw. Though Holiday played and recorded with many well-known black musicians, the editors feel it only necessary to mention that she made her first recording with Benny Goodman in 1933. She was known, Thornton and Bass write, "for the unique, bittersweet quality of her voice, her striking beauty, and the gardenia she usually wore in her hair;"[125] they neglect to comment on her work as one of the premier black recording artists of her day, and the fact that she was an outspoken critic of racism.

Bass and Thornton have, in effect, appropriated the writings of these black women and used them to further their own political agenda, albeit in the service of a good cause. In so doing they have compromised the integrity of both autobiographies, simplifying their complex messages and diluting their power. Neither Holiday nor Angelou writes about her experience of surviving child sexual abuse outside of the context of life as a black woman.

The excerpt from Angelou's *I Know Why A Caged Bird Sings* chosen for inclusion in the Bass and Thornton anthology interprets her experience through the lessons she had been taught as a child in the black church, internalizing her guilt as sin. Her abuser, a black man named Mr. Freeman, is murdered by her uncles in retaliation, since the white institution of a court of law failed, in their eyes, to provide justice. She believes she is responsible for his death:

> In those moments I decided that although Bailey [her brother] loved me, he couldn't help. I had sold myself to the Devil and there could be no escape. The only thing I could do was to stop talking to people other than Bailey. Instinctively, or somehow, I knew that because I loved him so much I'd never hurt him, but if I talked to anyone else, that person might die too. Just my breath, carrying my words out, might poison people and they'd curl up and die like the black fat slugs that only pretended.[126]

Her revelations about sexual abuse, like those of Susan Chute, are intimately involved with her racial identity. Angelou's power to harm others does not extend to white people, though she knows that she can harm her own black people by talking to white people. Likewise, she understands that black people are not protected by law. The white policeman – "taller than the sky and whiter than my image of God" – who informs her family of Mr. Freeman's death, has no mission beyond the delivery of the news. In Angelou's childhood world white people do not mete out justice, they simply pass judgment. She says of the policeman: "Although he looked harmless, I knew he was a dreadful angel counting out my many sins."[127]

The three-page excerpt from Holiday's memoir is a particularly abrupt abridgment, providing no context at all in which to examine her experience of sexual abuse. Holiday's life was filled with traumatic experiences, and her brief discussion of the sexual abuses she suffered is a clear indication of her belief that they were not the most notable wrongs inflicted upon her by a society that was both racist and sexist. As a child, Holiday was attacked by a neighbor, "Mr. Dick," who attempted to rape her with the assistance of a female accomplice. "I'll never forget that night," Holiday writes:

> Even if you're a whore, you don't want to be raped. A bitch can turn
> twenty-five hundred tricks a day and she still don't want nobody to rape
> her. It's the worst thing that can happen to a woman. And here it was
> happening to me when I was ten.[128]

She is acutely aware that the callous treatment afforded her by the police is
a result of the combination of her status as black and female. A white woman
attacked by a black man would not be treated in the same fashion:

> When we got [to the police station], instead of treating me and Mom
> like somebody who called the cops for help, they treated me like I'd
> killed somebody. They wouldn't let my mother take me home. Mr.
> Dick was in his forties, and I was only ten. Maybe the police sergeant
> took one look at my breasts and limbs and figured my age from that, I
> don't know. Anyway, I guess they had me figured for having enticed
> this old goat into the whorehouse or something. All I know for sure is
> they threw me into a cell. My mother cried and screamed and pleaded,
> but they just put her out of the jailhouse and turned me over to a fat
> white matron. . . . Mr. Dick got sentenced to five years. They sentenced
> me to a Catholic institution.[129]

Holiday declared that she refused to recreate the hierarchy of domination in
her own life, rejecting men who were not understanding and sympathetic
about her anger and hurt at being sexually abused. Thornton and Bass end the
excerpt on this note, suggesting that Holiday had the power to take control
of her life and that she used it positively. Such a conclusion also ignores the
many other hierarchies of domination that Holiday could not successfully
escape, the racist laws and attitudes which continued to humiliate and oppress
her, the economic difficulties faced by a black artist, the physical and psychological needs that drug addiction both satisfied and created.

The editors' deliberate decision to erase race issues from the text is also
reflected in their discussion of Hummy's short story, "A Totally White
World."[130] Though the short story describes a racially motivated sexual assault,
the editors choose to focus on Hummy's miraculous recovery from her
injuries, and her current status as a "successful businesswoman" rather than
on the questions of race and gender Hummy raises. The fact that Hummy
herself underlines the importance of race in her choice of a title for her story
seems to escape them.

Hummy begins:

> I think to myself, what is that awful smell? It's like old Prestone,
> antifreeze. I groggily try to open my eyes. Oh, this is a totally white
> world. I can't seem to move my right arm. It's all painted white and
> seems to be in cement. . . . I guess I must be dead. I wonder what I died
> of? I never thought it would be all white with the Sky People.[131]

Like Susan Chute and Maya Angelou, Hummy draws parallels between the idea of a white god and a white-ruled secular world. Told she is in a hospital by her beloved friend, Spring Flower, she asks what has happened to her. Spring Flower tells her she fell out of tree:

> You fell so hard that you tore yourself open. Part of your bowels were out of your body and your pelvic bone was crushed. Besides all that, you broke your jaw in four places. That's why your mouth is wired shut. Along with that, you broke nine ribs, your right arm is broken in three places, and the big bone in your left leg is broken. You have five cracks in your skull, and so many bruises.[132]

In this listing of her injuries it is quite clear that the consensus is that Hummy is responsible for hurting *herself*. She tore herself open, she broke her jaw, she broke her ribs. This catalogue of wounds appears rather extensive, even for a child who has taken a terrible fall from a tree, but Spring Flower relates it as if it is a documented truth. However, our belief in the accuracy of this assessment is undermined when Spring Flower reminds Hummy:

> It's important that you speak in the white tongue so that the nurses and doctors can help you with what you need. Besides, I have told you before, it's not polite to speak in our tongue when the people around can't understand what you are saying. You are in the white world now, so speak the white tongue.[133]

Hummy, even at five, is sensitive enough to understand her situation. She thinks, "Somewhere deep inside of me, I really didn't want them to know what I was saying."[134]

Hummy refuses to speak English and tells her story only to Spring Flower. Two white men kidnapped her took her into an old shed. They beat her, and one of them broke her arm over his knee. They tied her between two posts by her wrists and ankles, "spread out like you would stretch a hide to dry." When she fought them they beat her some more and knocked out her teeth. They raped her, and urinated and defecated on her body. Then they beat her some more, breaking bones and causing internal injuries. Though the story is told through the child's eyes, it is clear to the reader that both men use Hummy as an object to excite each other – the homoerotic quality of their violence is made obvious by Hummy's description of "Ernie . . . doing something to Floyd. You know, like dogs do,"[135] and by her relation of Floyd's comment, "Go come in her face so I can watch."[136] They refer to Hummy only as "Indian," "Toots," "cunt," "heathen," "slut," and "pussy," making it clear that her racial and sexual status makes her less than human in their eyes.

Hummy's decision not to tell her story in English is reasonable, given her position. She overhears Spring Flower speaking angrily to the doctor, demanding that the men be brought to justice. The doctor replies, "She would have to identify them. It would be her word, a five-year-old Indian child against two adult white men. . . . I don't think you could ever bring it to trial."[137] Spring Flower's answer suggests that Hummy's story will have a conclusion similar to the sexual abuse incident in Maya Angelou's autobiography:

> "Doctor, you're misunderstanding me," Spring Flower said. "I definitely do not want her involved in any way. I just want to know where they can be located. You can help me or not. These men will be found and will be treated accordingly. We, too, have our justice."[138]

Though the law does not mete justice out to most men who sexually abuse women, communities of American minorities suffer an additional burden of discrimination within the justice system. Women of color are rarely aided by white-controlled courts and police when they are sexually abused. Men of color are most likely to be prosecuted for the crime of sexual abuse when they are accused of abusing white women. Many people of color have learned that it is safest to avoid the U.S. court system entirely, and they often rely on community-based moral and ethical codes, as well as community enforced systems of punishment for infractions to solve their legal dilemmas. Such codes are frequently sexist, yet they often offer more useful guidelines than the dominant white practice of law and order.

Incest and sexual abuse survivor literature written by women of color reflects the complex interplay of gender and race within minority communities, and between the minority community and white mainstream culture. The elision of these differences in the early sexual abuse and incest survivor literature is an indication of the power hierarchy that exists in the community of women who produce such literature. Black feminist critic bell hooks warns us that we must question our motivations, and be aware of the uses to which we put women's personal narratives. Otherwise, we run the risk of misunderstanding and misinterpreting them:

> Feminist thinkers in the United States use confession and memory primarily as a way to narrate tales of victimization, which are rarely rendered dialectically. . . . We must . . . be careful not to promote the construction of narratives of female experience that become so normative that all experience that does not fit the model is deemed illegitimate or unworthy of investigation. Rethinking ways to constructively use confession and memory shifts the focus away from mere naming of one's experience. It enables feminist thinkers to talk about identity in relation to culture, history, politics, whatever and to challenge the notion of identity as static and unchanging. . . . In early feminist consciousness-raising, confession was often the way to share negative traumas, the experience of male violence for example. Yet there

remain many unexplored areas of female experience that need to be fully examined, thereby widening the scope of our understanding of what it is to be female in this society.[139]

hooks succinctly sums up the problems with the early attempts to publish and promote literature by sexual abuse survivors. *Kiss Daddy Goodnight, Voices in the Night* and *I Never Told Anyone* do embody a "normative" narrative of female experience of sexual abuse. Each of these books either omits stories that deal with racial identity, or includes such stories in an abridged or carefully decontextualized manner meant to prevent them from interfering with the explicit "message" of the volume.

As Louise Armstrong found, much to her dismay, the publication of these normative narratives have been ineffective in altering the patriarchal structure. They have, in fact, raised a new set of problems, which Armstrong describes in the introduction to *Kiss Daddy Goodnight: Ten Years Later* – a 1987 reissue of her landmark publication with a new foreword and afterword:

> [I]t was not our intention merely to start a long conversation. Nor did we intend simply to offer up one more topic for talk shows, or one more plot option for ongoing dramatic series. We hoped to raise hell. We hoped to raise change. What we raised, it would seem, was discourse. And a sizable problem-management industry. Apart from protective service workers, we have researchers, family treatment programs, incest offender programs, prevention experts, incest educators. . . . It was not in our minds, either, ten years ago, that incest would become a career option.[140]

Armstrong believes that while making incest a topic of public discourse has not reduced the number of children who are incestuously abused, it has resulted in the "medicalization" of incest and the "creation of an incest industry."[141]

Medicalization has reduced incest from crime to "disease"; a psychological illness which involves the entire family. Contemporary psychology, Armstrong claims, places an inappropriate amount of responsibility for incest on the mother of the abused child:

> From the outset, all the heavy artillery was aimed at this mother. The entire construction of the "family disease" model depended on her existence. . . . Without this abstract "her," we would have been forced to confront the political/power abuse as we had posed it. We would have had to hear the peculiar harmony between the victims' testimony and that of the offenders. We would then have had to confront head-on the moral dilemma: How wrong is it to molest your own child, within the context of our value system today? Worse than molesting the neighbor's kid? . . . Less bad?. . . .[142]

By looking at incest as a "family" problem, the status quo could be preserved – the problem could be explained so that it lay in the dysfunctional nature of a particular family, rather than in the abusive behavior of one man, or of many men towards many female children. In the classic Freudian tradition, family problems stem from the "neurotic mother," neatly repackaged as the "incest mother." Incest mothers caused their own problems by choosing husbands over children, being fearful of abandonment, and denying that abusive relationships existed in their families. Armstrong explains:

> [I]t pointed to an unfortunate (but apparently acceptable) assumption about family life: that mom's main job was to control pop's behavior. It suggested the need for a beady eye trained on the nursery door. It suggested that health was a lack of trust in the person you'd married.[143]

Laws were passed that criminalized the behavior of these mothers: "failure to protect" clauses, and statutes that punished mothers who "knew *or should have known*."[144] At the same time, a "pro-incest lobby" (which included a number of researchers, psychologists and academics) began to state publicly that "Incest between children and adults can sometimes be beneficial," and that its very prevalence made prohibition impossible.[145] Disheartened, Armstrong writes:

> Our voices, by now, had been almost entirely drowned out. It was becoming more and more unfashionable to appear to notice the fact that every study showed the perpetrators to be almost universally male, whether the victims were small boys or small girls. Indeed, by the time of this writing, even to mention the fact is to set off an explosion against such obvious retrograde feminist man-hating. As one Highly Placed Personage in the sexual-abuse-expert chain bellowed at me recently: "I am sick and tired of hearing about this as a gender issue!"[146]

Armstrong also mentions the male obsession with the notion that women use cries of incest to somehow oppress men. Just as the courts protect men from false accusation so enthusiastically and with such dedication that cases of "simple" rape are almost never prosecuted, so the mechanisms of law protect husbands and fathers from accusations of incest and child sexual abuse. Such accusations are often thought to be merely a tactic in divorce and custody cases, a ploy used by a bitter wife to "get back" at her husband. Armstrong concludes, "Speaking out was a first step only."[147]

> There are tremendous forces working against real change. A limited, but apparently constant portion of the male population obviously enjoys acting on the tacit privilege to molest children who are "theirs." Whether in open advocacy of children's "rights" to sex with adults, or behind

the cant of family privacy, preserving the family, and traditional values, or by counter-accusation when they are caught, these forces will continue to wage war.[148]

Armstrong's new ending for *Kiss Daddy Goodnight* is not nearly as strong and optimistic as the thanks she uttered in her first edition. Driven to frustration and despair, she concludes the book with an inarticulate wailing. The last word in the book is a scream, not so different from an infant's cry: "*Waaagh.*"[149] In a society where violence against women is supported and condoned, excused and rationalized, the testimony of survivors of sexual abuse is silenced, ignored, distorted, and drowned out by the thundering voices of the patriarchs.

Susan Brownmiller wrote in 1976, with a certain irony, "Man's discovery that his genitalia could be used as a weapon to generate fear must rank as one of the most important discoveries of prehistoric times."[150] Anthony Wilden concurred, and added that "Male control over women and their bodies is the oldest form of private property; the division of productive labor by sex is the oldest form of class distinction; male monopolies of myth, ritual, and religion are the oldest forms of ideology; male supremacy is the oldest form of imperialism."[151] Andrea Dworkin suggested that the male sexual act is inevitably a dominance ritual, that the urge to penetrate was inextricably tied to the urge to conquer and rule the penetrated, and that the one penetrated is inevitably feminized: "Fucking requires that the male act on one who has less power and this valuation is so deep, so completely implicit in the act, that the one who is fucked is stigmatized as feminine during the act even when not anatomically female."[152] Robin Morgan argued that to save the planet from certain destruction we must transform ourselves completely, refiguring "all forms of perception, including remembering, imagining, intuiting, hallucinating, dreaming, and empathizing."[153] Biologist and naturalist Irene Elia observes:

> [I]t now appears that in order to fundamentally alter any systems in which men dominate women, the rule of perpetuation of the successful (or natural selection) would have to be denied, contravened, manipulated, or abolished. While religions may deny ("transcend") this rule, utopians try to contravene it, and science manipulate it, nothing, it seems, will abolish the rule of natural (including social) selection short of that which would abolish differential reproduction and differential death.[154]

We bear witness not simply to individual crimes of abuse and brutality, but to an entire system of oppression that keeps women and many men in thrall, subject to the whims and desires of a privileged masculine class – a system in which maleness and violence are closely linked. Our testimony challenges that system, though it does not overthrow it. Bearing witness, we have learned, is just the beginning:

> The change we have wrought is a change in consciousness. The actual condition of rape continues, as do all the conditions of women's lives which cannot be separated from rape. . . . Yes, we do not yet have the end of rape. All we have is the feat of naming rape a crime against us.[155]

7

This Is about Power on Every Level

Three Incest Survivor Narratives

I will not say again
I sat on his lap. No.
He had me on his lap.
You were not raped: he raped you.
Memory moves as it can, freedom is yours
to place the verb.
And yes, the oppressor's language
sometimes sounds beautiful,
always dies hard. Let us move on.

                        – Margaret Randall[1]

The woman writer walks a stony path. Joanna Russ outlined the difficulties faced by women who enter the literary sphere in her now classic work, *How to Suppress Women's Writing* (1983).[2] Over a decade later, these obstacles are still in place. Women's works are ridiculed, trivialized, appropriated, scorned, or ignored, rarely engaged sympathetically and infrequently appreciated. In addition to literary skills, a woman writer needs determination and courage, and even the possession of all three does not guarantee success. This chapter focuses on the work of three women who have chosen to write and to publish narratives of incest; who have chosen to break not only the taboos against women writing, but the taboos against acknowledging and discussing sexual abuse.

Louise Wisechild's *The Obsidian Mirror: An Adult Healing from Incest* is the story of a woman who reconstructs her fragmented self piece by piece – assembling a whole woman out of the child shattered by incestuous abuse. *Enter Password: Recovery. Re-Enter Password* is Elly Bulkin's record of her

struggle towards self-consciousness and memory and of her efforts at generating a balance between herself and her community. Margaret Randall's
This is About Incest combines prose, poetry and photography in a work carefully
constructed to provide the reader with a chronological re-enactment of her
struggle to heal from incest. These narratives are dedicated to transforming
a personal journey into a matter of public record.

Sociologist Inger Agger and psychiatrist Søren Buus Jensen describe the
act of testimony as a ritual with dual purposes. When a survivor testifies, she
both purges herself of an internal "evil," and bears witness to a social or
political injustice:

> The word "testimony" has in itself a double connotation of both some-
> thing objective, judicial, public, or *political,* and of something subjective,
> spiritual, cathartic, or *private.* . . . Thus the use of the word "testimony"
> in itself in a psychotherapeutic setting with victims of political repres-
> sion implies that the subjective, private pain is to be seen in an objective,
> political context.[3]

Agger and Jensen believe that the drive to testify is a "universal phenomenon,"
and promote the use of the "testimony method" of psychotherapy in cross-
cultural treatment of trauma survivors. A therapist who uses the testimony
method is concerned with both "the cognitive and emotional levels in the
process of bearing testimony."[4] The therapist becomes involved in a multi-
level relationship with the patient, first as her psychotherapist, and subsequently in a public political role "as a joint advocate against political oppression and the violation of human rights."[5]

The sexual abuse survivor narratives discussed in this chapter are all products of this personal/political therapeutic process. Within the supportive environment of the feminist movement, writing workshops and therapy groups
for survivors of sexual abuse have evolved and multiplied. Survivors are both
going about the business of personal healing and publicly documenting atrocities against women. This work is difficult, and, as Agger and Jensen explain,
it is most successful with survivors who have a strong ideological commitment to bearing witness. Many of the women who engage in the process of
testifying to experiences of sexual abuse are white lesbian feminists and
activists, and share a certain set of beliefs and practices. Literary critic Lillian
Faderman explains:

> There is a good deal on which lesbian–feminists disagree. . . . But they
> all agree that men have waged constant battle against women, com-
> mitted atrocities or at best injustices against them, reduced them to
> grown-up children, and that a feminist ought not to sleep in the enemy
> camp. They all agree that being a lesbian is, whether consciously or
> unconsciously perceived, a political act, a refusal to fulfill the male

image of womanhood or to bow to male supremacy. . . . [Lesbianism] is a choice which has been made often in the context of the feminist movement and with an awareness of the ideology behind it. It has seemed the only possible choice for many women who believe that the personal is political. . . .[6]

Wisechild and Bulkin describe themselves as lesbians; Randall, though she does not state her sexual preferences, is clearly woman-identified.[7] The disproportionate representation of white lesbian women in the ranks of those who bear witness to surviving sexual abuse is liable to be misinterpreted, and a discussion of the phenomenon is in order. It is crucial that the student of sexual abuse survivor testimony reject the heterosexist assumption that lesbianism is deviant behavior. Approaching these writings with the idea that lesbian women are simply "normal" women who have "gone wrong" will prevent the critic from fully understanding the implications of lesbian testimony to surviving sexual abuse.

Lesbian sexual abuse survivors are not potentially heterosexual women who have been turned into "manhaters" by their terrible experience. As lesbian philosopher Sarah Hoagland explains in her text *Lesbian Ethics,* "Certainly many lesbians hate men, and there is reason to believe that manhating is important to moving out of oppression."[8] But manhating is not the defining characteristic of lesbians. According to Hoagland and other lesbian feminist theorists, *woman-identification* is the chief characteristic of lesbianism. Lesbian separatist Harriet Desmoines explains:

"Lesbian consciousness" is really a point of view, a view from the boundary. And in a sense every time a woman draws a circle around her psyche, saying "this is a room of my own," and then writes from within that "room," she's inhabiting lesbian consciousness.[9]

In order to fully understand the implications of lesbian testimony, we must refuse to trivialize lesbianism by defining it as a "bedroom issue," and expand our understanding into the realm of the political.[10]

The importance of woman-identification is clear to feminist therapists who work with sexual abuse survivors. *The Courage to Heal* (1988), a popular, mass-market, 500-page "handbook" for women survivors of child sexual abuse, contains the testimony of lesbian survivors, as well as a section entitled "On Being a Lesbian and a Survivor."[11] Edited by Ellen Bass and Laura Davis, *The Courage to Heal* is strongly supportive of lesbian women, and contains testimony that supports the idea that lesbianism is a viable option for women:

I had believed that I was a lesbian because I had been so badly abused by my father. I thought maybe it was a point of being stuck in my emotional growth. I thought that until I met a lesbian . . . who had never been abused in any way. . . . [T]hat's when I realized my lesbianism didn't have to have a cause. It's got nothing to do with what happened to me.

I'm a lesbian because I love women, not because I hate men. I'm not a separatist. I have a male child who I think is terrific. There are men in my life I care a great deal for. I'm not a man-hater. In fact, I think heterosexual women have a lot more reason to hate men than I do.[12]

Bass and Davis explain that although "some survivors still believe that there is something wrong with them that caused them to be lesbian," this is far from the truth. "Being lesbian," they state firmly, "is a perfectly healthy way to to be, not another effect of the abuse you need to overcome."[13] They suggest that women who are not comfortable with their lesbian identity look for support within the lesbian community: "Subscribe to lesbian journals and magazines. Get on the mailing list for women's music festivals and conferences. . . . Reach out. You're not alone. For many women their lesbian identity is a strong, positive anchor in their lives."[14]

Woman-identification serves as a strong, positive anchor for the three women whose works are discussed in this chapter. In their narratives we can find the essential elements of the same testimony method employed by women who serve as therapists both in a professional and peer group setting. The white lesbian feminist community provides a safe and supportive environment within which these sexual abuse survivors can come to terms with their pain and anger. The existence of this environment most likely accounts for the high proportion of sexual abuse survivor testimonies written by white lesbians. Heterosexual women may testify in smaller numbers than their lesbian sisters because they do not often have access to a close-knit communal support system that validates and encourages a strong ideological commitment to bearing witness to sexual abuse.

Therapeutic healing is at the heart of both the Wisechild and Randall narratives, where the relationship between survivor and therapist is central to the text. Though Bulkin is not in therapy, her lover and her friends take on the role of therapist, and she embarks on a journey of healing and self-discovery. These narratives parallel the three-stage process for treating Post-Traumatic Stress Disorder described by psychologist and art therapist David Read Johnson:

> First, the patient needs to gain access in a safe and controlled way to the traumatic memories, to overcome denial or amnesia for the events. Second, the patient needs to engage in a lengthy working-through process in which the trauma can be acknowledged, re-examined, and conceptualized, resulting in a modification of its intensity. The trauma is transformed from an intrusive re-living of the event into a memory that can be recalled when one wishes. Third, the patient needs to re-join the world of others through interaction with other trauma victims, to

find forgiveness from others for what happened, and to be able to go on with one's life.[15]

But where Johnson envisions a carefully managed therapeutic environment and an unequal patient–therapist relationship, the authors of these personal narratives describe a situation in which personal healing and public perception are inextricably intertwined. Patients and therapists are feminists dedicated to bringing about profound change in the political order. As Agger and Jensen suggest, the therapist is engaged in the process of reconstructing reality – her exposure to the testimony of the survivor may strengthen her own ideological commitment, and she may "choose to join the struggle against the injustice and evil [she has] witnessed."[16] The reader becomes part of this reconstruction when she participates in the testimonial process. Persuaded by the authenticity and power of a narrative generated by the collaborative efforts of therapist and survivor, she may revise her own views of reality or be moved to take an active role in the struggle.

The involvement of the reader in the testimonial process depends upon her willingness to participate in communal struggle and to identify with the survivor. The white lesbian feminist writer expects such commitment from her sister readers, whom she assumes are also feminists and involved in the work of interpreting and understanding women's writing with sympathy and respect. Literary critic Patrocinio Schweickart explains, "Feminist reading and writing alike are grounded in the interest of producing a community of feminist readers and writers, in the hope that ultimately this community will expand to include everyone."[17] Feminist ideology promotes and supports the testimonial process, and a community of feminists will create an environment in which testimony may be both given and received.[18] Women's testimonies are often dismissed by the masculine critical community as mere "confessional" narratives, "personal" rather than "literary."[19] But feminist critics are committed to a kind of testimony of their own, speaking "as a witness in defense of the woman writer. . . . The feminist reader takes the part of the woman writer against patriarchal misreadings that trivialize or distort her work. . . ."[20]

It is in this spirit of sisterhood and communal support that I undertake to analyze and comment upon the works of Wisechild, Bulkin, and Randall. I read, as Schweikart suggests, to "connect," to recuperate, and to formulate "the context, the tradition, that would link women writers to one another, to women readers and critics, and to the larger community of women."[21] Schweikart's cautions echo in my ears: I must respect the autonomy of the text; I am a visitor and must observe the requisite courtesies; I must be careful not to appropriate what is not mine.

Louise M. Wisechild's *The Obsidian Mirror: An Adult Healing from Incest* was published in 1988 by Seal Press, a feminist press that features a series of

"self-help and theoretical works for battered women and movement work-
ers."[22] Its lavender cover, and the excerpt from Judy Grahn's favorable
review,[23] identify it as a lesbian narrative to those who are able to pick up the
signals, though the lesbian perspective of the author is not advertised. Seal
markets the text to those interested in "Psychology/Self-Help/Women's Studies" and places the following comments on the back cover:

> In this affirming and inspiring book, Louise Wisechild describes her
> personal journey as an adult survivor of incest – the pain of her ex-
> perience and the power of her healing.
>
> Exploring the process of remembering, the author explains how she,
> like many other survivors, was unable to recall incidents of childhood
> abuse until well into adulthood. With the support of friends, counselors
> and her own work with body therapy, she begins her recovery: the
> movement from fear and grief to rage and resolve, the spiritual reawak-
> ening and growing understanding of her creativity, and the ultimate
> reclamation of self.
>
> Deeply personal and powerfully universal, *The Obsidian Mirror* gives
> validation and hope to survivors of incest and abuse and those working
> with them.

The Seal publicist writes in terms strikingly similar to Agger's and Jensen's,
demonstrating an awareness that the testimonial act has both personal and
political implications. Furthermore, by directing her remarks to "survivors of
incest and abuse and those working with them," she underlines the point that
abused women and their supporters form a community with specific interests. The Grahn quote reinforces this notion, emphasizing the fact that
many women belong to this community when she notes that the common
experience of women who are sexually abused is "one of the more spectacular
revelations of modern women – that a quarter of us and more are raped as
children."

The Acknowledgements page – the first page of the text – once again
affirms the communal nature of the testimonial act. Friends and therapists are
equally important and at times they are indistinguishable; both are an active
part of Wisechild's life. Furthermore, Wisechild is herself a therapist and
works with other sexual abuse survivors, so that her role as survivor is now
inseparable from her role as therapist: she is a therapist *because* she is a
survivor, and a survivor because she has entered into a therapeutic relationship with others. She has become both the healer and the healed. Wisechild
writes:

> Many people helped me as I wrote this book. I am grateful to the
> wisdom, humor and support of my friends and therapists and their
> willingness to be included in my life and in my writings.

The women I've seen as clients helped me keep writing by telling me
their stories and sharing their pain and their healing.[24]

The healing process is located in the acts of storytelling, and of listening
to stories. Wisechild acknowledges her debt to the women who have served
as her support network, and affirms that writing her healers into her stories
has enabled her to grow strong. She also acknowledges a debt to the clients
who have told her their own stories. It is both possible and desirable to share
pain and healing within the community through the process of testimony
with acknowledgment.

Wisechild divides her narrative into 20 parts. The introduction is entitled
"The Story," and it is followed by nineteen chapters, all, presumably, part of
the "story": "The Voice," "The Body," "The Well," "The Touch, "The Rock,"
"The Threat," "The Response," "The Stare," "The Fire," "The Mask," "The
Song," "The Fist," "The Mirror," "The Hand," "The Pit," "The Cord," "The
Dust," "The Climb," "The Gift." These titles indicate the mystical and
spiritual nature of Wisechild's journey and its connection to New Age phil-
osophy, for they call to mind the names of the Tarot cards – The Moon, The
Lovers, The Tower, The Star – and they are laid out, like cards. Feminist
Tarot interpreters Sally Gearhart and Susan Rennie explain that the Tarot is
"an instrument for women's self-discovery and self-exploration":

> Reading the Tarot is an attempt to perceive and understand the con-
> scious and unconscious reality surrounding a particular question or
> circumstance. What is important in a Tarot reading is whatever is
> discovered. The discovery is limited only by the reader's openness and
> sensitivity to the meaning of the cards. Sensitivity grows with acquaint-
> ance with the deck and practice in exploring relationships of symbols to
> particular questions.[25]

Wisechild is engaged in an attempt to perceive and understand the conscious
and unconscious reality which surrounds her incest experience.

Instead of using the symbols and archetypes pictured on a Tarot deck,
Wisechild gazes deep into an obsidian mirror, which reflects images she must
interpret. In the European mystical tradition fortune-tellers used crystal balls
to reveal the future to paying customers, and in fairy tales witches sometimes
possess magic mirrors which perform at their command, revealing secrets and
providing answers to specific questions. Wisechild's mirror is black, suggesting that it is a window into an internal, rather than external universe.[26] She
rejects the New Age answers offered by Western magic and turns, instead, to
an idealized notion of the magic of a native American population – the
Mexican Indians. In her Introduction, Wisechild explains the symbolism of
the obsidian mirror:

When obsidian is polished, it is reflective; a glossy black mirror of volcanic glass. Looking at myself in an obsidian mirror, I see my face circled with black. After several minutes of looking into the obsidian, my eyes turn inward, peering inside myself, meeting the blackness within me. Ancient Mexicans used mirrors of obsidian for visions. Some believe that gazing into polished obsidian brings whatever an individual needs to deal with the the surface of consciousness. Looking into the mirror, I saw buried scenes from my past. As I continued to look, I found new possibilities. I saw that darkness is a sacred part of my woman's body. I learned that I could reclaim this body as my own.[27]

The notion of looking inward for answers rather than turning to the outside world is powerfully attractive to Westerners who seek spiritual enlightenment in what can only be called a kind of *faux* native-American "style." Carlos Casteneda expresses his fascination with the Yaqui sorcerers who he alleged have taught him to "gaze," to "see" rather than to merely "look." To see, he learned to accept darkness, to overcome his Western fear of the night, and to find in it truth and clarity. In Castenda's narrative, the woman sorcerer Lidia explains to Casteneda that her magical powers enable her to see truth by looking at the shadow of an object, rather than at the object itself: "Now I never look at anything anymore; I just look at their shadows. Even if there is no light at all, there are shadows; even at night there are shadows. Because I'm a shadow gazer I'm also a distance gazer. I can gaze at shadows even in the distance."[28] Wisechild has also accepted the notion that dreams and visions are a gateway to a broader reality, and that the inability to see and interpret mystical signs makes personal growth difficult or impossible.

Wisechild perceives her healing process as a totality, a world where the "search through memory, the confrontation of my family and my subsequent growth could not be separated from my life as a whole. Instead healing was woven into my work, into my changing relationship with my lover and my friends and into my search for a new understanding of spirituality."[29] Lidia, the character of the Yaqui sorcerer, explains the manner in which she came to "see":

Dreamers must gaze in order to do *dreaming* and then they must look for their dreams in their gazing. . . . Gazing and *dreaming* go together. It took me a lot of gazing at shadows to get my *dreaming* of shadows going. And then it took a lot of *dreaming* and gazing to get the two together and really *see* in the shadows what I was seeing in my *dreaming*.[30]

Lidia's success in bringing her internal symbolic world into parity with the external natural world is matched by Wisechild's own. Wisechild gazes into the mirror, which is both real and symbolic, to see and *dream* her past. She moves toward wholeness as she integrates the symbols of memory – Well, Pit,

Dust, and Tree – with the kinesthetic memories of tension and pain. Changes in internal symbolic relationships affect changes in Wisechild's relationships in the physical world. By gazing she sees herself. By *dreaming* herself different, she changes herself. When she is healed, the physical image she sees reflected in *The Obsidian Mirror* is the same as the symbolic image she sees in the metaphorical obsidian mirror of her *dreams*.

Wisechild's first chapter, "The Voice," begins with her declaration of mutiny: "Since it is inappropriate to discuss religion, I will begin there."[31] But her rebellion is incomplete, for Wisechild believes "God is out to get me," and though she pretends to have outgrown her mother's cautions – "Never talk about religion or sex or politics in front of company" – she still finds herself bound by them:

> I still don't talk about religion. I think that I should have matured enough to stop worrying about God and to start putting my energy into something constructive. But God is a shadow. He even followed me here, to Stanford.[32]

Wisechild's first paragraph states her problem – she must come to terms with God. "He" is a shadow she must gaze at and understand. She makes clear at this point that she has only looked at God and not yet seen "Him," for "He" is indistinguishable from other authorities and "His" rules appear similar to the rule of other patriarchal authorities in her life:

> As it turns out, religion and graduate school have a lot in common. Each has a set of rules and acceptable standards. Like church, the classroom has an aura of solemnity. A hush descends when the elder professor enters the classroom, like a minister taking his place behind a pulpit. If I'm not on my best behavior, I'll get punished, just as my grandfather delivered God's punishment if I played too much when I was a kid. I'm afraid that I still don't know how to be good enough.[33]

The preoccupation with being "good enough," with living up to standards imposed by others, prevents Wisechild from gaining access to her own inner truth. "It's disturbing," she writes, "to admit that I became a graduate student for the same reasons I prayed to Jesus nineteen years ago. I want someone to tell me I'm good enough. I need saving. I lack the nerve to try something else."[34]

An inner voice, "The Voice" of the chapter title, tells Wisechild she is "bad." Wisechild has named this voice "Sarah," and she describes her as "a prematurely old woman with a tight mouth and worried forehead," who "quotes God and my grandfather against me."[35] Grandpa and God were, to the four-year-old Wisechild, the same entity – old men with "fierce white hair and stern blue eyes" – and Grandpa spoke with the voice of God, frequently quoting the Bible, especially "sow as ye shall reap." Like God, Grandpa dispensed judgment and punishment. An understanding of neither was accessible to a child:

> He had a lot of rules, but only grownups got to know exactly what they were. As a child, I discovered them only after breaking one, like the correct interpretation of an essay question revealed after the test.[36]

An instant acceptance of masculine authority has been conditioned in Wisechild, and she fears her professors "just as [she] feared [her] grandfather."[37] Sarah is Wisechild's internalized masculine authority, reminding her that a woman is nothing, and that she is doomed to failure. "Sometimes," Wisechild says," "Sarah talks like my mother."[38] Wisechild's mother reinforced patriarchal authority, speaking to her in an echo of her grandfather's "loud, mad voice."[39]

Sarah is not the only voice who lives inside Wisechild. At twelve she rebelled against her parents and a new part of her began to speak, chanting "I don't care, I don't care, I don't care" like "a demonstrator shouting slogans." Wisechild calls this new voice "Fuckit:" "Fuckit hates being told what to do. 'Fuck you!' she says, 'Leave me alone! I won't listen to Sarah! I don't care if I do go to hell!' "[40] The battle between Sarah and Fuckit is unending. Sarah pushes Wisechild to accept the judgment of her parents and grandparents – that she is a failure. Fuckit drives her to reject their judgments, but can offer nothing that promises fulfillment. Her spiritual and emotional agony takes the form of

> a dark, rotting mass that spreads from the secret recesses of my stomach into my chest. The heaviness is like dough that cannot rise. I imagine it smelling like an open sewer. . . . I know it's an evil that lives inside. It keeps growing bigger like a curse. I feel trapped and small inside of it. I don't know when it began because I don't remember when I didn't feel this way. I can't seem to make it go away. I can't ever let anyone know it's inside of me. . . . I know it's not normal. It keeps me from fitting in. If anyone likes me, it's only because they don't know about the darkness and the smells.[41]

Wisechild opens her story at the moment she can no longer repress or ignore the darkness inside. Though she has attempted "converting" from fundamentalist religion to academia, she has failed to divorce her mind from her body. When she reaches the point of seriously considering suicide because she "can't imagine any other solution," a third voice speaks to her, a voice without a name, but one which offers the possibility of hope: " 'I thought you had other visions once,' the voice says. 'I recall you deciding to pursue a creative path. You were determined to make a difference.' "[43]

"Do you think I'll make it?" I finally ask. "I've always thought I would
die before I turned thirty."

"Sure," the voice says. "I'm sure."[44]

"Sure Voice" names herself, the first of Wisechild's voices that spring from
her own needs and desires; neither an internalization of the codes imposed
upon her, or a reaction to those codes. Able to hear herself for the first time,
Wisechild decides to act on her own desires and to leave graduate school. Her
decision brings her face-to-face with "The Body."

Sure Voice is associated with a new freedom for Wisechild, and she finds
herself revising her notion of authority:

> I was led to expect burning bushes and stone tablets with rules and
> regulations on them. Sunday school had established a firm polarity:
> God the destroyer, Mary with her arms full of Jesus. No one men-
> tioned a firm, clear voice from the stomach. No one ever hinted at a
> woman's voice in any sort of divine capacity. For a while I under-
> estimated her. But I find myself feeling strangely confident when I hear
> her, as if I'm in tune with myself. She says she's a part of me, but she's
> greater than me in some way I don't understand. She feels old, but
> somehow without an age. Sure Voice asks questions I've never thought
> about before.[45]

For the first time Wisechild considers an authority who may ask questions
rather than provide answers. Sure Voice tells Wisechild, "You do not understand power," and Wisechild begins to consider the notion that power might
be generated internally, rather than exercised externally:

> It's hard to imagine power without thinking of war, football or having
> the final words in disputes like my grandfather and stepfather did.
> Power means that someone is controlling someone else. Power feels
> like a bad word. It's never been connected to being a woman.[46]

This voice without precedent teaches Wisechild about vision, explaining
"When vision joins emotion you learn and everything is changed."[47] Gazing
and dreaming go together. Combining them, Wisechild begins to see shadows
in a new way.

The new voice within her teaches Wisechild how to feel with her body, to
experience the physical pleasures of simple movement. She finds that when
she listens with her body, the voices within are temporarily stilled. But with
her newfound ability to experience the present comes a less pleasant tendency
to flash back, to reexperience the past. Sure Voice explains that this is natural,
the result of Wisechild's new efforts to understand herself. She suggests
Wisechild take a massage course, that this will help her come to terms with
her own body. Despite her fears, Sarah's warnings that she is doomed to

failure, and Fuckit's disdain for "mellow carrot-juiced sissies" and "health freaks," she begins the course. At the end of the day a new voice is born, one whose first words are, "Gentle. Be gentle."[48] "Who are you?" asks Wisechild as she thinks, "I'm not sure how many more voices I want to have."[49] The voice responds:

> Carrie. I was born in the pulsing of your hands. I began in touch when you felt another's body without hatred. I was birthed in the space of the table. I can travel under the skin, finding muscle. Textures and colors are alive for me. I like activities that are restful and herb tea, especially peppermint. I hold your dreams about the future.[50]

Carrie becomes devoted to massage, and to healing others, helping Sarah to know her own body by responding to the bodies of others with patience and awe. All bodies, she discovers, are not the same.

Wisechild fears her own body, and hates it, because of the darkness she perceives as lurking within it – a feeling of decay, a "misery without a name."[51] When she thinks of her body and the evils she feels it contains, she remembers moments where men's words and looks have made her feel dirty and afraid. She realizes that she has attempted to bury her body in fat, to become thin enough to make herself invisible, to "turn her body into stone" in order to save her spirit. Wisechild, crying, remembers a scene from her infancy, remembers her mother's impatience and anger: "She hits me across the mouth a couple of times, which makes me cry harder; she yanks me out of the cart by the arms and I am afraid my arm will come off. She is so big."[52] For the first time she can remember, memories of childhood are accessible and they overwhelm her with fright and misery. She writes:

> Even though I cried for the first time in a long time, I am still weighted. Heavier than before I started crying. Now what? I wish someone would hold me.
>   Despair. There is no apparent direction: I think of suicide to still the hopelessness. Thinking of self-destruction makes the darkness larger, blacker. I always consider suicide when I don't know what else to do.[53]

But she is no longer without resources. Sure Voice, calm and reassuring, suggests she go to see a healer.

Wisechild's therapy begins in "The Well," a place with rough obsidian walls "which climb straight up for miles."[54] Her therapist, Kate, works with her to explore the Well, and Wisechild finds herself adjusting to the darkness within. She has, she explains, "acquired a peculiar kind of night vision":

> What once felt like a dark rotting mass in my stomach has specific features. The rocks lining the Well are dusty, jagged chunks of obsidian. The inner fire dims and quickens. Sarah, Fuckit and Carrie take form

in the Well which houses them. Even more curious is that the more clearly I see the Well, the more I understand about how I move in the world.[55]

Wisechild's new sight resembles Lidia's – both are shadow gazers. Wisechild has discovered that she has the talent to see in the dark, and that the darkness is not always what it seems. With her newly sighted eyes, Wisechild looks within the Well and discovers a Pit, so deep and dark she can't see the bottom of it. Beside the Pit is perched an infant of six months, filthy and wailing. The infant, whom Wisechild names YoungerOne, is a child part of herself.

Therapy brings more than one child part to consciousness, and the infant in the Pit is soon joined by a miserable thirteen-year-old. Wisechild, desperate and in pain, again thinks of suicide: "I keep coming back to dying. It's a familiar place. I don't ask why I wanted to die." Her ability to heal others sustains her, keep her alive, but does not relieve her pain. Caught in a cycle of depression, she is unable to break out of it until Kate convinces her that she is able to begin to nurture herself. For the first time, she moves to comfort the YoungerOnes within her: "I see the clear-eyed twenty-six-year-old part of myself holding two children on her lap. I rock back and forth, hugging a pillow against my belly. I didn't know I could hug myself and feel comforted." This is "The Touch," Wisechild's ability to reach out to her inner children: "I feel my own strong arms around my shoulders."[57]

Once she is able to nurture herself, Wisechild is able to discover an important aspect of her sexuality. She decides she is a lesbian, and that she wants an intimate relationship with another woman. In therapy she explains how she felt at a women's potluck: " 'I just know that I liked being a woman when I was with them,' Carrie tells Kate. 'I felt strong and proud.' "[58] On the heels of this revelation comes Kate's announcement that Wisechild has learned from her all she can. At their last therapy session, Wisechild writes and performs a play for Kate which recapitulates all she has learned. All goes well. "I thought I was done," writes Wisechild. "Sure Voice didn't tell me we were just resting."[59]

"The Rock" begins with a celebration of Wisechild's new relationship with Stephanie, as she glories in her rediscovered ability to play. But as quickly as she praises the relationship, she voices her doubts and fears:

I get uncomfortable thinking about intimacy. I feel stimulated and accepted when I'm with Stephanie. But parts of me are hiding. My heart closes so that I don't feel anything. My genitals seem lost in the bottom of the Well. Sometimes Stephanie gets too close and I tell her I don't want to see her for a week. Sometimes I'm not sure I want to see her at all. Then I remember all the friends and lovers I've lost in the past because I ran away from them instead of trying to work things out.[60]

Sex troubles Wisechild. It makes her feel used and dirty. When she is sexual, her good feelings go away. Stephanie, also a healer, hypnotizes Wisechild in an attempt to explore the problem. The results are startling:

> A man stands in the Pit. He is naked, his penis is erect. . . . He is my stepfather. . . . I am sixteen years old in my bedroom. I am in the bed, but I am not alone. I've been asleep and at first, I think I'm dreaming. But the weight is too real: it presses me into the bed. He puts a pillow over my face, catching my mouth open. Inside I think, I can't breathe, can't breathe, I will die, it doesn't matter, I want to die, I want it to end. . . . My body is underneath a rock, but it's not a rock because there is hair, it is rough and scratches. And there are hands pushing my legs apart and I can't get my legs to stay together. My legs are weak. Hardness. Tearing. The weight pounds against me. . . . He doesn't seem to see me.[61]

Wisechild's first thought is that she must be crazy – such things don't happen to people. But Sure Voice explains that her memories of incest are the Pit in the Well: "The only way out of the Well is to know the secrets held within the obsidian, seeing what you have hidden from yourself."[62] With Stephanie's help and support, she will begin to find her way out.

Flashbacks are a common phenomena in women who have suffered sexual abuse, just as they are in combat veterans, holocaust survivors, and other PTSD sufferers. Liz Kelly, who works with sexual abuse survivors, explains that both flashbacks and intrusive dreams occur in women who are in the "forgetting or minimizing phase, perhaps functioning as an internal reminder that there was something important the woman needed to resolve."[63] These flashbacks may occur often. Sometimes they are uncontrollable, and at other times they can be summoned by a woman who is attempting to work through her abuse by remembering suppressed events. In Wisechild's case, she experiences both controlled and uncontrolled flashbacks. The latter terrify her.

The sixth chapter begins with the words, "I don't know how to be safe."[64] The onslaught of memories awakened by hypnosis terrifies Wisechild. She lives in fear that her stepfather, Don, will carry out "The Threat" to kill her if she ever tells anyone about his abuse of her. Unable to function within her relationship to Stephanie, and haunted by unwanted memories, she makes the decision to begin therapy again. She shares the memories of Don with her new therapist, Jean, who gives her a book about incest, perhaps one similar to *Voices in the Night* or *I Never Told Anyone*. Wisechild writes:

> I open the book. I read myself in another woman's words when she talks about being so afraid of the world and of everything around her; of feeling like she has no self-confidence. I close the book again. I don't want it to remind me of how I am.[65]

But still she is comforted by the knowledge that "someone else felt this way too."[66]

Every step forward seems to bring a new and unbearable memory to light. In her bodywork sessions she is overwhelmed with the memory of her grandfather forcing her to suck on his penis and later raping her. "The Threat" concludes with her reevaluation of a scene she has "always remembered":

> [M]y grandmother pulled my pants down and held me on the bed while my mother probed inside my vagina. I was nine years old. They said they saw blood on my underwear and I must have fallen from my bike. I screamed that I didn't fall from my bicycle. They weren't listening to me. Now I wonder if they knew what Grandpa was doing. I don't know what they found. I don't know how the blood got there. No one stopped him.[67]

"The Response" which follows "The Threat" is anger. Wisechild, consumed by her painful memories, feels ugly and violated. "The incest has become part of me," she writes, "absorbed into my skin, my vagina, my mind."[68] She shares her feelings with her woman friends, who are supportive and comforting, but, again, her progress is interrupted by another intrusive memory – her mother's brother, "Uncle Kevin" rapes her in the garage when she is eleven:

> He lies on top of me after unzipping his pants. He pushes up and down, wrapping his arms around my ribs. I can't breathe. . . . "You cunt," he says. His anger comes out on his breath. . . . My body is confused. . . . But Kevin feels horrible. He feels hating. He feels old. This is dying. It seems like he will crush my body underneath his weight. I cannot breathe. I cannot move. Every time he bears down on me he calls me a name. No one has ever called me these names before. But I know what they mean. They mean I'm bad. "Bitch. Cunt. Whore." My body stops feeling. I become vacant. He is sneering. "You're liking this aren't you?" he whispers. I can't talk. . . . I have no room.[69]

Yet this last memory, which would once have been devastating, can now be survived because of her new strengths. For the first time she can envision a different ending to the scene, Carrie and Fuckit storming the garage and taking Kevin prisoner, carrying her away to safety. Her anger is cleansing and she is full of hope: "I don't know all the steps to healing. I only know that each step follows the one before it."[70]

More memories unfold. Wisechild recalls her Uncle Kevin trapping her in a closet and shoving small toys – "Red hotels from a monopoly game, Scrabble letters, plastic animals" – into her anus; her mother walking in on Kevin as he raped her from behind. "How could something like this happen," she asks:

I never read about things like this, other than in Amnesty International reports of the torture of political prisoners. Or newspaper accounts of rapes by strangers. But this was happening within my own house. No one drank, no one was in jail. Everyone went to church. I feel crazy trying to fit this into the "perfect" family I was told I had . . . there was so much abuse and no one seemed to notice it.[71]

Her confusion is understandable. Sarah Hoagland comments, in *Lesbian Ethics,* that "Except for radical feminists, no one in the United States perceives the phenomenal rate of incest (daughter rape), wife beating, rape, forced prostitution, and the ideology of pornography . . . as any kind of concerted assault on women."[72] Instead, each incident of sexual abuse is perceived of as unique, a particular pathology within a particular family. The victim has no connection with other victims, and believes that she is the only one in the world suffering such pain and humiliation.

Psychologists Ashurst and Hall explain that because children do not conceive of the abuse on any more than an individual level, abused youngsters internalize blame, and do not expect help and sympathy from others. This repression is not countered by assistance from doctors or other professionals, who either "[do] not enquire about them, or disregard or make little of them, leaving the distress to persist, sometimes for years."[73] Wisechild writes: "No one at school talked about anything like this. None of my friends, none of my teachers. My mind took the words away, the words didn't fit how I felt. I wouldn't know how to tell. It's hard to tell you, fifteen years later."[74]

Feminist theorist Dale Spender believes that women have difficulty talking about rape and sexual abuse because there is

no name which represents the trauma of being taken by force. . . . When an act cannot be accurately named it cannot be readily verified, to oneself, or to others. . . . Unable accurately to symbolize the event, rape victims can be victimized still further by the dominant reality, which may lead them to believe that they are responsible for this terrible act which they themselves do not perform.[75]

Wisechild's preoccupation is with memory, naming, description of the abuse she has survived. Since her therapist, Jean, is unable to take away the pain, Wisechild must content herself with telling Jean what she does remember. "I'm tired of running away from myself," Wisechild tells Jean.[76] "The Stare" takes shape as she looks Jean in the eye. Wisechild has begun the work of creating a new name for sexual abuse, one which, as Spender suggests, "is not neutral" and "does not rationalize the facts."[77] Refusing to accept the blame for her abuse, Wisechild is intent on creating the new definition Spender calls for, one "which is more consistent with female-generated meanings," one "named by women as they applied to women, and with women central to their meaning."[78]

The reclamation of anger is inseparable from the reclamation of memory. Anger is "The Fire," consuming Wisechild. It both attracts and terrifies her; she is afraid: "If the feeling gets out nothing will be left of me."[79] Wisechild is unable to cope with her anger, she explains, because "The fury of my family was funnelled through unacknowledged channels." Her mother and grand-mother, unable to show rage, would not acknowledge anger but would threaten Wisechild, telling her that she was "bad" and that God would punish her. The men in her family were not acceptable targets for rage, but instead presided over arguments, and deflected the women's anger onto each other. Her own anger, once acknowledged, seems endless and is accompanied by a flood of memories and physical sensations, including abdominal bloating, nausea, and muscle pain. These crystallize in a single, horrifying flashback as Wisechild remembers her Uncle Kevin forcing her child self to chew and swallow his shit. Her own reaction to the revelation is disbelief: "I've never heard of anything like this. What's wrong with my mind and body that I see such things? Why do I have to feel so horrible?"[81] In a session with her therapist Jean, she explains:

> Sometimes I feel crazy because this stuff is so bizarre and hateful. . . . After I remembered Kevin forcing me to eat feces I thought that I'd lost my mind, because I'd never heard of anything like that. When I went to a workshop on incest at the Association of Women in Psychology conference, one of the presenters said that ten percent of the abused children she worked with were forced to eat fecal matter. I didn't feel so crazy then. . . .[82]

She is reassured when she finds that she alone did not suffer such abuse, that other children have survived similar horrors. Such reassurance is found, however, only in a feminist environment – one in which incest is considered a suitable topic for discussion, and in which the experiences and beliefs of women are considered important, relevant and truthful.

Wisechild's repressed rage has exploded because, for the first time, she has experienced an environment where her anger is seen as legitimate and ap-propriate. Without the presence of a supportive lesbian feminist community, she would have been forced either to continue repressing her rage, or, if she could not repress it, would have viewed her anger as inappropriate and unacceptable. Child psychiatrist Alice Miller suggests that the most damaging abuse of children occurs in homes where the child is unable to express her anger, and where her distress and pain are considered unimportant or in-trusive:

> As I have repeatedly stressed, it is not the trauma itself that is the source of illness but the unconscious, repressed, hopeless despair over not being allowed to give expression to what one has suffered and the fact that one is not allowed to show and is unable to experience feelings of

rage, anger, humiliation, despair, helplessness, and sadness. This causes many people to commit suicide because life no longer seems worth living if they are totally unable to live out all these strong feelings that are part of their true self. . . . Pain over the frustration one has suffered is nothing to be ashamed of, nor is it harmful. It is a natural, human reaction. However, if it is verbally or nonverbally forbidden or even stamped out by force and beatings . . . then natural development is impeded and the conditions for pathological development are created.[83]

It is only when Wisechild's emotions are given legitimacy by the process of therapy that she can reclaim her rage, and accept her "true self." Jean's work as a feminist therapist is to allow the adult Wisechild to experience her powerlessness and her inability to prevent her childhood sexual abuse as a condition imposed *from the outside*. Wisechild must learn, in a safe environment, that she is not to blame for her own pain, that she is not "bad," but rather the victim of an externally imposed oppression which is both personal and political. Reduced to its simplest form, Wisechild has internalized the belief that "It's bad . . . to be a girl."[84]

Once she can articulate this basic assumption, she is free to reject it as false. Freedom from psychic bonds is accompanied by a new physical sense of well being:

The old reason for being bad leaves my body as I exhale. A hidden dishonesty that can be rejected once I've defined it. The shame of being female was poured inside of me, not born in. It was injected through incest, through my families belief that boys were more important, and through the messages of this culture. My arms and legs tingle as if the old ideas were moving out through my hands and feet.[85]

Accompanying this shift in perception is a shift in the imagery Wisechild uses to symbolize her plight, for gazing and *dreaming* are intertwined. Anger, which Wisechild once viewed as evil – a fire that might consume her – becomes a tool by which she claims her freedom. Fire metamorphoses from foe to friend when she shifts her perspective from masculine-oriented to a woman-centered:

The small fire in the Well brightens as if dry wood has been added. The fire has always been inside me. The fire planted questions about what was happening to me even when the Well seemed inescapable. The flames represent my desire to embrace myself.[86]

A newfound sense of self-esteem empowers Wisechild, and she is ready to direct her struggles outward as well as inward. A visit to her family on Christmas day enables her to understand "The Mask" of normalcy which her family dons both in public and private. In her home, Wisechild wears the mask of the "crazy" child – a child who lives out lies and fantasies – so that her mother is never is forced to consider the idea that Wisechild's accusations are true. Her abusive stepfather, Don, wears the mask of the perfect husband; he doesn't drink, or get angry, he earns a good living and supports his wife and family. Wisechild's mother wears the mask of "a poor, defenseless woman,"[87] a model primary school teacher, a good wife and mother. Her brother Jim wears the mask of "the older brother;" his assigned role is to protect their mother:

> Jim takes care of mother. I take care of Jim. Don takes care of mother, but she really takes care of him, feeding, clothing, arranging a social life. I take care of Don, not telling, protecting. No one takes care of themselves. Hands reach out to give while trying to take.[88]

Wisechild realizes that being conscious of the mask makes all the difference. She is able to go home and interact with her family and come away unscathed because she has gained insight into herself. Once the mask becomes a self-conscious symbol, she can choose to wear it and, more important, choose to take it off. As her internal voice Carrie comments, Christmas with Wisechild's lover Stephanie can be more enjoyable than her visit home. Wisechild can choose to create her own family and to interact with her new, chosen family members in a healthy and positive manner: "We won't have to wear a mask."[89]

Once the mask is dropped, Wisechild is able to both feel and articulate her own perceptions of the world. She is also able to begin to integrate her perceptions of her body with her new understanding of herself. "The Song" she tries to capture when she sings and plays her guitar, is a consonance of mind and body. Her body has been co-opted by the men who have sexually abused her. They have penetrated her mouth, vagina, and anus, filled her with foreign matter, forced her to orgasm without her consent, restrained her from movement, bruised and wounded her. Wisechild's feelings about sex and sexuality are connected to her feelings about being oppressed and abused, and she is unable to separate them out, "self-conscious, crawling with the wrong body,"[90] until Jean helps her to realize that she was a helpless victim and not a responsible party to the abuse. Her Fuckit voice helps her to understand that, although she was unable to say "no"

> We never said "yes" to him either. He didn't give a shit about what we thought and felt. The orgasm was a part of us that he stole, just like he took our body and our right to feel safe in our own room. No one thought the feelings of teenagers were important. But the danger was the adults who denied their sexuality while raping us. We were just trying to stay alive around that loony bin.[91]

Fuckit tells Wisechild that she resisted her abusers, that she was not complicit in the act. Liz Kelly, who counsels women who have survived sexual violence, explains that though resistance always involves active opposition to abuse, "The extent and form of women's resistance to particular assault(s) is dependent on the circumstances of the event(s) and on the resources that they feel they can draw on at the time. . . . Resistance is a coping strategy which denies the abusive man certain forms of power over the woman."[92] Fuckit is Wisechild's resisting voice, but the cost of her resistance was the rejection of her physical self. Sure Voice, who represents the part of Wisechild's psyche which is guiding the healing process, counsels her: "Without a body . . . you could not make music or write poems. You would not feel the earth moving when you walk. The voices would have no home. The body houses the inner and takes you beyond yourself. You are a player in a complex puzzle which changes as you respond do it."[93] Wisechild must bring her *dreaming* and gazing selves together and unite them in her body. "I don't want," writes Wisechild, "to hate myself for what he did to me."[94] Instead of internalizing blame she projects it onto a more appropriate object; her stepfather, Don: "I hate him. . . . Right now, I'd like to kill him."[95]

When Wisechild begins to project blame onto the persons responsible for abusing her she discovers that she too is guilty of abusing others. Memories surface: at seven she inserted a stick into her kitten's anus and pushed it in and out until she was caught and reprimanded by a cousin; at thirteen she struck an infant she was babysitting and was overcome by guilt when the father of the child rebuked her for her act. She remembers verbally abusing her lover. Fuckit, the part of her who resisted abuse most strongly, is also the part of her that is most often abusive. "The Fist" belongs to Fuckit, who raises it to threaten and hurt. Fuckit "moves toward Stephanie, using her mouth like my mother. She forgets about caring. . . . The memories of my own abusiveness line the Well like unwanted photographs. I am ashamed of my hitting and hurting, and of my tongue."[96] Along with this revelation comes a larger connection. Wisechild comes to believe that incest "makes violence."[97] Like Virginia Woolf, she chooses to "reflect on the patriarchs,"[98] and concludes that incest is "not so different from war or beating people up or throwing sewage into drinking water."[99] And patriarchy, Wisechild must admit, is the structure that shapes her world. Part of the price of Wisechild's reclamation of self is the awful knowledge that she is a member of a systematically oppressed and disempowered group:

> Incest is not so crazy. For a large part of the population, sexually abusing children is a silent routine. Children growing into lessons of abuse, becoming victims and abusers again, forgetting how to love. In order to call incest crazy, I would have to believe that the world is only a wonderful, just, loving place where people know how to respect each other. I know that isn't true. . . . The crazy feeling is the denial, the figures pretending that nothing has happened.[100]

This realization drives Wisechild to demand a confrontation – she will face the forces which have dominated and exploited her and declare herself free of them.

But as long as Wisechild lives, she will never be free of the threat of masculine violence. She finds, when she seeks reparations from her family, that they are no more willing to acknowledge her present pain than they were willing to protect her in the past. The importance of the confrontation does not lie in the promise that Wisechild can, by facing the past, free herself in the present. Rather, the confrontation becomes "The Mirror" in which Wisechild learns to see herself, and accept herself, for what she is – a sexually abused woman, a lesbian, a woman-identified woman with a certain limited number of choices in a mostly hostile world. As she writes a letter to her stepfather detailing his abuse and her response to it, Wisechild notes a shift in her internal imagery. She finds, in the Pit, "a loose slab of obsidian."

> Unlike the rocks which form the walls of the Well, this is polished. A shiny black triangle of volcanic glass that reflects a clear image. I stare into the black reflective mirror, looking into my twenty-nine-year-old face. "This rock holds both the past and the future," Sure Voice says. "It will remind you of where you have been. There is always somewhere new to explore; this mirror holds those mysteries also. The past leads to the future." Looking into *The Obsidian Mirror* I see the faces of my friends circling me as YoungerOnes moved through tears and rage and terror.... Taking courage with them.... I look into the mirror of obsidian. I hold the stones in my hand. They pulse in the rhythm of my changing.[101]

"The Hand" that Wisechild reaches out to her younger brother Jim is tentatively accepted and Wisechild is heartened by his belief in her story. She makes an appointment to meet her stepfather, Don, at a restaurant, so that she can confront him in a public place. They meet, and she reads him the letter she has written. He denies that he ever assaulted her, though he agrees to join her in a session with her therapist: " 'I'll do that,' he says, 'but I didn't do it.' "[102] A phone call from her brother follows the meeting; Jim has entirely withdrawn his support.[103] "Why did you have to tell me in the first place?" he asks. "Why did you have to come in and mess up my life? . . . What do you think this is going to do to Mother? . . . You're always stirring up trouble. . . . Why couldn't you just let things be?"[104] Wisechild is still trapped in "The Pit," but she comes to the realization that her friends – her lover, Stephanie, and her close friend Paul – are more strongly bonded to her than her family: "My friends and I chose each other. We aren't forced to be together. I may have lost Don and Jim, but I haven't lost the people who really know me."[105] She has abandoned the ideal of the nuclear family as one that is unworkable for a woman who wishes to heal from childhood sexual abuse, and has redefined her concept of "family" in a manner which frees her to reshape her future.

The last link that remains to be broken is "The Cord," which "stretches from my belly, from the place where we were connected, daughter to mother. . . . A cord that feels like a chain."[106] Wisechild longs for resolution, for a chance to tell her:

> [W]e're past being mother and daughter. . . . Those were roles that never allowed us to see each other. But we are both women. I want to tell her how I felt about my life with her. . . . Because we're both women, I want to understand her. I have to tell her how betrayed by her I feel and that I'm angry. . . . I don't know how I'll feel about her after that. Maybe nothing will be left then and we'll never see each other. But I'll feel completed with her. Or perhaps we will surprise each other and begin a new relationship.[107]

But she is denied that opportunity. A short note from her mother arrives in the mail. All that is written on it is: "Louise, I don't want to hear any more or see you again, Carol."[108] Her mother is inaccessible to her, for she refuses to believe her. Wisechild's mother listens to Don's denials, trusting "the words of men" over a woman's truths, just as she has always done. The cord has been ungently severed, and the Well is disintegrating:

> I feel tentative as the rock breaks into boulders and an avalanche of pebbles. . . . I have a hole in my belly where the rocks of the Well held the echoes of past pain. I used to believe that if I held onto these rocks, my essence couldn't be sucked out by invaders. I used the pain to remind me that I was alive. Now there's nothing to hold onto.[109]

The Well gives way to "The Dust," whirling in the air outside. "I cry for the loss of the Well," writes Wisechild, "even though I fought so hard to free myself from it. Now, being outside of the Well reminds me of what I don't know."[110] Wisechild begins to visualize herself as a tree, able to root in the Dust, and to grow there. Four months pass. She visits a lake and performs a ritual similar to those she had imagined occurring in the Well, burying the evils of the past which she has magically contained within a rock. When she is finished, she looks into the water and sees reflected both her face and green alder trees: "I look at my reflection for a long time. It wrinkles when the wind blows, but does not fade. I have not lost everything."[111] Eight months pass, and she discovers that the last of the Dust has blown away. Her internal landscape is no longer a barren, rocky place – it is fertile and rich, filled with a Tree covered in "new bunches of colossal, freshly opened leaves."[112] The Tree is another Mexican Indian image, the Tree of Life:

> [T]he Tree pushes outward, feeding from my breasts, returning breath

to the air sacs that hang within my lungs. Its trunk grows deep into my belly, sending roots through my legs, into ground. The branches press upward, winding through unexplored areas of my mind, reaching to the sunlight over my head. I imagine that if I climbed this Tree, I would have adventure and perspective.[113]

"The Climb" begins with Wisechild's decision to perform publicly at the women's cultural festival, almost two years after her break with her family. Her new joy at singing in public is entwined with the difficult process of ending her relationship with Stephanie. "I want my body to myself," she says to Stephanie. "I can't keep feeling like I should be sharing it with you."[114] Sure Voice reminds her that being free does not mean that everything works out the way you want it to: "You sought healing so that you could fully be yourself. . . . It is not easy to be faithful to your path. But you have learned to go where you need to go."[115]

Wisechild joins a writing workshop, and she emphasizes its importance: "We gather as women writing and learning. We study our craft. We read the women who have written before us and beside us."[116] Wisechild is preparing herself for her new work, the writings she begins in this class will become the text of *The Obsidian Mirror*. Perhaps it is even a workshop run by Ellen Bass or by Elly Bulkin. She celebrates her new community: "In my family, the father held power at the expense of everyone else. Here, I learn that we can all be powerful. Speaking uplifts all of us. I learn that respect is at the expense of no one. I see beauty in what makes us different as well as what brings us together."[117] Wisechild believes that a community of women who can share experiences and ideas can free each other:

> I hear women reclaiming their inner children, honoring their feelings and rediscovering the desire to grow and love. I see women moving out of isolation to support each other in groups, to take the risks of telling and to search for healers who empower them. I know women who have grown wiser in their journeys; who have broken the patters of genera-tions in their lifetime. Around me, as women speak about the violence in their families, they are creating a new awareness that is changing how we create families now. Violence within the family is not so different from the violence that haunts our lives in a wider sense. As we confront the denial of our personal pain, we also face the denial of our collective planetary wounds.[118]

The work of building a community of women, of making changes in the world, is inseparable from the work of healing the individual. "Incest split my mind from my body," writes Wisechild.[119] "The different parts of my self took on attributes of the abuse: victim, abuser, fighter and healer. As I heal the divisions in my self mend. The diverse aspects of my personality join together in deepening cooperation, creating a new whole instead of a collection of competing parts."[120]

Wisechild's yearning for wholeness is symbolized in a story that bears an eerie similarity to that told by another survivor. *The Obsidian Mirror* of the book title was shattered when Wisechild propped it up so that she could see her face in it when she was writing music:

> When I struck the first chord, the obsidian mirror fell backwards, breaking into four pieces. I cried because the stone was precious to me and I knew it would never be the unblemished looking glass that it had been. I glued it together. I looked mournfully at the long cracks until I understood that the mirror is a reflection of me: scarred from the fall and joined together in a new whole.[121]

This story closely resembles the tale told by another incest survivor, Lillian Kelly. A close friend of Kelly's received two antique vases in the mail:

> One arrived whole, the other hopelessly shattered. My friend labored . . . all through that year piecing together the delicate porcelain. When her cat knocked the half completed reconstruction from her desk, breaking it in new places . . . my friend saw it as a minor and interesting setback. . . . She completed the project, but the vase she produced could hardly be called complete. Tiny and large chips, once part of the original, had inevitably been lost. . . . This vase was more a product of my friend's labor than that of the original artist. Strangely, though, the new vase, for all its disfigurement, scars, chips, and ragged lip, for all the horror of the shattering and an imperfect mending, when set beside its unblemished twin, was the more splendid of the two. My friend presented her vase to me as a graduation gift, and I have it still.[122]

The journey of the survivor is from fragmentation to wholeness, but the whole is marked by the struggle. The survivor works to integrate her experiences and her beliefs, to create a space in the world where her truths can be heard, to see rather than to merely look. Wisechild's triumph is the amalgamation of her shattered selves, the achievement of unity: *dreaming* and gazing she sees the same sights.

The Obsidian Mirror is comparable to W. D. Ehrhart's prose works – *Passing Time* and *Vietnam-Perkasie* – in its insistence on tracing the protagonist's development in a chronological fashion, and in its refusal to generate an all-knowing narrative voice to serve as the interpreter of the story. Both authors insist firmly on allowing the protagonist to speak for himself/herself, and on situating the reader in the same state of "unknowing" as the main character. Both convey the disintegration and fragmentation of the young self in the traumatic setting, and use the device of flashback to demonstrate the connection between the healing process and the process of recovering and integrating the past and the present. Both leave their protagonists in a state of movement, a journey toward recovery which, they intimate, the character will travel without end. These works challenge the reader to share a transformative experience undergone, they suggest, by both main character and real-life author/survivor. This invitation is both intimate and public and marks the act of "bearing witness" or giving testimony in environments as diverse as survivors' groups, Alcoholics Anonymous sessions, religious meetings, and courts of law.

Wisechild's and Ehrhart's choice not to privilege reader or narrator prevents them from offering a coherent political analysis of the traumatic event. Ehrhart's protagonist's ideas and explanations often seem to the reader naive and ill-formed. This is not because Ehrhart-the-author lacks a sophisticated understanding of American politics, culture, and society. Rather, it is the result of his considered decision not to impose his current views upon the character that represents his younger, immature self. Such imposition, he knows, would be useful in helping the reader understand the context of the American involvement in Vietnam, but it would inhibit his audience's ability to identify with and, by proxy, *become* his younger, traumatized self. Wisechild has taken a similar course: her involvement in the lesbian feminist community, and her work with other survivors, indicates that she is far more aware of the political, social, and economic implications of widespread child sexual abuse than her personal narrative suggests. Wisechild and Ehrhart see testimony as a powerful and moving force and choose not to dilute the impact of their testimonial act by offering the reader an analytic framework within which it can be contained and interpreted. They hope – as Terrance Des Pres claims that those who write Holocaust survivor narratives hope – to create "an image of things so grim, so heartbreaking, so starkly unbearable, that inevitably the survivor's scream begins to be our own."[123]

Other survivor-authors have made different decisions. Margaret Randall's collection of prose, poetry and photographs, *This Is About Incest,* is a confrontational work dedicated to creating a context for the interpretation of child sexual abuse. She is concerned with sharing her own experience of trauma and healing only in order to expose and dissect the power structures that support and condone acts of violence against women and children. Unable to fully embrace the rhetoric of hope, she cannot ignore the institutionalized sexism and racism that determine the course of her life and the lives of other women. Re-vision is, for Randall, a process in which she clarifies the relationship between her personal suffering and the forces of oppression and injustice that operate in the world.

Randall is a white U.S. journalist, poet, and photographer who has lived for two decades in Mexico and Central America, working as a feminist activist and a supporter of the Sandinista revolution. Her other books have titles like *Part of the Solution, Cuban Women Now, Inside the Nicaraguan Revolution, A Poetry of Resistance, Nicaragua Libre!* Clearly, *This is About Incest* is a departure from the norm, though it is also a product of her experiences in Latin America, as well as intimately involved with her successful struggle to force the U.S. Immigration and Naturalization Service to allow her to remain in the United States. (Because she was a political "undesirable" and a known communist sympathizer, the INS claimed Randall had renounced all rights as an American citizen during her self-imposed 23-year exile, and they sought to have her deported when she resettled in New Mexico.)

This is About Incest is dedicated to her therapist Becky Bosh, "who helped retrieve the memory" and to her parents "who (knowingly and unknowingly) provided a buffer of love, and for my sisters and brothers working to survive." Like Wisechild, Randall has expanded her notion of "family" to include those whom she has grown to love and value, and she weaves her thoughts and feelings about her communal family into the text of the book. Feminist theorist Robin Morgan suggests that this radical redefinition of family as a consciously constructed communal relationship, rather than as a "naturally" occurring biological unit depends upon a reevaluation of female sexuality, and that this redefinition will have a profound effect on both domestic and international politics as well on on interpersonal relationships:

> The powers of female sexuality, in all of their expressions *and* redefinitions (maternal, celibate, bisexual, lesbian, and heterosexual) have the potential of forming completely different relationships in the twenty-first century. . . . This would mean an end to terrorism, its causes and effects and self-propagation, because it would mean an end to the sexuality of terrorism – which has given violence its power to destroy us all.[124]

Political scientist Cynthia Enloe also believes that shift in family and relational structures will affect international political and economic changes. She takes the 1970s feminist claim that "the personal is political" several steps farther, suggesting that the assertion is a palindrome: it makes as much sense read backward as forwards. When applied to world politics, Enloe suggests, "the personal is international" as well:

> The implications of a feminist understanding of international politics are thrown into a sharper relief when one reads "the personal is international" the other way round: *the international is personal.* This calls for a radical new imagining of what it takes for governments to ally with each other, compete with and wage war against each other.
>
> "The international is personal" implies that governments depend upon certain kinds of allegedly private relationships in order to conduct their foreign affairs. Governments need more than secrecy and intelligence agencies. . . . They need not only military hardware, but a

steady supply of women's sexual services to convince their soldiers that they are manly. To operate in the international arena, governments seek other governments' recognition of their sovereignty; but they also depend on ideas about masculinized dignity and feminized sacrifice to sustain that sense of autonomous nationhood.[125]

Randall's belief in the notion that the personal is international is apparent in her prose essay, "The Story," which precedes the poetry and the photographs in the text.

Randall has entitled her nine-part introductory essay "The Story" – the same title Wisechild chose for her introduction. Such consistency is not likely to be coincidental. The decision to precede the text with "the story" is rooted in the desire to shape both the narrative *and* its interpretation. As cognitive scientists Weber, Harvey, and Stanley suggest,[126] one reason for generating stories is to take control of the past, to "retrospectively understand and make sense out of an experience that at the time must have seemed very senseless and ridiculous."[127] Thus, moral lessons can be extracted from painful experiences. Both Randall and Wisechild create a story which places their text in context, and suggest that there is a correct reading of the work. Both writers and critics of their own works, they simultaneously situate themselves inside and outside of the discourse, insisting – in the words of feminist historian Carroll Smith-Rosenberg – on the "separateness and inseparability of material and discursive practices, of 'actions in the world' and symbolic gestures."[128] These incest survivors create self-histories which, as Smith-Rosenberg claims, help us to gain a "more precise understanding of the ways social and linguistic difference take shape and power" as they trace the ways in which the history of and discourse around the sexual abuse of women "weave in and out of one another, powerful yet mutually dependent."[129] Smith-Rosenberg writes:

> Considerations of power are central to the interaction of the physical body and the body of language. Sexuality produces power, at the same time as the discourse of the powerful constructs sexuality. We must not collapse sexuality, power, and discourse upon each other. It is their interpenetration not their interchangeability that is critical within the abstractions of poststructural debate, within the affective world of the emotions – and within the political arena.[130]

To make her position as guide and interpreter even more clear, Randall offers the following information to her readers. The comment is separated from the rest of the text, placed alone on the page that precedes "The Story":

> If the following prose, poems, and photographic images are taken in the order in which they are offered, the reader/viewer will have the chro-

nological journey as close as possible to that which I experienced and wish to share.[131]

Randall has assured that her position of authority is inviolate when she reminds us that she knows things which we do not.

The first section of "The Story" proclaims "1. This is about the language." Prefaced by a quote from Audre Lorde's *Sister Outsider,* in which Lorde declares that she is committed to reclaiming language,[132] this first section establishes the primacy of the interaction between public and private memory, oral and written language. "Writing about incest," explains Randall,

> is at once necessary (exploration, exorcism?) and painful for the writer. It is also often tenuous – the source itself floating somewhere just beyond consciousness. For the listener or reader it is uncomfortable, perhaps demanding, especially if the revived experience taps into something of her own, until now safely stored, adroitly camouflaged.[133]

Randall is engaged in a struggle between the dominant masculine discourse and the needs of women to represent their own experiences. In the words of sexual assault counselor Liz Kelly, there is "a conflict between men's power to define and women's truth."[134] The international community of feminists has been engaged in this battle over language for years. They are aware of the pain and damage suffered by the individual woman who loses this fight – the consequences are articulated by Quebequoise sexual abuse survivor and feminist Elly Danica in her personal narrative, *Don't: A Woman's Word:*

> Years of silence. Silence wrapped around life like a cocoon. I learn to live in a world where nothing is as it seems. Nothing is as I think it ought to be. Silence. Fear. . . . There is something wrong with me. Everyone tells me. The world is not how you imagine it to be. You've imagined everything. Your pain is imaginary. You are imaginary. You are crazy.[135]

Craziness is a mask on the truth for Danica, just as it was for Wisechild. Randall and other feminists are committed to dropping the mask and giving voice to truth as women experience it. They wish to take control of language. Monique Wittig, one of the most articulate of the French feminists dedicated to revising language, wrote:

> The women say, the language you speak poisons your glottis tongue palate lips. They say, the language you speak is made up of words that are killing you. They say, the language you speak is made up of signs that rightly speaking designate what men have appropriated.[136]

Wittig's celebration of *The Lesbian Body* made use of new words and structures to "embody" the previously inarticulable love between women.[137] In the tradition of Wittig and other language-oriented feminists, Randall seeks to redefine language, to re-appropriate the terms of discourse.

"2. This is about the small me" is just such an articulation. "The small me" is Randall's characterization of those internal children Wisechild named "YoungerOnes." Abused by her maternal grandfather, Randall's small me was unable "to define, fight back, or reveal."[138] Unlike Wisechild, however, Randall's small me was raised by supportive parents and was not entirely cut off from her mother. Randall comments:

> I have moved back and forth in my need – no, not in my need but in my ability – to talk with my mother about the incest issue. She has wanted to be supportive, and has been, far beyond what many mothers would have mustered. It is clearly painful for her as well. One day we can speak; the next her concern for a dead father – the aggressor – shuts my doors again. It has been beautiful to have the opportunity of seeing her legitimate love, she who so rarely expresses unedited feelings. Then, after a conversation particularly moving to me, she gets a migraine. And I retreat once more.[139]

The vacillation described by Bass and Davis is manifest in Randall's description of her family's response to the subject of her incest, but they do not reject her entirely as Wisechild's family did.

For Randall, the incest was symbolized by mushrooms – pale, soft fungi that flourish in the dark. She developed a phobia and took extreme measures to avoid coming in contact with mushrooms in their natural setting, in supermarkets, and even in pictures in books:

> All my conscious life I have feared mushrooms – their sight, their smell, the possibility of their presence, something to be found in unexpected places and that grow so quickly, almost while one watches. The terrifying thought was that I might come into actual physical contact with them. Worse, one might somehow enter me. Even now my body orifices close almost automatically at the thought (threat).[140]

Such fear is the stuff that Far Side cartoons and Woody Allen plots are made of, but Randall approaches the subject with the utmost seriousness, identifying incest as the source of her phobia and offering the reader the opportunity to forego laughter and seek with her the source of her terror. She allows us to choose – accept the simple scorn of her friends and psychiatrists ("Well, I'm sure if you just confronted the fear . . .") or venture with her in a new direction. Those of us who wish to proceed may be ready for her next declaration: "4. I am a woman."

Her declaration is not simply biological, for the section begins with the words, "Feminism was essential." Randall makes it clear that without a feminist perspective, she would have been unable to achieve the self-knowledge that has led to her perception of her own worth as a woman *and of our worth as women*. For the feminist, one's worth as a woman is inseparable from the worth of women as a group. With a feminist's belief that the personal is political, Randall assumes the political nature of her own phobia. "[M]y fear," she writes, "is rooted in a part of my woman's history denied in order that I function in the world as it is."[141] Minimizing experiences of sexual abuse, and repressing the details are coping strategies for women in a society that does not define sexual violence as "serious." An anonymous rape survivor explains, "I survived through my dubious ability to push things to one side, which I suppose you could say I'm paying for now. I think women do that. They have to otherwise they just don't survive."[142] But minimizing, as Liz Kelly explains, "seldom prevents women being affected and the effects of what is described as 'not serious' may well be."[143]

Randall believes that patriarchy denies the value of women and children, and that capitalism works in tandem with patriarchy in a white, male, upper- and middle-class conspiracy to oppress. Power, Randall suggests in an argument that bears great similarity to Cynthia Enloe's proposition, is primarily divided along gender lines, and then complicated by issues of class and race: "Feminist theory reminds us that even as we deal with individual acts of sexual and physical violence committed by men, it is the power concentrated in the hands of one gender that is the fundamental social problem."[144] Female children, "double commodit[ies] in a consumer society," are invisible victims of male abusers, "disappeared" by the patriarchy that refuses to accord them human worth. Reclaiming that worth necessarily requires, in Randall's words, "a reclamation of memory."[145]

The idea of reclaiming memory is familiar. Critics and interpreters of Holocaust literature suggest that Holocaust survivors who bear witness are participating in a communal, reconstitutive act. According to Des Pres, individual testimony introduces new information into public consciousness and the moral order is revised. Des Pres argues that testimony is part of "a collective effort to come to terms with evil, to distill a moral knowledge equal to the problems at hand."[146] Lawrence Langer concedes that such a collective effort may indeed be underway, but suggests that the trend is more reactionary than revisionary. The reading public may "misuse" the testimony of the survivor – interpreting the survivor's words in ways that help them "feel better" rather than "see better." The tendency of the audience, warns Langer, is to "conjure up a principle where none existed and reduce the complex survival ordeal to a matter of mere inner strength, of clinging to values that somehow insured continuing existence."[147]

This appropriation of the survivor's experience is possible because the experience has been translated into symbols manipulable by the reader – suffering has ceased to be suffering; it is, instead, merely a sign that stands for suffering, and could just as easily stand for something else. Popular culture critic John Carlos Rowe describes a similar appropriation of the symbols generated by survivors of combat in Vietnam:

> It is, of course, no revelation that marginal, counter-cultural, critical discourses are "quoted" or "translated" in more popular forms of representation. . . . When military fatigues and boots migrate from the soldiers to anti-war demonstrators to Vietnam veterans protesting the war to high-fashion models to punkers and, finally, to adolescents, the path of metonymic displacement is hardly direct or simple.[148]

Aware that her words are liable to be appropriated and misinterpreted, Randall works to make it difficult for her readers to revise her meanings. Unlike Wisechild, she takes control of both the retelling and interpretive processes.

Memory, for Randall, transcends the intellectual task of reconstituting the past in symbolic form. She uses the the tools of feminist theory – its holistic approach to "knowing" and its conflation of personal and political – to find truths which are buried in her mind *and* in her body. Randall's insistence that her body plays an active part in her re-vision of the trauma of incest makes it difficult for the reader to reduce her re-telling to the merely symbolic. Her reclamation of her body's role as a participant in the interpretive process suggests to the reading audience that they also have a body – and a memory – to reclaim. "True to my conditioning," she explains, "there is a disjuncture between my mind and body in their separate ways of touching my history. . . . Now I am teaching my body to go back, to identify the act, to work through the terror and anger . . . and to understand how the abuse informed other areas of my action and reaction as well."[149] This process, which Randall calls "coming whole," is intimately related to her perception of international politics – the politics of oppression. Randall writes: "An oppressive system's most finely honed weapon against a people's self-knowledge is the expert distortion of that people's history."[150]

"6. This is about memory" explores the ways in which the oppressor culture coopts and revises the history of the peoples they control, "disappearing" the history and influence of minorities, rewriting the past in their own image.[151] Reclaiming her personal history, Randall asserts, is an essential part of reclaiming the history of the female gender: "When memory stood as the key to my absence and presence in this world, I looked at the ways in which our collective memory is manipulated – at times mutilated – in order that we forget who we are, what we have done, our feelings."[152] When she examined her mushroom phobia in that context, she found to her surprise that her fear was constructed in order to contain her memories of incest, and to store them for later retrieval and use.[153]

Writing was, for Randall, an essential part of the retrieval process. She used poetry and prose in combination with photography to help her visualize and concretize the memories she needed to confront and integrate. At the same time she continued her therapy, and used it both as inspiration for her artistic work and as a means of interpreting the symbols and images she generated. At the end of her introductory essay, Randall reiterates the need to understand her work as an artistic vision of the journey toward healing, the "process of unfolding." Psychiatrist Deborah Golub, who has used art therapy in the treatment of posttraumatic stress disorder, suggests that "the creation and transformation of symbols" provided her Vietnam veteran patients with "a new approach toward achieving self-integration and mastering the trauma."[154] Randall's process is not radically different from the one Golub describes. Like the combat veterans in Golub's workshop, Randall has "abstracted mental images from feeling states, organized the images into concrete art forms, reflected upon symbols and amplified them with associations, and manipulated imagery in an attempt to reframe and discover alternative solutions to problems."[155] It is in this context that we must read Randall's description of *This is About Incest* as a set of "images and words speaking a language we must take the power to change."[156]

The first poem in *This Is About Incest*, entitled "Killing The Saint," is addressed to her mother, and voices Randall's distress at her mother's inability to fully acknowledge the incest. "Once you say yes, / maybe he also forced my brother. / Maybe he forced me. / But now again you don't remember. / I didn't say that, you tell me, tonight. / I never said that."[157]

Randall uses the same mirror imagery that Wisechild employs. Both women struggle to see themselves; both women are afraid that when they look in the mirror they will see their mother's face. Randall and Wisechild generate images of mothers who place their own needs before the needs of their children. Like Wisechild, Randall faces her need to break the cord, writing: "Mother you are larger now. / Awkward, we split. / The mirror goes."[158] They must reject their mothers' anger and fear before they can care for their own inner children, before they can, as Randall writes, bring "my children back, circling / their size."

Randall's next five poems are addressed to her abuser, her grandfather, and make us of the second person singular. These poems are angry and strong, reminiscent of much of the poetry in the early incest anthologies edited by Thornton and Bass, McNaron and Morgan:

I don't want your business suit,
flat white face too close to mine.
Your rimless glasses
get in my way.

. . . .

I need to kill you *my* way.[159]

★ ★ ★

Learning to remember,
learning against all odds
to break your chain in me.[160]

★ ★ ★

There are things we will never do together,
you who have hidden so long
in death,
I who wrench you from my flesh
breathing or not.[161]

★ ★ ★

It was you who used my tender baby flesh and mind,
hid behind your patriarchal privilege
and left me to figure it out,
left me to wonder who abused you,
and how to clean the fear.[162]

The sixth poem, "Someone Trusted Has Used Force" abandons the device of direct accusation and is, instead, contemplative as Randall considers the consequences of her grandfather's actions. "Someone trusted has used force / to enter this space," she writes:

Memory tears and shreds.
Life and memory
have both been sacrificed.

Nothing is as it was.[163]

With these words she begins to explore the shape and form that the reclamation of memory will take. "The Green Clothes Hamper" is strongly imagist – its invocation of William Carlos William's "The Red Wheelbarrow" is almost certainly intentional.

Williams rejected the literary devices of Pound and Eliot, rejected their reliance on classical languages and allusions to classical literature, maintaining that there were "No ideas but in things. The poet does not . . . permit himself to go beyond the thought to be discovered in the context of that with which he is dealing. . . . The poet thinks with his poem. . . ."[164] Williams wrote evocative poetry in an American idiom, poetry which refused to accede to the primacy of "the great subject." He chose instead to make clear "how any object, rightly regarded, can display its special signature."[165] "The Red Wheelbarrow" is a sparse poem, a mere eight lines comprising a single sentence. Randall's "The Green Clothes Hamper" is a longer work – 20 lines arranged in four-line stanzas – but contained within it is a single sentence which, when slightly rearranged, conforms perfectly to Williams' original:

This is
the

green lucite
top

of a clothes
hamper

where rape impaled
diapers.[166]

As Williams explains, "The particular thing offers a finality that sends us spinning through space. . . ."[167]

Williams had an interest in freeing himself from the traditional constraints of language, and in generating new poetic forms: "I propose sweeping changes from top to bottom of the poetic structure. . . ."[168] Randall would have found Williams' preoccupation with reshaping language so that it might contain and clarify an "eternal moment" appealing.[169] She might have considered it to be consonant with her own desire to reconstruct language and to create a place within it for women's reality, but she would also have found his sparse descriptions insufficient to convey the complexities of the incest experience. Imagist poems work only when the audience and the author share reference points. H.D. relied on her readers' knowledge of Greek mythology,[170] and Williams depended on the notion the reading public would be able to create a context for the red wheelbarrow. Randall places the imagist construct at the heart of her poem, but surrounds it with contextualizing references, suggesting that new languages are not born full-blown from the forehead of Zeus. They are, instead, carefully constructed as the poet creates explicit ties between "This lost green hamper" and "My body coming home." Without her intervention we would miss the importance of the green clothes hamper, upon which so much depends. She cannot, like Williams, depend on the fact that much goes without saying. To Randall, nothing must go without saying – too often the words of women are left unspoken. She fears that it is ". . . impossible / to cut this silence with the words."[171]

The notion of silence has preoccupied feminist scholars and writers. Literary critic Susan Gubar explained that women's unwritten stories are symbolized by "the blank page [which] contains all stories in no story, just as silence contains all potential sound and white contains all color."[172] Feminist theorist Susan Griffin has written about the silence of women:

Silences. Not the silences between notes of music, or the silences of a sleeping animal, or the calm of a glassy surfaced river witnessing the outstretched wings of a heron. Not the silence of an emptied mind. But this other silence. That silence which can feel like a scream, in which there is not peace. The grim silence between two lovers who are quarreling. The painful silence of the one with tears in her eyes who will not cry. The silence of the child who knows he will not be heard. The silence of a whole people who have been massacred. Of a whole sex made mute, or not educated to speech. The silence of a mind afraid to admit truth to itself.[173]

Books such as Tillie Olson's *Silences* (1983) and Adrienne Rich's *On Lies, Secrets and Silences* (1986) focus on the ways in which spoken and written language fail to articulate women's experience.[174] Concerned with similar issues, Randall aims to reclaim her voice, both by restructuring the language itself and by creating a new context – one which alleviates her readers' culturally inculcated inability to hear what women say.

"Let Us Move On" articulates Randall's philosophy about language. It begins with an excerpt from Adrienne Rich's essay "Split at the Root," in the anthology *Nice Jewish Girls* (1982): ". . . The poet who knows that beautiful language can lie, that the oppressor's language sometimes sounds beautiful."[175] "Having found the event / I looked for the man," writes Randall. "Having discovered the man / I needed the meaning."[176] In "Let Us Move On," Randall reminds herself to substitute the word "rape" for the word "abuse," and to reread her grandfather's affectionate words to her child self so that his apparently loving birthday note – "This is for my little sweetheart Margaret / who has set back the clock / for her 'Grandpa' " – is exposed for the vicious hypocrisy it is. "Moving on" is a re-visionary process: "I will not say again / I sat on his lap. No. / He had me on his lap. / You were not raped: he raped you. / Memory moves as it can, freedom is yours / to place the verb."[177] She is no more seduced by her grandfather's words than she was seduced by William Carlos William's attractive invitation to allow images to speak for themselves. She must speak or be spoken for.

"Easier To Match His Face" and "Guilty of Innocence" connect Randall's personal experience of incest with institutionalized oppression. In the first poem, her grandfather's hands become the hands of "that man in the White House / who calls himself a contra, Joe McCarthy's ghost, / Jerry Falwell, Rambo, the District Director / of INS." She links right wing politicians (living and dead), religious fanatics, popular culture manifestations of American militarism, and the bureaucrats of the Immigration and Naturalization Service to her traumatic incest experience in the same way W. D. Ehrhart ties his Vietnam war trauma to the Kent State massacre, the My Lai massacre, the dropping of the atomic bomb on Hiroshima, police brutality, capitalism, and other evils in his poem "To Those Who Have Gone Home Tired."[178] "Guilty of Innocence" equates institutionalized violence against women to the Holocaust, the archetypal trauma experience, as Randall allows Holocaust survivors Abraham Bomba, Motke Zaidl, and Itzhak Dugin to speak for her, quoting their words in her poem.[179] She, and they, speak together, bearing witness to atrocity: "The rape of language, the rape / of meaning. / Guilty of innocence. Innocent guilt. / Memory hibernating / when memory threatens life. / Memory coming back returns survival."[180]

Comparisons between the suffering of contemporary American women and the suffering of the Nazi victims strikes horror into the hearts of some Holocaust scholars. Alvin Rosenfeld, for example, writes of the "pathology" embodied in Sylvia Plath's poetry – referring to the poem "Daddy" (1966), which invokes images of German atrocities including lampshades made of human skin, mass executions and cremation.[181] Rosenfeld calls Plath a "confessional" poet – a label that McNaron and Morgan specifically condemn when they discuss the ways in which male critics have marginalized women's writing – and he accuses her of appropriating these powerful images to make her own "individual suffering" seem more important.[182] Rosenfeld failed to consider that Plath might have good reason to make use of Holocaust imagery. He prefers to see her as a bad girl – a spoiled child who employs these metaphors without understanding them, sheerly out of a desire to shock the grown-ups. His smug dismissal is, however, rooted in the assumption that women have "personal" rather than "political" problems, and that, whatever these problems are, they are not important enough to discuss in connection with an event as "serious" as the Holocaust. As James Young reminds us, though, "The Holocaust exists for [Plath] not as an experience to be retold or described but as an event available to her (as it was to all who came after) only as a figure, an idea, in whose image she has expressed another brutal reality: that of her own internal pain."[183]

Feminist scholars take issue with Rosenfeld and his ilk. The most radical feminists claim that other atrocities pale in comparison to the systematic oppression of women. Andrea Dworkin suggests that the Holocaust is too *mild* a metaphor to use in connection with the subjugation of women:

> There is no analogue anywhere among subordinated groups of people to this experience of being made for intercourse; for penetration, entry occupation. There is no analogue in occupied countries or in dominated races or in imprisoned dissidents or in colonialized cultures or in the submission of children to adults or in the atrocities that have marked the twentieth century ranging from Auschwitz to the Gulag.[184]

Whether or not Dworkin is correct, feminist poets like Plath and Randall make use of Holocaust metaphors because they find that these comparisons are useful in illuminating the traumatic experiences in their own lives. The codified trauma of the Holocaust may echo Plath's pain in language that is close to representing her reality.

Holocaust metaphors are not the only ones that occur to Randall. In "The Language of What Really Happened," Randall connects her memories of incest with the "underground memories" of the Vietnam War. She feels her own inability to remember "what really happened" most deeply as she stands before the Vietnam War memorial wall, sure that these hidden truths would help her ". . . connect / Quang Tri 1974 with Washington 1986."[185]

"The Language of What Really Happened" is the final poem in *This Is About Incest,* and it claims the authority to tell a "true" story, displacing official accounts and allowing suppressed memories to rise to the surface. But her newborn memory cannot yet successfully banish the official story, cannot yet find the words to express her thoughts "in a language they'd understand." Instead she stands silenced in the face of the enormously symbolic wall – she can only think of her memory "way off there in the mountains / waiting me home."

The text of *This is About Incest* is interspersed with a series of photographs that parallel the story of Randall's journey towards wholeness. The first set of photos appears 38 pages into the book, when Randall has established the context in which they are to be interpreted. The first photo is full portrait of her grandfather, seated at his desk holding holding a magazine (*Town and Country*) and looking into the camera with a faint smile. Three subsequent photos trace the progress of a mushroom across this portrait as it creeps up her grandfather's body and comes to rest on his chest. Randall has switched the terms of her relationship with her abuser, forcing him to carry the burden of fear.

The second portrait is placed adjacent to a poem entitled "The Second Photograph." The poem interprets and contextualizes the photo, explaining that her grandfather's hand circles her buttocks with its "fingers strangely held, as if in secret sign."[186] Randall writes of this seemingly innocuous portrait:

> I am reading this into the image.
> I am reading it because I know.
> I am telling it because now, half a century later,
> I understand. . . .[187]

Her reinterpretation gives the next photograph an ominous overtone. Once again we see the original portrait of her grandfather, accompanied by the mushroom, which now lies, like a long-stemmed rose, across the bottom. To the right of the portrait, beside the mushroom, is a small portrait of Randall seated alone on a step, with her own book in her hands. The similarity of the pose held by grandfather and granddaughter is somehow oppressive, as if he were recreating her as a smaller image of himself. The mushroom, the only three-dimensional object in the frame, dominates the picture. A series of two more photos follows. The first contains an upper-body portrait of her grand-father as a young man, and a photograph of another small child (perhaps Randall or her own mother) in a similar position to the portrait of Randall in the previous photo. Beside those two portraits lies a third portrait – her grandfather, now much older, holding two naked and vulnerable infants. The mushroom is again prominently featured at the bottom of the frame. The final photograph of the series contains the youthful portrait of her grandfather and, arranged upon his chest, three portraits of Randall as a young girl. The portrait occupies only the upper right third of the frame. To the left of the portrait lie three discarded mushrooms, and the lower right hand of the frame is filled with Randall's sandaled foot, which crushes a fourth mushroom.

The next photo is a close-up of Randall seated on her grandfather's lap, but superimposed over the photo are Randall's own hands hovering above a mushroom. It appears as if she is reaching into her own past and reshaping it. The final three photographs accomplish a complete restructuring of authority. In the first of the three a large and powerful female figure dominates most of the frame – the portrait of her youthful grandfather and several mushrooms are crowded into the right-hand side of the frame. In the second a battered, one-eyed teddy-bear sprawls in the upper right-hand corner of the frame, flanked by strewn mushrooms, a General Electric scale, and a small portrait of Randall as a child. The final photograph of the text normalizes the mushroom, placing it carelessly beside a telephone on her nightstand. It no longer dominates the frame, or even intrudes upon it.

The movement in the text is from patriarchal power, represented by her grandfather and embodied in Randall's mushroom images, to a new woman's power, represented by Randall's reclamation of her voice, her powerful female doll, and her demystification of the mushroom. Her prose essay, "This Is About Power," interprets the photographs for the reader and titles them. By appropriating existing portraits and arranging them with carefully chosen props she revises the past and then reinterprets it with her prose. The process is complete even before the film is developed – the images that actually appear on the film have a predetermined meaning generated and explicated by Randall herself. "Now I am developing this film," she writes. "It's secrets are still locked inside the canister, suspended in sixty-eight degree chemicals."[188]

These are secrets kept from us – Randall is privy to the answers and will choose, as she notifies us in the beginning, just which images she wishes to share. She concludes, and we – successfully manipulated – must agree: "This is about power, on every level."[189]

Randall is primarily concerned with the relationship between the powerful and the powerless. She believes that the power relationship is a gendered relationship. In her analysis, the archetypal drama of dominance and subordination is played out between men and women, and all other forms of discrimination derive from and are interpreted within the framework of that essential division of the sexes. A number of white feminist scholars heartily concur with her, among them historian Joan Scott, who writes:

Power relations among nations and the status of colonial subjects have been made comprehensible (and thus legitimate) in terms of relations between male and female. . . . Gender is one of the recurrent references by which political power has been conceived, legitimated, and criticized. It refers to but also establishes the meaning of the male/female opposition.[190]

Randall's goal is to dethrone the men in power, claiming equality and freedom from fear and oppression. In Randall's new world, no one will walk in fear.

Because she believes that the power relationship is gendered, Randall thinks that women can and should unite in common cause. Randall's pain at her mother's refusal to unequivocally support her in her condemnation of her maternal grandfather runs through both prose pieces and poetry. The conflict in *This is About Incest* is between women and men, and between women-identified women and the women who (through fear, or self-hatred) support the patriarchal power structure. Such a simple construction elides the differences *between* women and comes dangerously close to obscuring the race and class issues for which gender is supposed to serve as archetype. Such an elision is far from Randall's intent, but it is a result of her decision to place patriarchal power on one side and femaleness, Jewishness, blackness, homosexuality, disability, and youth on the other.[191]

Enter Password: Recovery. Re-enter Password, Elly Bulkin's survivor narrative, is also concerned with questions of power. But where Randall is interested in the relations between the men in power and the women who are oppressed by them, Bulkin is specifically concerned with the interactions between women. Bulkin belongs to several different communities that at times overlap and at times diverge: she is Jewish, lesbian, feminist, and a sexual abuse survivor – simultaneously a member of several of the categories of oppressed persons Randall refers to in *This Is About Incest*. Concerned with questions both of autonomy and community, Bulkin explores the differences between women that Randall elides. She begins her narrative with the word "**Recovery**" in boldface: "That word."[192] Bulkin wrestles with language, sure, like Randall, that she must build something new, but not at all sure of how to go about it: "Moved finally to a different use of language. Using it too, still, in the old way, as cover, as distance."[193] Afraid she is off to a bad start, she wonders if she ought to begin again, to break her silence in a different way:

> . . . I have been silent. Which is, after all, the issue. Or one of them. I'm a writer who does not write. Who said only yesterday, in response to a well-meaning question, that I've written one review in the past four years. Who had a panic reaction two springs ago when a woman tried to engage me in the common language of the lesbian–feminist literary

scene. . . . And I left, rudely, compulsively, needing to go *right away,* not five minutes later. "Like rape trauma," a friend said to me a month later; she had once been raped and knew the real thing, whereas I only knew the irrationality of my response and had no words for it.[194]

Bulkin's difficulty is not in understanding her relationship to hostile, masculine power structures, but her connections to the community of lesbian feminists with which she identifies. How can we, she asks, talk to each other about ourselves. She notes, ". . . as a prime instance of male violence and power, childhood sexual abuse (mine and others') has begun to be an acceptable topic for feminist discussion, [while] the complexity and pain of women's interactions with each other remain taboo."[195]

Enter Password is written in journal form – all of the entries bear dates and Bulkin writes in a familiar, first-person style. In addition to her own notations, she includes correspondence to and from other women, excerpts from her writings, and quotes from the works of other writers. The book is divided into two main sections: "Part One" and "Part Two." "Part One" contains her short introduction (which bears the same title as the book, and could as easily have been called "The Story"), dated April, 1987. Following the introduction are seven numbered sections, most beginning with a quote, which bring us up to October, 1987. "Part Two" is comprised of three sections, begins in January of 1988 and ends in October of the same year. By shaping her work to resemble a journal, Bulkin exerts the same control over the reading process that Randall seeks in *This is About Incest* – a chronological journey that reflects, in as much depth and detail as Bulkin chooses to share, the healing or "recovery" process.

Bulkin begins her first section with a quote from Perri Klass, in which Klass describes his reaction to his discovery that the *New York Times Book Review* contained letters accusing him of "some crime I hadn't committed." Klass explains that, wrongly accused, he felt "a little bit the way the victim of rape must feel . . . anyone I told would have at least a split second of wondering whether the accusation was true. . . ."[196] Underneath the quote, Bulkin writes, "I've always called it 'the cloud.' "[197] "The cloud" has followed her since a publisher responded to her lover's submitted manuscript by describing it as "the most anti-Semitic writing she had ever read"[198] and circulated an 11-page memo filled with angry criticism within the feminist community. Bulkin explains:

In all this time, the memo implied, I'd apparently been living – quite unknown to me – with a rabid anti-Semite. . . . It felt, I imagined, like having trash dumped all over the lawn, words scrawled on the walls – the 3 a.m. act, not of the Klan or some local kids, but of the neighbors who for years had been dropping by for coffee. I felt furious and vulnerable. Not just unwanted by Jewish feminists, but discarded, rendered a virtual enemy of my people. . . . I raged, and, having no outlet for that anger, lapsed into depression.[199]

Her response was to write furiously, first long letters to feminist journals, then a 150-page manuscript. Bulkin was propelled by the thought that unless she got "everything right," she was liable to be publicly pilloried. But no one can rest assured she has "everything right," and so Bulkin wrote "in a state of fear,"[200] suffered from stress-induced illness, and was finally admitted to a hospital because she was unable to speak or breathe – her vocal cords had swollen up and filled her throat.

After the publication of her long manuscript as an article in the anthology *Yours in Struggle: Three Feminist Perspectives on Anti-Semitism and Racism,*[201] Bulkin stopped writing. Perplexed, she found herself in a crisis of faith, finally giving in to her "irrational" desire to seek spiritual satisfaction. A scholar, Bulkin turned to books for answers, and found, in a volume entitled *God's Fierce Whimsy: Christian Feminism and Theological Education,* a partial explanation of why "the cloud" had knocked her "so solidly onto her emotional back that [she'd] been unable to pick [herself] up again."[202] What illuminates Bulkin is not a brilliant theological argument, but a simple exchange between Carter Heywood, a white lesbian, and Katie Cannon, a black woman whose sexuality is not identified. Heywood and Cannon were survivors of childhood sexual abuse and told their stories in *God's Fierce Whimsy.* Cannon's summation of the abuse – "It wreaked havoc in our psyches"[203] – strikes Bulkin to the heart and her own childhood memories "bubble up, loudly, insistently, no longer to be quieted."[204]

The quote that heads the third section of *Enter Password* was penned by Judith McDaniel, a feminist activist and a friend of Bulkin who had been taken hostage by the contras in Nicaragua. McDaniel's description of splitting off from her body, looking down at herself "from a safe spot about six-feet overhead"[205] is reminiscent of Wisechild's descriptions of her incest experience, and of many of the writings in *Voices in the Night* and *I Never Told Anyone.* The contradiction between the "gentle face" of her contra captor and the terrible power he wields is similar to the contradiction between a person who is both a "loving" family man and a violent rapist. Bulkin addresses two letters to McDaniel in this section. In the first she communicates her new understanding of the ways Bulkin herself helped create the environment that prevented her from coping with "the cloud" and integrating that experience into her life:

> As I've known for a long time, I hadn't laid the groundwork for friends to know that I wasn't just upset, but that, in addition to taking care of myself, I needed some way to be taken care of. And because I hadn't done the work of setting groundrules or precedents, no one would've even thought to offer and I'd pretty much have to ask for something

which I'd already established as the sort of thing I couldn't possibly need.[206]

In the second letter, Bulkin declares herself, for the first time, a sexual abuse survivor. "Except for a two-or three-sentence comment to two Bronx friends (probably ages eight or nine)," Bulkin writes, "I have quite literally never discussed this experience with anybody."[207] Bulkin's perception of her decision to repress, to "forget" her experience is complicated by her position as a feminist, a woman who has "read all the books, can offer all the analyses" about sexual abuse. She is troubled by the fact that one can know and not know at the same time.

Bulkin was abused by a male acquaintance, the superintendent of her apartment building ("white, not Jewish, probably early thirties"[208]), who invited her to his room and traded her stacks of comic books for sex ("my touching him until he came; his hand guiding mine"[209]). There was, she says, "No violence, no threats, no undressing."[210] This occurred, Bulkin writes, some three or four times. Her memories of her feelings included shame, fear, guilt, isolation, and abandonment, and she finds them strangely entwined with her feelings about her brother, who was, at the same point in time, having certain difficulties "never to be discussed"[211] and was subsequently sent away to a special school. Her unresolved emotions about the abuse and about her relationship with her family are mirrored in her reaction to "the cloud." When her lover's manuscript was attacked, Bulkin felt "complicity," "fear," "loneliness," "isolation," and "abandonment." Her realization of the continuity of her emotional response brings her to a new stage of self-consciousness.

Margaret Randall's voice weaves through Bulkin's narrative. Bulkin begins her third section with Randall's words: "Not everything is recorded here. It is important to remember that. Not everything can be said."[212] Though it is true that not everything can be said, Bulkin realizes the importance of telling and re-telling stories of sexual abuse, and offers an example of her own dependence upon the words of other women. Bulkin struggles to take control of her tale, to choose what she will say and what she will not say, and she learns how to shape her story from other writers. She finds, in a Brattleboro bookstore, a copy of I Never Told Anyone, which she "inevitably" purchases. She also reads Randall's work and is inspired to adopt her technique of using journal entries to tell her story. She converses with Judith McDaniel about rape trauma and child abuse, and is deeply affected by an article published in the women's journal Sojourner by women who remembered having been sexually abused.[213] Gradually she begins to reconstruct her story, beginning with a letter to Sojourner:

> I recalled . . . that in a 1983 essay I had described myself "as a feminist who has counseled rape victims, had spoken with and found shelter for battered women, and who, like women all over the world, know wom-

en among those I love who have been raped and abused." And I knew
that my failure to include myself among their number was one measure
of the power of that forgotten experience.[214]

When Bulkin sees the published letter, "prominently placed" in the journal,
she regards it as a new kind of "coming-out" experience and purchases a
"Child Abuse Kills" button from the bookstore. Still ambivalent, however,
she buries the button in her pocket instead of wearing it.

Only after she publicly declares herself a sexual abuse survivor does Bulkin
discover the title of her work – the prompts displayed by her computer when
she opens her word-processing documents. The title seems to Bulkin symbolic of her effort to get "past something (a door, a block, silence, loss of
memory." The request for re-entry of the password indicates to her "that it
isn't enough to do it once and be done with it."[215] Recovery is a process and
it takes time to find the right word to open each door. For inspiration she
always returns to the work of other women:

> . . . I started to think more about writing and recovery. Writing both as
> part of healing and as a way of taking control of what's happening. The
> sense that publishing makes some piece of one's life "finished" in a way:
> Many examples: my letter to *Sojourner,* Joan's poems, Judith's writing
> about alcoholism and being captured in Nicaragua, Dorothy's "The
> Women Who Hate Me," Audre's prose and poetry on cancer and
> racism, Margaret's incest poems, Cherríe on Latina sexuality, Adri-
> enne's "Contradictions: Tracking Poems." There are lots of other ex-
> amples – but I'm thinking primarily about women who *are* writers, who
> see writing as necessary to their lives. Recovering the ability to write, or
> to write about what's most difficult.[216]

She seeks guidance not only in understanding what she *can* say, but in what
she is permitted to omit, "The difference between our actual lives and both
our own and other people's public presentations of them."[217]

The impact on Bulkin of the early anthologies of sexual abuse survivor
testimony is clear. Images from *I Never Told Anyone* and *Voices in the Night*
appear throughout the text. Bulkin begins section five with an epigraph from
Anne Lee's "Untitled Incest Piece" in *Voices*: "To remember is to regress – to
remove the careful, clanking armor of adulthood, and say finally, this is how
it was."[218] She accepts and works with the images of "the child me," the
fragmented self, the journey toward wholeness. As a part of her own healing
process she decides to teach a writing workshop she calls "Risky Writing," a
"non-fiction prose workshop focusing on writing about experiences which
participants might find personally difficult."[219] Bulkin explains:

> I'm beginning to understand how my sense of identification with other
> women is making possible my own writing and recovery. Writing now,

I'm struck by the extent to which my risks are inseparable from theirs. For me, the movement out of depression, into some sort of slow healing has much to do with other women's stories, with what women have told *me* when I said, "I never told you this, but. . . ."[220]

Bulkin places her biography on the flier advertising "Risky Writing," and describes her life in a manner that is not, strictly speaking, correct: "For the past year," the flier reads, "she has been writing about recovering from childhood sexual abuse."[221] In truth, her problem is that she has *not* been writing, and she hopes that this workshop will force her to produce new work. She sees her decision to run the workshop as a turning point in her healing process, and end the first half of *Enter Password* on that note.

"Part Two" opens on a completely different topic. Bulkin, distraught and angry, asks the reader, "How not to simplify? Not to rant?" as she relates the story of the end of her 12-year relationship with her lover, Jan. Her feelings of rage and hurt are shared with the reader as Bulkin – returning from a conference – discovers that Jan has had sex with a man in the apartment she shares with Bulkin, "twice, without benefit of safe sex or birth control, with a man she'd met a few weeks earlier."[222] Her sense of betrayal is great, and it is heightened by the complex interplay of emotional, sexual, social, and ideological factors. Bulkin is infuriated "about men, about roles, about women who could pass as straight."[223] She sees Jan's act of infidelity as both personal and political; in Randall's words, "this is about power on every level." In a final paroxysm of agony, Bulkin exclaims, "And we had been dykes together."[224]

The relationship between Jan and Bulkin does not dissolve immediately. "I waited in silence," Bulkin writes, "the few months when we hoped – against emotional logic and the downward slide of events – for things to work out. Except for telling a few friends, I waited silently."[225] Only when the end of the partnership is in sight does Bulkin choose to write, "having had too much already of my own silence."[226] The composition process is crucial: she writes to express her feelings, and then reads and re-reads her writings in order to "notice what I've left out, or not highlighted."[227] In a manner similar to that which Randall described in *This Is About Incest,* Bulkin takes control of both the writing process and the interpretation of her work. From this privileged position she is able to discern an important truth: "I've been here before. Not in this exact spot, but very close to it."[228]

On February 19, 1988 Bulkin writes, "I'd not expected to write so soon about these things. I don't yet have the language to explain what it was like. . . ."[229] On February 21 she corrects herself, saying of that last sentence, ". . . I know it's inaccurate. For in truth, I'd *never* expected to write about these things."[230] In discussion with Jan during a last vacation together, Bulkin had wrestled with an important question: "What of our life together (and breaking

apart) could we write about, and when?"[231] They negotiated, and, in deference
to Bulkin's wishes, had agreed on "a ten-year limit on memoirs and explicit
writing which describes the other person (or submit for approval)." Bulkin
observes:

> Only later did I realize what this meant: I'd have to stop writing this
> piece. I couldn't finish it or think about publishing it. I couldn't use it
> as a way of getting certain things behind me. Out of my own fears, my
> own desire for some control over the written record of my life, I'd
> acquiesced in my own silencing.[232]

Caught up in the "irreversible" process of articulating the "unsayable," Bulkin
asks that Jan agree to her request to remove the restrictions on their writing
about each other. When Jan agrees, Bulkin is both relieved and afraid. She is
face to face with the fact that the words she writes are solely her responsibility:
"*My* words. *My* risk. Soloing in yet another way."[233]

The Ellen Bass poem that opens the next section can be used to interpret
Bulkin's writing up to this point, and to suggest the new direction her writing
is taking. "You do not know the breaking through as it happens," reads the
epigraph. ". . . After, after you will look. You will acknowledge. You will see
through the opening you have cleared."[234] This growth is apparent in Bulkin's
discussion of the "Risky Writing" workshop:

> I didn't expect to receive so much from the six women and one man
> who stayed with the workshop: who started with fragments of journals,
> or prose about impersonal topics . . . who ended with writing so direct
> and painful that I felt near tears at our last workshop, overwhelmed both
> by what they were wiling to say and by my ability to hear them into
> speech. For me, as for them, a measure of change.[235]

Taking a lesson from the writers in her workshop, Bulkin sends her manuscript to a feminist publisher. But despite her brave gesture, she still agonizes
over the choice to make her work public. "To publish under a pseudonym,"
she writes, "would just reinforce my feeling that I shouldn't be talking about
any of these things. But to publish under my name is unsettling. What will
it mean to my future interactions with women I don't already know well that
they have ingested this personal information about me?"[236]

Though Bulkin emphasizes her emotional connection to her work, she is
also concerned with the literary quality of her writing. She comments on
Randall's manuscript, *This Is About Incest,* that the "prose worked better than
the poetry,"[237] and in a discussion with a publisher she agrees that her own
manuscript is not "crafted enough"[238] – that its structure and presentation are
not yet complete. Style, for Bulkin, is composed of a set of consciously
adopted techniques (the journal entry form, the familiar address, etc.) that can

be used to convey a particular set of meanings in a carefully engineered environment. So conscious is she of the impressions and emotions written words can evoke that a trip back to the house she once shared with Jan stimulates a desire in her to find and remove from Jan's possession all of the letters Bulkin had sent her over the years. She would like to disappear these documents, dump them at "some roadside rest-stop,"[239] and thereby rewrite (unwrite) the story of their relationship, as Jan rewrote that story by telling Bulkin about her affair. She eschews this retroactive rug-pulling for a clean break; stealing her words back will only cause more words to be uttered, "outraged phone calls or letters trailing,"[240] pursuing her without end.

Soon after she has begun "to sink into the simple rhythm of a single life led in a single place," Bulkin finds herself in the Lesbian Herstory Archives giving her first public talk "about how my young dykehood had shaped my sense of being Jewish."[241] As a young woman Bulkin had read lesbian novels and then burned them, erasing their words in the same way she considered disappearing her letters to Jan. (Adrienne Rich writes about this in a letter to Bulkin: "I think of you as you described yourself burning lesbian novels in the incinerator; finding the words you needed but then having to destroy them."[242]) In the Archives, she is surrounded by these lost words, miraculously reconstituted, there for her to use when she needs them. Bulkin's awareness of all of the books never published, the books burned and suppressed and ruined, is crucial in her decision to pen, now, words she does not intend to destroy.

Bulkin's decision to write for a public audience entails a second decision – to share her words with her daughter Anna. Though Bulkin is determined to provide a healthy and supportive environment for Anna, and is careful to encourage her daughter to grow and develop in her own way and at her own pace, she is unable to entirely prevent herself from projecting her own fears onto the child. She dreams that Anna has been abused by a man. In this dream she looks for Anna but cannot find her; she knows that something has happened, but she does not know what it is. Bulkin describes this as "a dream in which, on several levels, the little girl got totally lost."[243] This entry brings to mind W. D. Ehrhart's prose-poem "The Dream," in which he witnesses, and then becomes the perpetrator of, the massacres of his friends and loved ones.[244] Like Ehrhart, Bulkin cannot escape the suspicion that she is the embodiment of her own worst fear. The little girl of her dream is simultaneously Anna and Bulkin herself; the "something" that happened represents Bulkin's inability to fully remember and articulate her own past – she is afraid of failing herself and of failing others. Even her journey toward healing causes Bulkin to doubt her fitness as a mother. "In this journal," she writes, "I was for months the mother who was leaving her daughter, or waiting for her to go off someplace so I could write or collapse or be alone. . . ."[245]

Instead of succumbing to the notion that she is a "bad mother," however,

Bulkin retells her story from another perspective, once again taking control of the interpretation of her own life and work. Up to now, she notes, she has "been near-silent as a mother," but a simple revision can change the reader's perception. She reminds us that what we have read so far has been what she has chosen to tell us. It is not the whole truth. "[T]here are other stories."[246] *Enter Password* is dedicated to Anna. Through the recovery process Bulkin has learned to be what she she calls "a consenting mother."[247] She has chosen to raise her child in an atmosphere of "parental speech" rather than "parental silence" and to cede to her daughter the right to forgive or condemn her for her decision. This marks Bulkin's acceptance of full responsibility for her actions and it is embodied in a new perception of her intimate relationships.

Her relationship with Jan, Bulkin realizes, was predicated on the notion that *she* could change while Jan remained the same. All change has its price, as Randall and Wisechild both confirm. The notion panics Bulkin, immobilizes her. How much will each change cost? The next decision that faces Bulkin, whether or not to become involved with the Jewish feminist literary project *Gesher,* terrifies her. Unable to continue throwing away the words of the past, Bulkin knows that she must carry "the cloud" with her into this new group, that she must explain "the ... implications of my tangled Jewish-feminist history."[248] It would be safer to be silent, to use "language in the old way, as cover, as distance."[249] But Bulkin is no longer able to take the safe way out, no longer able "to simply walk away."[250]

> As I write this, I finger for the first time the rage behind my recent depression: cup in my hands my just-found anger and its source. I have talked and written myself into this word I can no longer even pretend to control: am furious *at myself* for having let my shell slip so far from its secure, familiar spot (soft vital organs, hard-to-the-touch vertebrae – all unguarded). The loss of armor. The end of safety.[251]

Faced with a future that holds no promise of security, she acknowledges the presence of her fear. She may never walk without fear again. The world is not a safe place for any woman, and it is a downright dangerous place for a Jewish lesbian feminist activist. "My fault. My responsibility. My move," writes Bulkin. The decisions are her own, but she cannot control or even predict the consequences.

Wisechild, Randall, and Bulkin have constructed survivor testimonies that force us to confront the damaging power of male violence. Wisechild has recreated the experience of her terror and pain, and the first years of her healing, in order that we might exercise our ability to empathize, to understand on an emotional level her experience of childhood sexual abuse. Randall has shared her therapeutic process – her literary and photographic depiction of her unfolding recognition of her status as an incest survivor enables us to interpret her experience and place it within the feminist theoretical context she creates. Bulkin brings us face-to-face with "the cloud" and then gives us the tools to dissipate it: honesty, openness, frank speech between sisters, the acknowledgement of our different needs and goals.

The final line of *Enter Password* embodies the contradictions contained within the personal narratives of sexual abuse survivors. "I don't know if I'm ready," Bulkin writes, unsure about her decision to publish her story. Yet the published book in my own hands belies her claim to uncertainty. Bulkin's words and her actions are composed in counterpoint to create the final composition: Ready or not, here we come.

This Is Not
a Conclusion

For quite some time I puzzled over how to end this book. It seemed, in fact, to have no end – each "last chapter" I conceived of led to another "last chapter," which in turn led to the next. It came to me, finally, after a year of deliberation – one needs, after all, to *finish* a book or else it is *not* a book – that to write a "last chapter" would be to commit the same sort of grievous sin of appropriation and disappearance that George Bush committed when he named the Gulf War the cure for the "Vietnam syndrome." The process of analysis is neverending, but it is not a *story*.

"Holocaust," "Vietnam," and "rape" are still floating signifiers, still contested ground. I anticipate that they will remain unfixed for some time to come, the battles over their meaning revealing far more about our contemporary culture than about any sort of historical truth. What I have done with this book, I hope, is to provide my readers with a *way* of watching these contests over meaning, and of recognizing other contests over similar signifiers (and there are many, ranging from "drugs," to "guns," to "terrorism"). I wanted to demonstrate the connections between these signifiers (signifiers float for a *reason*), and to show, from as many angles as possible, the investments different groups of people have in their interpretation. I wanted to make it clear why I believe that traumatic metaphors – the stories of survivors – are always political, even when they are most earnestly intended (or pretended) not to be. And I wanted to demonstrate that at the same time they are political, they are intensely personal – that the personal *is* political, without exception.

If I have accomplished any of these things, that is good. But meanwhile, ideological battles over the meaning of the Holocaust continue to be fought. Despite normalization of U.S. relations with Vietnam, "winning" the Vietnam War and the Vietnam-veteran-as-victim/hero continue to fascinate the American public. And a woman is raped every five minutes – in the time it takes you to read a few pages. There is no plot. There is only the passage of

time, from moment to moment, and, in each moment, what we choose to do,
choose to do, choose to do.

> every three minutes
> every five minutes
> every ten minutes
> every day.[1]

Notes

Chapter 1

1. Alice Miller, *For Your Own Good: Hidden Cruelty in Child-Rearing and the Roots of Violence* (New York: Farrar, Straus, Giroux) 1983: 197.
2. Gregory Bateson, "Metalogue: What is an Instinct?" in *Steps to an Ecology of Mind* (New York: Ballantine) 1972: 47.
3. Nadine Broznan, "Chronicle" column, *The New York Times* (30 Nov 1991): A20.
4. Terrence Des Pres, "The Authority of Silence in Elie Wiesel's Art," in *Writing into the World: Essays 1973–1987* (New York: Viking) 1978/1991: 25.
5. Elie Wiesel, *From the Kingdom of Memory* (New York: Summit) 1990: 15.
6. Elie Wiesel, "For Some Measure of Humility," *Sh'ma: A Journal of Jewish Responsibility* (31 Oct 1975): 5.
7. Elie Wiesel, *Legends of Our Time* (New York: Holt Rinehart Winston) 1968: 178.
8. Elie Wiesel, *From the Kingdom of Memory* (New York: Summit) 1990. From "Kaddish in Cambodia," originally published in *The Jewish Chronicle* (18 Apr 1980).
9. Ben Kiernan, "The American Bombardment of Kampuchea, 1969–1973," *Vietnam Generation 1:1* (Winter 1989): 4–41; William Shawcross, *The Quality of Mercy: Cambodia, Holocaust and Modern Conscience* (New York: Simon & Schuster) 1984.
10. Terrence Des Pres, "The Authority of Silence in Elie Wiesel's Art," in *Writing Into the World: Essays 1973–1987* (New York: Viking) 1991: 30.
11. Philip Hallie, "Writing About Ethical Ambivalence During the Holocaust," in Berel Lang, ed., *Writing and the Holocaust* (New York: Holmes & Meier) 1988, pp. 93–109; 105–106.
12. No doubt the order in which I choose to reveal this information about myself is significant, though I will leave it to the reader to generate an interpretation.
13. Valerie Smith, "Gender and Afro-Americanist Literary Theory and Criticism," in Elaine Showalter, ed., *Speaking of Gender* (New York: Routledge) 1989: 57.
14. Joan Cocks, *The Oppositional Imagination: Feminism, Critique, and Political Theory* (London: Routledge) 1989: 87.
15. Ibid.: 13.
16. Ibid.: 14.

17. Terrence Des Pres, *Writing Into the World: Essays 1973–1987* (New York: Viking) 1991: 3.
18. Gerald Graff, "Why Theory," in, Lennard J. Davis and M. Bella Mirabella, eds., *Left Politics and the Literary Profession* (New York: Columbia University Press) 1990, pp. 19–35 (Series: The Social Foundations of Aesthetic Forms): 23.
19. Rosenfeld: 172–173.
20. Michel Foucault, "Two Lectures," in Colin Gorden, ed. and trans., *Power/Knowledge: Selected Interviews and Other Writings, 1972–1977* (New York: Random House) 1980: 90.
21. Goleman: 116.
22. Terrence Des Pres. Introduction to Jean-François Steiner's *Treblinka*, in *Writing Into the World: Essays 1973–1987*. (New York: Viking) 1991: 53–62 (page 54).
23. James E. Young, *Writing and Rewriting the Holocaust* (Bloomington: Indiana University Press) 1988: 99.
24. Miriam Greenspan, "Responses to the Holocaust," in: Richard S. Gottlieb, ed., *Thinking the Unthinkable: Meanings of the Holocaust* (New York: Paulist Press) 1990: 393–394.
25. Ibid.
26. The following joke was making the rounds during the Persian Gulf War: Kurt Waldheim meets with Saddam Hussein. Waldheim is outraged – he shakes his finger at Saddam Hussein and says, "Saddam, Saddam, I *knew* Adolf Hitler. Adolf Hitler was my friend. And let me tell you, *you're no Adolf Hitler!*"
27. Literature produced by persons engaged in those activities belongs to the category of "Resistance Literature" – a genre distinct from survivor literature. See Barbara Harlow, *Resistance Literature* (New York: Methuen) 1987.
28. I do not mean to imply that Americans bore the brunt of the suffering inflicted in the Vietnam War. A simple comparison of numbers of American and Vietnamese dead (approximately 60,000 U.S. soldiers and over 2 million Vietnamese) puts American losses in perspective. The population of the U.S. did not endure devastating bombing campaigns, deforestation, destruction of arable land, economic blockade, or contamination of food and water supplies. Any study of the Vietnam war itself should emphasize that the Vietnamese paid a terribly high price for their independence. Research on the effect of the traumatization of both Vietnamese soldiers and civilians should be supported and encouraged by both U.S. and Vietnamese scholars.
29. Though it can be argued that many noncombat veterans define themselves as members of this group, it is quite clear that there is a line of demarcation between combat and noncombat veterans. This division between "grunts" and "REMFs" has been catalogued in some detail by bibliographer and novelist David Willson, author of the novels *REMF Diary* and *The REMF Returns*.
30. John Kerry and the Vietnam Veterans Against the War, in David Thorne and George Butler, eds., *The New Soldier*, (New York: Macmillan) 1971.
31. Myra MacPherson, *Long Time Passing: Vietnam and the Haunted Generation* (New York: Doubleday) 1984: 64.
32. Timothy W. Luke, *Screens of Power: Ideology, Domination and Resistance in Informational Society* (Urbana: University of Illinois Press) 1989: 171.

33. Steven Gomes, personal communication with the author in the form of hand-written notes on manuscript, April, 1993.

34. Telford Taylor, America's chief counsel for the prosecution at the Nuremberg Trials in 1946, wrote a book entitled *Nuremberg and Vietnam: An American Tragedy* (New York: Bantam, 1970) in which he concludes that "the anti-aggression spirit of Nuremberg and the United Nations Charter is invoked to justify our venture in Vietnam, where we have smashed the country to bits, and will not even take the trouble to clean up the blood and rubble.... Somehow we failed ourselves to learn the lessons we undertook to teach at Nuremberg, and that failure is today's American tragedy." (p. 207)

35. Vietnam Veterans Against the War (Anti-Imperialist). "Statement from Vietnam Era Veterans," in *About Face 1; 5* (November 1982): 1. See also Robert Jay Lifton, "Beyond Atrocity," in *Crimes of War:* 25.

36. Eric Norden, "American Atrocities in Vietnam, " in *Crimes of War:* 278.

37. Jean-Paul Sartre, "On Genocide," in *Crimes of War:* 547.

38. Edward M. Opten and Robert Duckles, "It Didn't Happen and Besides, They Deserved It," in *Crimes of War:* 441.

39. Michael Clark, "Remembering Vietnam," *Cultural Critique 3* (Spring 1986): 47.

40. Marvin E. Gettleman, Jane Franklin, Marilyn Young, and H. Bruce Franklin, eds., *Vietnam and America: A Documented History* (New York: Grove) 1985: xv.

41. Peter Davies, "A 1990 Postscript," in Susie Erenrich, ed., *Kent and Jackson State, 1970–1990,* a special issue of *Vietnam Generation* 2(2) 1990: 37.

42. Ibid.

43. Peter Davies, "Four Students," in Susie Erenrich, ed., *Kent and Jackson State, 1970–1990.*

44. James William Gibson, *The Perfect War: Technowar in Vietnam* (Boston: Atlantic Monthly) 1986: 3.

45. Ibid.: 3–4, 6.

46. Ibid.: 462.

47. Ibid.: 466–467.

48. Harry Haines, "Disputing the Wreckage: Ideological Struggle at the Vietnam Veterans Memorial," *Vietnam Generation* 1.1 (1989): 149.

49. Ibid.: 150.

50. Clark: 76.

51. Chaim Shatan, "Afterword – Who Can Take Away the Grief of a Wound?" in Ghislaine Boulanger and Charles Kadushin, eds., *The Vietnam Veteran Redefined: Fact and Fiction* (Hillsdale, NJ: Erlbaum) 1986: 172.

52. Émile Beneviste, "The Semiology of Language," in Robert E. Innis, ed., *Semiotics: An Introductory Anthology* (Bloomington: Indiana University Press) 1985: 242.

53. Ibid.: 235.

54. Paul Fussell, *The Great War and Modern Memory* (New York: Oxford University Press) 1975: 169–170.

55. Ibid.: 170.

56. Elie Wiesel, "To Believe or Not to Believe," in *From the Kingdom of Memory* (New York: Summit) 1990: 33. Originally published in the *Jerusalem Post,* September 15, 1985, translated from the French by Judy Cooper Weill.

57 Roland Barthes, "Rhetoric of the Image," in Robert E. Innis, ed., *Semiotics: An Introductory Anthology,* (Bloomington: Indiana University Press) 1985: 197.

58. Ibid.

59. I use this term advisedly, since I believe that these interpretive "flashbacks" are linked quite closely to the phenomenon of flashbacks described in the psychological literature, which appear to be triggered by body-memories of traumatic experiences. I address this in more detail in the next chapter.

60. Joan W. Scott, "Deconstructing Equality-Versus-Difference: Or, the Uses of Poststructuralist Theory for Feminism," in Marianne Hersch and Evelyn Fox Keller, eds., *Conflicts in Feminism* (New York: Routledge) 1990: 135.

61. See, for example, David Bleich, *Subjective Criticism* (Baltimore: Johns Hopkins University Press) 1978; Stanley E. Fish, "Working on the Chain Gang: Interpretation in the Law and in Literary Criticism," *Critical Inquiry,* 9 (1982); Norman Holland, *Laughing: A Psychology of Humor* (Ithaca: Cornell University Press) 1982; Wolfgang Iser, *The Act of Reading: A Theory of Aesthetic Response* (Baltimore: Johns Hopkins University Press) 1978; Hans Robert Jauss, *Aesthetic Experience and Literary Hermeneutics* (Minneapolis: University of Minnesota Press) 1982; I. A. Richards, *Practical Criticism: A Study of Literary Judgement* (New York: Harcourt Brace) 1952.

62. Jorge Luis Borges, "Pierre Menard, Author of Don Quixote," in *Ficciones* (New York: Grove) 1962: 53.

63. Ibid.

64. The idea that married women have the right to say no to their husbands was recently ridiculed by the Louisiana legislature. When Rep. Odon Bacque of Lafayette brought his marital-rape bill up for consideration in the house "... hooting and hollering began. The House chamber crackled with jokes about scenes in the marital bedroom after the men returned from their democratic duties in Baton Rouge. Rep. Carl Gunter (D), a country boy from Pineville, declared that the bill would inspire women to falsely accuse their husbands of rape. 'Women know what a man is when they marry him,' he said as colleagues snickered and guffawed. With no serious discussion the bill was tabled." (The *Washington Post,* 30 Jun 1990: A3.)

65. "In New York, for example, researchers studying police files found that 24% of the rape complaints in nonstranger cases were judged by the police to be without merit, compared with less than 5% in the stranger cases." [Susan Estrich, *Real Rape* (Cambridge, MA: Harvard University Press) 1987: 16. The study she mentions is Duncan Chappell and Susan Singer, "Rape in New York City: A Study of Material in the Police Files and its Meaning," in Duncan Chappell, Robley Geis, and Gilbert Geis, eds., *Forcible Rape: The Crime, the Victim, and the Offender* (New York: Columbia University Press) 1977].

66. Ibid.: 18.

67. "Freud may have been right in regarding incest as central in the development of young girls – but, if so, he was right for the wrong reason. Incest may be central in the development of young girls because the maturation of every little girl may be affected by the incestuous urges – overt, covert, or repressed – that the males in their families often feel toward them. ... Just as the source of incestuous feelings has been projected onto children, so has seductive behavior been pro-

jected onto young girls. It seems likely that this perception of young girls as seductive may be a rationalization for the desire of many fathers and older male relatives to make sexual advances toward them." [Diana E.H. Russell, *The Secret Trauma: Incest in the Lives of Girls and Women* (New York: Basic Books) 1986: 395.]

68. Judith Herman, "Recognition and Treatment of Incestuous Families," International Journal of Family Therapy 5(2) 1983: 81–91.

69. Ibid.

70. There is no need to make a long list of popular books and films which feature "romantic" rape scenes. *Gone With the Wind* has become a classic of this type, and this hackneyed cliché shows up even in "progressive" films like as Spike Lee's *She's Gotta Have It,* where "nice-guy" Jamie finally gives Nora what she really wants. The image of the pint-sized seductress wasn't invented by Nabokov, though his *Lolita* certainly serves as a paradigm case. Films such as *Pretty Baby* and *Taxi Driver* carry on the tradition.

71. Andrea Dworkin, *Pornography: Men Possessing Women* (New York: E.P. Dutton) 1989: xxxviii.

72. Anthony Wilden: 165.

73. Natalie Shainess, M.D., "Foreword," in Eleanore Hill, *The Family Secret: A Personal Account of Incest* (New York: Dell) 1985: vi.

74. Appelfeld: 86.

75. Claudia Tate, *Black Women Writers At Work* (New York: Continuum) 1983: 104.

76. John Ketwig, . . . *And a Hard Rain Fell* (New York: Pocket) 1985: xiii.

77. Des Pres, "Holocaust *Laughter?*": 219.

78. Jonathan Morse, *Word by Word: The Language of Memory* (Ithaca, NY: Cornell University Press) 1990: 2.

79. Ibid.: 5.

Chapter 2

1. Jerry Samet, "The Holocaust and the Imperative to Remember," in Richard S. Gottlieb, ed., *Thinking the Unthinkable: Meanings of the Holocaust* (New York: Paulist Press) 1990: 418.

2. The following T-shirts are popular products: 1) a shirt printed with the American flag, subtitled "Burn This!"; 2) a shirt printed with a large peace symbol, subtitled "Footprint of the American Chicken"; 3) a shirt bearing the logo "Nuclear reactors are built better than Jane Fonda."

3. The shirt bears a prominent copyright mark at the bottom of the design which reads © 1990 Wes Caton. I was unable to locate the artist for permission to reproduce the graphic. In the author's collection.

4. At the time, I was a consultant for the U.S. Holocaust Memorial Museum where I worked with the staff of the "Learning Center" to design the interactive multimedia computer displays intended to educate Museum visitors.

5. Jochen Schulte-Sasse and Linda Schulte-Sasse, "War, Otherness, and Illusionary Identifications with the State," *Cultural Critique,* Number 19, Fall 1991 (Special Issue: "The Economies of War"), pp. 67–96: 85.

6. Mario Benedetti finds "ominous resemblances between Bush's 'New World Order' and the 'Neue Ordnung' and 'Ordine Nuovo' of Hitler and Mussolini." *La Epoca* (4 May 1991), quoted in Noam Chomsky, "'What We Say Goes': The

Middle East in the New World Order," in *Collatal Damage: The 'New World Order' At Home and Abroad*, Cynthia Peters, ed. (Boston: South End Press) 1992: 51.

7. Jonathan Culler, *On Deconstruction: Theory and Criticism after Structuralism* (Ithaca: Cornell University Press) 1982: 17.

8. Joseph Natole, "Tracing a Beginning through Past Theory Voices," in Joseph Natoli, ed., *Tracing Literary Theory* (Urbana: University of Illinois) 1987: xix.

9. Livant, Bill, "The Imperial Cannibal," in Ian Angus and Sut Jhally, eds., *Cultural Politics in Contemporary America* (New York: Routledge, Chapman & Hall) 1989: 26–36. Livant claims that "Cultural politics in contemporary America" is "politics of the passions."

10. See Lucy S. Dawidowicz, "Lies About the Holocaust," *Commentary* 70 (December 1980): 31–37. For an extensive treatment of Holocaust-deniers see Deborah Lipstadt, (forthcoming). Also see Pierre Vidal-Naquet, ed., *Assassins of Memory: Essays on the Denial of the Holocaust*, Jeffrey Mehlman, trans. (New York: Columbia University Press) 1992.

11. See *Chronicle of Higher Education* tracked this throughout the late 1980s and early 1990s. Revisionists have also carried their arguments to the broad audience of Usenet and Bitnet electronic bulletin boards, where they have sparked heated debate in such arenas as soc.history, and alt.activism. Their strategy is to "post" an inflammatory revisionist article, and then to wait for the myriad angry responses of readers. Then they can legitimately "answer" every response, thus involving the entire electronic community in the argument with their ubiquitous postings. When bulletin board users complain about the huge amount of space taken up by the revisionist group, the revisionists can cry censorship and provoke a second debate on that topic, keeping themselves in the eye of the reader.

12. Lucy Dawidowicz, "How They Teach the Holocaust," *Commentary*, December 1990: 25–32.

13. Ibid.: 25.

14. Ibid.: 31.

15. Margot Stern Strom and William S. Parsons, *Facing History and Ourselves: Holocaust and Human Behavior* (Watertown, MA: Intentional Educations, Inc.) 1982: 13.

16. Dawidowicz, "How They Teach the Holocaust": 25.

17. Strom and Parsons: 383.

18. Kobena Mercer, "'1968': Periodizing Politics and Identity," in Lawrence Grossberg, Cary Nelson, and Paula Treichler, eds., *Cultural Studies* (New York: Routledge) 1992: 424–425.

19. Ibid.: 427.

20. Daniel Landes, "Anti-Semitism Parading as Anti-Zionism," in Michael Lerner, ed. Tikkun: An Anthology (Oakland, CA: Tikkun Books) 1992: 367.

21. Ibid.

22. Ibid.: 368.

23. Ibid.

24. Noam Chomsky, *Language and Politics*, C. P. Otera, ed. (New York: Black Rose Books) 1988: 528.

25. Ibid.: 528–529.
26. Ibid.: 529.
27. Ibid.
28. Noam Chomsky, *Deterring Democracy* (New York: Verso) 1991: 378. Though Chomsky has political views diametrically opposed to conservatives such as Charles Krauthammer and William Safire, his choice of metaphors is strikingly similar. Krauthammer, writing in the Washington Post six days before the Iraqi invasion of Kuwait, claims that what makes Hussein "truly Hitlerian is his way of dealing with neighboring states. . . . The diplomacy practiced by the fascist powers of the '30s was to accumulated massive military power for translation into immediate gain – territorial, economic, political – through extortion and, if still necessary, war." Charles Krauthammer, "Nightmare from the Thirties," editorial in the *Washington Post,* 27 July 1990.
29. Robert I. Friedman, "War and Peace in Israel," in Micah Sifry and Christopher Cerf, eds., *The Gulf War Reader: History Documents Opinions* (New York: Times Books) 1991: 433. This article, originally titled, "Israel's Peace Movement Calls for War," was published in the 26 February 1990 issue of *The Village Voice.*
30. Stephen J. Solarz, "The Case for Intervention," in *The Gulf War Reader:* 271. This essay was originally published in the 7 and 14 January 1991 issue of *The New Republic* under the title "The Stakes in the Gulf." Solarz has been extremely active in the movement to revise the Vietnam war, and his intent in this essay was to overcome "the Vietnam Syndrome" that caused the U.S. to hesitate before engaging in war in the Gulf. His theme: "In Vietnam no vital American interests were at stake. The crisis in the Gulf poses a challenge not only to fundamental American interests, but to essential American values." (p. 269)
31. John B. Judis, "Jews and the Gulf: Fallout from the Six-Week War," *Tikkun: An Anthology:* 131. This article originally appeared in Tikkun, May/June 1991.
32. Cornel West, "Black-Jewish Dialogue: Beyond Rootless Universalism and Ethnic Chauvinism," in *Tikkun: An Anthology:* 89.
33. Ibid.: 90.
34. Harold Cruse, *The Crisis of the Negro Intellectual* (New York: Quill) 1967/1984: 484.
35. An exemplary text is *Israel and South Africa,* by Donald Will and Sheila Ryan (Trenton, NJ: Africa World Press) 1990. *Israel and South Africa* is sold in quite a few bookstores specializing in African-American, black nationalist and Afrocentric texts. I purchased my copy at Pyramid House Books, Washington, DC. Simply because I have come across no African-American literature using the Nazi/Jew Israeli/Palestinian analogy does not mean this literature does not exist. It is a good indication that such a comparison is rare, even in the literature sold in bookstores that cater explicitly to the black community.
36. Ibid.: 483.
37. Ibid.: 486.
38. bell hooks, *Yearning: Race, Gender, and Cultural Politics* (Boston: South End Press) 1990.
39. Though there is certainly an enormous amount of evidence of genocidal inter-tribal behavior on the African continent, this topic is rarely broached in discussions of "comparative" holocausts. For example, the genocidal war waged by the

Tutsi against the Hutus in Burundi in 1972 resulted in the massacre of upwards of 200,000 Hutus in a three-month period, and in Rwanda (where the situation was reversed) the Hutus murdered about 100,000 Tutsis in 1959 and continued to persecute the Tutsi through 1964. Those who have observed the results of the African genocides have not hesitated to make comparisons: Stan Meisler, the African correspondent for the *Los Angeles Times,* wrote of his visit to Bujumbura, the capital of Burundi, "It is a little like entering Warsaw after World War II, and finding few Jews there" and that inveterate critic of atrocity, Bertrand Russell, called the killings in Rwanda "the most horrible and systematic human massacre we have had occasion to witness since the extermination of the Jews by the Nazis." However, such references have not entered the common discourse on the nature of the "Holocaust." See David Lamb, *The Africans* (New York: Vintage Books) 1983: 12–14.

40. Nina King, "What Happened at Duke," in Patricia Aufderheide, ed., *Beyond PC: Toward a Politics of Understanding,* (St. Paul, MN: Greywolf Press) 1992: 120.

41. George F. Will, "Literary Politics," in *Beyond PC:* 24. Conservative critics like Will claim that there is an absolute standard by which "literature" can be judged – most often called an "aesthetic" measure – which is presumed to have no political location. Just as Dawidowicz asserts that the study of the Holocaust does not fall into the category of "oppression studies" because of its universal importance, Will and his ilk claim that the "great" books that have traditionally comprised the canon taught in U.S. colleges and universities are selected sheerly on the basis of an objective standard of excellence – a standard that it just so happens no works by minority and/or female authors meet. In what must be one of the most arrogant assertions of the P.C. debate, Mortimer J. Adler (editor-in-chief of the 1990 edition of the *Great Books of the Western World*) boldly claims that "great books are relevant to human problems in every century, not just germane to current twentieth-century problems. A great book requires reading over and over, and has many meanings; a good book need be read no more than once, and need have no more than one meaning." (Mortimer J. Adler, "Multi-culturalism, Transculturalism, and the Great Books," in *Beyond PC:* 60.) In response, I refer the reader back to the Jerry Samet quote which heads this chapter.

42. Nancy Armstrong and Leonard Tennenhouse, eds., *The Violence of Representation: Literature and the History of Violence* (New York: Routledge) 1989: 24.

43. Terrence Des Pres, "Holocaust *Laughter?*" in *The Writer Into the World: Essays 1973–1989* (New York: Viking) 1991: 277–278.

44. Terrence Des Pres, *The Survivor* (New York: Oxford) 1976: 155.

45. Elie A. Cohen, *Human Behavior in the Concentration Camp 1954* (London: Free Association Publishing) 1988; Bruno Bettelheim, *The Informed Heart* (Glencoe, IL: Free Press) 1960.

46. A Dutch citizen, Cohen was arrested and assigned as a transport doctor at the Westerbork transit camp from December 1942–September 1943. Cohen was imprisoned in Auschwitz I until January 1945, and he survived the death march to Mauthausen to be interned in Melk until April of that year. (Cohen: xxi) He was liberated by the Americans at Ebensee in May, 1945. Bettelheim was an Austrian citizen; he was arrested and imprisoned in Dachau within a few weeks

of the annexation of Austria by Germany in 1938, transferred to Buchenwald, and then released by the Gestapo in 1939, when he immigrated to the United States. (Des Pres, "Bettelheim Problem": 63).

47. Des Pres, *The Survivor:* 155.
48. Ibid.: 156.
49. Ibid.: 157.
50. Ibid.: 161.
51. Ibid.
52. Ibid.: 164.
53. Ibid.: 167.
54. Ibid.: 170.
55. Ibid.: 176.
56. Bruno Bettelheim, "Surviving," in *Surviving and Other Essays* (New York: Vintage Books) 1979: 274. The essay originally appeared under the same title in *The New Yorker*, 2 Aug 1976: 31–52. The original essay was slightly different from this anthologized version, but it is the anthologized version to which Des Pres responds.
57. Ibid.: 274.
58. Ibid.
59. Ibid.
60. Ibid.: 275.
61. Ibid.: 276.
62. Ibid.: 278.
63. Ibid.
64. Ibid.: 279.
65. Ibid.
66. Ibid.
67. Ibid.: 281.
68. Ibid.: 285.
69. Ibid.
70. Ibid.
71. Ibid.
72. Ibid. 287.
73. Ibid.
74. Ibid.: 289.
75. Ibid.
76. Ibid.: 290–291.
77. Des Pres, *The Survivor:* 157.
78. Ibid.: 158.
79. Ibid.: 160. The reference is to Eugene Kogon, *The Theory and Practice of Hell,* translated by Heinz Norden (New York: Farrar, Straus, Giroux) 1953.
80. Ibid.
81. Bettelheim, "Surviving": 296.
82. Ibid.: 297.
83. Des Pres, *The Survivor:* 37–38.
84. Ibid.: 42.
85. Ibid.: 49.

86. Ibid.: 39.
87. Ibid.: 47.
88. Bettelheim, "Surviving": 313–314.
89. Certainly, textual critics are often annoyed when amateurs see a film or read a book and feel qualified to offer their opinions as if they constituted a serious analysis. This may be one of the reasons that literary criticism has joined other professions in its tendency to employ a lot of jargon. There is a valid argument that complex ideas require complex structures of theory and language not easily accessible to the layperson, but an excess of jargon may also indicate a desire to exclude outsiders and preserve "secret" knowledge.
90. Des Pres, "The Bettelheim Problem": 63.
91. Ibid.
92. Ibid.: 63–64.
93. Ibid.: 64. Des Pres is himself an academic theorist, of course, and with the benefit of distance, the reader may find him or herself remarking on the peculiar strategy of undermining one's own authority in order to advance one's viewpoint. This is, however, a common practice in the arena of debate about the Holocaust (and about other traumatic events, such as military conflicts) where the authority of those who were "there" is accepted by all parties without question. In such circumstances, those who were not "there" have to content themselves with asserting, in the manner of feuding schoolchildren, that "my survivor can lick your survivor."
94. Ibid.
95. Ibid.: 65. That Des Pres' analysis might have been more accurate even than he suspected was suggested by a series of articles wthat appeared in the national press following Bettelheim's death in 1990. Charles Pekow, a writer who as a child had attended the Orthogonic School, wrote: "The Bettelheim I knew was a man who while publicly condemning violence, physically abused children. And the Orthogonic School I knew was an Orwellian world where mail and reading was censored, where staff tried to monitor conversations, and few were permitted outside unescorted." William Blau, a counselor at the school (1949–50), concurred: "I would characterize the atmosphere at the Orthogonic School, at that time, as the beginnings of a cult, with Dr. B. as the cult leader." Blau also commented on Bettelheim's "limitless ability for self promotion." Alida Jatick, a computer programmer who had been an inmate of the Orthogonic School, clams that "Bettelheim once pulled her out of a shower and beat her, wet and naked, in front of a room full of people." Charles Pekow, "The Other Dr. Bettelheim," in *The Washington Post,* Outlook section (26 Aug 1990): C1–C4.
96. Ibid.: 65. Italics mine.
97. Ibid.: 66–68.
98. Ibid.: 67.
99. Ibid.
100. Ibid.: 68.
101. Ibid.: 69.
102. Ibid.: 73.
103. Ibid.: 74.
104. Ibid.: 75.

105. Ibid.: 76. Des Pres makes an interesting aside in the text at this point: he uses Bettelheim's rage at student antiwar protests in the 1960s, and his equation of those students with fascists of the "pre-Hitler days" as yet another illustration of his point.
106. Ibid.: 76–77.
107. Ibid.
108. Ibid.: 86.
109. Terrence Des Pres, "The Authority of Silence in Elie Wiesel's Art," in *Writing Into the World*: 32.
110. Ibid.: 25.
111. Des Pres, *The Survivor*: v–vi.
112. Ibid.: vi.
113. Ibid.: 184.
114. Ibid.: 49.
115. Ibid.: 47.
116. Ibid.: 199–200.
117. Ibid.: 13–14. The most fascinating part of this argument is that the cleansing is accomplished by a literal "immersion in shit," the excremental assault to which Des Pres devotes an entire chapter of *The Survivor*. His rather bizarre reference to the Jewish tradition of ritual bathing passes without remark in most critical analyses.
118. Bruno Bettelheim, "The Holocaust – One Generation After," in Richard S. Gottlieb, ed., *Thinking the Unthinkable: Meanings of the Holocaust* (New York: Paulist Press) 1990: 381–382.
119. Ibid.
120. James E. Young, *Writing and Rewriting the Holocaust: Narrative and the Consequences of Interpretation* (Bloomington: University of Indiana Press) 1988; Lawrence Langer, *Holocaust Testimonies: The Ruins of Memory* (New Haven: Yale University Press) 1991; Shoshana Felman and Dori Laub, *Testimony: Crises of Witnessing in Literature, Psychoanalysis, and History* (New York: Routledge) 1992.
121. Young: vii.
122. Ibid.
123. Ibid.: 4.
124. Ibid.: 5.
125. Ibid.: 23.
126. Ibid.: 24–25.
127. Ibid.: 37.
128. Ibid.: 39.
129. Ibid.: 55.
130. Ibid.: 60.
131. Ibid.: 80.
132. Ibid.: 98.
133. Ibid.: 99.
134. Ibid.: 109.
135. Ibid.: 130–132.
136. Ibid.: 132.
137. Ibid.: 192.

138. Lawrence L. Langer, *Holocaust Testimonies: The Ruins of Memory* (New Haven: Yale University Press) 1991: 3.
139. Ibid.: 2.
140. Ibid.: 21.
141. Ibid.
142. Ibid.: 61.
143. Ibid.: 69.
144. Ibid.: 36.
145. Ibid.: 161.
146. Ibid.: 197.
147. Ibid.
148. Ibid.: 201.
149. W. E. B. DuBois, *The Souls of Black Folk,* reprinted in *Three Negro Classics* (New York: Avon) 1965: 214–215.
150. Barbara Johnson, "Metaphor, Metonymy and Voice," in *"Their Eyes Were Watching God," Black Literature and Literary Theory,* H. L. Gates, ed. (New York: Methuen) 1984: 218.
151. Young: 158.
152. Ibid.: 171.
153. Ibid.: 166.
154. Shoshona Felman and Dori Laub, M.D., Testimony: *Crises of Witnessing in Literature, Psychoanalysis, and History* (New York: Routledge) 1992: xiv.
155. Ibid.
156. Ibid.: 1.
157. Ibid.
158. Ibid.: 5.
159. Ibid.: 15.
160. Ibid.: 41.
161. Monique Wittig, "The Straight Mind," in Russell Ferguson, et al., eds., *Out There: Marginalization and Contemporary Culture,* (Cambridge, MA: MIT Press) 1990: 52.
162. Felman and Laub, ibid.: 48.
163. Ibid.: 50.
164. Ibid.: 52.
165. Ibid.: 53.
166. Ibid.: 54–55.
167. Ibid.: 58.
168. Ibid.
169. Ibid.: 72.
170. Ibid.: 76.
171. Wittig: 52.
172. Felman and Laub, ibid.: 79.
173. Ibid.: 78.
174. Ibid.: 82.
175. Ibid.
176. Ibid.: 121.
177. Ibid.: 123.

178. Ibid.: 135.
179. Ibid.: 139.
180. Ibid.: 238.

Chapter 3

1. George Bush, "Remarks to the American Legislative Exchange Council," March 1, 1991, *Public Papers of the Presidents of the United States, 1991,* Book I: January 1 to June 30, 1991 (Washington, DC: Government Printing Office) 1992: 197.
2. George Bush, "Radio Address to United States Armed Forces Stationed in the Persian Gulf Region," March 2, 1991, ibid.: 207.
3. George Bush, "Remarks to Veterans Service Organization," March 4, 1991, ibid.: 209.
4. James William Gibson, *The Perfect War* (New York: W.W. Norton) 1986: 5.
5. Ibid.: 433–435.
6. Ibid.: 435.
7. Ibid.: 6.
8. Lisa Kennedy, "The Body in Question," in Gina Dentz, ed., *Black Popular Culture,* (Seattle: Bay Press) 1992: 107.
9. Jan C. Scruggs and Joel L. Swerdlow, *To Heal a Nation* (New York: Harper & Row/Perennial) 1985: 101.
10. Ibid.: 129.
11. Gibson: 6.
12. See, for a list of memorials, Jerry L. Strait and Sandra S. Strait, *Vietnam War Memorials: An Illustrated Reference to Veterans Tributes Throughout the United States* (Jefferson, NC: McFarland) 1988.
13. "Four Writers Try to Make Sense of the Vietnam-Book Boom." *The New York Times* (4 August 1987).
14. Philip D. Beidler, *American Literature and the Experience of Vietnam* (Athens: University of Georgia Press) 1982: 19.
15. Ibid.: 195.
16. The words "real" and "reality" are extremely troublesome in this context. I assume that a certain set of events actually took place, which was the war, and that these events are the "real" ones. But it seems important to point out that acknowledging the existence of the reality of the Vietnam War is not the same thing as claiming to know what "really" happened.
17. Ibid.: 202.
18. Ibid.
19. James C. Wilson, *Vietnam in Prose and Film* (Jefferson, NC: McFarland) 1982: 7.
20. Ibid.: 100–101.
21. Ibid.
22. Ibid.
23. Ibid.: 102.
24. John Hellman, *American Myth and the Legacy of Vietnam* (New York: Columbia University Press) 1986: 207.
25. Ibid.: 135.
26. Ibid.: 137.
27. Ibid.: 208.

28. Ibid.
29. Richard Slotkin, in *Gunfighter Nation: The Myth of the Frontier in Twentieth-Century America* (New York: HarperPerennial, 1992), describes *Star Wars* continuing the "myth of the frontier" – "a myth of historical progress similar to that in the progressive Westerns and 'empire' movies of the 30s and 40s. The tale of individual action (typically a captivity/rescue) is presented as the key to a world-historical (or cosmic-historical) struggle between darkness and light, with perpetual happiness and limitless power for the heroes and all humankind (or 'sentient-kind') as the prize of victory." (p. 635).
30. Ibid.: 222.
31. Ibid.: 223–224.
32. Thomas Myers, *Walking Point: American Narratives of Vietnam* (New York: Oxford University Press) 1988: 10–11.
33. Ibid.
34. Ibid.: 13.
35. Ibid.: 32.
36. Ibid.: 142.
37. Ibid.
38. Susan Jeffords, *The Remasculinization of America: Gender and the Vietnam War* (Bloomington: Indiana University Press) 1989: 53.
39. Ibid: 5.
40. Ibid.: 30.
41. Ibid.: 51.
42. Ibid.: 77.
43. Kathleen Puhr, "Four Fictional Faces of the Vietnam War," *Modern Fiction Studies* 3.1 (Spring 1984): 104.
44. Jacqueline Lawson, ed., *Gender and The War: Men, Women and Vietnam* (Vietnam Generation, Inc., 18 Center Rd., Woodbridge, CT 06525) 1989. Published as *Vietnam Generation* 1(3–4) 1989.
45. This is most striking in the chapter entitled "Do We Get to Win This Time? Reviving the Masculine," Jeffords: 116–143.
46. Philip H. Melling, *Vietnam in American Literature* (Boston: Twayne Publishers) 1990: xiv.
47. Ibid.: 15.
48. Ibid.: 16.
49. Perry Miller and Thomas H. Johnson, eds., *The Puritans: A Sourcebook of Their Writings, Volume One*, revised edition, 1938 (New York: Harper Torchbooks) 1963: 1.
50. Melling: 72.
51. Ibid.: 76.
52. Miller: 5.
53. Melling: 39.
54. Ibid.: xviii.
55. Ibid.: 94.
56. Ibid.: 199.
57. Ibid.: 112.
58. Ibid.: 121.

59. Ibid.: 133.
60. Ibid.: 171.
61. Ibid.: 194.
62. Ibid.
63. Ibid.: 53.
64. Philip D. Beidler, *Re-Writing America* (Athens: University of Georgia Press) 1991: 12.
65. Ibid.: 19.
66. Ibid.: 20.
67. Ibid.: 39.
68. Ibid.: 39.
69. Ibid.: 86.
70. Ibid.: 148.
71. Ibid.: 254–255.
72. Ibid.: 69.
73. Ibid.: 97.
74. Ibid.: 207.
75. Ibid.: 208.
76. Ibid.: 208.
77. Ibid.
78. Ibid.: 223.
79. Ibid.: 238.
80. Ibid.: 266.
81. Ibid.: 207.
82. Wilson: 101–102.
83. Hellman: 221.
84. Beidler: 195.
85. Myers: 147.
86. See Slotkin, *Gunfighter Nation,* especially Part V: "Gunfighter Nation: Myth, Ideology, and Violence on the New Frontier, 1960–1970": 489–663.
87. Carroll Smith-Rosenberg, "The Body Politic," in Elizabeth Weed, ed., *Coming to Terms: Feminism, Theory, Politics* (New York: Routledge) 1989: 101.

Chapter 4

1. W. D. Ehrhart, "The Farmer," in *The Outer Banks and Other Poems* (Easthampton, MA: Adastra) 1984: 17. All poems printed and quoted are used with the permission of the author.
2. Ehrhart, *Going Back* (Jefferson, NC: McFarland) 1987: 185–186.
3. Lawrence L. Langer, *Versions of Survival: The Holocaust and the Human Spirit* (Albany: State University of New York Press) 1982: 88.
4. Samuel Delany, The Motion of Light in Water (New York: Arbor House) 1988.
5. Ibid.: xviii.
6. Larry Rottmann, Jan Barry, and Basil T. Paquet, eds., *Winning Hearts and Minds: War Poems by Vietnam Veterans* (Brooklyn, NY: 1st Casualty Press) 1972.
7. Ehrhart, *A Generation of Peace* (New Voices Publishing Company) 1975: 13.
8. Langer, *Versions of Survival:* 12.

9. Jan Barry and W. D. Ehrhart, *Demilitarized Zones: Veterans After Vietnam* (Perkasie, PA: East River Anthology) 1976.

10. Ehrhart, *A Generation of Peace*. Revised and reprinted under the same title by Samisdat Press, 1977.

11. Alvin H. Rosenfeld, "The Problematics of Holocaust Literature," in Rosenfeld and Greenberg, eds., *Confronting the Holocaust: The Impact of Elie Wiesel* (Bloomington: Indiana University) 1978: 26. Rosenfeld is a Holocaust literary critic whose work bridges Des Pres reliance on the authenticity of the survivor experience and Young's second-generation perspective.

12. Robert Jay Lifton, "Beyond Atrocity," in Richard Falk, Gabriel Kolko, and Robert J. Lifton, eds., *Crimes of War: A Legal, Political-Documentary, and Psychological Inquiry into the Responsibility of Leaders, Citizens, and Soldiers for Criminal Acts in War* (New York: Random House) 1971: 18–19.

13. Lawrence Langer, "The Divided Voice: Elie Wiesel and the Challenge of the Holocaust," in *Confronting the Holocaust:* 31.

14. Ibid.: 33.

15. Sidra DeKoven Ezrahi, *By Words Alone: The Holocaust in Literature* (Chicago: University of Chicago) 1980: 73.

16. Des Pres: 100.

17. The main character of Ed Dodge's novel, *Dau* (New York: Berkley, 1984) is haunted by the ghosts of dead friends and murdered mistress. Chris Starkmann, the protagonist of Philip Caputo's *Indian Country* (New York: Bantam, 1987) is visited by the ghosts of D.J., Hutch, and Ramos, who urge him to join them. And, of course, Larry Heinemann's prizewinning novel *Paco's Story* (New York: Penguin, 1986) is narrated to James, Paco's dead comrade.

18. Des Pres: 88.

19. Rosenfeld: 53–54.

20. Samisdat Press, 1977.

21. Samisdat Press, 1978.

22. Michael Herr, *Dispatches* (New York: Avon) 1978.

23. Book review, *Win* (18 May 1978).

24. Ibid.

25. "The accommodations that documentary art has made to the imperatives of an extreme and unprecedented historical experience can be seen as part of the general trend toward fictional journalism which came to be known in the sixties as the New Journalism. . . . For the survivor of the A-bomb or the Nazi Holocaust, the documentary approach suggests a faith in memory over imagination and a loyalty to one's dead over the creations of one's mind. . . . It may be seen as an extension of the regard for the primacy of the report that was exemplified during the war years by Thomas Mann and other writers who served as broadcasters or journalists devoted to publicizing the little-known facts of the atrocities. . . . Nearly every documentary writer prefaces his narrative with the claim that nothing in his story is invented. . . . The aesthetic and moral implications of what amounts to the author's abdication of creative responsibility rest not in the verifiability of individual facts but rather in the premises which underlie an ostensibly undoctored reconstruction of historical events. The very claim to historicity lends such works a certain authority." Ezrahi: 24–25.

26. Rosenfeld: 6–7.
27. Ehrhart, *The Samisdat Poems* (Samisdat Press) 1980.
28. Ehrhart, *To Those Who Have Gone Home Tired: New and Selected Poems* (New York: Thunders Mouth) 1984: 70.
29. Ibid.: 72.
30. Ibid.: 71.
31. Ehrhart, "Preserving the American Myth," *Intervention*, 1.1 (Spring 1984).
32. *Samisdat Poems:* 48.
33. Book review, *Win* (20 September 1979).
34. Ehrhart, "Stealing Hubcaps," keynote speech delivered at the Conference on Youth, Militarism and Alternatives, Chicago (3 June 1988).
35. Ibid.
36. Ehrhart, letter to *Win,* (1 June 1980): 2.
37. Ehrhart, *Matters of the Heart* (Adastra Press) 1981.
38. Ibid.
39. Ibid.
40. "Briana," ibid.
41. Ehrhart, "The Long Road Home to Intimacy," *Win* (1 March 1980): 16.
42. Ehrhart, *Channel Fever* (Backstreet Editions) 1982.
43. Thomas Bulfinch, *Bulfinch's Mythology* (Toronto: Modern Library) nd: 295.
44. Margaret Atwood, "Circe/Mud Poems," *You Are Happy* (New York: Harper and Row) 1974: 51.
45. Estella Lauter, *Women as Mythmakers: Poetry and Visual Art by Twentieth Century Women* (Bloomington: Indiana University) 1984: 64.
46. "Cowgirls, Teachers & Dreams," ibid.
47. "Everett Dirksen, His Wife, You & Me," ibid.
48. "... the light that cannot fade ...," ibid.
49. "Climbing to Heaven," ibid.
50. " ... the light that cannot fade ...," ibid.
51. "Everett Dirksen, His Wife, You & Me," ibid.
52. "The Vision," *The Outer Banks.*
53. Ehrhart, *Vietnam-Perkasie* (New York: Kensington House) 1983: 11.
54. Rosenfeld: 21–22.
55. Ehrhart, *Vietnam-Perkasie:* 19.
56. Ibid.: 39.
57. Klaus Theweleit, *Male Fantasies, Volume 1: Women Floods Bodies History* (Minneapolis: University of Minnesota) 1987: 284–285.
58. Ehrhart, *Vietnam-Perkasie:* 382.
59. Ehrhart, *Marking Time* (New York: Avon) 1986; retitled *Passing Time* and reprinted (Jefferson, NC: McFarland) 1989.
60. Elie Wiesel, *Night* (New York: Bantam) 1960.
61. Lawrence Langer, *Versions of Survival: The Holocaust and the Human Spirit* (Albany: SUNY Press) 1982: 132.
62. *Marking Time:* 21.
63. Langer: 148.
64. *Marking Time:* 56.
65. Ibid.: 57.

66. Langer: 168.
67. *Marking Time:* 111.
68. Ibid.: 137.
69. Ibid.: 185.
70. A different version of this camping trip appears in "A Confirmation," from Empire, where Ehrhart offers an image of Gerry that emphasizes the unbearable connection between two men whose pain is too great for them to share and who have chosen different paths to peace. The poem, unlike the novel, gives us a final image which suggests that though separated, these two men share one soul.
71. Ibid.: 271.
72. See *Win* (1 March 1980).
73. *Marking Time:* 295.
74. Ehrhart, book review, *Philadelphia Inquirer* (17 Mary 1987): Section S.
75. Ehrhart, "Who Will Apologize for Vietnam?" *Philadelphia Inquirer* (4 July 1989): 8A.
76. *Going Back:* 24.
77. Ibid.: 70.
78. Ibid.: 96.
79. Ibid.: 175.
80. Ibid.: 180.
81. Ibid.: 5.
82. "Winter Bells," in W. D. Ehrhart, *Winter Bells* (Easthampton, MA: Adastra) 1988: 5.
83. "Parade Rest," ibid.: 10.
84. "Last Flight Out From the War Zone," ibid.: 12.
85. "For Mrs. Na," and "Twice Betrayed," Ibid.: 13–14.
86. Ehrhart, "This Is Not A Poem About the War," *Samisdat* (1989).
87. Ehrhart, private correspondence with the author, 6 December, 1991.
88. Langer: 125.
89. "Stealing Hubcaps."

Chapter 5

1. Daniel Goleman, *Vital Lies, Simple Truths; The Psychology of Self-Deception* (New York: Simon & Schuster) 1985: 21. See also Roger Schank, *Dynamic Memory* (Boston: Harvard University Press) 1982.
2. Chaim Shatan, "Afterword," in Ghislaine Boulanger and Charles Kadushin, eds., *The Vietnam Veteran Redefined: Fact and Fiction.* (Hillsdale, NJ: Erlbaum) 1986: 179.
3. Philip Beidler is a Vietnam veteran, which makes his decision to enter into the critical discourse on the same level as Wilson, Hellman, and Myers quite interesting. In none of his critical writing does he claim that the viewpoint of the combat veteran is essentially different fro the viewpoint of the nonveteran reader, writer, or critic. The insistent burial of the fact of his own veteran status implies a rejection of the notion that veterans have a privileged viewpoint, and his identification with the "objective" analytic techniques of the literary critic.
4. Eric J. Leed, *No Man's Land: Combat and Identity in World War I* (New York: Cambridge University Press) 1979: 193–194.

5. Ibid.: 14.
6. Ibid.: 194.
7. Ibid.: 208.
8. Ibid.: 212.
9. Ibid.: 213.
10. Gerald Linderman. *Embattled Courage: The Experience of Combat in the American Civil War* (New York: Free Press) 1987: 267.
11. Ibid.: 268.
12. Ibid.: 280.
13. Ibid.: 297.
14. Veterans Administration. *Selected Bibliography 2: Post-Traumatic Stress Disorder with Special Attention to Vietnam Veterans,* Revision 25 (Phoenix: VA Medical Center) 16 January 1986.
15. Lawrence L. Langer, *Versions of Survival: The Holocaust and the Human Spirit* (Albany: State University of New York Press) 1982: 88.
16. Elie Wiesel. "Why I Write," in Rosenfeld and Greenburg, eds., *Confronting the Holocaust: The Impact of Elie Wiesel,* (Bloomington: Indiana University Press) 1978: 205.
17. Langer: 185.
18. Robert J. Lifton, *History and Human Survival* (New York: Random House) 1970: 206.
19. Wiesel, "Why I Write": 200–201.
20. The Winter Soldier Investigation was convened in Detroit, Michigan on January 31 and February 1 and 2, 1971 by Vietnam Veterans Against the War to provide a forum for soldiers who wanted to testify to having committed or witnessed war crimes in Vietnam. The quote is from the testimony of Lt. Larry Lee Rottmann, veteran of the 25th Infantry Division in Vietnam Veterans Against the War, *The Winter Soldier Investigation: An Inquiry into American War Crimes* (Boston: Beacon Press) 1972: 163–164. Rottmann became a Vietnam War writer in his own right, founding, with Wayne Karlin and Basil Paquet, the Vietnam veteran-owned and run First Casualty Press. Since then he has authored a novel, poetry, memoir and nonfiction about the Vietnam War.
21. Quoted in Louise Thornton, "Preface," in Ellen Bass and Louise Thornton, eds., *I Never Told Anyone: Writings by Women Survivors of Child Sexual Abuse.* (New York: Harper & Row) 1983: 20.
22. Wiesel, "Why I Write": 201.
23. Terrence Des Pres, *The Survivor: An Anatomy of Life in the Death Camps* (New York: Oxford University Press) 1976: 42.
24. Hellman: 206–207.
25. Wiesel, "Why I Write": 201.
26. Larry Heinemann, *Close Quarters* (New York: Warner) 1977: 289.
27. A number of French feminists, such as Monique Wittig, Luce Irigary, and Hélène Cixous have written extensively on the subject, and American feminists such as Elizabeth Meese, Alice Jardine, and Barbara Johnson (among others) have also produced essays dealing with the topic.
28. *Sister,* Los Angeles (December 1977).
29. Andrea Dworkin, *Intercourse* (New York: Free Press) 1987: 65.

30. Dworkin: 134–135.

31. Sidra DeKoven Ezrahi, *By Words Alone: The Holocaust in Literature* (Chicago: University of Chicago Press) 1980: 11.

32. Ibid.

33. Ibid.

34. Paul Fussell, *The Great War and Modern Memory* (New York: Oxford University Press) 1975: 131.

35. Alvin H. Rosenfeld, "The Problematics of Holocaust Literature": 19.

36. "I encountered among Hiroshima survivors a frequent sense of being 'as-if dead,' or what I called an 'identity of the dead,' which took the following inner sequence: I almost died; I should have died; I did die or at least I am not really alive; or if I am alive, it is impure of me to be so and anything I do which affirms life is also impure and an insult to the dead, who alone are pure. An expression of this sense of themselves can be found in the life-style of many survivors, one of marked constriction and self-abnegation, based upon the feeling that any show of vitality is in some way inappropriate for them, not inwardly permissible. They retain a sense of infinite culpability, and even, ironically enough, of guilt and responsibility for the catastrophe itself, despite being victims rather than perpetrators of that catastrophe." Robert J. Lifton, *Boundaries* (New York: Random House) 1969: 13.

37. Des Pres: 38.

38. Ibid.: 46.

39. Ezrahi: 13–14.

40. Ibid.

41. Ibid.

42. Most of the literature of the Holocaust actually appeared almost twenty years after the end of the war (see Ezrahi: 67–68). A quick check of the publication dates of most World War I, World War II, and Vietnam War literature will support the claim of the elapse of over a decade before the publication of most major works. I have not yet come across a pieces of rape or incest literature that was *not* published at least ten years after the event.

43. A number of Jews who had not, before their persecution, identified very strongly with the Jewish community, changed their minds in the camps or after. Being persecuted as Jew had the effect of making some victims see themselves, for the first time, as belonging to the Jewish community. Becoming what one is named is a common coping mechanism for those who are persecuted and abused.

44. Langer: 44.

45. Natalie Shainess, "Foreword," in Eleanore Hill, *The Family Secret: A Personal Account of Incest* (New York: Dell) 1985: vi.

46. Micheline Beaudry, *Battered Women. Translated by Loren Huston and Margaret Heap* (Montreal: Black Rose Books) 1985: 19.

47. Louise Wisechild, *The Obsidian Mirror: An Adult Healing from Incest* (Seattle: Seal Press) 1988: iv.

48. Remember the earlier Lifton quotation about Hiroshima survivors.

49. Louise Thornton, "Preface," in Ellen Bass and Louise Thornton, eds., *I Never Told Anyone: Writings by Women Survivors of Child Sexual Abuse* (New York: Harper & Row) 1983: 22.

50. Ibid.: 59.
51. Peter G. Bourne, "From Boot Camp to My Lai," in Richard Falk, Gabriel Kolko, and Robert J. Lifton, eds., *Crimes of War: A Legal, Political-Documentary, and Psychological Inquiry into the Responsibility of Leaders, Citizens, and Soldiers for Criminal Acts in War,* (New York: Random House) 1971: 463–464.
52. Ibid.: 465.
53. Leed: 78.
54. Robert Jay Lifton, "Beyond Atrocity" in Richard Falk, Gabriel Kolko, and Robert J. Lifton, eds., *Crimes of War: A Legal, Political-Documentary, and Psychological Inquiry into the Responsibility of Leaders, Citizens, and Soldiers for Criminal Acts in War,* (New York: Random House) 1971: 23.
55. Robert Jay Lifton. "Victims and Executioners" in *Crimes of War:* 422.
56. Langer: 122–123.
57. Al Hubbard, Sgt. 22 Troop Carrier Squadron, August 1965 to June 1966. In John Kerry and Vietnam Veterans Against the War, *The New Soldier* (New York: Macmillan) 1971: 92.
58. Kerry: 4.
59. Ibid.: 116.
60. Bestor Cramm, Lt. 7th Eng. Br., USMC, March 1968 to April 1969. In Kerry: 152.
61. Jim Weber, Sgt. "A" Company, American Division, November 1967 to November 1968. In Kerry: 38.
62. Linderman: 281–282.
63. Patrocinio P. Schweickart, "Reading Ourselves: Toward a Feminist Theory of Reading," in Elaine Showalter, ed., *Speaking of Gender* (New York: Routledge) 1989: 25.
64. This brings up the interesting question of "cross-traumatic reference," or the way in which the survivor of one trauma (for example, rape or sexual abuse) might write about the experience of a different trauma (for example, the Holocaust). This is a subject area that is largely unexplored.
65. Though Weber, Harvey, and Stanley formulated this theory of storytelling specifically to explain why people told stories about failed relationships, it is also useful for understanding why people tell stories about other man-made traumatic experiences. Failed relationships, in fact, are a subset of the larger category of traumatic experiences and I will be discussing some of these relationships in the section of my work which deals with rape and incest. [Ann L. Weber, John H. Harvey, and Melinda A. Stanley, "The Nature and Motivations of Accounts for Failed Relationships," in Rosalie Burnett, Patrick McGhee, and David Clark, eds., *Accounting for Relationships: Explanation, Representation and Knowledge* (New York: Methuen) 1987.]
66. Kenneth J. Gergen and Mary M. Gergen, "Narratives of Relationship," *Accounting for Relationships:* 270–271.
67. Ibid.
68. See Natalie Dehn, *Computer Story Writing: The Role of Reconstructive and Dynamic Memory,* Ph.D. thesis, Computer Science Department, Yale University, December 1989. For more information on the cognitive process of storytelling, see also Robert Wilensky, *Planning and Understanding* (Reading, MA: Addison Wes-

ley) 1983; and, Edward Hovy, *Generating Natural Language Under Pragmatic Constraints,* Ph.D. thesis, Computer Science Department, Yale University, March 1987 (Technical Report #YALEU/CSD/RR521).

69. Aharon Appelfeld, "After the Holocaust," in Berel Lang, ed., *Writing and the Holocaust,* (New York: Holmes & Meier) 1988: 84.

70. Ibid.

71. Gregory Bateson, "Conscious Purpose Versus Nature," in *Steps to an Ecology of Mind* (New York: Ballantine) 1972: 429.

72. Ibid.: 432.

73. Umberto Eco, *The Name of the Rose* (New York) 1980: 491.

74. Terrence Des Pres, "Holocaust *Laughter?*" in *Writing and the Holocaust:* 232.

75. Lawrence Langer, *Versions of Survival: The Holocaust and the Human Spirit* (Albany: State University of New York Press) 1982: 12.

76. In this dissertation, I have limited my discussion to what I call "man-made" trauma. This is trauma that results from the deliberate exercise of violent power by one human being over another human being. Not under discussion here, though certainly related and deserving of study on their own merits, are the other two classes of trauma: environmental trauma and incidental trauma. Environmental trauma (caused by earthquakes, floods, lightening strikes, etc.) and incidental trauma (car and boat accidents, death of a loved one from natural causes, etc.) have been studied by psychiatrists and sociologists. There exists a large body of literature on the subject.

77. Langer: 88.

78. See Karl Abraham, Ernest Jones, et al., *Psychoanalysis and the War Neurosis* (London, Vienna, and New York) 1921; John Appell, M. C. Gilbert, et al., "Comparative Incidence of Neuropsychiatric Casualties in World War I and World War II," *American Journal of Psychiatry* 103 (1946–1947): 196–199; F. X. Dercum, "So-called 'Shell-Shock': The Remedy," *Archives of Neurology and Psychiatry* 1 (1919): 65–70; M. D. Eder, "Psychopathology of the War Neurosis," *Lancet* (12 Aug 1916): 279–288; Great Britain, Army, *Report of the War Office Committee of Enquiry Into "Shell-Shock,"* (London) 1922; G. W. Howland, "Neuroses of Returned Soldiers," *American Medicine,* New Series 12A (May 1914): 312–319; Ernst Simmel, *Kriegsneurosen un psychisches Trauma* (Munich) 1918.

79. See Lawrence C. Kolb, "The Post-Traumatic Stress Disorders of Combat: A Subgroup with a Conditioned Emotional Response," *Military Medicine* 149(3), May 1984: 237–243.

80. A Veterans Administration handout, given away at Veterans Outreach Centers all over the country, describes the following symptoms. Emotional Response Symptoms: psychic or emotional numbing; feelings of helplessness; apathy combined with being withdrawn; dejection; anger, rage, hostility that is repressed; anxiety and fears associated directly with combat experiences; emotional constriction and unresponsiveness; tendency to react under stress with combat survival tactics; sleep disturbances and recurring nightmares; loss of interest in work, activities; fatigue and lethargy; hyperalertness, irritability; avoidance of activities that arouse memories of Vietnam; suicidal thoughts and feelings; self-destructive behavior; survivor guilt; flashbacks to stressor events or part of event experienced in war; rapid turnover in employment; running away

from involvement (at times, literally driving long and fast at night). Interpersonal Relationships: difficulty in establishing or maintaining intimate relationships; tendency to have difficulties with authority figures; emotional distance from children; self-deceiving and self-punishing patterns of relating to others; inability to discuss war experiences with others; fear of losing others; inability to deal with significant others without alcohol or drugs to relieve anxiety. Cognitive Functioning: fantasies or retaliation and destruction; confusion in value systems; memory impairment; negative self-image; hypersensitivity to issues of equity, fairness; alienation, feeling "different," sense of meaninglessness. (VA Handout, no date, in possession of author.)

81. American Psychiatric Association. *Diagnostic and Statistical Manual of Mental Disorders,* 3rd edition (Washington, DC: APA) 1980: 236.
82. Ghislaine Boulanger, et al., "Posttraumatic Stress Disorder: A Valid Diagnosis?" in Boulanger, ed., *Vietnam Veteran Redefined: Fact and Fiction* (Hillsdale, NJ: Erlbaum) 1986: 25.
83. J. O'Connor, "Conference on Posttraumatic Stress Covers Effects of Combat, Crime, and Sexual Abuse," *Hospital and Community Psychiatry* 36 (1985): 309–319.
84. See the excellent collection edited by Susan Rubin Suleiman, *The Female Body in Western Culture: Contemporary Perspectives* (Cambridge: Harvard University Press) 1986.
85. Alice Jardine, "Men in Feminism: *Odor di Uomo or Compagnongs de Route?"* in Jardine and Smith, eds., *Men in Feminism* (New York: Methuen) 1987: 58.
86. Sedelle Katz and Mary Ann Mazur, *Understanding the Rape Victim* (New York: John Wiley) 1979: xi.
87. Menachem Amir, *Patterns in Forcible Rape* (Chicago: University of Chicago Press) 1971: 27.
88. Nancy Gager and Cathleen Schurr, *Confronting Rape in America* (New York: Grossett & Dunlap) 1976: 1.
89. Robin Warshaw, *I Never Called it Rape: The Ms. Report on Recognizing, Fighting and Surviving Date and Acquaintance Rape* (New York: Harper & Row)1988: 11.
90. Margaret T. Gordon and Stephanie Riger, *The Female Fear* (New York: Free Press) 1989: 36.
91. Diana E. H. Russell, *The Secret Trauma: Incest in the Lives of Girls and Women* (New York: Basic Books) 1986: 93.
92. Des Pres, "Holocaust *Laughter?":* 219.
93. Claudia Tate:, *Black Women Writers at Work* (New York: Continuum) 1983: 156.
94. Egendorf: 193.
95. Adrienne Rich, "Blood, Bread and Poetry: The Location of the Poet," *Massachusetts Review* (1984): 540.
96. Stephen Wright, *Meditations in Green* (New York: Bantam) 1983: 322.
97. James Webb, *Fields of Fire* (New York: Bantam) 1978.
98. John DelVecchio, *The Thirteenth Valley* (New York: Bantam) 1982.
99. Ken Miller, *Tiger the Lurp Dog* (New York: Ballantine) 1983: 224–225.
100. Ron Kovic, *Born on the Fourth of July* (New York: Pocket) 1976: 189.
101. Egendorf: 159.
102. See Shulamith Firestone, *The Dialectics of Sex* (New York: Morrow) 1970; Simone de Beauvoir, *The Second Sex* (New York: Vintage) 1974; and self-help texts

such as *The Assertive Woman*. Other excellent examples of this kind of writing can be found in some of the early collections of essays by women of color, including Moraga and Anzaldúa, eds., *This Bridge Called My Back: Writings by Radical Women of Color* (New York: Kitchen Table) 1981.

103. See John Blassingame, *The Slave Community,* revised and enlarged edition, (New York: Oxford University Press) 1972/1979; WEB DuBois, *The Negro,* (New York: Oxford University Press) 1915/1970; Eugene Genovese, *Roll Jordan, Roll: The World the Slaves Made,* (New York: Vintage) 1972/1974; Lawrence W. Levine, *Black Culture and Black Consciousness,* (New York: Oxford University Press) 1971/1977.

104. Chaim Shatan, "Afterword," in *Vietnam Veteran Redefined:* 175.

105. Gustav Hasford, *The Short-Timers* (New York: Bantam) 1979: 94.

106. Philip Caputo, *A Rumor of War* (New York: Ballantine) 1977: xvii.

107. Egendorf: 130.

108. Teresa DeLauretis, "Feminist Studies/Critical Studies: Issues, Terms, and Contexts," in *Feminist Studies/Critical Studies* (Bloomington: Indiana University Press) 1986: 10.

109. Vietnam Veterans Against the War, *The Winter Soldier Investigation: An Inquiry into American War Crimes* (Boston: Beacon Press) 1972.

110. DeLauretis: 11.

111. Egendorf: 224–225.

112. Richard B. Fuller, "War Veterans' Post-Traumatic Stress Disorder and the U.S. Congress," in William E. Kelly, ed., *Post-Traumatic Stress Disorder and the War Veteran Patient* (New York: Brunner/Mazel) 1985: 6.

113. Ibid.: 7.

114. Ibid.

115. Richard A. Kulka, et al., eds., *Trauma and the Vietnam War Generation: Report of Findings from the National Vietnam Veterans Readjustment Study* (New York: Brunner/Mazel) 1990: 53.

116. Charles R. Figley, M.D., "Post-Traumatic Family Therapy," in Frank M. Ochberg, M.D., ed., *Post-Traumatic Therapy and Victims of Violence* (New York: Brunner/Mazel) 1988: 86.

117. Robert J. Lifton, "Advocacy and Corruption in the Healing Profession," in Charles R. Figley, ed., *Stress Disorders Among Vietnam Veterans: Theory, Research and Treatment* (New York: Brunner/Mazel) 1978: 213.

118. Ibid.: 217.

119. Jacob D. Lindy, *Vietnam: A Casebook* (New York: Brunner/Mazel) 1987: xv. The tendency to use "Vietnam" as a metonym for the experience of American soldiers in the Vietnam War is almost universal in the psychological literature as it is in fiction, nonfiction, and memoir.

120. Ibid.

121. Ibid.: 14–15.

122. Ibid.: 40.

123. Ibid.: 58.

124. Ibid.: 63.

125. Ibid.: 71.

126. Ibid.: 72.

127. Michael Anderegg, ed., *Inventing Vietnam: The War in Film and Television* (Philadelphia: Temple University Press) 1991: 1.
128. John Hellman, "Vietnam and the Hollywood Genre Film," ibid.: 59.
129. Leonard Quart, "The Deer Hunter: The Superman in Vietnam," in Linda Dittmar and Gene Michaud, eds., *From Hanoi to Hollywood: The Vietnam War in American Film* (New Brunswick, NJ: Rutgers University Press) 1990: 167.
130. Klaus Theweleit, *Male Fantasies: Volume 1: Women, Floods, Bodies, History*, Conway, Stephen, trans. (Minneapolis: University of Minnesota Press) 1987. Originally published as *Männerphantasien*, Volume 1. *Frauen, Fluten, Kœrper, Geschichte*, by Verlag Roter Stern, 1977: xi.
131. Sarah Haley, "Some of My Best Friends Are Dead: Treatment of the PTSD Patient and His Family," in William Kelly, ed., *Post-Traumatic Stress Disorder and the War Veteran Patient* (New York: Brunner/Mazel) 1985: 63.
132. Lindy: 27.
133. Ibid.: 65.
134. Leonard Quart: 166.
135. Lindy: 218.
136. Lindy: 218.

Chapter 6

1. Louise Armstrong, *Kiss Daddy Goodnight: Ten Years Later* (New York: Pocket) 1987: 264.
2. See *Public Papers of the Presidents of the United States: George Bush, 1990, Book II – July 1 to December 31, 1990* (Washington, DC: US Government Printing Office) 1991: "Remarks at a Republican Campaign Rally in Manchester, New Hampshire," 23 Oct 1990; "Remarks at a Republican Fundraising Breakfast in Burlington, Vermont," 23 Oct 1990; "Remarks at a Campaign Rally for Gubernatorial Candidate Pete Wilson in Los Angeles, California," 26 Oct 1990; "Remarks at a Republican Party Fundraising Breakfast in Burlington, Massachusetts," 1 Nov 1990; "Remarks at a Republican Reception in Cincinnati, Ohio," 2 Nov 1990; "Remarks at a Reception for Gubernatorial Candidate Pete Wilson in Thousand Oaks, California," 3 Nov 1990; "Question-and-Answer Session With Reporters Following Discussions With President Václav Havel in Prague, Czechoslovakia," 17 Nov 1990; "The President's News Conference," 30 Nov 1990. My thanks to Nancy Kendall for locating these remarks for me, and for kindly supplying me with copies.
3. See Susan Brownmiller, *Against Our Will: Men, Women and Rape* (New York: Bantam) 1975.
4. Anthony Wilden, *Man and Woman, War and Peace* (New York: Routledge) 1987: 168.
5. Brownmiller, ibid.
6. Louise Armstrong, *Kiss Daddy Goodnight* (New York: Hawthorne Books) 1978.
7. By "self-conscious sexual assault narratives," I mean narratives in which the authors have taken as their primary subject the specific incident(s) of sexual assault that traumatized them, and then attempted to describe and contextualize the assault for the reader.
8. See Sally Emerson, "Sins of the Fathers," *Washington Post Book World*, 9 June

1991: 11; Richard Eder, "An American Tragedy," *The Los Angeles Times,* Book Review Section (28 April 1991): 3.

9. *New York Times Book Review,* 23 June 1991: 16.

10. Mary Helen Washington, "'Taming all that anger down': Rage and Silence in Gwendolyn Brooks's *Maud Martha,* " in H. L. Gates, Jr., ed., *Black Literature and Literary Theory* (New York: Methuen) 1984: 249–250.

11. Emerson, "Sins of the Fathers."

12. Eder, "An American Tragedy."

13. Ibid.

14. Donna Britt, "The Author, the Relative and a Question of Incest: Carolivia Herron's Disputed Tale of Childhood Horror," *Washington Post,* Style section: D1.

15. bell hooks, *Yearning: Race, Gender and Cultural Politics* (Boston: South End Press) 1990: 225–226.

16. Susan Willis, *Specifying: Black Women Writing the American Experience* (Madison: University of Wisconsin) 1987: 159.

17. Mary Helen Washington, "'Taming All That Anger Down': Rage and Silence in Gwendolyn Brooks' *Maud Martha,* " in Henry L. Gates, Jr., ed., *Black Literature and Literary Theory* (New York: Routledge) 1984: 258.

18. Michelle Wallace, *Invisibility Blues: From Pop to Theory* (New York: Verso) 1990: 215.

19. Angela Y. Davis, "We Do Not Consent: Violence Against Women in a Racist Society," *Women, Culture, Politics* (New York: Vintage) 1989: 47.

20. Ibid.: 43.

21. Armstrong: 1.

22. Ibid.: 4.

23. Ibid.

24. Ibid.: 5–6.

25. Ibid.: 7.

26. Ibid.: 8.

27. Ibid.: 9.

28. Ibid.

29. Ibid.: 10.

30. Ibid.: 11.

31. Ibid.: 17.

32. Ibid: 17–38, quoting from L. Bender and A. Blau, "The Reaction of Children to Sexual Relations with Adults."

33. "[I]t is not surprising that Sigmund Freud had to conceal his surprising discovery of adults' sexual abuse of their children, a discovery he was led to by the testimony of his patients. He disguised his insight with the aid of a theory that nullified this inadmissible knowledge. Children of his day were not allowed, under the severest of threats, to be aware of what adults were doing to them, and if Freud had persisted in his seduction theory, he not only would have had his introjected parents to fear but would no doubt have been discredited, and probably ostracized, by middle-class society. In order to protect himself, he had to devise a theory that would preserve appearances by attributing all "evil," guilt and wrongdoing to the child's fantasies, in which the parents served only as

objects of projection. We can understand why this theory omitted the fact that it is the parents who not only project their sexual and aggressive fantasies onto the child but also are able to act out these fantasies because they wield the power. "[Alice Miller, *For Your Own Good: Hidden Cruelty in Child-Rearing and the Roots of Violence,* (New York: Farrar, Straus, Giroux) 1983: 60. Originally published in German under the title *Am Anfang war Erziehung* (Frankfurt am Main: Suhrkamp Verlag) 1980.]

34. Armstrong: 20.
35. Ibid.: 41.
36. Ibid.: 13.
37. Ibid.: 48–49.
38. Ibid.: 102–103.
39. Ibid.: 57.
40. Ibid.: 131.
41. Ibid.: 132–133.
42. Ibid.
43. Ibid.: 167.
44. Ibid.: 193–194.
45. Ibid.: 211.
46. Ibid.: 231.
47. Ibid.: 260.
48. Ibid.: 263.
49. Ibid.
50. Toni A. H. McNaron and Yarrow Morgan, eds., *Voices in the Night: Women Speaking About Incest* (San Francisco: Cleis Press) 1982: back cover.
51. Ibid.: 11.
52. Ibid.
53. Ibid.: 12.
54. Ibid.: 13.
55. Ibid.
56. Vivian Gornick, "Woman as Outsider," *Woman in Sexist Society: Studies in Power and Powerlessness* (New York: Basic Books) 1971: 128–129.
57. Ibid.
58. Ibid.: 14.
59. Ibid.
60. Ibid.: 16. Here the editors renounce their claim to all "literature" and "statistics." I assume that they believe the new writings are something different, but I am troubled by this wholesale renunciation of the past, which included a great many useful writings by women.
61. This is similar to the process of art therapy for Vietnam veterans. See Deborah Golub, "Symbolic Expression in Post-Traumatic Stress Disorder: Vietnam Combat Veterans in Art Therapy," *The Arts in Psychotherapy* 12(4) 1985: 285–296.
62. McNaron and Morgan: 17–18.
63. Ibid.: 18.
64. Ibid.: 19.
65. Ibid.: 23.
66. Ibid.: 25.

67. Susan Marie Norris (Cygnet), "Cross My Heart," ibid.: 30.
68. Ibid.: 56.
69. Ibid.
70. Yarrow Morgan, "Mommy," ibid.: 110.
71. Toni A. H. McNaron, "For My Mother," Ibid.: 176.
72. Yarrow Morgan, "Remember," ibid.: 180.
73. "Cross My Heart," ibid.
74. Toni A.H. McNaron, "Mother-Rite," ibid.: 47.
75. Donna J. Young, "Phoenix," ibid.: 85.
76. Joanne Kerr, "Process Piece: A Story of Telling My Truths: Revealing and Transforming Myself. Incest Secret: A Story of Telling My Truth: Naming My Reality," ibid.: 91.
77. Kate Muellerleile Darkstar, "To Mike," Ibid." 124.
78. Ran Hall, "Five After Incest," ibid.: 118.
79. "Incest Story," ibid.: 33–34.
80. Susan Chute, "Black Girl Learn the Holiness of Motherhood," ibid.: 59.
81. Ibid.
82. Ibid.
83. Ibid.: 60.
84. Ibid.
85. Ibid.
86. Ibid.
87. Ibid.
88. Ibid.: 61.
89. Elizabeth V. Spelman, *Inessential Woman: Problems of Exclusion in Feminist Thought* (Boston: Beacon Press) 1988: 162.
90. Ibid.: 163.
91. Ibid.: 175–176.
92. Ibid.: 167.
93. The Personal Narratives Group, ed., *Interpreting Women's Lives: Feminist Theory and Personal Narratives* (Bloomington: Indiana University Press) 1989: 13.
94. Ibid.: 264.
95. Elie Wiesel, *Night* (New York: Bantam, 1982) 1960.
96. Thornton addresses the decision to divide the sexual abuse pieces into four categories in her Preface. She explains that sexual abuse by fathers is unique "in terms of betrayal and devastation." She describes the last category, sexual abuse by strangers, as important because it breaks down sinister stereotypes and suggests that an abusive stranger can come from any part of society. (Thornton, "Foreword," Thornton and Bass: 21.)
97. J. R. Conte, "Progress in Treating the Sexual Abuse of children," *Social Work May/Jun 1984:* 258–262.
98. Florence Rush, "Foreword," Thornton and Bass: 13.
99. Ibid.
100. Diana E. H. Russell, *The Secret Trauma: Incest in the Lives of Girls and Women* (New York: Basic Books) 1986: 312.
101. Rush, "Foreword," Thornton and Bass: 13–14.
102. Ibid.: 14.

103. Ibid.
104. Ibid.
105. Pamela Ashurst and Zaida Hall, *Understanding Women in Distress* (New York: Routledge) 1989: 70.
106. Louise Thornton, "Preface," Thornton and Bass: 16.
107. Ibid.
108. Ibid.: 16–17.
109. Ibid.: 19.
110. Ibid.
111. Ibid.: 22.
112. Ellen Bass, "Introduction: In the Truth Itself, There is Healing," Thornton and Bass: 27. Like Rush, she leaves no room in her analysis to explore the mechanism of the sexual abuse of boys by adult males.
113. Ibid.: 30.
114. Ibid.: 33.
115. This metaphor is more apt than one might expect. Bass explains: "Our forests, our rivers, our oceans, our air, our earth, this entire biosphere, are all invaded with poison – raped, just as our children are raped. . . . To stunt a child's trust in people, in love, in her world . . . to desecrate children so is consistent for people who desecrate all life and the possibility of future life." (Ibid.: 42–43.)
116. Ibid.: 44.
117. Ibid.: 50.
118. Ibid.: 53.
119. Ibid.: 60.
120. Maggie Hoyal, "These Are the Things I Remember," Thornton and Bass: 85.
121. Jean Monroe (pseud.), "California Daughter/1950," Thornton and Bass: 91–102.
122. R. C., "Remembering Dream," Thornton and Bass: 105–106.
123. Marty O. Dyke (pseud), "Yeah I'm Blaming You," Thornton and Bass: 112–113.
124. Ibid.: 120. (Italics mine.)
125. Ibid.: 175.
126. Maya Angelou, from *I Know Why the Caged Bird Sings,* ibid.: 134.
127. Ibid.: 133.
128. Billie Holiday, from *Lady Sings the Blues,* Ibid.: 176.
129. Ibid.: 177.
130. Hummy, "A Totally White World," ibid.: 240–249.
131. Hummy, ibid.: 241–242.
132. Ibid.: 242.
133. Ibid.: 243.
134. Ibid.
135. Ibid.: 246.
136. Ibid.
137. Ibid.
138. Ibid.: 249.
139. bell hooks, "feminist politicization: a comment," *Talking Back: Thinking Feminist Thinking Black* (Boston: South End Press) 1989: 110.
140. Armstrong, *Kiss Daddy Goodnight: Ten Years Later:* ix.

141. Ibid.: 266.
142. Ibid.
143. Ibid.: 269.
144. Ibid.: 273.
145. Ibid.: 275.
146. Ibid.: 277.
147. Ibid.: 288.
148. Ibid.
149. Ibid.: 291.
150. Susan Brownmiller, *Against Our Will: Men, Women and Rape* (New York: Bantam) 1976.
151. Wilden: 207.
152. Andrea Dworkin, *Pornography* (New York: Perigee) 1981: 23.
153. Robin Morgan, *The Demon Lover* (New York: Norton) 1989: 327–328.
154. Irene Elia, *The Female Animal* (New York: Henry Holt) 1988: 266.
155. Susan Griffin, *Rape: The Politics of Consciousness* (San Francisco: Harper & Row) 1986: 34.

Chapter 7

1. From "Let Us Move On," in *This is About Incest* (Ithaca, NY: Firebrand Books) 1987: 54.
2. Joanna Russ, *How to Suppress Women's Writing* (Austin: University of Texas) 1983.
3. Inger Agger and Søren Buus Jensen, "Testimony as Ritual and Evidence in Psychotherapy for Political Refugees," *Journal of Traumatic Stress* 3(1), Jan 1990: 116.
4. Ibid.: 118.
5. Ibid. Agger and Jensen cite, as an example of this process, the use of testimony as a therapeutic tool by the underground in Chile: "In this work, psychologists, at the risk of their own lives, collected testimonies from former prisoners who had been subjected to torture. These testimonies were drawn up by the therapist and the ex-prisoner together, and they form part of the evidence which the underground movement collected of the regime's repressive techniques. The drawing up of a complete and precise testimony became a therapeutic process for ex-prisoners, as through this, they were able to relate to their pain in a new way. They could see the universal in pain which had been experienced as personal encroachment. The bearing of the testimony became a cathartic process in which the common goal acted as a means of reestablishing the connection to reality. The collection of testimonies was also a research process for therapists who continuously learned more about the regime's methods against its opponents" (118–119).
6. Lillian Faderman, *Surpassing the Love of Men: Romantic Friendship and Love Between Women from the Renaissance to the Present* (New York: William Morrow) 1981: 413–414.
7. Firebrand Books, the press that published This is About Incest, identifies itself as a lesbian feminist press [Andrea Fleck Clardy, *Words to the Wise: A Writer's*

Guide to Feminist and Lesbian Periodicals & Publishers, revised second edition, Firebrand Sparks Pamphlet #1 (Ithaca, NY: Firebrand) 1987. Furthermore, she has influenced and been influenced by lesbian writers such as Elly Bulkin (*Enter Password*) and Adrienne Rich ("North American Tunnel Vision," and "Blood, Bread, and Poetry: The Location of the Poet," in *Blood, Bread, and Poetry: Selected Prose 1979–1985* (New York: Norton) 1986: 160–166; 167–187].

8. Sarah Lucia Hoagland, *Lesbian Ethics: Toward New Value* (Palo Alto, CA: Institute of Lesbian Studies) 1988: 4.

9. Harriet Desmoines, "Notes for a Magazine II," *Sinister Wisdom* 13 (Spring 1980): 16.

10. Lesbian psychologist Coralyn Fontaine writes on the sexualization of lesbianism, and the need for students to learn about patriarchy, heterosexism and woman-identification in courses on the psychology of women in her essay, "Teaching the Psychology of Women: A Lesbian-Feminist Perspective," in Margaret Cruikshank, ed., *Lesbian Studies: Present and Future* (Old Westbury, NY: The Feminist Press) 1982: 70–80.

11. Ellen Bass and Laura Davis, *The Courage to Heal: A Guide for Women Survivors of Child Sexual Abuse* (New York: Harper & Row) 1988: 268–269.

12. Ibid.

13. Ibid.

14. Ibid.

15. David Read Johnson, "The Role of the Creative Arts Therapies in the Diagnosis and Treatment of Psychological Trauma," *The Arts in Psychotherapy* 14 (1987): 8.

16. Agger and Jensen: 129.

17. Patrocinio P. Schweickart, "Reading Ourselves: Toward a Feminist Theory of Reading," in Elaine Showalter, ed., *Speaking of Gender* (New York: Routledge) 1989: 39.

18. Feminist testimonial narratives proliferate. In addition to the incest and sexual abuse survivor narratives discussed in this text, one may find, in any women's literature or women's study section in any bookstore, a variety of personal narratives, anthologies of personal narratives, oral histories, novels using testimonial devices, and "reclaimed" narratives of long "lost" women. A few examples include: Maxine Alexander, ed., *Speaking for Ourselves: Women of the South* (New York: Pantheon) 1984; Rita Mae Brown, *Six of One (New York: Bantam) 1978; Lillian Halegua, The Pearl Bastard* (Boston: Alyson Publications) 1959; Hall Carpenter Archives Lesbian Oral History Group, *Inventing Ourselves: Lesbian Life Stories* (New York: Routledge) 1989; Erica Jong, *Fear of Flying* (New York: New American Library) 1973; Audre Lorde, *The Cancer Journals* (San Francisco: Spinsters Ink) 1980; Cherríe Moraga, *Loving in the War Years: Lo Que Nunca Pasó por sus Labios* (Boston: South End Press) 1983; Alice Walker, *The Color Purple* (New York: Washington Square Press) 1982; Ida B. Wells, *Crusade for Justice: The Autobiography of Ida B. Wells* (Chicago: University of Chicago Press) 1970; Harriet E. Wilson, *Our Nig: Or, Sketches from the Life of a Free Black* (New York: Vintage) 1859/1983.

19. McNaron and Morgan challenge male and male-oriented critics who call the testimonies collected in their text "confessionalism": "Male and male-oriented

critics have often attempted to devalue women's art either by saying that it is not crafted enough, i.e., does not fit established male forms; that it is innovative; or that it is not universal. 'Universal' means that it is about or from a male perspective. Since much of women's literature is about defining what our experience is, it is invalidated as private and therefore not of interest. Since we as editors are passionately convinced of the necessity and excitement of rendering women's lives into art as healing, enriching and affirmative experiences, there is little or no dialogue possible with the critic who will attempt to silence us in this way." [Toni A. H. McNaron and Yarrow Morgan, *Voices in the Night: Women Speaking About Incest* (San Francisco: Cleis) 1982: 17–18.]

20. Ibid.: 31.
21. Ibid.: 32.
22. Clardy: 17.
23. Judy Grahn is a lesbian feminist and the author of a number of books, including *Another Mother Tongue: Gay Words, Gay Worlds* (Boston: Beacon Press) 1984. Her name would be familiar to most lesbian feminist readers.
24. Louise Wisechild, *The Obsidian Mirror: An Adult Healing from Incest* (Seattle: Seal) 1988: Acknowledgements.
25. Sally Gearhart and Susan Rennie, *A Feminist Tarot, revised and expanded edition* (Watertown, MA: Persephone Press) 1981: xix.
26. The blackness of the obsidian mirror parallels the black granite mirror of the Vietnam Veterans memorial Wall in interesting ways.
27. Wisechild: xiii.
28. Carlos Casteneda, *The Second Ring of Power* (New York: Pocket) 1977: 307. There is a strong and persuasive argument to be made that Casteneda fabricated the Yaqui "sorcerers" out of whole cloth, that they are the fictitious creations of a skilled writer. Casteneda's books have been the subject of quite a bit of debate in the anthropological community and have come in for a great deal of criticism from Native American scholars such as Ward Churchill for their alleged appropriation of nonwhite cultures. Their popularity in the New Age spiritual community, however, is undeniable and – true or not – they have influenced a great many readers. For the purposes of this study, they can be regarded as powerful fictions that describe archetypal characters and imagined ways of being in the world.
29. Wisechild: xii.
30. Casteneda: 308.
31. Wisechild: 3.
32. Ibid.
33. Ibid.: 4.
34. Ibid.
35. Ibid.: 4–5.
36. Ibid.: 5.
37. Ibid.
38. Ibid.: 6.
39. Ibid.
40. Ibid.: 7.
41. Ibid: 8–9.

42. Ibid.: 11.
43. Ibid.
44. Ibid.: 13.
45. Ibid.: 15.
46. Ibid.: 15–16.
47. Ibid.: 16.
48. Ibid.: 20.
49. Ibid.
50. Ibid.: 21.
51. Ibid.: 23.
52. Ibid.: 25.
53. Ibid.: 27.
54. Ibid.: 30.
55. Ibid.: 33.
56. Ibid.: 49.
57. Ibid.: 51.
58. Ibid.: 52.
59. Ibid.: 55.
60. Ibid.: 57.
61. Ibid.: 61.
62. Ibid.: 65.
63. Liz Kelly, *Surviving Sexual Violence* (Minneapolis: University of Minnesota) 1988: 193.
64. Ibid.: 67.
65. Ibid.: 80.
66. Ibid.
67. Ibid.: 85.
68. Ibid.: 88.
69. Ibid.: 102.
70. Ibid.: 104.
71. Ibid.: 117.
72. Hoagland: 36.
73. Ashurst and Hall: 2.
74. Wisechild: 118.
75. Dale Spender, *Man Made Language,* second edition (London: Routledge & Keegan Paul) 1985: 179–180.
76. Wisechild: 119.
77. Spender: 180.
78. Ibid.
79. Wisechild: 121.
80. Ibid.: 122.
81. Ibid.: 127.
82. Ibid.: 129.
83. Miller: 259.
84. Wisechild: 133.
85. Ibid.
86. Ibid.: 134.

87. Ibid.: 142.
88. Ibid.: 146.
89. Ibid.: 148.
90. Ibid.: 160.
91. Ibid.: 162.
92. Kelly: 162.
93. Wisechild: 162–163.
94. Ibid.: 163.
95. Ibid.
96. Ibid.: 175.
97. Ibid.: 177.
98. "Reflect on the patriarchs. True, they had money and power, but only at the cost of harboring in their breasts an eagle, a vulture, forever tearing the liver out and plucking at the lungs – the instinct for possession, the rage for acquisition which drives them to desire other people's fields and goods perpetually; to make frontiers and flags; battleships and poison gas; to offer up their own lives and their children's lives." [Virginia Woolf, *A Room of One's Own* (New York: Harcourt, Brace, World) 1929: 38–39.]
99. Wisechild: 177.
100. Ibid.: 178.
101. Ibid.: 193.
102. Ibid.: 215.
103. Bass and Davis mention that this is a common scenario for incest survivors who confront family members. An initially sympathetic response does not indicate that the survivor can expect continued support. Often sympathy changes to rejection, denial, and anger when the implications of the accusation sink it. (Bass and Davis, *The Courage to Heal:* 140–141.)
104. Wisechild: 218–219.
105. Ibid.: 220.
106. Ibid.: 226.
107. Ibid.: 227.
108. Ibid.: 228.
109. Ibid.: 234.
110. Ibid.: 236.
111. Ibid.: 247.
112. Ibid.
113. Ibid.: 248.
114. Ibid.: 263.
115. Ibid.: 264.
116. Ibid.: 265.
117. Ibid.: 267.
118. Ibid.: 272.
119. Ibid.: 276.
120. Ibid.
121. Ibid.: 278.
122. Thornton and Bass: 197–198.
123. Des Pres: 50.

124. Morgan: 327.
125. Cynthia Enloe, *Bananas, Beaches and Bases: Making Feminist Sense of International Politics* (Berkeley: University of California Press) 1989: 196–197.
126. See Chapter 2 for a detailed explanation of their claims.
127. Weber, Harvey and Stanley: 124.
128. Carroll Smith-Rosenberg, "The Body Politic," in Elizabeth Weed, ed., *Coming to Terms: Feminism, Theory, Politics* (New York: Routledge) 1989: 101.
129. Ibid.
130. Ibid.: 101–102.
131. Emphasis mine.
132. "Each of us is here now because in one way or another we share a commitment to language and to the power of language, and to the reclaiming of that language which has been made to work against us. In the transformation of silence into language and action, it is vitally necessary for each of us to establish or examine her function in that transformation and to recognize her role as vital within that transformation." [Audre Lorde, "The Transformation of Silence into Language and Action," in *Sister Outsider* (New York: Crossing Press) 1984.
133. Randall: 14.
134. Kelly: 13.
135. Elly Danica, *Don't: A Woman's Word* (San Francisco: Cleis Press) 1988: 77.
136. Monique Wittig, *Les Guérillères, translated by David Le Vay* (Boston: Beacon Press) 1985. Originally published 1969 in French under the same title by Les Editions de Minuit. For other French feminist discussions of language (in English translation) see also Elaine Marks and Isabelle de Courtivron, eds., *New French Feminisms: An Anthology* (New York: Schocken) 1980.
137. Monique Wittig, *The Lesbian Body*, translated by David Le Vay (New York: Bard) 1975. Originally published 1973 in French under the title *Le Corps Lesbien* by Les Editions de Minuit.
138. Randall: 16.
139. Ibid.: 16–17.
140. Ibid.: 18.
141. Ibid.: 19.
142. Kelly: 191.
143. Kelly: 147.
144. Randall: 20.
145. Ibid.
146. Des Pres: 47.
147. Langer: x.
148. John Carlos Rowe, "'Bringing It All Back Home': American Recyclings of the Vietnam War," in Nancy Armstrong and Leonard Tennenhouse, eds., *The Violence of Representation: Literature and the History of Violence* (New York: Routledge) 1989: 203.
149. Randall: 21.
150. Ibid.: 22.
151. See Frances FitzGerald, *America Revised* (New York: Vintage) 1979; Oscar Handlin, *Truth in History* (Cambridge, MA: Harvard) 1979, especially Chapter 16, "Ethnicity and the New History; " and, David Thelen, ed., *Memory and American*

History (Bloomington: Indiana University Press) 1990, especially David Low-enthal's essay "The Timeless Past: Some Anglo-American Historical Preconceptions."

152. Ibid.: 24.
153. "The phobia became the safeguard of my memory, the place where it could be stored, the memory bank from which I would someday be able to retrieve it, retrieve and deal with it." (Ibid.)
154. Deborah Golub, "Symbolic Expression in Post-Traumatic Stress Disorder: Vietnam Combat Veterans in Art Therapy," *The Arts in Psychotherapy* 12(4) 1985: 285–296.
155. Ibid.
156. Randall: 29.
157. Ibid.: 33.
158. Ibid.
159. From "Enter the White-Faced Man," ibid.: 36.
160. From "Learning to Remember," ibid.: 37.
161. From "Watching It Grow Between Your Legs," Ibid.: 42.
162. From "The Letter," ibid.: 46.
163. Ibid.: 48.
164. Quoted in Richard Ellmann and Robert O'Clair, eds., *The Norton Anthology of Modern Poetry* (New York: W.W. Norton) 1973: 286.
165. Ibid.
166. Randall: 52.
167. Ellmann and O'Clair: 286.
168. Ibid.: 287.
169. Ibid.: 286.
170. Think, for example of the title image in "Oread." (Ibid.:373).
171. Randall: 52.
172. Susan Gubar, "'The Blank Page' and the Issue of Female Creativity," in Elizabeth Abel, ed., *Writing and Sexual Difference* (Chicago: University of Chicago Press) 1982: 89.
173. Susan Griffin, "Thoughts on Writing: A Diary," in Janet Sternburg, ed., The *Writer on Her Work* (New York: W.W. Norton) 1980: 117.
174. Tillie Olson, *Silences* (New York: Dell Laurel) 1983.
175. Evelyn Torton Beck, ed., 1982 (New York: Crossing Press) 1983.
176. Randall: 53.
177. Ibid.: 54.
178. See Chapter 3.
179. Survivor testimonies, from *Shoah,* Claude Lansmann's oral history of the Holocaust (New York: Pantheon) 1985.
180. Randall: 160.
181. Ellmann and O'Clair: 1295–1296.
182. Alvin H. Rosenfeld, "The Problematics of Holocaust Literature": 175.
183. James E. Young, *Writing and Rewriting the Holocaust: Narrative and the Consequence of Interpretation* (Bloomington: Indiana University Press) 1988: 118.
184. Dworkin, *Intercourse:* 123.
185. Randall: 71.

186. Ibid.: 45.
187. Ibid.
188. Ibid.: 67.
189. Ibid.
190. Joan W. Scott, "Gender: A Useful Category of Historical Analysis," in Elizabeth Weed, ed., *Coming to Terms: Feminism, Theory, Politics* (New York: Routledge) 1989: 99.
191. Randall: 59.
192. Elly Bulkin, *Enter Password: Recovery. Re-enter Password.* (Albany, NY: Turtle Books) 1990: 11.
193. Ibid.
194. Ibid.: 11–12.
195. Ibid.: 12.
196. Ibid.: 13.
197. Ibid.
198. Ibid.
199. Ibid.: 14–15.
200. Ibid.: 18.
201. Elly Bulkin, "Hard Ground: Jewish Identity, Racism, and Anti-Semitism," in Elly Bulkin, Minnie Bruce Pratt, and Barbara Smith, *Yours in Struggle: Three Feminist Perspectives on Anti-Semitism and Racism* (Brooklyn: Long Haul Press) 1984: 91–230. Reprinted by Firebrand Books (Ithaca, NY).
202. Ibid.: 21. The Mud Flower Collective (Katie G. Cannon, Beverly W. Harrison, Carter Heyward, Ada Maria Isasi-Diaz, Bess B. Johnson, Mary D. Pellauer, and Nancy D. Richardson), *God's Fierce Whimsy: Christian Feminist and Theological Education* (New York: The Pilgrim Press) 1985.
203. Bulkin: 22.
204. Ibid.
205. Ibid.: 23.
206. Ibid.: 25.
207. Ibid.: 26.
208. Ibid.: 27
209. Ibid.
210. Ibid.
211. Ibid.: 29.
212. Ibid.: 31.
213. "Recovering Our Memories of Child Sexual Abuse," *Sojourner* (September 1986): 15–17.
214. Bulkin: 34–35.
215. Ibid.: 39.
216. Ibid.: 40.
217. Ibid.: 41.
218. Ibid.: 42.
219. Ibid.: 48.
220. Ibid.
221. Ibid.: 51.
222. Ibid.: 62.

223. Ibid.
224. Ibid.
225. Ibid.
226. Ibid.: 63.
227. Ibid.
228. Ibid.: 66.
229. Ibid.
230. Ibid.: 67.
231. Ibid.
232. Ibid.: 68.
233. Ibid.: 70.
234. Ibid.: 72. Epigraph is from Ellen Bass, *Of Separateness and Merging* (Brookline, MA: Autumn Press) 1977.
235. Bulkin: 33.
236. Ibid.: 75.
237. Ibid.: 36.
238. Ibid.: 79.
239. Ibid.: 82.
240. Ibid.: 83.
241. Ibid.
242. Ibid.
243. Ibid.: 91.
244. See Chapter 3, p. 123.
245. Ibid.: 92.
246. Ibid.
247. Ibid.
248. Ibid.: 99.
249. Ibid.: 100.
250. Ibid.
251. Ibid.: 101.

This Is Not a Conclusion

1. Ntozake Shange, "With No Immediate Cause," in *Nappy Edges* (New York: St. Martin's Press) 1978: 117.

Index

The following titles are out of print: